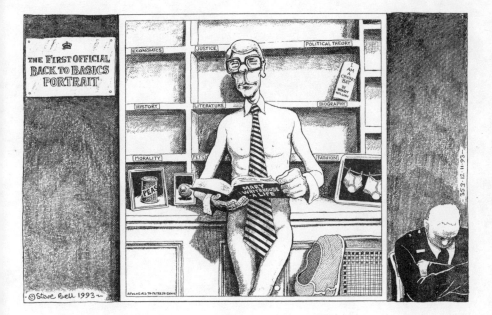

The **Guardian Year**

The Guardian Year
'94

Introduction by **Jeremy Paxman**
Edited by **Alan Rusbridger**

FOURTH ESTATE · *London*

First published in Great Britain in 1994 by
Fourth Estate Limited
289 Westbourne Grove
London W11 2QA

Copyright © 1994 by Guardian Newspapers Ltd
Introduction © 1994 by Jeremy Paxman

The right of Alan Rusbridger to be identified as the
editor of this work has been asserted by him in
accordance with the Copyright, Designs and
Patents Act 1988.

A catalogue record for this book is available from
the British Library.

ISBN 1–85702–265–3

Typeset by Books Unlimited (Nottm), Rainworth, NG21 0JE
Printed in Great Britain by the Bath Press Ltd, Avon

Contents

Introduction by *Jeremy Paxman*   ix

At home
For queen and country *Maggie O'Kane*   1
Pass Notes: Elizabeth Hurley   6
Rich pickings for an eyesore at the races? Don't bet on it *Vivek
    Chaudhary*   7
Natalie's neighbours *Nick Davies*   9
'I want my kids' *Nick Davies*   16
The will and the way *Leader*   22
In hock to family values *Maureen Freely*   23
Goldmine Sachs *Ian Katz*   26
It is no good asking me, I was only Prime Minister *Matthew Engel*   30
The Scott Inquiry *Steve Bell*   31

Lobby terms
Apply here for top job: portly rightists will have priority *Michael
    White*   33
The choice between two Labour lettuces *David McKie*   35
A demagogue's lost empire shrouded in myths *Hugo Young*   37
A happy snapper steals scene from PM's Pollyanna *Simon Hoggart*   40
Major picks a fight with the big boys and gets a bloody nose *Hugo
    Young*   41
The man who expressed a strong interest in the European voting
    rights affair *Steve Bell*   42
A psychopath, a mega-nerd and now Bambi *Steve Bell*   44
Wealth of happiness may be in store *Will Hutton*   46
The big lie *Martin Kettle*   50
PS *Geoffrey Wheatcroft*   57
Major's pay-off line has them roaring *Simon Hoggart*   59
Triviality breeds content for MPs *Simon Hoggart*   60

Abroad
Letter from Key West: the etiquette for unzipping the fly *Barbara
    Ehrenreich*   62

Thanks be to the OJ show *Barbara Ehrenreich* 63

Inside the forbidden forests *Tim Radford* 65

Pass Notes: Carlo Maria Martini 70

Solzhenitsyn slides into his place in Russia's pantheon *Jonathan Steele* 71

Staring death in the face and blind to all error *Chris McGreal* 73

The black knight *Gary Younge* 74

South African election diary: making history through a haze *Rian Malan* 81

Glitterati's procession watches fairy-tale ending *David Beresford* 85

An epic to live in the memory *Leader* 88

Death on the road marked Whitewater *Leader* 89

Italy's tawdry pleasure palace *Ed Vulliamy* 92

Media moguls *Alan Rusbridger* 95

The trouble with Hillary *Barbara Ehrenreich* 105

Close to the edge *David Hirst* 107

A quiet day in Jericho *Derek Brown* 113

Bottom line *John Vidal* 114

The media village

Caught in the net *Kevin Kelly* 116

Connections from Essex to Sarajevo *Clancy Sigal* 119

The search for sleaze which demeans Western societies *Martin Woollacott* 121

Royal front page *Steve Bell* 124

Gotcha! Well, perhaps not *Barry Norman* 124

Restless country that Gerry built *Catherine Bennett* 126

It's a mad, mad multi-media world *Richard Neville* 129

The diet of worms *David Mellor* 131

Strong, thick and glossy *Matthew Engel* 133

Arts, books, culture

Coronation tales of soap, sex and secrets *Nancy Banks-Smith* 136

BBC builds new house of Eliot on traditional foundations *Edward Pearce* 137

Pass Notes: Albert Camus 140

Junking the image *Will Self* 141

An eye on the afterlife *Andrew Clements* 144

Preacher woman *Jenny Turner* 146

Landmark for the information age *Deyan Sudjic* 153

My mother's story *Anna Karpf* 156

Rock of sages *Sebastian Faulks*   158
Darling, you were wonderful *Catherine Bennett*   163
Fatherhood in its funday best *James Wood*   169
Boor with a big heart *Tony Tanner*   171
Comrade Pushkin's myth *Elaine Feinstein*   174
A sentence *Steve Bell*   175

Sex: war and peace
A prophet and porn *Catherine Bennett*   177
Pass Notes: Sister Wendy Beckett   187
Sloth about the house *Suzanne Moore*   188
I do, I do, take you and you *Sally Weale*   190
Bush blazes that inflamed the sex war *Richard Neville*   194
Taking the law into our own fists *Suzanne Moore*   196

Miscellany
Politics, paper bags and nasal penetration *Armando Iannucci*   199
Pass Notes: New Zealand   201
Why the young need their single ticket to freedom *Germaine Greer*   202
Whose D-day is it anyway? *Richard Gott*   204
Spam and flim-flam *John Ezard*   209
Boring in the gloaming *Leader*   211
Take a few pigs along to the Pie in the Sky café and watch
    payment go bob-bob-bobbin' along *John Vidal*   212
One down, thousands more to go *John Perkin*   215
Didn't he do well? *Centipede*   220
Major on a sticky wicket with plan to cap special friendship *Martin
    Walker*   222
A frenzy of goodness *Paul Foot*   224
Back to the front with Tommy *Sebastian Faulks*   226
Crowned heads of the kitchen *Catherine Bennett*   230
The dismal diary of Adrienne Mole *Nancy Banks-Smith*   237

Sporting life
Short-change final *Stephen Bierley*   242
Sampras cops the long and short of it *Stephen Bierley*   243
Lara joins the greats *Mike Selvey*   245
God's gift to the game simply born to be great *John Mullin*   248
Pass Notes: Ray Illingworth   253
Five-ton Lara rewrites every record in the book *David Foot*   254

Death and the risk business *Matthew Engel*   256
From Mr Irascible to Master Olazabal *David Davies*   258
Eccentric England 'rest in pieces' with worst performance since
   1887 *Matthew Engel*   260
Cobblers nobbled *Matthew Engel*   262
Soccer? Who's a succer? *Matthew Engel*   264
A limit to Sky's appeal *Matthew Engel*   270

Gone before
Dennis Potter *Kenith Trodd*   272
      Melvyn Bragg   273
      Michael Grade   274
      Alan Rusbridger   274
      Gavin Millar   275
      Lynda La Plante   276
Smoke screen *Dennis Potter*   276
John Smith *Hugo Young*   277
Sharper wit with inner fire *Simon Hoggart*   280
His mark, one stride from the pinnacle *Leader*   282
A thoroughly English dissident *W.L. Webb*   284
'Controversialist' Jarman takes his final bow *Mike Ellison*   288
The vibrant voice *John Humphrys*   289
Raging at the dying of the light *Polly Toynbee*   291
Talking a very good game *Frank Keating*   298

Introduction

Jeremy Paxman

It is what the Irish call 'a soft day' in August. Which means the sky is gun-metal grey and the rain is falling in stair-rods. As I look out of the window, a black and white cow has turned her back to the wind the better to graze on the spidery west Cork grass.

On the radio by the fire, a voice so soft you wonder how he ever gets to the end of a sentence without having eaten all the words he hoped to utter, is auctioning a hurling stick. It has been autographed by the whole of the Limerick team. He has raised £35 so far.

'That £35 means the difference between life and death for someone,' he says. 'So thank you all. Lor, did you ever see anything like those pictures of the poor people in Rwanda? Would you think it could happen in this day and age?'

Around the world, similar auctions are taking place, no doubt, as involuntary spectators to catastrophe try to relieve the suffering of the millions of Rwandan refugees. Six months ago, how may of us could have stuck a pin in a map of Africa and had any confidence we'd be within a thousand miles of Rwanda? Yet now, nightly, we watch its people dying in our own homes. Television makes spectators of us all.

It is of course, technology which has made it all possible – specifically, in the case of Rwanda, portable satellite transmission dishes and satellite telephones. The considerations which drive the media are not editorial but electronic. A generation late, we are at the edge of McLuhan's global village, where nothing of consequence happens anywhere in the world without our being able to watch it, live, in our front rooms.

We have not begun to tackle the implications of this high-voltage familiarity. We know, as Alan Rusbridger discovered on his assignment in New Delhi, that the impetus for encircling the world by satellite is commercial. The great Molochs of the television age – Murdoch, Turner and the rest of them – would clasp old William Randolph Hearst to their bosoms as a kindred spirit. (It was Hearst who sent a reporter to Cuba to 'cover the war' and, when the reporter said, 'But Mr Hearst, there isn't a war,' replied that the reporter's job was to get there: Hearst would make sure the war happened. He did.)

Aid workers will tell you that nothing does more to raise money and put pressure on governments than for their own disaster to be the subject of saturation media coverage. Which means, incidentally, that it's best if it occurs when there's not too much else going on in the world. But if the charity auctions are a positive consequence of exposure to world events, there may be just as great a danger that, for some people, a permanent ringside seat merely induces passivity.

Which is why we need newspapers like the *Guardian* to make sense of the world. Raw news meets no British Standard, contains no agreed list of ingredients. Buy a bar of high-tensile steel and you know exactly what it's made of. News is just an accretion of events. So newspapers are a matter of judgement. For the most part, those decisions obey age-old laws. 'Dog bites man, no news. Man bites dog: that's news.' 'News is whatever someone somewhere doesn't want you to know.' Even the most enlightened news editor carries a tribal memory made up of a thousand clichés coined by green eyeshades who went before. The *Guardian*'s strength – and what makes it so irritating – is its readiness to strike an attitude.

When you look back over the events which made the news this year, what an oddly trivial country we seem; how thin is the line between drama and farce. Headlines dominated by news that a Tory MP has shared a bed with a male friend while on a 'gastronomic tour' of France, that another Tory MP has fathered a child out of wedlock, even, for heaven's sake, that a newspaper columnist's amanuensis served him smoked salmon while dressed in black suspenders. When it comes to sex, the popular press has all the *savoir-vivre* of a fourteen-year-old. Yet at times, as Hugo Young, Michael White and Simon Hoggart frequently remind us, British public life seems to merit no better. How anyone can watch Prime Minister's Question Time, with its rehearsed questions, rehearsed answers, rehearsed name-calling and pathetically rehearsed waving of order papers, and then repeat the age-old adage about the mother of parliaments is an eternal mystery. Reading the recital of excuses and obfuscations which characterised the investigations into how we came to sell arms to Malaysia and Iraq in breach of public guidelines speaks volumes about 'open government'. And are we really supposed to consider John Major's much-trumpeted 'triumph' in blocking the appointment of a portly Belgian as the European Union's top bureaucrat a Churchillian achievement?

Far away from the Westminster-obsessed world of the London media is another Britain where, unreported except when tragedy strikes, millions try to avoid a cycle of diurnal desperation. It is this dislocated world of deprivation, early unplanned pregnancies and easy drugs which falls most readily to sensationalist reporting and quick political platitudes. I hope when this collection appears the simple-minded tub-thumpers back home from the party conferences will read Nick Davies's accounts of life in this overstressed underclass.

Individuals or even families may have an *annus mirabilis* or *horribilis*. But it is rare to find a year which can so easily be summarised for the world at large. I always tend to look at the obituaries first. Most prominently mourned this year was John Smith, who will doubtless be raising a quizzical eyebrow in the heaven to which he aspired and wondering why it was that politicians and journalists of all hues were only prepared to admit once he was dead that the caricature they had drawn in his life of a dour and solid bank manager was so far from the truth. Other afflicters of the comfortable to pass on were the historian E. P. Thompson and *Guardian* alumni Brian Redhead and Jill Tweedie.

We shall not find their match among the detritus of Comet Shoemaker Levy such as Bienvenida Buck or Radio 4's Gerry Anderson, the only man who can make Bruce Forsyth sound like Spinoza. But other arrivals this year were more substantial, like the magical Brian Lara, the man who broke cricketing records as if they'd been set by village elevens.

Yet it was the fate of two old men which most symbolised change for better in the world. Having been booted out by a government which could not stand the contagion of his ideas, Alexander Solzhenitsyn made a triumphal return by train across Russia. He will, doubtless, find plenty to be grumpy about in the years left to him, but we should not lose sight of the significance of his freedom.

Nor can we ignore Nelson Mandela, who returned from prison to rout and rule the kingdom of the damnable and inspire some of the most exuberant reporting of the year. All the gloomy prognostications about nemesis when expectations cannot be met may turn out to be true. But if so, it will not be the fault of the first legitimate government but an accumulated debt crisis thrust on its shoulders by generations of racists. For the moment, though, we should just be glad of the great achievement of peaceful change.

A couple of hours have gone by since I started reading this collection of pieces about the year past. It is still raining. On the radio, the news is that an outbreak of cholera among the Rwandan refugees has been followed by the beginnings of a dysentery epidemic. There is more fatuous spluttering from foreign governments at the Bosnian Serbs' total disregard of the 'final' peace plan. The last foreign airliner has left Port-au-Prince.

Events go on. The man with the soft voice has just started to auction a hurling stick autographed by the Cork team. It would be easy to get depressed. But not necessarily necessary.

Skibbereen, August 1994

At home

Maggie O'Kane

19 October 1993

....

For queen and country

He drives into Belfast's Catholic ghettos to kill with a six-inch cardboard cut-out of a Celtic football player swinging gently from his back window screen, partly as a decoy, partly because it amuses him. He selects the targets himself. Tells his hit team where to meet and allows no time for leaks or set-ups. The police have stopped him cruising on the Catholic Falls Road. 'I'm taking a short cut,' he says. Then he taunts them – lets them know he knows: 'That's so and so's place over there, isn't it?' he says, pointing to the home of a Sinn Fein councillor or a well-known Catholic. Any Catholic will do. It's better, he will admit, if they are Republicans. But the bottom line is that Mad Dog and his men are in the business of 'spraying Taigs' (Catholics).

The police call him Mad Dog and the IRA will probably kill him. Police intelligence say he has shot twelve Catholics in raids on bars and houses and arranged the murders of at least eight others in the past two years. He leads an organisation which, besides shooting Catholics, is perfecting its explosives capabilities: 'They are near there,' said a senior police intelligence officer in Belfast last week, distractedly stirring his coffee. 'And then ...'

It is 12.30 on Monday afternoon. Mad Dog's silver-grey Volvo is pulling gently on to the kerb in a cul-de-sac off Belfast's Shankill Road. The neat red brickwork sits uncomfortably underneath a huge wall mural to the 2nd Battalion of the UFF. On each side of Mad Dog's double-fronted local authority house, a huge Union Jack hangs from a white flag-pole. He is turning off the ignition and saying that everybody believes in God. And the commandment Thou Shalt Not Kill? 'Thou shalt not be caught killing,' he says.

He is twenty-nine and his short hair has blond highlights. He stands about five feet seven inches in his white striped training shoes and has the body of a stocky full back beginning to go to seed. He wears a gold earring in his right ear and a light denim shirt covers an arm sheathed in tattoos in honour of the Ulster Freedom Fighters. To the left of Mad Dog's front door, the neat red brickwork is sprayed with bullet holes. There have been four attempts on his life: three by the IRA, a fourth, he says, by a plainclothes member of the security forces. In a police cell in Castlereagh not long ago, he told a detective he knew he would be killed, but he would 'take a lot of Taigs with him' before he went.

The front door of his house is lined with metal and has four locks. Behind the door is a steel roller shutter, the type used for extra security on shops. In the corner of his sitting room a close-circuit TV is showing a snowy black and white picture of his front doorstep. Along one side of the room is a six-foot-long tropical fish tank, lit by a neon strip light and built into the wall. Below it is stretched a woman on a black leather sofa watching *Neighbours*.

The mother of his three children left long ago and the woman on the couch says the IRA is after her as well. 'They call me the Orange bitch,' she says proudly. And is she worried about her lover's end? She shrugs her shoulders and turns her fine-boned face back to the TV while Mad Dog reads out his death warrant from *An Phoblacht*, the Republican newspaper. He jabs his finger at a headline: 'UDA death squad leader targeted.' In a slow, faltering voice he begins to read: '... the IRA said: "We are absolutely determined to make this Loyalist mass murderer pay for his crimes."' 'That's me,' he says, showing his six column inches, and his chest puffs a little under his denim shirt.

In the last year the police have arrested six UFF death squads but Mad Dog has evaded them, according to one police source, because he never tells anyone on the team about jobs beforehand. The UFF has learned from the IRA and organised into tight cell structures. Mad Dog is not an easy man to catch or kill. He goes alone to choose the targets and always works with the same two men. There are three cars in each operation. A surveillance car that goes up front and, using walkie-talkies, checks there are no police or army patrols; then the hit car with three men inside, and finally the gun car. When they get to the scene, the guns are handed over. The other cars leave and the two hitters go in.

Like the IRA, the Protestant paramilitaries have what they call legitimate targets. Until 1991, the leadership generally exercised some discretion in their killings. The new leadership reflects a growing extremism among hardline Loyalists – extremism partly fuelled by a perception that since Unionists lost their veto on Northern Ireland politics, their powerbase has been slowly eroding. Since the signing of the Anglo-Irish agreement, which officially gave the Dublin government a say in the running of Northern Ireland, the alienation of the Protestant community has been steadily increasing. In July this year Protestants on the Shankill Road rioted in protest against 'police harassment' and the level of surveillance. Old friends in the RUC and British Army became enemies. Earlier this year a Protestant prison officer was murdered by Protestant paramilitaries in a parole protest. The most recent thorn in the side of Ulster Loyalists was the announcement of secret talks between the Social Democratic and Labour Party leader, John Hume, and Sinn Fein's Gerry Adams. The 'pan-Nationalists' conspiracy was upon them and the UFF, bolstered by this latest betrayal, began murdering Catholics with vigour. As Sinn Fein announced its decision to set up office in Brussels the Protestant paramilitaries were insisting that if the IRA has shot its way to a position of strength, they can follow.

'The IRA have shown us how to get what you want,' said a former UFF volunteer.

The first meeting with the UFF inner council takes place in the back room of a Loyalist club on a Protestant housing estate. Here, among the 1950s houses with satellite TV dishes, gardens planted with beech trees and Austins and Vauxhalls parked behind smooth hedges, the leaders gather. Introductions are brief: 'This is the OC (officer commanding) North Belfast, OC North West, OC West Belfast. (Mad Dog is OC West Belfast.) Please take a seat. You have half an hour, these are busy men.'

Mad Dog says little during the interview, he is bored by the Loyalist rhetoric flowing over a Formica coffee table. A barman hovers with a pot of freshly brewed coffee and tuna and salad sandwiches cut in neat triangles are handed round.

The young men explain why they have no regrets, no remorse about killing Catholics, although over 90 per cent of the targets are people with no involvement in Republican politics: 'We are out to terrorise the terrorists. To get to the stage when old grannies up the Falls will call on the IRA to stop, because it is ordinary Catholics that are getting hit, not the Provos behind steel security doors.'

'Every death is regrettable,' says one of the old guard. About fifty and affable, he is the PR man, the guy who passes round the tuna sandwiches and nudges in on the questions when the answers go a bit astray. He's there to wrap the political framework around the shoulders of his young killers. 'Our document is called "Common Sense",' he says.

'Common Sense' was published in 1987 and was the Protestant paramilitaries' response to Mrs Thatcher's 'betrayal' in signing the Anglo-Irish agreement. 'Common Sense' was praised all round. It guaranteed power-sharing with Catholics and was greeted with excited cries of a breakthrough in newspaper editorials. But Ulster's crusty old Unionists knocked it back and it was forgotten until the Loyalist paramilitaries dusted it down and presented it as the ideological overcoat for killing Catholics.

'The bottom line now is this,' says the UFF's PR man. 'The Northern Ireland state has failed in its duty to protect Ulster Protestants and we will protect ourselves.' No surrender. 'We have our self-respect, we will not allow ourselves to be wiped out like the Jews in Germany. For twenty-three years we have been taking it lying down. Protestants in the Republic were "ethnically cleansed" (by intermarriage). We cannot allow the same thing to happen to us. We will fight fire with fire.'

Mad Dog is bored with it all. Speak up, the PR man keeps saying, but he can't be bothered.

He's driving downtown with a steady eye on the back mirror. His Volvo is a smart job. Police intelligence says he's dipping – creaming off extortion profits. He says: 'We have support among the middle classes. There are businessmen backing us, supporting us financially.'

We are driving on to the Shankill Road, away from the steadying hand of the older leadership. Mad Dog is suspicious. 'So how did you know to get in touch with us then?' he asks. He has a steady Mona Lisa smile and looks ahead or checks the mirror all the time, never making eye contact. So did he ever have a Catholic in his car before? 'Only a dead one,' he says. We drive on in silence.

There's a craziness about the drive. We go into car-parks, around back alleys, under ten-foot-high Loyalist murals that read: 'One Faith, One Crown. Ulster/ Scotland We Are United.' Along pavements painted in red, white and blue, he stops to talk to men strolling along the Shankill. 'Get in,' he says to Norman.

In his house behind the bullet-proof glass windows, one says: 'She's not from London.' 'No, she's from Dublin,' says Mad Dog. Silence again in the room, as the tropical fish swim up gently under the neon light and the pretty woman on the couch turns for a better look. Across the road from the red brick house is a bar. It's about 1.30 pm but most of the men have been in there for the morning. From behind the wheel of the Volvo, Mad Dog sends a runner to summon the men he wants. The show is on for the one from the English paper.

'Got the piece, Jackie.'

'Have you a weapon on you? Here's Joe, he'll have one.'

A man sways gently across the road from the bar. He's one of us, says Mad Dog, ready to go any time. The man with six pints in his eyes smiles in a friendly sort of way into the car. He strokes the lapel of his combat jacket. 'All ready to go,' he says. 'What do we do with Taigs?' Mad Dog asks. 'We spray them,' obliges the combat jacket with a friendly drunken grin.

Ask Mad Dog what he is and he says an 'Ulsterman'. Ask him what he is going to die for and he says: 'The Crown. If you didn't support that, what would you support? Dublin? The Pope?' He shrugs his shoulders.

'He is not long for the road,' says the detective. 'He has a death wish but it means he's not afraid of anything because it doesn't matter any more.'

'I know they will get me,' says Mad Dog. But he doesn't lose sleep over it. He has no remorse for the killing and now no pity for his victims. He says he is proud of the job he does. 'Once you get your first Fenian blood it is easy after that.'

Mad Dog understands about the first blood – 'the blooding'. On 8 September, Sean Hughes was finishing up for the day in the hairdresser's he had worked in on the corner of the Falls Road and Donegal Road for nineteen years. A car carrying two men wearing baseball caps and hoods pulled up outside. Hughes's customers said later that the men who killed Hughes looked to be no more than eighteen years old. That night the UFF claimed responsibility. He had been their third Catholic that week and the first kill for two young members of the Ulster Young Militants. Their blooding.

'They are blooding young people all the time to bring them in. They get their first easy kill and they get the taste of it,' said a senior police detective. The IRA knows who Sean Hughes's killers are but, says a Republican source: 'The IRA won't get drawn into a sectarian tit-for-tat attack. They won't kill the boys because they were being "blooded".' They want Mad Dog.

His Volvo is pulling up at traffic lights on the Shankhill. Suddenly a car pulls out fast behind us. 'Do you think that bastard is grassing me?' he asks the man in the back of the car as a black sports car speeds by. A moment of panic, then he's back safely on Sandy Row.

In Rathcoole housing estate, built in the 1950s and trumpeted as the largest in Europe, the men in the Cloughfern Arms bar speak of him in hushed tones. One has a tattoo on his arm that reads, 'KAI, Kill All Irishmen', and he is patiently explaining that he supports the British National Party because they hate the IRA and Loyalists need all the support they can get. Just before 8 pm the door opens and five boys in black baseball caps stride into the bar. Ulster's Young Militants, says the tattoo proudly, and you wonder which of them was blooded on Sean Hughes. The Cloughfern Arms flute band is the breeding ground of good Loyalist paramilitaries. A young and handsome drummer of around eighteen says he can't explain but he just hates Catholics. He has delicate cheekbones and fine teeth. 'That was the way I was brought up,' he says.

Lying beside the gearstick of Mad Dog's car is a photograph taken two weeks ago in the Maze prison outside Belfast. In the centre is a man in a blue shirt with long black curly hair. Michael Stone secured his place in the pages of Loyalist history when he chucked two grenades into the mourners at an IRA funeral. He killed three and wounded sixty-eight, and said to the police when they told him of the toll, 'Brilliant – I'm game for anything.'

The man standing beside him in the photograph is Mad Dog. 'Stone,' he says, 'he's a hero – a real hero.' •

Pass Notes

3 August 1994   Elizabeth Hurley

Age: 29

Physical condition: Tip top!

Colour of hair: Brown.

Colour of bottom: Pink.

How would you know? See last week's *Sunday Times* Magazine.

Profession: ATGTPTIBN.

Eh? Actress turned girlfriend turned pin-up turned interviewee in broadsheet newspapers.

Never heard of her: Come come. You must remember her in That Dress.

Who else was in it? She wasn't in a film, dummy, she was at a film. In That Dress.

What dress? You know, the one by that designer, Janny Whatsisname – the one with safety pins down the side and half her chest poking out.

What of it? Well, she goes out with that Hugh Grant.

Never heard of him: Impossible. Haven't been to *Four Weddings and a Funeral*?

Yes – but it's a common surname: No, the film, the famous British film. He starred in it. And she goes out with him. And she wears sexy clothes.

Anything else? She trained as a dancer, was once a punk, went to school, grew up, had boyfriends, owns a mink coat, went to drama college, starred in *Cristabel*, loves her dog, knows how to make custard, appeared in some other films no one remembers, likes tapestry, goes out with Hugh Grant.

You've left something out: Her bust measurement is an estimated 36C.

Women say: 'Lousy legs, shameless minx, nothing special, can't think what he sees in her, I could do that.'

Men say: 'An English rose with a Mediterranean temperament' (Toby Young); 'Has the slightly gangly grace that only the over-abundantly sexy can get away with' (Tom Shone); 'Almost enough to make a man forget his marriage vows' (David Thomas); 'Exuding sexual magnetism' (Derek Nimmo); 'She was so luminous' (Kenith Trodd); 'Wooorgh, you wouldn't get many of them in a bucket' (John Walsh); 'Nice' (John Major).

Hurley on men: 'I am only going to marry someone if he's a good cook.'

Watch out Hughie? Well, Keith Floyd has recently become available.

A brief setback: She recently appeared in a less sexy dress than Elle MacPherson's.

A tip for the girls: 'Hugh says English knickers just aren't as nice.'

And a warning: 'He's my best friend and I could not do without him now.'

Recommended career moves: Eliminate Elle MacPherson, write a novel, design a range of knickers, launch a perfume (Elizabeth Hurley's Sexual Magnetism), have a baby, visit Rwanda in That Dress, retire from public life à la Princess Diana.

Most likely to say: Is that a gun in your pocket or are you just John Walsh?

Least likely to say: Only if it's strictly necessary for the plot.

Vivek Chaudhary
2 June 1994

Rich pickings for an eyesore at the races? Don't bet on it

It was a good day for horse-racing but a bad one for begging. Outside the Queen's Stand at Epsom yesterday, the 'above stairs' classes were indulging in a bit of pre-Derby revelry.

Expensive cars were entering the car-park as finely dressed people sat round tables being served by waiters. Gypsies tried to sell good-luck charms and ticket touts plied their trade, but Britain's unashamedly decadent class were too busy idling the afternoon away. There was an abundance of champagne, salmon, caviare and upper-class accents, but a distinct lack of generosity.

Unshaven and shabby, I went cap in hand asking for money as gentlemen in spats, top hats and tails, and ladies decked out in all their finery chatted and drank waiting for the Derby to start.

'Excuse me, could you spare some loose change, please. I haven't eaten for days,' I asked a group of men standing round a brand-new Rolls Royce and sipping champagne. 'Oh, sorry, I never carry any loose change,' one of them replied. 'Why don't you ask my friend?'

By this stage the chauffeur had come round, gently pushing me away and saying: 'Look, just piss off, don't bother these people; they're very busy,' looking as if he was about to punch me.

Close by, a haystack of a man was strolling through the car-park with a fat cigar sticking out of his mouth.

'Could you spare any loose change, please?' I asked.

He just grinned from under his top hat, sucked on his cigar and walked on.

A small group of people drinking champagne and eating sandwiches had a bit more time for this eyesore of a beggar but little money.

'You look healthy enough to me. Why can't you go out and get a job?' said a lady wearing a wide-brimmed hat covered in feathers.

'Oh, you poor thing,' her friend said. 'It's absolutely criminal, and they say John Major's getting it right. Here, have a sandwich,' she said, offering me a tray of prawn sandwiches.

'You know, begging is not the way. You should try and get a job,' she added, offering me another sandwich.

The conversation was overheard by a group of men leaning on their Range Rover. 'Any spare change, please,' I asked them.

'Not a single penny. Can't do a thing for you, old boy, it's just tough luck,' one said, giving me a scornful look as he adjusted his cravat.

Forty-five minutes of begging and not a penny earned.

Salvation, however, came in the form of an Arab-looking gentleman who emerged from his limousine with two immaculately dressed women. 'Are you going to use the money for gambling?' he asked. 'No,' I replied, upon which he pulled out a wad of notes and handed me £5.

I was dumbstruck. 'Go and get yourself some food,' he advised me.

With my faith in human nature slightly restored I entered the fray again.

Round the corner from the Queen's Stand the 'below stairs' classes were ripping open tins of lager and munching burgers and chips. Most ignored my request for loose change but a group of men had a whip-round when I told them I was a Spurs fan.

'Here's £1.50. Go and get yourself a drink,' one, wearing a Spurs shirt, said.

Close by, an old woman sitting on a grass verge drinking tea gave me 50p. 'Get yourself a portion of chips,' she said gently.

After almost two hours I had made £7. Most people didn't see me as an eyesore but just seemed to ignore me.

With my pride bruised and feeling utterly despondent, I decided to put human nature to one final test. Unfortunately and unknowingly, I returned to a group of men I had approached earlier.

'Bugger off,' one, holding a glass of champagne, screamed. 'John Major's right. Not only are you an eyesore but you're also a bloody nuisance.'

I was not the only one to have had a bad day. The good-luck-charm sellers were complaining about trade being slow and a man selling *Big Issue*, the magazine produced by the homeless, protested that he had not sold a copy all day. •

Nick Davies
14 May 1994

Natalie's neighbours

For most of her life, Natalie Pearman was a walking portrait of an ordinary girl. She lived with her four brothers and sisters and her cat called Lucy in a neat little council house on the edge of a peaceful village in Norfolk. She liked ballet and horses and watching *Neighbours* after tea, she was good at drawing and painting and she had the idea that when she grew up, she would like to go into the air force so that she could be independent and travel around the world.

Her family was indistinguishable from any other in their street: the father, Chris, going off to work each day as an engineer in a plant-hire firm; the mother, Lin, who had given up her career as a nurse to manage the home; the children clambering on to the bus that took them down the road to school; all of them running through the routines of an ordinary existence.

Then it changed – at least, Natalie did. It was as if she had decided to take a knife to that ordinary portrait of herself and hack it to shreds and start all over again. She was fourteen when it happened and, when she re-emerged, everything had changed: her clothes, her hair, her likes and passions, her friends, even her name. Natalie Pearman vanished. And no one really knew why.

In place of the skinny little schoolgirl with the mousy brown hair, there now stood a willowy blonde who called herself Maria, who drank and smoked and played around with dope. She no longer lived in the little council house or had anything very much to do with her family at all. All they knew was what they heard from the police when she was picked up from time to time – for breaking and entering, for stealing a car, and then for soliciting on the streets of Norwich. Maria was a whore.

The last time she came home, her mother barely recognised her. Lin hadn't seen her for more than a year and it was like having a stranger in the house. When Lin made her a cup of tea, she had to ask her whether she took milk and sugar. She could barely understand the things that Natalie talked about – pimps and punters and the guys in the vice squad. And when Lin looked at her daughter, she saw what she could only describe as a fog of evil hanging around her.

All this might have remained a private mystery, distracting only to those who were closest to her, if there had not been a terrible sequel to the story. A few days after that final visit home, Natalie died. In the small hours of a dark November morning, somebody used her for sex and then choked the life out of her and dumped her body in a lay-by outside Norwich. She was sixteen.

Her murder turned the riddle of her life into a public puzzle. In many ways, it seemed to be a classic story of self-destructive youth, corrupted by drugs and ruined by reckless self-indulgence, the kind of case that has adults sadly shaking their heads in despair. The local paper wrote her epitaph: 'Hooked on drugs, and on the streets at the age of 14. Dead by 16. That was the sum total of Natalie Pearman's tragic life.' But it wasn't quite that simple.

The key to the mystery lies in the very ordinariness of Natalie's childhood. Police and social workers and neighbours, too, have taken a long, hard look at her past, but they have found only the everyday tensions of family life: Natalie used to fight with her brother, Jon, who was two years older than her and inclined to push her about, like older brothers always do; and she sometimes resented Chris, because she knew he was not her real father. She and Jon had been fathered by Lin's first husband, an oil worker named Rod Earp. But the marriage had collapsed when Natalie was only one, and Chris had played the part of her father since she was eight. They were things that might have upset her sometimes, but no worse.

There was something else which was equally common but which appears to have upset her more. The Pearmans were poor. They were not starving and they were nowhere near that state of sordid desperation which envelops the destitute, but they were trapped at the bottom of the financial cliff, with Chris working full-time and bringing home only £120 at the end of the week, and Lin juggling her child benefit to fill in the gaps. They had enough to get by, but no more. They had no car, so if they wanted to go anywhere they had to travel by bus, and since there were only four of those a day, they tended to stay in the village. They had no holidays abroad or any extravagance at all. Life was strictly limited.

And when Natalie was twelve, it got a little worse. Lin had fallen pregnant with her youngest child and began to have a very difficult time. She needed twenty-four-hour care and the only person who could provide it was Chris. He asked his employers if they would let him take time off to look after her and then come back when the baby was born, but they wouldn't have it, so he was forced to give up his job. When the baby was born and Lin had recovered, he went out to look for more work. There was the canning factory in North Walsham, the gas terminal at Bacton, a couple of pig farms, but no one was hiring. Once, he was offered shifts at a place near Cromer, but he had no way of getting there. Another time, he signed up with a friend who was starting his own business, but there was no money in it, and it all went sour.

Natalie hated being poor. It was not that she was ashamed of it, it was the simple practical fact that she could not enjoy the things she wanted, even simple things. There were times when she came home from school asking if she could go on a day trip with the other children and she had to be told that they couldn't afford it. Some of her friends went to Brownies, but Natalie didn't; there was no money for the uniform. She had to give up her ballet lessons.

And then there was Mundesley, the kind of village that looks right in the rain. It is a tiny place, with a population of 1,500, perched on the cliff-tops overlooking the muddy brown sea about half an hour's drive north of Norwich. There are a couple of caravan parks, which fill up with trippers in the summer months and then sit soaking up the drizzle for the rest of the year. There's the Haig Club with its star cabaret night featuring compère and vocalist Phil St John; a pub or two; a scattering of guest houses pleading for business ('All rooms en suite'); and the Coronation Hall, built of red brick and pebble dash, with four concrete tubs of ageing flowers collecting dust outside, and a poster that says 'Come to Sunny Mundesley'.

Natalie spent most of her life here and never found much to do. There was the little amusement arcade with the sign over the door telling local children to stay away unless they could demonstrate to the satisfaction of the management that they were on holiday. No cinema, no youth club. There was the beach, bristling with rules: no dogs on the beach, no parties on the beach, no barbecues on the beach unless they take place in the designated area with the written permission of North Norfolk District Council. The nearest town was a £6 taxi-ride away. Natalie stayed at home. She'd sit in her room and draw. Sometimes, on a Saturday morning, she'd go to a jumble sale with Lin. And for a long time, that was enough.

When Natalie started to change, she did so with dazzling speed. The beginning was simple: a few months after her fourteenth birthday, she got herself a weekend job at a little take-away hamburger bar next to the amusement arcade and earned herself pocket money for videos and clothes, and while she was working down there, she saw something that caught her eye – a group of village children having fun. To an outsider's eye, there was nothing to it, just a bunch of boys and girls on a sheltered bench, chewing gum and sharing cigarettes. But they had their little secrets, which Natalie soon discovered.

One of them was dope. There was an older boy who had a room of his own in the village who used to buy little lumps of hash in Great Yarmouth, and then they'd all sit around on their bench, spitting at the grass and giggling while they tried to get stoned. Then there was sex, lots of groping and screwing down on the beach. Natalie started to sit around with them on the sheltered bench and then to join in. Some of the adults from the village saw what she was doing but they had no worries about it. Village kids had always done it. What else was there to do in Mundesley?

Back in their neat little council house, Chris and Lin saw within weeks that something new was happening, but when they asked her, she shrugged them off. They told her to behave herself and wrote off to the RAF for glossy brochures about life in the air force, but Natalie wasn't that interested any more. Lin wasn't too sure what to make of it, until one of Natalie's friends came to see her and said she was afraid that Natalie was on drugs.

Now, Lin had always believed in what she calls 'tough love': you lay down the rules and you offer your children love, but on your own terms. The door is always open, but the child has to come to you. Lin told Natalie in no uncertain terms that there was no place in this family for anybody on drugs. But years of squabbling with her big brother had taught Natalie to stand up for herself. She said she wasn't on drugs – not the way her mother thought – and, anyway, she was having fun at last. Then she got pregnant.

She was ecstatic. It was the best thing ever. The father was seventeen, three years older than her, a local boy with his own motor-bike (and a more or less permanent plaster on the leg he kept breaking). She was in love. They'd have their own house together and both of them would go out to work so they could afford to buy furniture and, while she was at work, Lin would look after the baby. It was going to be great. But Lin said no: there was no way she was going to look after Natalie's baby. If she wanted to have the baby, that was up to her, but she would have to take responsibility for it herself or give it up for adoption. And that was final. Natalie turned to her boyfriend for help, but he took fright and told her he didn't really want to get involved. She said that was fine, she'd bring up the baby with her friend Julie. When she was ten weeks pregnant, she miscarried, and so the dream was over.

Natalie started to stay out late at night. Chris used to go out at midnight, fishing around in the dark corners of Mundesley until he found her and brought her back for a good ticking-off. Lin was going through a rough time herself. She had just miscarried and was feeling bad, her eldest son had joined the army and been posted to the Falklands, and Chris's mother was dying very slowly from cancer. She told Natalie they really didn't have time to deal with her silliness. Natalie started drifting further afield, to North Walsham and Great Yarmouth, so that Chris couldn't find her when he went out looking, and, without a car, they ended up calling the police to find her.

They decided to get tough. One night when two boys brought her home full of cider, Lin took off her slipper and beat her from one end of the house to the other. They started locking her indoors, but Natalie fought to get out, smashed a window once, tried to squeeze herself through the cat flap another time and nearly succeeded. By now, the family was at war with itself. The tighter they pulled at Natalie, the further she ran away. The more they shouted, the less she heard. When the police brought in a social worker to try to help, Natalie gritted her teeth and announced she wanted to be taken into care.

She found a new boyfriend, Simon, a young farm worker, five years older than her, with a ring in his ear and an old Vauxhall Cavalier and two best mates. The four of them hung around together, smoked a little dope, got stopped by the police, got away with it, broke into an empty house and legged it when the police came, got caught, got cautioned, carried on having a laugh, while Chris and Lin sent out the police to bring her back.

The social workers talked to Natalie, who was full of anger for her family – for her real father who was lost in the past and for her stepfather who was too tough on her. She threw up a whisper of a hint that she had once been physically abused by a friend of the family. She said she couldn't care less: if people didn't like her, then she didn't like them. When she was out, Lin read her diary, scattered with little hints of dope and sex, and then she told Natalie straight that she did not like what she had read.

Once when she came home late, Chris hit her and she wore the bruise like a medal the next time she saw Simon. Then one night, she didn't come back at all and the police couldn't find her until the next morning when they spotted her wandering along a beach alone. They picked her up and called Lin and asked what she wanted them to do, and Lin said she didn't want Natalie home, she wanted her taken into care. The police agreed. And so Natalie was out of her family – less than six months after she first went to work at the hamburger bar and saw the other kids having fun.

Now the war became a stand-off. Lin stuck to her tough love: if Natalie wanted to come back, that was fine, but Natalie would have to make the first move. Natalie told her friends she couldn't be less bothered about being in care. She hated Chris and she was better off without them. In the children's home near Cromer, she was caught sniffing petrol.

That week, Chris's mother finally died and when the news reached Natalie at the children's home, she said she wanted to go to the funeral. Chris wrote to the social workers to say that his family did not want her there; she had caused too much upset. The social workers felt Natalie ought to be there, so they ignored Chris's letter and took her along to the funeral, where Natalie sat alone at the back of the church while Chris and Lin and their friends and relations pretended she was not there. Back at school, Natalie sniffed lighter fuel and was suspended for a week. Chris's family decided that she should no longer call herself Pearman; she should use her real father's name if she was going to be so bad.

Natalie spent just over a year in care, calm for months at a time, running around with Simon and the lads at weekends, occasionally pitched into sudden panics if things went unexpectedly wrong. Once, Simon wondered out loud if they should stop seeing each other so much, and Natalie went back to her foster home and said she'd swallowed fifty contraceptive pills. Simon raced over, but she was fine though she fell into a long sulk, snarling at others in the home until her foster mother said she should leave. Natalie didn't wait to be pushed; she ran and, from a phone box outside a pub, she called her family. Chris went and fetched her and took her back to the social services. When she returned to the children's home, she warned the social workers that she was full of heroin. They had her blood tested and found she was clean. She settled back into the stalemate. Her family did not visit her; Lin thought it would teach her a lesson. They were supposed to go for family therapy, but Lin couldn't afford anyone to look after the baby and, anyway, she had no transport, so the sessions fizzled out. At Christmas, Chris delivered some presents to the home, without seeing her. Natalie was alone.

She reached her sixteenth birthday, struggled free of social services, walked out of school and headed for Norwich. She had no job, she was too young to sign on, and for a while she lived in the YWCA. But she still had her mates – Simon and the lads and a whole network of other young people who had fallen out of the bottom of village life and drifted into the nearest big town. They showed her how to survive. For a girl, it was easy. Within weeks, she was working on the pavement. 'Maria' was born.

She used to stand outside a pub called the Ferry Boat in the middle of the network of streets which have been used by prostitutes for years and which are collectively known in Norwich as The Block. £15 for a hand job, £20 for a blow job, £30 straight sex. At first, she worked only part-time, selling just enough of herself to pay for her rent and food. But after a few months, she became more confident and started to work routinely and now, in a twisted upside-down kind of way, she began to find what she wanted.

She wasn't poor any more. She was pulling in £500 a week and then blowing it in great gushes of extravagance – videos, clothes and anything else she wanted. She talked about buying a flash new car and a mobile phone. No more strictly limited life. One of the girls who used to work round the corner from her, Louise, says that the two of them used to raid nightclubs together and get completely paralytic and then stumble into a taxi in a heapful of laughter. She was having fun. It wasn't the kind of fun she had dreamed of as a child, and often it was only the synthetic excitement of something she'd stuffed up her nostril, but it was more fun than she'd ever had in Mundesley.

Most important – and most upside-down – she was wanted. She could stand out there on The Block, cocking her chin at the cars rolling by, and she could watch them wanting her, circling round for a second look, stopping for her, asking her to come with them. If she wanted to, she could turn them away. If she went with them, they would pay her – pay her for her company. It wasn't real love — any more than a head full of coke is real life — but it was better than nothing. She used to say her real parents had been killed in a car crash.

Maria was not so much a new self-portrait as a caricature, a grotesque parody of the life that Natalie craved, but everyone who was with her at the time agrees on one thing, that she was happy. She wasn't the mad-eyed junkie whore of legend at all. In fact, she wasn't a junkie of any kind. All her friends say the same thing: that she smoked some dope and, when she was working on The Block, she played around with heroin and cocaine, but she was never very interested. She wasn't trapped and dragged down by sinister forces. She chose to do what she did, because when she looked at her life she saw she was trapped and when she looked at her future, it was even worse — getting pregnant, getting married, getting a house and stewing slowly in front of a television for forty years. What else was there?

When she went back to see Lin on that last visit, just before she died, she wasn't interested in going home. She went back to collect her birth certificate because she wanted to get a passport and go off to France or Spain. 'There's nothing here for me any more,' she said. And she glided round the house with her dyed blonde hair and her skin-tight trousers with her nails all polished and her eyes painted up, and she was saying she'd won the war with her past. Her visit wasn't an offer of peace, it was a victory roll.

The next night, she was back on The Block. Just before midnight, a taxi driver picked her up and used her for half an hour. At about one in the morning, a man paid her £30 to come back to his house where his baby daughter was asleep upstairs. Then, just after half past three, a lorry driver who was working his way through a narrow road to the north-west of the city, spotted a bundle of clothes in a lay-by. He stopped to look and, in the lights of his lorry, he found Natalie Pearman, stripped from the waist down, scarlet bruises round her neck.

The police set up the biggest inquiry in the history of Norfolk, but the killer eluded them. They collected her property and found she had acquired almost nothing — a few tacky dresses, some make-up and a little box in which she had kept the medals she had once won for ballet — just the possessions of an ordinary girl.

Lin Pearman was devastated. She blamed social services. She said she had only allowed them to take Natalie to keep her away from the friends who were leading her astray, but they had let her run wild. When the police were finished, she buried Natalie behind the church on the cliffs overlooking the muddy brown sea at Mundesley, and sometimes now she goes back there and cries over the hummock in the grass and catches herself asking out loud: 'Natalie, Natalie. How could you do this to us?' •

Nick Davies
19 January 1994
....
'I want my kids'

In the early hours of Monday morning, 3 January, five small boys from Leeds were taken into care. They were brothers, aged between six months and six years, their mother was only twenty-two, and they lived together in a council house which was said to be so dirty, so littered with dog mess, that police were physically sick at the smell and senior social workers compared it to a toilet.

It was not a big story but it ran in all the nationals – another case of Home Alone at Christmas, another horror story from the underclass, another single mother spawning children at the expense of the state, another good reason to go back to basic family values. In reality, however, it was not quite like that.

The story was catapulted into the headlines by sheer fluke. The foster parents who were called in to look after four of the boys were due to appear on BBC Radio Leeds later that Monday and when they phoned the radio show's presenter to explain that they couldn't appear because they had suddenly inherited four more children, he told them to come on in and tell everyone about it. So they did. By Tuesday morning it was a national story.

Back in Leeds, the social workers could hardly believe it. There was nothing special about the case at all. In an average week, they were used to dealing with fifty cases of children in need of protection – 2,500 of them a year – some not so bad but some much worse than this one. And when they saw the angle the story was taking, they began to feel angry.

According to one senior official: 'This was not a Home Alone case at all. The mother was with the children all the time. The concern here was neglect, and society reacts in a very odd way to cases of neglect. People prefer not to know about it. Sex abuse is different: they can blame someone. But with neglect they can't, because it is linked to poverty and changes in the benefit system and people do not want to admit that. It opens up too many questions. So if a case like this does become public, they look for scapegoats – either the parents or the social services.' In this case, it was the parent.

From the dual carriageways that sweep through the suburbs of Leeds, the sprawling red-brick housing estates look like the models of welfare planning which they were when they were built in the 1950s and 1960s. Closer up, they are a portrait of deprivation.

The house where Tina Sampson lives has two front windows on the ground floor, both of them boarded up. The chunks of broken glass still lie where they fell on the concrete path in front of the house, with a couple of broken beer cans and an old towel. The back garden is littered with the remains of two burned-out cars and several charred bed frames. Inside, there are holes in the hall walls that go clean through the brickwork, puddles of water in the bathroom from three leaking pipes, mould running up the front wall, no source of heat in any of the upstairs rooms, no carpets, no curtains, no lampshades, no wallpaper, almost no furniture.

But this place is the end of the story, not the beginning. Tina Sampson's troubles began in 1979, just at the start of the great sea change in social policy that was to transform her surroundings. That was the year her mother put her into care. She was seven. 'My mam broke up with my father and he went off and I never seen him. She got another man and he used to batter me. She did try and stop him, but he just wanted to batter me. So I got took into care and never saw my mam for three years. She had four more children, but they all stayed with her.

'I was in care till I was thirteen. I had seven different foster parents. I'd get one lot and then they'd need to take in some different children so I had to move on to make room. There was one lot of foster parents I was with for three years, but when I was thirteen, they said I had to choose. Either I could stay with the foster parents or go back to my mam. So I went back to my mam. Wrong choice.'

She swivels her head away to stare at the bare plaster on the wall for a moment. She is very thin, with pinched cheeks and baggy blue Levi's. 'I was leading a normal life when I was twelve or thirteen. I was a right little snob really but I had nice things and a nice house. When I came back here, I just got scruffy. I went downhill. I suppose it's my fault for mixing with the wrong people. When I came back, I wasn't close to my mam. We used to have arguments and I'd go right up against her. I'd say, "All right, hit me if you're gonna hit me." The social workers got involved. I've had social workers all my life – loads of different ones.

'I used to take overdoses of paracetamol so I could get time off school. I had my stomach pumped three times. Since I were taken off me mam, when I was little, I've always had a certain thing for dying. I used to cut myself, slash my arm.'

She rolls back her left sleeve and twists the underside of her forearm into the light of the naked bulb that hangs down from the ceiling. There must be fifty scars there and she points them out, the ones that dug right down into the thin blue vein until the ambulance came, the ones that were only begging for attention.

'The first time I fell pregnant, I were still at school. I were sixteen. Everything changed for me when I had kids. I had something to do. You know? It weren't just me on me own any more. I don't know if I loved the boy's father. It was half and half really. With me never having had a father when I was a kid, I was more into my boyfriends being one for me. He was twenty-three this one, quite a bit older than me. But he never wanted to stay. He was always off behind the sheds with me mates. Shagging. So that was that, really.'

She looks away again. 'They've all got different fathers, my boys. Some of them had jobs and some of them didn't. None of them wanted to settle down. Except one – the father of the third. We was going to get married. We was together a year or two and then one day I caught him in bed with me best mate and I threw him out. So ... '

All the time she talks, she flicks the end of her cigarette, hardly bothering to smoke it. 'I had trouble with looking after my first boy. I had stitches and piles and backache and I could hardly move and so my mam had to take over. Then my second one didn't want to eat, he couldn't get his food down and he kept being sick, so the health visitor said I should let my mam try with him, so she took over with him, too. They're still my kids, still call me mam, but she looks after them. It was the same thing with the next two.

'I did have my own house for a while and I lived there with my third child. It was good there. I had a shagpile carpet and a cooker and a fridge and a washer and there was a carpet in the boy's room with all clowns and aeroplanes on it. Then I got burgled and they nicked it all. They didn't take the shagpile carpet. But they nicked everything else and the water boiler, too, and when they was carrying it out, they spilled all oil and water all over the carpet, so it was ruined. I had to chuck it out. I had trouble with the neighbours and all. One of them used to batter her kids and I told her if she did it again, I'd bloody batter her, so she got all her mates on me. I just jacked it in and went back to my mam.'

Social workers have been continually involved with Tina since 1988. One of her boyfriends had a conviction for sexually abusing children and whenever he moved into the house, they registered the children as being at risk of sexual abuse. But for the most part they believed the family could survive as long as Tina's mother was there to hold the loose ends together. It was in the summer of last year that it began to drift into its final crisis. That was when Tina gave birth to her fifth boy, Jason. She had moved in with a boyfriend called Donnie who thought he was the baby's father. 'I told him loads of times that he wasn't but he just wouldn't take it in.' Donnie, who was only ten years old when he was first locked away for theft and violence, insisted that Jason belonged to him.

'He's always threatening me. I've broken up with him loads of times and he comes round threatening me, and my mam says "Look, we won't get no peace till you go back with him." So I have to go with him. Then we break up again. It was him that broke the windows at the front of the house. He's burned out stolen cars in the back garden, just chucks petrol at them and lights them to wind us up. He could have set the house on fire. He always makes trouble for me. I really hate him. And he's not my baby's dad.'

As Christmas approached, Donnie stepped up the pressure. 'He was phoning ambulances to come up here and calling out the fire brigade and ordering taxis to come out here and pick me up. Just winding me up. Then he starts sending the police round. He told them there was drugs here. Then he told them there was stolen property here. So we get the CID up here asking loads of questions.'

Shortly before Christmas, she says, Donnie came up with a new tactic. 'He started getting on to the police and telling them there was five kids left alone here and then they'd come round and see me and my mam here and they'd go away. I don't know why they listen to him. He always tells them he's the baby's dad. But he wasn't. I know he wasn't. He was in prison when I fell pregnant.' But Donnie persisted and went to court to apply for an order for Jason to live with him. He lost. His lawyer applied for an interim order. Donnie lost again. Social workers and health visitors were still in and out of the house. On 6 November, all five boys were examined by a doctor and found to be in good health. Visiting social workers found that the children were well dressed and warm and that conditions, though poor, were adequate, although on the most recent visit, on 30 December, Tina's mother was fed up and threatening to leave.

The next day Tina's mother moved to another daughter's house in search of peace. Two days later, on Sunday 2 January, the crisis broke when, shortly after midday, Donnie turned up at the house once more. 'He said he wanted to take the baby out. I thought, what with all these court cases he was bringing, it would help me out if I let him. So I said he had to wait while I bathed him and changed his clothes but he wouldn't wait, he said he had a taxi standing there, so he just took the baby. He never even took his milk.

'I told him to get him back by three. But he never turned up, so I started to get worried and I called the social workers and they said he'd taken the baby to hospital for nappy rash. I said I was treating it with baby cream. It was his fault, he wouldn't let me change the baby's clothes. I tried to get the baby from the hospital but he'd taken him away by then. So I called the police and put them on to him. The next thing I knew, about midnight, they was on my doorstep and I says, "Where's my baby?" and they say, "You're not having your baby, you haven't been looking after him, you're not getting him back."'

There are different versions of the argument that followed. The police say Tina then ran out of the house and could not be found. Tina says the police ordered her out of the house because she was trying to stop them taking her other children. The police say they had to hunt for her for forty-eight hours. She says she was standing on the street corner in the cold. 'I was just crying me eyes out there. I didn't know what to do. About half past one, I saw 'em bring my boys out. I could see 'em all in the back of the car. I was screaming and crying. I didn't know what to do.'

The next morning the foster parents broke the story on Radio Leeds. By the time it reached the national newspapers it had taken on a momentum of its own. Many reports suggested the children had been 'home alone'. The *Daily Telegraph* produced the most extravagant account: 'A young mother left her five children, all under the age of seven, to fend for themselves in appalling squalor for four days.' In spite of the evidence of social workers, the *Independent* reported that after being taken into care, 'the children were given warm clothing, fed and bathed – possibly for the first time in weeks'. The most shocking element in the story was the dog mess, which was said to have been spread throughout the house and over the children. Tina says that her sister's puppy had made a mess in two of the bedrooms, that she had kept telling her sister to clear it up and was leaving it because it was her puppy. 'It wasn't all over the house. The downstairs was just like normal. I clean, I wash, I look after my kids. I'm not some rich snob, but I'm not dirty either.' Some papers reported that the children had been naked in the street, begging for food, but the same papers described Tina's two sisters, who were living in the house, as men. These reports appear to have come from neighbours.

The courts issued interim care orders, sending the four oldest boys to a foster family and – to Tina's despair – ordering that the baby Jason should stay with Donnie's family. Social workers are now preparing detailed reports on the family for court hearings, which are due in February. The Social Services Department will not discuss the case, but they are clear about its context.

The city's Social Services chairman, Michael Simmons, said: 'We have seen a steady increase in poverty and a steady dismantling of the benefit system. The whole system has got tighter. They now get no benefits at all for their children aged sixteen to eighteen. If their cooker blows up, they used to get a grant to replace it. Now all they get is a loan and they have to pay that back out of income support, which is, by definition, already at the level of poverty. This is deprivation. And I am afraid deprivation and neglect go hand in hand.

'People in these circumstances become depressed – clinically depressed. Their physical health suffers: they eat bad food and wear inadequate clothing. They all suffer stress, children as well as adults. We have a young boy now who is literally chewing the ends off his fingers, breaking the flesh, drawing blood. We have numerous homes who live without electricity or gas, because the new privatised companies have put them on meters and they simply don't have the cash to pay for fuel. In a few cases, we find they don't even have water; they're running a hose pipe from the house next door.

'Their kids can't go to school because they can't afford school meals or proper clothing, and they don't have the know-how or the money or the energy to drag five children across Leeds to fill in complicated forms to get help. And now the schools have started turning them away. Since schools have been compiling league tables, there are headteachers in this city who are deliberately excluding children like this to avoid damaging their statistics. Some of these children just can't cope with school. There was one family who simply couldn't communicate. The children just cried all the time. Why? They were extremely unhappy. And who can blame them?

'It all flows from this extraordinary idea that we have to give rich people an incentive to work by giving them more money and poor people an incentive to work by taking money away from them. These people are not evil. If they're bad parents, it's not because they don't care about their children. It is because they cannot cope. We see cases like this every day of every week. You are talking about a fairly routine occurrence, but it is an area which most people are quite happy to ignore. They leave it to one side until they become sentimental at Christmas. It's the puppy syndrome.'

Tina Sampson sits alone in the bare bones of her house, behind the boarded windows. Her mother has not come back. She has no pictures of the children; she has never had a camera. She has nothing to do: there was a television but someone stole it after Christmas. The troublesome puppy has been given away. She's dragged her few sticks of furniture and scraps of carpet into the garden to burn them, in case anyone says they're too dirty to be near children. She wants to get drunk and cut her arm, but she can't in case anyone says that proves she's a bad mother.

The other night, she was asleep on a mattress in the front room and she woke herself up because she was crying in her sleep. It was about half past four in the morning and there was no one around and, anyway, she knew by then that no one was interested in what she thought. So she took a biro and she went to the bare plaster wall of the chimney breast in her front room, and wrote the names of her five boys. Then she wrote them again, and again. Finally, she wrote in square capital letters 'I love my kids' and then again 'I want my kids', as if somebody might see it and do something for her. •

The names of Tina Sampson, Jason and Donnie have been invented to conceal the identity of the family.

Picture: Richard Oliver

Marques of success ... Tony Harrison, aged fifty-two, has worked at the plant for twenty-two years. Some of the models that have vanished in his time could return, it is said.

Leader
2 February 1994

The will and the way

It is simply not an option for the British Government to tell the country's motor industry to make its own way in the world. Already there has been a dramatic decline in its fortunes: a loss of volume, with car production almost halved in fifteen years and trucks down by two thirds in less than a decade; and an increase in assembly operations, with Vauxhall now an assembler of Opel kits and Talbot (formerly Rootes) an assembler of Peugeot kits.

An ominous development has been an increase in foreign ownership and control. Foreign investment and interest is, of course, to be welcomed, but control has its dangers. For the major parts of the British motor industry to fall entirely into foreign hands would leave it a hostage to decisions in Detroit, Paris, Turin and perhaps Tokyo. Experience shows, time and time again, that when the going gets rough, as it always will in such a cyclical industrial sector, foreign subsidiaries (which in this case means subsidiaries in Britain) will bear the brunt of the cutbacks. The skills in research and development tend to be lost. That is why the future of the sole remaining British-owned and British-controlled motor manufacturer, Rover, will continue to be a matter for the Government. Otherwise the British motor industry will find itself further down the cul-de-sac to extinction.

Sometimes the writers of this column come across a statement of principle and perception by another hand which it is impossible to better. So it is with the two paragraphs above. They come from Where There's a Will, *published by Arrow in 1987. Author: Michael Heseltine.* •

Maureen Freely
6 January 1994

In hock to family values

O nce upon a time, when I was a respectable Oxford housewife, I shared a nanny with John Redwood. It was not a happy association. Neither he nor his wife betrayed a single human weakness: they were as clean and well groomed as their political mottos. They tried to forgive me for being scruffy but, six months on, when I had still not caught on to the importance of brushed hair and neatly tied shoelaces, they gave up on me in disgust.

Soon afterwards, they moved out of the neighbourhood and into power, while I drifted into divorce, adultery and the moral turpitude of single motherhood. When I heard John Redwood's first tirade against me and my kind, I was pregnant with my second illegitimate child. It made me mute with rage – and not just because of his political opportunism.

This man is not pretending. He is one of those appalling creatures who practises what he preaches. I remember thinking, 'If only I could use my privileged knowledge to accuse him of hypocrisy!' Alas, the only thing I could say against him was that he had once burned my fingers by serving a glass of boiling mulled wine.

This week I have had the pleasure of watching him struggle to cover for the transgressions of a less admirable colleague. Tim Yeo is not a hypocrite, he tells us, because he contributes to the support of his illegitimate child. 'I objected to men fathering babies with no intention of supporting them,' he said on the radio programme *Today*. 'Clearly this is not the situation in this case.'

Now, finally, I can accuse him of twisting his own words. I can use these same words to prove that he is not qualified to speak on the subject. Forget how the other half live – he doesn't even seem to know what his half gets up to. This is the norm, John. Good intentions do not always turn into happy marriages. When ministers fall in love, they sometimes forget to use condoms. The public is ready to accept that politicians are sexually fallible. The time has come for the Cabinet to come out of the closet.

I see no reason why Tim Yeo needed to be punished for having an affair or for having an illegitimate child. I'm not even inclined to see his behaviour, taken on its own, as foolish, or even irresponsible. Someone else in his position might have tried to make the problem go away by forcing the woman to have an abortion. But he's respected her wishes and accepted responsibility for the child. What I object to are his hypocritical comments about how the rest of us should live.

I refuse to forgive him for being human until such a time as he and his government accept that the electorate is also human. And not just human but trying very hard. If these people bothered to use their eyes, if only once a year while standing in a Christmas queue, they would see that divorcees and adulterers and single mothers and even most absent fathers are just as much in hock to the same stupid family values as they are.

Today, especially, as our December bank statements cast their horrible shadows over Twelfth Night, reprobates like me are aware of the cost of aspiring to this ideal. And so naturally we complain about being misunderstood. But as we do so, we are leaving it to the Redwoods and Yeos of this world to set the terms of the debate.

Let me give you a small example. Years ago, when I was first drifting into divorce and single motherhood, I suffered from chronic pneumonia. My doctor told me that the best thing for me to do was to take up swimming, and so I did. One day, when the children were on holiday, I took them along to the pool with me. I didn't want to leave them unattended in the wading pool. I had them sit in the bleachers so that I could see them while I did some lengths. The lifeguard objected. When I explained that I was swimming on doctor's orders, he reminded me that my job as a mother was to look after my children, not my health.

I get the same message every time I listen to a Tory family values pontificator. And I'll take this opportunity to say to them what I wish I had said to that lifeguard: that they grossly misunderstand what parents need to do a decent job.

If you're going to look after children in sickness and health, you have to look after your own health, too. If you need two pay cheques to keep a roof over their heads, you need schools and other institutions to see the two-pay-cheque family as normal. If you're going to make sure children outside wedlock get the best possible care, you set up a system that supports and rewards the parents who take their responsibilities seriously. Most important, you need to treat all parents as equals.

Here we come to the part of the doomed Yeo defence that I found the most laughable: his claim that he did not jeopardise Conservative policy on the family because his financial support meant that his child was costing the state nothing. I object to this not only because it is double-speak but also because it implies that money is all a child needs from his father.

He may well believe that paternal love is best administered through direct debit. It's a commonly held view. Despite the Children's Act, it continues to define family policy and the decisions in most of the country's courts. Care and control of children is still most likely to go to the mother in the event of a divorce. Divorced fathers have few real rights. Natural fathers have no rights at all. Not even if they do the right-wing thing like Tim Yeo and pledge support!

That's why I pity him for his hypocrisy instead of hating him for it. His moral short-termism has not just lost him his place in the Cabinet. It has weakened his entitlement to his own child.

Hasn't the time come to take family values away from the Tories and redefine them so that they help parents instead of tripping them up? Surely, the point of the exercise is not to punish people who live outside that impossible dream called the traditional family but to give all our children the best possible start in life. If the Tories thought beyond the corner shop, they would realise that this more pragmatic project would, in the long run, also be the cheapest.

A stable society is not made up of brittle, secretive families that are racked with shame every time they fall short of perfection, and that hide their faults until they turn into scandals and social problems. It is made up of families that are flexible enough to adapt to changing circumstances, and strong enough to be publicly accountable for their shortcomings.

Need I add that what works for families could also work for the Cabinet? Think how different the government would look today if philanderers did not always have to be hypocrites. •

Ian Katz
10 December 1993

Goldmine Sachs

Two years ago the people of the large east African country of Tanzania produced goods and services worth an impressive sounding $2.2 billion. Trouble is there were almost 26 million of them, so that if the cash had been distributed equally – and few imagine it was – each person would have pocketed less than $100. Not quite the sort of money to set you thinking about a new Merc, or even a modest Mediterranean holiday.

But imagine, if you will, that there were only 161 people in Tanzania. Granted, the bars might be a little empty; but life would be pretty cushy, wouldn't it? You don't need a GCSE in mathematics to work out that every Tanzanian would quickly become a multi-millionaire.

It's unimaginable, of course, that such a colossal sum could be divided between such a small group. What could they possibly have done to earn it? How could they possibly *spend* it? It was questions like these which engaged barstool philosophers this week as a flurry of press reports brought news of the record profits made by the American investment bank Goldman Sachs.

When all the sums had been done, we learned, the firm was expected to make a pre-tax profit this year of about $2.6 billion – give or take a few hundred million. We barely had time to calculate the National Insurance on this sum before we had been made privy to another staggering 'leak': the company would be rewarding up to 100 of its 1,500 London employees with $1 million bonuses. (In the world of high finance, it seems, few people count out more than their pocket change in humble pounds sterling.) The good times, City commentators declared, were back.

Delightful as the news of the new Christmas millionaires was for every luxury car dealer, florist and expensive restaurant within a five-mile radius of Goldman's Fleet Street European headquarters – not to mention the millionaires themselves – it missed the point. The real significance of the firm's zero-laden profit figures lies in its unique ownership arrangements.

Goldman Sachs is the last of the great investment banking partnerships. Most financial firms started that way but have long since passed into the hands of thousands of faceless shareholders. The conventional wisdom was that companies needed to raise enormous amounts of capital to compete in the vast new global market. They did it by floating their stock, and partners, who typically sold their stakes for many times their so-called 'book' value, rarely felt sentimental for long.

At Goldman's, though, there are no legions of shareholders eagerly awaiting their dividend cheques in the Christmas mail. That $2.6 billion? With the exception of a few hundred million going to a handful of institutions holding non-voting shares, it will be divided up between the firm's 161 'general partners'. Welcome to the other Tanzania.

Not that the loot will be shared equally between these Masters of the Universe, of course; some partners are more, well, equal than others. According to this week's reports, around $5 million will be par for the course among the twenty-six partners in the firm's London office. That, for instance, is the amount by which economist Gavyn Davies, Labour Party theorist and one of the earliest British Goldman partners, should be richer by the end of 1993.

Rival investment bankers who have long been plunged into Yuletide fits of depression by estimates of the payouts to their Goldman counterparts suggest the figures could be much higher. 'You only have to do the maths,' says one former Wall Street grandee. 'The top guys will be making $10 million easy. I had a friend there who was making $15 million back in the eighties.'

Understated or not, the bonus leaks are said by staffers to have sent the firm's management 'ballistic'. Marcus Goldman, its founder, supposedly walked around Manhattan with a selection of promissory notes tucked into the headband of his high silk hat. But they may have been the last shreds of information the company willingly revealed.

At least throughout the second half of its 125-year history, the firm's name has rarely appeared in print far from the qualifying adjective 'discreet'. To be sure, you could be forgiven for thinking Messrs Goldman and Sachs were partners in a small south London dental practice to judge from the firm's minuscule entry in the phone book.

A genial press officer will tell you, pleasantly enough, that he can tell you just about nothing: 'Private partnership, you see ... not, between you and me, very pro-publicity.' Any chance of a peek, at least, into the award-winning office building Goldman had grafted on to the listed façade of the former *Daily Telegraph* office? 'Absolute no-noer.' (An anonymous staffer is helpful here: 'It's sober – grey and wood finishes – understatedly expensive, certainly not flash.')

The culture of discretion runs deep at Goldman. As a private firm it is not required to publish any annual reports. Profit figures – and just about anything else you might want to know – must be teased from information provided to other firms or regulatory bodies. Employees exhibit near-Masonic reticence when talking about the company; those prepared to say anything, always on condition of anonymity, grudgingly part with bland reflections on office management that might apply to any institution employing more than twenty people.

Former employees, even those who left years ago, are guarded too, talking as though they are somehow still subject to its strictures. Even rivals insist on anonymity, for heaven's sake. Those willing to speak refer to the firm with a mixture of envy, awe and something approaching terror. A source at a leading UK rival is unusually effusive: 'It's a phenomenal company. Don't even think that people look on them other than as an awesome company.' A handful venture a tentative dig at the firm's reputation for hard work. 'They're known as the Moonies because they have this very driven, almost cultish thing about them,' says the British banker. 'It is said they warn the better halves of people they employ that they should assume they won't see them again for five years.'

'They are an extremely hard-working, highly organised, highly disciplined organisation that would probably be best described as a sweatshop,' says a bold American rival. 'They are bores because they have no outside life.'

Tales of Goldman's fanaticism are common currency in the City's wine bars. There is the one about a partner who said of a recent hiring: 'I am so glad he has decided to join us: his wife will really fit in.' Another is the one about a group of Goldman employees who attended a meeting on a rainy weekend in London last year; as other bankers hailed cabs afterwards, the Goldman team donned track-suits and ran off together.

Rivals enjoy caricaturing the 'mentor' system under which new recruits are placed under the close supervision of a partner. In the firm's global headquarters at 85 Broad Street these guardian figures are said to be known as 'rabbis'. Others point to the Big Brother-like reports which employees are required to file on the performance of their colleagues – these are used as part of what the firm's chairman, Stephen Friedman, calls 'a very difficult set of matrices' with which the management committee of eleven decides how much it should reward each employee. (Goldman's prides itself on the fact that performance bonuses are not based on anything so crude as the amount an individual has earned for the firm; that might discourage the teamwork which it tries to foster.) Some even giggle about the fourteen-point 'bible' of so-called business principles issued to every recruit.

Any rival's volunteered insights on life at 133 Fleet Street must be treated with great caution for one simple reason, however. Goldman's has been running rings around most of them for years and this year it has run even more rings than usual.

All the help the firm will provide a journalist is to supply a few media cuttings charting its apparently inexorable rise through the financial stratosphere. End-less graphs and tables catalogue Goldman's pre-eminence in terse categories such as 'advisory', 'underwriting' and 'trading'. The figures speak for themselves: since the early eighties the firm's staff has increased from fewer than 3,500 to more than 7,000. Profits have increased from $400 million a year to this year's estimated $2.6 billion.

In keeping with its claim to the moral high ground, Goldman's refused, during the corporate take-over frenzy of the mid-eighties, to represent hostile bidders. But in recent years the firm has matched its rise through the investment banking league tables with a spirited debut in those controversy leagues to which it had long been a stranger.

First it was drawn into the Milken–Boesky insider trading scandal through links between its senior arbitrageur, Robert Freeman, and Martin Siegel, the Wall Street financier who admitted he had passed confidential information to Ivan Boesky. Later it was singed by its role in facilitating Robert Maxwell's crooked dealings; after a lengthy investigation, the City watchdog, the Securities and Futures Authority, fined it £160,000 for a minor technical transgression, absolving it of more serious wrongdoing.

There are other, more esoteric, complaints about the robust way in which the firm solicits business, and then executes it. Did it perhaps misjudge an $843 million issue of shares in China Steel, considered a flop? Was the placing of its giant $1.5 billion Ford Motor Credit bond (a device used to raise money for the auto-firm) a little 'lopsided' in favour of the US? Perhaps.

But there is no getting away from the fact that in 1993, the men and women of Goldman played a blinder. (The year before, after all, they made a mere $1.5 billion.)

Competitors are quick to point at the ways in which 1993 was a highly unusual year – 'unsustainable', they say. The US bond market has been booming as companies take advantage of low inflation to raise cash through low interest bond issues. Then there have been the extraordinary currency fluctuations: 'Soros made $1 billion out of the pound and I'm pretty sure Goldman's wouldn't have made much less,' says one US rival.

Like other big American banks, blessed with vast capital reserves, Goldman's is making more and more of its money from dealing with its own money – so-called 'own-account trading' – as opposed to through its traditional roles of advising other firms and acting on their behalf. 'They are eating off the merchant banker's table but they are also cleaning up in the kitchen,' says one City source.

Both rivals and former employees insist that the limited ownership is at the heart of Goldman's success. 'The partnership system breeds a very close-to-the-bone attitude,' says one US competitor. 'Everyone's proverbials are on the line.' Another suggests Goldman's traders are prepared to take bolder positions because they are not gambling shareholders' money.

The bank approaches the business of recruitment with characteristic zeal and attention to detail. Graduate trainees are subjected to a selection procedure reminiscent of exclusive London social clubs – more than twenty interviews with 'everyone from the desk secretary up to a partner' are typical according to one former Goldman trader. If any one of them rejects the candidate, they may not be taken on.

'It's open warfare to get in but once you get in, you're part of a club,' says another ex-staffer. 'They spend a long time telling you that you are the best. They make you feel that you belong, that you're part of this great engine.'

And at the end of the long tunnel of late nights and Sundays spent analysing offer documents lies the ultimate reward: partnership. Sometimes the tunnel is not so long. Star performers are typically admitted to the inner circle in their early or mid-thirties.

The joke among initiates is that new partners generally take a pay cut when they are first appointed because they are required to plough most of their colossal earnings back into the firm's capital reserves. For the same reason many retire young, so that they can extricate their paper millions and live it up. There are few partners over fifty.

'You can't draw out enough cash to display your wealth ostentatiously while you're still in the firm,' says one rival. Just like Tanzania. •

Matthew Engel
9 December 1993

It is no good asking me, I was only Prime Minister

Lord Justice Scott told Lady Thatcher they were anxious to draw on her 'almost unparalleled experience in government'. But nothing in her experience had remotely prepared her for the Scott inquiry.

There was this barrister with the funny name, a pleasing simper and the hint of a lisp, Presiley Baxendale QC, precisely the kind of smart young woman who might have impressed Lady Thatcher in a meeting at No. 10, asked some penetrating questions and done her career a lot of good.

Miss Baxendale asked lots of questions. Lady Thatcher was sorry but for the most part these were matters of detail and she was not able to help. And, being a busy person, she seemed very anxious to leave.

'I don't think I can add any more,' she said at 10.25 am. The questioning had hardly started. She couldn't leave.

The day wore on. Outside, behind the shutters, the traffic roared by in Buckingham Gate, darkness fell and the wind got up. Spectators nodded off or wandered out. But the Great Stateswoman was trapped as if arrested.

Of course, she is accustomed to answering questions: fifteen minutes twice a week in the House, fifty minutes now and again with Walden or Dimbleby. But here she was not in command of the situation. It went on and on. And Miss Baxendale kept asking her to find page 2,456 or Project 1,728.

It was very unBritish. There are no wigs and no oaths at the Scott inquiry, which is lucky because 'the whole truth' is a concept with which Britain's rulers have some difficulty. Most important, Britain's former leaders expect to be left to flog their memoirs in peace, not to be called to account.

So Lady Thatcher had to rely on guidance from overseas models. Her performance was part Nixon, who took the responsibility but not the blame, part Reagan, who remembered nothing, and part Ceausescu, who regretted nothing and how dare they?

She might have done better to have copied Honecker, who acquired a cancer of convenience, or Idi Amin, who vanished. There was a touch of General Salazar, who so terrified the Portuguese that no one dared tell him he had been ousted. So he kept giving orders from his sick-bed till he died.

Lady Thatcher kept using the present tense. 'I do not substitute my own judgement unless I have great reason to do so. There are nineteen departments and eighty-three ministers.' This was the theme: Lady Thatcher concerned with policy not administration. Miss Baxendale kept asking the questions about MoD

24.1 page 299, and paragraph 7, and (my favourite) Guideline Little Three. Lady Thatcher kept saying she had never seen any of these; how could she cope with all this detail?

'Miss Baxendale, if I'd seen every minute that was ever written in government, I'd have been in a snowstorm.

'I'm not going to comment,' she said at one point, 'on a background note to a minister who had great responsibilities who was capable of discharging those responsibilities. I accept the Foreign Secretary's judgement.'

This was a reference to Sir Geoffrey Howe, whose judgement is dealt with in some detail in the memoirs.

'Delegation matters in government,' she said later.

'I have to say,' said Robin Cook, who was one of the more gleeful observers, 'that I don't remember this style of government.'

Lady Thatcher's initial response was to be patronising. Then she grew tetchy. Twenty minutes after the start she used the third worst insult known to an English courtroom: 'With respect'. Twenty minutes after that she skipped the second worst ('With great respect') and went straight on to the worst: 'With the greatest possible respect...' As the exchanges wore on, she grew less combative.

12.28 – Lady T (wearily): Can I help any more?

Miss B (bouncily): Certainly. We've got *lots* more.

12.50 – Miss B (routinely): We're nearly at the end of this correspondence.

Lady T (very weakly): Good.

3.30 – Lady T (with an air of finality): There were big things, this was dealt with very briefly.

Miss B (rapidly): Can we go on to MoD 40 part 3 page 43 ...

4.00 Lord Justice Scott (solicitously): I don't know if you're flagging.

Lady T (almost inaudibly): No, no.

Should this have been on television? Of course, but only the edited version will seem like truly great theatre. Huge amounts of time were taken up dealing with the subjects that obsess the Iraqgate buffs, such as the Cohen Question (asked by Harry Cohen MP in 1989) which has become the grassy knoll of the conspiracy theorists.

Personally, I have always thought that conspiracy theories are just things concocted by MI5, the Freemasons and the Kremlin. But when the cock-ups become sequential and interlinked, well, who knows? Not Lady Thatcher. She was only Prime Minister. •

Lobby terms

Michael White

25 June 1994

Apply here for top job: portly rightists will have priority

The World's most exclusive JobCentre opened for business on the sun-drenched shores of the Mediterranean yesterday to interview candidates for one of the few employment opportunities created on the continent in recent years: the presidency of the European Commission.

The post having been held by a small socialist from a large country – the Frenchman, Jacques Delors – European rules specify that it must next be held by a large conservative from a small country, preferably Jean-Luc Dehaene.

The portly prime minister from Belgium advertised his suitability for the post yesterday by trying to pick his nose on television.

Tension over the appointment mounted all day, insofar as tension does on an island covered in bougainvillaea where everyone lives to be ninety. Mostly it mounted over the World Cup.

Ever sensitive to popular feeling, the Euro heads of government did not rush their decision. Before getting down to the big one over a working dinner in the Achilleion Palace, they ate their way through working breakfasts and lunches, and slept through some important treaty-signings as well as a two-hour Greek siesta – which is like a Spanish siesta, only less energetic.

This was appropriate. Nothing has happened in Corfu for centuries except that most of the twelve member states of the European Union have taken it in turns to capture, rebuild and bombard the Old Fort where four new members signed on yesterday.

The siesta also seemed sensible since the summit's Greek host, Andreas Papandreou, aged seventy-five, looked fragile even by Euro standards.

It must be quite a worry having such a young wife – Mimi, the blonde in red, having to sit so close to the French president, François Mitterrand, that is, in the same room. You can never be too careful with seventy-seven-year-old fellow socialists: they are so competitive and weak on property rights.

A lot of time has been devoted here to being nice to Boris Yeltsin, the only one to bring his own warship.

The Russian president signed something called a partnership agreement,

WELL, YOU CANT VOTE FOR NELSON MANDELA, AND THAT'S THAT.

which everyone said was frightfully important but actually did not have a cheque attached. In any case, Mr Yeltsin is part of the European jobs problem, persistently late for work and trained to turn out a product no one wants: communism.

Mr Yeltsin behaved impeccably. All the same, the contrast with Silvio Berlusconi was a cruel one. The media mogul has become so successful that, instead of sacking his presidents and prime ministers from time to time – as Rupert Murdoch does – he has decided to cut out the middleman and do the job himself.

This was his summit debut. Mr Berlusconi signed the treaty of accession with a huge egotistical B, whereas John Major provided a somewhat cramped and repressed handwriting sample.

The two prime ministers breakfasted to discuss who to support for Mr Delors's job. British officials refused to disclose the result, so it must have been someone who would appeal to Mr Berlusconi *and* Mr Major's Eurosceptics – probably Kelvin MacKenzie.

Officially Britain has a cunning plan to increase its influence in Europe by supporting Sir Leon Brittan, 'His Oiliness' as he is known in Brussels.

The weakness of Sir Leon's candidacy is twofold. One, no one likes him. Two, Sir Leon comes from Mars, not even an associate member of the EU yet. You can tell from that haircut, that voice, that accent (his English accent is even worse).

Any doubt on that score was resolved here on Thursday night, when Sir Leon announced a press conference to coincide with Italy's critical World Cup tie. No one attended, not even Sir Leon.

The summit survived and even managed to discuss such trival matters as Bosnia and Italian milk quotas.

Never mind. What with the heat, the security wilted into pleasing informality.

Corfu will be a hard act to follow, and the Germans are not even going to try. Their summit will be in the industrial Ruhr. Not much bougainvillaea in Essen in December. •

David McKie
27 June 1994

....

The choice between two Labour lettuces

A preacher who came to my school asserted that if you took a rabbit, and set it down at a point equidistant between two lettuces, the creature would die of starvation before it decided which lettuce to go for. For years, I believed this was true, until some scientific person declared it nonsense.

But the contest for the Labour deputy leadership is making me reconsider. Take the case of Joe Stubbs: Joe in the constituency, although Joseph Stubbs on the cover of his 1986 publication, *Tribalism and alignment in the British Labour Party, 1980 – 82* (Recondite Press, £40). Stubbs came into the House in 1987 as member for Gritdyke. Since then, it's become quite a safe seat, though that hasn't stopped him worrying about it.

The Labour deputy leadership contest has been making Joe very worried indeed. He's spent an unusual amount of time at home over the past few weeks because of his injury. Something wrong with his foot. He blames an accident with a trowel, though some Westminster colleagues say it got trampled on in the stampede to be first to nominate Blair. Joe has no doubts about Blair, since he, too, is a moderniser. There's been some trouble over this preference with his partner, Sarah. (They've been together for several years now, since he separated from Miriam. Pressures of Westminster life. Drifted apart after he got elected.) Sarah, who, to be honest, is nowadays a bit to the left of Joe, doesn't take to Blair at all. Can't understand what brought him into the party, she says. Couldn't even bring himself to promise John Humphrys that he'd tax back some of the money the Tories had given the rich through tax cuts. Talked of 'not taking sides' in the rail dispute. Not taking sides! Between Railtrack and the union?

Sarah was so incensed that she seized the copy of Etzioni's *Spirit of the Community* which Joe was quietly reading and hit him over the head with it. 'What on earth do you expect him to say?' Joe remonstrated. 'We can't go back to doctrines of class solidarity now. The Labour Party's evolved.' 'I'll tell you what's evolved,' Sarah said, *'you've* bloody evolved. You've become a bloody right-winger. Remember the publication you were selling on the street corner the day we first met?' (And, of course, he did. But he's grown out of all that now.)

But they don't argue too much over Blair, since they both assume he has won already. The problem is over the deputy. Why is Joe so reluctant to commit himself to Beckett? Male chauvinism, Sarah insists, though Joe denies it: as he

told her the other day (she at the stove, he reading Blair's policy document), Joe
is Pure New Man.

How could he even *consider* voting for Prescott, Sarah demanded. That *antique*
macho image! That sense of being ready to pick a fight? All right, he didn't hit
people, but he went round looking as if he would like to. And the incoherence!
'An incoherent tongue,' Sarah says, 'is the mark of an incoherent mind.' She's a
liberal studies lecturer at Gritdyke Poly. Sorry, university.

Sometimes, Joe begins to worry whether it even matters. What's a deputy
leader? The title was only invented because Herbert Morrison felt the world
undervalued him. (The poor old chap wasn't to know that he'd one day be
remembered as Peter Mandelson's grandfather.) Given the choice, Joe would
have liked Gordon Brown as Blair's number two. They were a natural team.
Failing that, he'd have gone for Cook, who might look like a gnome, but had a
mind like a gimlet and terrified the Tories. Still, here we were with Margaret
and John.

And, of course, Sarah was right. There were very good reasons for backing
Margaret. First (though you couldn't say so in quite these terms, in case it
sounded like tokenism), she was a woman. Also, she was the incumbent: did she
really deserve, on her record, to be replaced? And shouldn't she have some credit
for putting her job on the line, instead of sitting tight, declining to enter a
leadership contest with Blair, and so ruling out any contest for the deputy
leadership? Also you had to admit she had done a splendid job as stand-in leader.
So incisive at Question Time; and outside the House, so dignified and serene.

Was it really male chauvinism which caused him to nurse bad feelings about
Margaret? The very thought sent a pang of guilt through him. But her record
troubled him. He'd been in the Dome at Brighton that awful night when Margaret accused Neil Kinnock of selling his political soul for a few pieces of silver
(after Kinnock had declined to back Benn against Healey in 1981). He remembered her taking the job which Joan Lestor had just resigned on a point of
principle.

And he hadn't last year liked the way that Margaret had distanced herself from
John Smith over OMOV. 'Truckling to a union vote she may one day need,' he'd
recorded in his notebook. As a columnist for the *Gritdyke Gazette*, and a writer
from time to time in the *Guardian*, he collected words like 'truckling'.

It was Brighton last year which made him warm to Prescott. That defence of
Smith: 'This man has put his head on the block; we've got to support him.'
Wonderfully stirring. The language might not have been quite as coherent as
that, but the message was unmistakable. It had been the saving of Smith; had
he lost, John would have quit the leadership. Joe had a lump in his throat at that
moment, he didn't mind telling you.

What finally made up his mind was Margaret on radio sounding appeasing towards the unions; also saying she felt she was better than Thatcher at a similar stage. So here is what he is doing. He is casting the vote he holds as a Member of Parliament for John Prescott. But his five other votes, as a party member both in Gritdyke and London, and as a member of three affiliated organisations (two unions and the Fabians) are going to Margaret. Admittedly his MP's vote is worth roughly 200 times as much as the others, but at least it redresses the balance.

He hasn't got round to breaking the news to Sarah, but that is what he will do. Unless between now and then, someone moves one of the lettuces. •

Hugo Young
3 May 1994

A demagogue's lost empire shrouded in myths

In a disillusioned age, four characters offer themselves as a committee of national salvation. They are emblematic figures, creatures of our time, favoured by the *Daily Mail*.

First up is the Sentimentalist. He locates the source of Britain's disillusion with itself a long time ago. It all began with the end of empire. This was the moment the British began to lose themselves. But it wasn't the British, as such. The end of empire was an élitist conspiracy, the first of many, about which the British were not consulted. And this tyranny of the governors stretched further. Neither Africa nor India really wanted self-government. They weren't consulted either, and wish it had never happened. Britain let the empire down. 'It had the financial and military resources to carry on,' the Sentimentalist asserts. 'All it lacked was the will.'

But if there was an economic problem, he adds in caveat, it had a simple cause. The block vote of trade unions was responsible for the end of empire, just as for every other British economic shortcoming, including the trade deficit with the infamous European Community. Trade unions were another élitist folly. The people never wanted them, never had the slightest interest in redressing the power of capital. For the world of the Sentimentalist is wonderfully simple. He has lists of other laws as well which only go to prove that modern government is a conspiracy against the governed. Food standards, environmental protection, health and safety at work, a hundred other monstrous statutes: none, 'so far as I can discover', have any basis in popular demand.

A natural bed-fellow for the Sentimentalist, it will be apparent, is the Paranoiac. In this universe of hatred for all that Britain is, the paranoid style has much to bite on. It finds a world of soft judges, lax prosecutors, tormented policemen and not enough hanging – preferably in public. In describing this world, the Paranoiac is driven to lard an admittedly bad situation with some extravagant assertions: for example, that 'in many areas' people are victims of crime 'once a week', and that there is 'an increasing ideological reluctance to send anyone to prison at all'. He also neglects to favour us with an explanation of why, in this land of 'undemocratic' liberalism, there are more people in jail than anywhere else in Europe; and fails, equally, to address the topical issue of innocent persons who might have been wrongly hanged, whether in public or private. For the Paranoiac, such quibbles must be mere distractions, confirming the very malignity against which he proposes himself as saviour.

Another such is the cost of the policing and imprisoning state he recommends – perhaps because this tedious detail would inconvenience a mind already eaten up with selective rage against public spending. Gazing upon the failure even of his late-heroine to effect a permanent decimation of the budget, the Paranoiac briefly flirts with the complicating fact that public services are popular, before lighting on the axiom that present tax levels are an 'undemocratic defiance of what the public wants and is universally known to want'. Detesting the welfare state, but unable to discover how much of its cost goes on fraud, he supplies some research. 'A billion? Five billion? Twenty billion? It could well be the last figure.' Rather like the belief that it is 'not only common but usual' for Oxbridge dons 'to exclude systematically' pupils from fee-paying schools, hallucination is more pleasing than verifiable fact to a serious loather of the modern age.

Alongside this character, thirdly, sits the Philistine. He, too, is enraptured with the past. He laments the fact that Charlotte Brontë is not writing at this hour, nor Constable painting. Without exception, all creations in the name of art are now a fraud and a failure. The public patronage of art in any form, far from opening the eyes of many millions who once hardly knew what art or drama was, is another of these ever more pervasive conspiracies against the people that define what Britain has become.

Our Philistine is rigorous in his dislikes. He has no conception of modernity as a life-force for the creative process, and cannot contemplate the possibility that work to which his own cauterised sensibilities disqualify him from responding might have merit. He believes that the only test of a novel's literary value is whether as many people buy it as bought J. B. Priestley in the pre-television age. For proof that modern poetry has disappeared up an unintelligible cul-de-sac, he delivers a name to render the world prostrate at his feet: Philip Larkin.

Binding together the Sentimentalist, the Paranoiac and the Philistine is the Demagogue. The Demagogue is indispensable to the other three, because through him they enlist the will of the people. He is the guarantor of their political position, their link to the 'democracy' that entitles them to their rage.

The Demagogue, however, turns out to be a little confused. From time to time, he posits the utopian world which the curses of modernity – experts, pressure groups, interest groups, politicians – have destroyed. In that world was born the system since followed 'by every country in the world which practises democracy'. This was medieval England, where 'towns and shires selected representatives and sent them to Westminster, a nation of two or three million delegating its authority to a few hundred'. Repeatedly, the Demagogue summons the time when knights and burgesses brought the message from their constituents, or Queen Elizabeth I was forced to bend to her petitioners. This was the elysium the Demagogue desires to re-create: indeed, is one to which he imagines the British – 'their judgements are usually right, their brains are as sharp and their muscles as strong as ever' – leading the rest of Europe, once they have shed the incubus of all we now call politics.

No irony strikes the Demagogue here. Purporting to revive democracy, he offers an account in which the only world he finds undeficient is one where democracy did not exist. He calls 'instant democracy' unworkable and ignoble, but then proposes the push-button populism soon to be made possible by the electronic super-highway as an escape from the manifold corruptions, not to mention the grey failures of leadership, he discerns all around him.

Modern Britain is an imperfect country. Its governing system needs reform, its frontiers need expansion. The Demagogue and his friends offer narrowness, torpor and a series of loud illusions: the world of a dead élite masquerading as the popular will. •

Wake Up Britain by Paul Johnson, is published by Weidenfeld & Nicolson (£9.99) •

Simon Hoggart
22 April 1994

A happy snapper steals scene from PM's Pollyanna

You can tell a truly unfortunate government, one which has bad luck stamped through it like seaside rock, when it gets even the smallest things wrong.

Yesterday, towards the end of Prime Minister's Questions, Mr Major was engaged in one of his lengthy round-ups of the good news. On and on he blithely rambled: long period of growth, low interest rates, record exports ... nothing would stop him, not even the remarkable fact that not a single MP was looking his way.

Instead they were all craning their necks up to the very back of the Press Gallery. It was as if they had been following a tennis match in which time had stood still and the ball was frozen to Steffi Graf's racquet. The reason was that a young woman, a foreign visitor, had shamelessly pulled a camera out of her handbag and taken a flash photograph of the scene below.

You might think that since all the Commons deliberations are converted into electronic images at the rate of twenty-six frames per second, one solitary snap would hardly matter. In fact, taking a picture anywhere in the Commons is a solecism somewhere between organising a spam-frying contest to mark D-Day, and what the *Guinness Book of Records* calls history's greatest *faux pas*: the man who, on meeting his future in-laws for the first time, rode in on horseback and doused their living-room fire by peeing on it.

The woman was hustled out (no doubt, one of my colleagues remarked sourly, they'll use it as an excuse to ban the press from the Press Gallery too) and the MPs were suddenly released from their spell. But it was too late. Mr Major's Parade of Pollyannaisms had entirely passed them by.

It's a small symbol of a government which simply doesn't see what is going on in front of its face. For instance, I don't blame the National Heritage people for contracting out some of the organisation – they are badly understaffed – but I do blame them for choosing a PR company, and especially for choosing Sir Tim Bell.

All public relations men are crass because they do not want to understand public opinion, only how to manipulate it. Churchill would no more have asked a PR man to organise a public commemoration than he would have had the fellow who drained his cesspit serve dinner to his guests. But times have changed, now we have a government which contracts out its most sensitive judgements to the sleaziest profession of them all. No wonder Mr Major was greeted by a jeering chorus of 'We'll Meet Again' when he arrived in the Chamber.

Afterwards Mr David Evans (C., Hatfield) let off a rant against past Labour governments, on the topic of topping. Some 3,000 people had committed murder since 1985, he raved, and if the British people were the Home Secretary they'd have hanged the lot of them – in other words their feet wouldn't have touched the ground.

I suppose there are people who find Mr Evans amusing, though in my view people who imagine themselves well-loved national characters are invariably boring beyond words. Mr Evans yammered on for so long that the Speaker was obliged to interrupt him, saying wearily to the minister: 'Mr Maclean, do your best with that.'

Here's something they could ponder. In the discussion of the young American condemned to caning in Singapore, it's assumed on all sides that these horrible punishments do at least serve their purpose. Yet last year, Singapore had a murder rate of 21.5 per million – almost *twice* as high as soggy, spare-the-rod, do-gooding Britain. How can that be? •

Hugo Young
29 April 1994

Major picks a fight with the big boys and gets a bloody nose

I t is John Major's conceit that he is the essential prime minister. If he had not been in the chair, the Cabinet would have fallen apart. And this indeed is why he got where he is today. He soothed the most, and enraged the fewest, members of his party. He was neither opinionated nor autocratic, and they were very relieved. Fewer of them would say the same today, but Mr Major himself continues to see that as his strength. He holds the ring, listens to the voices, and remains the only man who can be relied upon to do so. That's why he is confident of still being where he is today, tomorrow and next week and next year.

For a while, this style was a strength. But now it is a weakness. You could call

THE MAN WHO EXPRESSED A STRONG INTEREST IN THE EUROPEAN VOTING RIGHTS AFFAIR

© Steve Bell 1994 — with apologies to H.M. BATEMAN   417·29·3·94

it weak leadership personified. It subcontracts the task of decision-making from one man to the lowest common denominator of twenty-two men and women, not led virtuously from the centre but ignominiously from the rear. The charge often made against Mr Major is that he lacks charisma. That is something he cannot help, and anyway it didn't lose him an election. The charge now fully exposed concerns something he can help, and was, in fact, the reason for his elevated existence. The retreat from Ioannina concludes an exercise of stunning political folly, with a signal that reaches ominously far into the distance.

It should become a textbook study. First, take a position you cannot win. It was obvious to all observers that the EU would never buy the continuance of a twenty-three-vote blocking minority in an enlarged community. The analogy of the Maastricht opt-outs did not apply. Mr Major was impressed by those, but deceived by his own achievement in securing them. Over voting power, unlike the social chapter, hardly anybody else was able to see objective merit in the British line. They weren't prepared to sacrifice either their own preference or the programmed passage towards enlargement in favour of one nation's eccentric opinion.

And why was this opinion so eccentric? The British answer is instructive. Asked why France and Germany, the other big countries, were less fearful of a dilution of their negative power, the British say: Ah, the Germans and French have natural allies. Benelux and Spain will usually support their respective demands, therefore they don't need to care about defending the blocking minority in the way we do. Britain, it seems, has no similar allies. Out of Britain's alienated past, in other words, grows her solitary future. What a commentary on these years of proud isolation!

Second, take your impossible demand and make it (a) late and (b) public. Although the voting issue was still open, hardly anyone was prepared for the absolutist stand the British took three weeks ago. The chance was reduced still further of gaining anything more than the cosmetic concession Douglas Hurd squeezed out at the weekend. Nobody had the strategic wisdom to take the opposite line: welcome enlargement as a British achievement, and stand proud on the status quo as far as voting was concerned – retaining the 30 per cent block, pending a wholesale review in 1996. Mr Major told me last week that this had nothing to do with party politics. It reflected his own judgement of the British national interest, especially the baseline from which the 1996 negotiation should begin. But the motive scarcely alters the quality of the error. The prime minister chose to negotiate for twenty-three by taking unambiguous public positions whose rejection has left him bereft of almost all face. If he was Chinese, he'd have the choice of exile or the bullet.

Third, add to this misbegotten tactic a lesson in how not to be a leader. At no stage in the piece has Mr Major been prepared to set down his own position and dare his party to reject it. He did not say – does not say now – that there comes a moment when foreign policy has to be made by the Prime Minister and Foreign Secretary, and the Cabinet can like it or lump it. Incredibly, this line has been maintained up to and past the eleventh hour. Even yesterday, when it was apparent that Downing Street and the Foreign Office had decided to live with the deal, they were not prepared to say so. Has there ever been a statement quite like Mr Hurd's, summoned to the Commons to answer a question but then replying that he would not give his opinion until the Cabinet had met? When does collective government turn into awe-struck grovelling before party opinion whose refinements have not yet been exactly added up?

We are witnessing a parody of the Major style, but one without any laughs. It is not merely his predecessor who did things differently. Most prime ministers would have been ashamed to exhibit such self-abnegation to so little effect. None would have offered so many opportunities to the disparate elements round the table to make their disparities known. Collegiate leadership has been transformed into an exercise that almost invites the worst result: push me, the leader invites his colleagues, and I will respond to the side that pushes hardest.

We will see whose weight is assembled best today. The Secretary of State for Social Services must be amazed to be given his opportunity. He probably won't use it to deploy the terminal threat Mr Major would appear almost to be begging him to exercise, although he came closer than anyone to doing so at the time of Maastricht. It seems most likely that the Prime Minister will get what he wants:

collective endorsement for a climbdown from the position which they did, after all, collectively agree on 17 March. Tacticians might say how clever he has been, locking everyone in at every stage. Do they not all look equally forlorn, the more so in the knowledge that Mr Heseltine and, above all, Mr Clarke put their stentorian Europhiliac voices behind the unobtainable demand for twenty-three?

This should be no consolation to anyone, in or out of the Conservative Party. Inside the party, it exposes a leader who now seems almost chronically unable to lead without first looking at every one of the angles on the 360-degree circumference of his position, wondering from which of them the fiercest shots will come.

Beyond the party, the cause of Britain-in-Europe goes into further recession. By raising their expectations, Mr Major has made more enemies in the party, bitching at his failure to satisfy them. His only gain is to postpone the day when another reckoning is made. These days come at shorter intervals. The sceptic pressure feeds relentlessly on the concessions he has desired, without success, to make to it. Meanwhile, the truth about what 'Europe' can be and should mean gets buried under the delusions the leader has encouraged his enemies to discharge upon him. •

Steve Bell
21 July 1994

....

A psychopath, a mega-nerd and now Bambi

How does a cartoonist de-Follett Tony Blair? When I first saw him in the flesh at a Labour press conference I thought: 'That young man has spiky hair and too many teeth.' Then I saw him on TV. I can't remember what he was talking about, but I remember the smile. Dazzling, there's no other word for it. John Major has a nice smile, one of his few strengths; it switches on and says: 'I am Nice.' It's precisely one half of his armoury of facial expression. The other is his gormless but inscrutable look. Tony Blair's smile says: 'I have too many teeth. I am dazzling. I am dangerous.'

The next thing I remember Tony Blair for is a Labour Party conference speech. It was in the Kinnock years during the year-long run-up to the 1992 election. The words 'agenda', 'values', 'challenge', 'freedom', 'opportunity', 'empowerment', 'modernised', 'issues', 'democracy', 'achievement' and 'change' featured prominently in a speech that hinted at meaning and sought to please without actually saying anything. There were a lot of speeches like that that year, but Blair's effort struck me as an archetype.

I thought no more about him apart from the famous 'Tough on crime; tough on the causes of crime' soundbite (which made me think: 'that sounds like a good soundbite') until John Smith's death, and suddenly there he was all over everything everywhere. I'm sure this wasn't entirely of his own volition but there has been a definite snowball effect. Now I know that he's two years younger than me, he's the first 'post-Modern' labour leader, he used to sing in a rock band, and somebody or other started calling him 'Bambi' – which of course is a gift to any self-respecting cartoonist.

Why 'Bambi'? Extreme youth? Forty-one is well on the way to middle age. He's definitely wide-eyed with big lashes. He's shortly to become king of the forest. He's also got enormous ears. Drawing Blair as Bambi does present problems, however, because even though they both have big eyes and big ears, they have completely different shaped heads. Then there's the problem of teeth: Blair has loads, Bambi doesn't have any. Just splicing a human head on to an animal's body is rarely very satisfactory in a political cartoon (unless it's about vivisection).

The truth is it's difficult to do anyone until you're fairly sure what sort of political animal they are. It took several years before I realised that Margaret Thatcher was a psychopath. Conversely it took less than a month to see that John Major was mega-nerd. Margaret Thatcher definitely connived in her own depiction as the Iron Lady. It was an image she built for herself and played up to. She first impressed me as a small-minded and extremely right-wing hoarder of tinned food. The actual structure of her face took a long time to work out. It's largely to do with the angle of her nose in relation to her eyeballs, one of which is half hooded, the other swivels free. Once this is established, all else – the quiff, the neck, the pearls – falls into place.

While Major has never connived in his depiction as mega-nerd, he does play up to the image of plucky little ordinary chap, rather in the manner of Chaplin or Hitler. He wears glasses which for me always makes caricaturing more easy because it's a ready-made structure on which you can build the likeness. (In life drawing classes you're always told the likeness doesn't matter.) Above all, he has a unique upper lip structure which, when I first drew him, tended to spread out in a duck-like manner until I saw a side view of him and realised that it swoops inwards and wraps itself around his front teeth. Add the weak chin poking out underneath and here you have him.

The underpants are simply a metaphor for uselessness. I stumbled on them when, just after his accession to the leadership, I was looking at his record in office hitherto. It was a sorry tale of non-achievement, ranging from the cold weather payments fiasco through to his ballsed-up entry into the ERM, so I drew him as a crap Superman. Superman wears sleek red briefs outside his tights; naturally John Major would wear aertex Y-fronts outside his trousers. Only later did I hear the vile rumour as to where he tucks his shirt-tails.

Kinnock I always found impossible, partly because he had the most difficult head, which seemed to change shape radically from every angle you looked at it. I wasn't helped by his lack of political definition and the strangulated foggy verbiage which characterised his journey rightwards.

Physically, Blair is more promising: teeth, ears, eyes and spiky hair are a sound basis for caricature. Politically, who knows? He's passionate about Europe: that's rather like being passionate about garden furniture. Along with everybody else on earth apart from Margaret Thatcher, he believes in 'community' and 'the individual backed by the power of society', and he's a Christian. Some of my best friends are Christians. Maybe there's scope here for a few lion gags.

Will Bambi lead us to salvation? As the man on the News at Ten used to say: only time will tell. Never mind Bambi, I'd vote for Goofy, Dumbo, Pinocchio or even Digby the Biggest Dog in the World in order to consign this present bunch of clowns to the oblivion they so richly deserve. •

Will Hutton
8 November 1993

Wealth of happiness may be in store

Are you happy? Do you expect to get any happier? You might think economics allowed such questions to intrude into its deliberations: after all, the pursuit of happiness is central to the economic project. No such luck.

Economics does not want to worry about what makes human beings happy. That might compromise its attempt to be a value-free science. Instead, it offers a set of guidelines about how happiness might be attempted but makes no judgement about what happiness itself might be. As long as we know what we like and can organise a pecking order of such preferences, it is the exercise of free choices that will make us happy – and economically efficient – says economics.

By dodging the happiness question, by insisting that we only have to choose, economics disables itself in two ways. It surrenders itself to being captured by the right – and it imposes upon itself a wholly artificial construction about how human beings behave. In short, economics becomes an ideology whose predictions about the real world are frequently wrong.

But, for the new right the proof that choice is the key to happiness is a godsend which it has seized upon with enthusiasm. The privacy of choice and its individual nature were attractive enough, but if choice meant economic efficiency the circle was squared. It was not for nothing that Professor Milton Friedman entitled his proselytising book *Free to Choose*, and born-again Conservatives everywhere hammered on about the morality and efficiency of choice. Markets were deregulated and public activity privatised to allow us to make those efficient and happiness-making choices.

But fifteen years on, there are growing doubts about the results. Choosing has not led to either happiness or economic welfare, and the more reflective economists have begun to wonder whether economics' famous dodge works. What if individuals do not possess the mental equipment to be rational about why and what they choose? Maybe economists have to wonder what it is that makes us happy after all; and at the Happiness Conference at the London School of Economics last week, some of the best and brightest in the profession gathered to ponder whether that might be the case – and what would be the consequences. It was a revelatory experience.

What would Michael Portillo, the high priest of choice, make of the results of Daniel Kahneman's exhaustive tests at the University of Princeton about whether the human memory and the psychology of choice are consistent with rational economic behaviour in markets? He showed that even in controlled situations individuals make choices which are persistently and painfully wrong, and which require the intervention of a paternalist figure to correct.

Mr Portillo and his ilk had better hope that Mr Kahneman is mistaken, for the case for tax cuts and deregulated markets depends upon our ability to organise rational choices so that basically the choosers get things right. But Mr Kahneman shows that because our memories are so distorted by the peak experience of any episode – whether good or bad – and what we felt like when the experience stopped, there are even doubts about whether we can be rational about what we have liked or disliked.

Our memory of a painful hospital operation, for example, is dictated wholly by how we felt at the end of the operation – and what the worst feeling of pain was during the course of it. The operation's duration has virtually no impact on our recollection. Thus, our memory will rank a short and relatively painless operation which ends on a painful note as worse than an operation which ends on a painless note – even if it lasted longer and was overall more painful. As Mr Kahneman concludes, most of us are simply incapable of maintaining the coherence and consistency in our choices that allow us to be conceived of as being able to maximise outcomes – which is rather a serious blow to economics.

But even if we exclude areas that depend on the rationality of our memories, we cannot be relied upon to choose to maximise our outcomes. Economics demands that our happiness equals our capacity to maximise profits – so that if, for example, we were given £20 and offered two options – split it 50/50 or keep £18 and give away £2, economics predicts that, as profit maximisers, most of us would opt to keep the £18.

But when Mr Kahneman does the experiment, he finds that three quarters of respondents choose to split the money 50/50 – a completely irrational response in terms of profit maximisation. This happens even under conditions of complete anonymity so that the respondent does not know with whom they are sharing; or who is offering the choice! A large number of us choose to be happy not by doing down our fellow men and women but by being altruistic and fair-minded. Horrors!

What this means, of course, is that many of the predictions of economic theory relying on maximisation of outcomes and willingness to put one's own interests first fall apart – and so they do. Professor Truman Bewley of Yale, one of the US's leading econometricians, frustrated by the incapacity of economics to predict actual outcomes in the real world, interviewed 183 managers and people professionally involved in the jobs market in an attempt to understand its real dynamics.

Labour market economics relies heavily on economics' assumptions about choice and rationality. In particular, it predicts that employers' first preference is to lower wages in recessions rather than lay off workers; that unemployment is essentially a matter of choice; and that the unemployed worker who chooses to lower his or her wages will quickly be hired; and that well-qualified workers get hired more quickly than poorly qualified workers. But Prof Bewley's work challenges the received wisdom. He finds these predictions are wholly wrong – and do not succeed in forecasting what firms and workers actually do.

Labour market theory insists that firms bend every muscle to make workers' wages exactly equal to the incremental value of their output – so that firms produce up to that point where the last unit of output equals wages. Unions, social habits, inefficiency and monopoly power may get in the way, but good firms know that is what they should be trying to do. Above all, wages should be flexible.

But as Prof Bewley notes, wages are not flexible – even in hire-and-fire, non-union America. Piece rates, the classic free-market wage contract, are surprisingly stable throughout the economic cycle – and in recessions firms will lay off workers rather than reduce everyone's wages. At the same time, employers are wary about taking on unemployed workers who have dropped their wage below what their skill level commands. The 'flexible' job-seeker is less likely to get work than the one who is inflexible. Labour market economists fail to describe what is going on.

Employers find that workers have a conception of fairness which they simply have to respect to preserve their firms as ongoing social organisations. Cutting wages is not seen as 'fair'; nor is it possible to pay a worker either above or below what is deemed to be fair inside the internal pay hierarchy without others insisting on parity or deploring the unfairness. Taking on a group of unemployed people at below the firm's going wage rate – to 'price them into jobs' – proves to be impossible.

And if firms disregard these injunctions, even the most capitalist find themselves encountering problems of low morale and staff disaffection, causing low productivity, that require the decision is reversed – or at least never repeated. When Henry Ford invented his $5-a-day rate on the new lines at Ford, he never changed the rate in recessions; and it was that which won him the productivity gains. Workers could trust the rate and thus gave of their best. Prof Bewley captures why Ford's strategy worked – and why employers today are reluctant to lower wages and change piece rates; but economists are necessarily perplexed.

One of the saddest by-products of the new-right revolution is that, under the barrage of propaganda, some employers are beginning to believe that respecting fairness and creating trust are economically irrational – and are trying to make wages flexible, as the economists recommend. But, as the recent debate over why performance-related pay produces less good performance shows, the initiatives are not raising productivity. The new right's world does not work.

Human beings, economists and managers alike are discovering value fairness. As social animals we like esteem and being ranked highly in our firms' pecking orders. We need to be able to trust the social networks in which we are embedded; and unless we can trust them we perform less well. We are not happy simply choosing and maximising our individual preferences – which is just as well, given that so many of our choices must be mistaken.

In the meantime, we must live with the world economics is inventing: nasty, brutish and unproductive. But economics can no longer take refuge in the fiction that the route to happiness is choice; it must confront reality. In that, maybe – just maybe – lies hope. •

Martin Kettle
26 February 1994
····················
The big lie

Our town centre is a busy place on a Saturday. From 9 o'clock onwards it heaves for a solid eight hours. The shops are packed and the market is crammed with stalls. You can get anything you can carry in this market, and there's no shortage of customers. There's even one stall that sells nothing but sticky tape. More kinds of sticky tape than you imagined possible or necessary. Rolls of every width, texture and colour. In the two years I've lived in this town I've bought a grand total of two rolls here. A wide cream-coloured roll for the backs of picture frames. And a roll of blue insulating tape for a radio lead. When I bought the insulating tape last year I asked the sticky tape man how he managed to survive with people like me who only spent a pound a year at his stall. He said I would be surprised how many people have a call for sticky tape and that it was a good living. And sure enough, whenever I pass his stall there are always one or two customers.

This is more than can be said for the *Socialist Worker* sellers. Perhaps it's because they have made their pitch halfway between the gents lavatory and the hot-dog van. This is an area of the market which you are either very keen to visit or to avoid, depending on the state of your bladder or your appetite. But it's not a place to linger and I am fairly sure that I have never seen them actually selling a copy of their paper, even though it is said to be a different issue each week. The other Saturday I almost broke the habit of a lifetime and bought a copy of *Socialist Worker*. It was the headline which caught my eye. It said: WE CAN FINISH THEM OFF – THE TORIES ARE IN TATTERS – NOW IS THE TIME TO FIGHT. But then I saw the nearby crowd, clustered five deep around what turned out to be a man demonstrating his new carpet cleaning kit and like any other normal human being I needed to see what was going on. I didn't buy a *Socialist Worker*. And nor did anyone else, pretty much as usual.

But the headline stayed with me. I couldn't get it out of my mind. I ought to explain that our town is a fairly typical southern town. It's a busy place, as the market proves. A lot of people here work in London, as I do. But there are lots of things going on all the time in the town. It's not dead at all. It is pretty prosperous, but not as prosperous as you might think.

Politically, it is pretty typically southern too. It has a Tory MP with a big majority, but a hung local authority. Most of the wards in the town are Liberal now. The town voted Labour once, in 1945, but never since. If there was a by-election here, the Liberal Democrats would sail in.

But of course that's the point. There isn't a by-election. There isn't going to be a by-election. And, more importantly, there isn't going to be a general election either. The Tories are certainly in tatters, just as the headline on *Socialist Worker* claimed. You would be hard put to find any enthusiasm for the government at the moment, even in our town or in any of the dozens like it. Most people would like the Tories out, if they think about such things at all. The trouble is, there is absolutely no straightforward way of doing it. As Rousseau said, as soon as the English have elected their MPs they are enslaved until the next election – which isn't due until April 1997. And unlike the SWP, most people don't fancy a fight.

It is hard to tell whether many people are greatly fussed by their inability to do anything about their political anxieties, but to me this problem goes right to the heart of what we mean by democracy. The opinion polls don't help. They report every month on the state of opinion in answer to the question: if there were a general election tomorrow, which party would you vote for? The results are interesting as far as they go, but since there isn't going to be an election tomorrow the answers don't go very far. Above all, the polls don't explain the degree of importance which people attach to their political views. This is why the recurrent news that Labour has a 20 point lead over the Tories each month leaves me cold. The question they should really ask is whether people think their choice of party actually matters. The conventional wisdom is nowadays that most people are not much interested in politics and – though it is not necessarily the same thing – that they have no faith at all in political parties or leaders. This does not mean that people are not interested at a generalised level. The same polls which show that politicians are no longer believed (though not as little believed as journalists) also show that people rate their rights and freedoms highly. The problem is that these rights, though powerful and absolute in theory, are non-existent for much of the time. Voting is not an integral part of daily life. It is hugely reassuring – and important – to be able to continue in the knowledge that, every now and again, we will have the opportunity to kick our rulers out if we want to. But it is a depressing thought that, 250 years after Rousseau, we still have to show that there is more to democracy in the modern world than periodic elections.

People would certainly be angry if their right to vote were taken from them, but neither their existing rights nor the representatives whom they elect loom large in their lives, for the simple reason that they are not as important or meaningful as they ought to be. The belief in liberty and citizenhood which Rousseau noticed in the English two centuries ago is still very real, even if we spend more time thinking about cleaning the carpet than changing the constitution. But it is surely time for something more, much more.

The defects of our representative system have been laid bare many times. But they are none the less devastating for that. As the Labour MP Tony Wright – one of several new parliamentarians who seem at last to recognise the urgency of reform – has pointed out, our system perpetuates itself on the basis of 'fictions and elisions'. Members of Parliament claim to represent all their constituents, but in most cases a majority of them voted for someone else. Our parliamentary majorities claim to represent the people as a whole, in spite of the fact that they are elected only by a minority of those voting and by an even smaller majority of those entitled to vote. Governments claim a mandate for their policies, but there is no way that they can know who voted for what reason. Parliament claims legitimacy for being representative, even though the upper house is entirely neglected and though both it and the elected house are made up quite disproportionately by the old, the wealthy, the educated – and by men.

It is no wonder that such a system fails to command universal admiration and support. Its theoretical weaknesses are also compounded by a whole set of practices and traditions which discredit the parliamentary process still further. Once again, these are mostly quite familiar and well rehearsed: the power of the executive and the whips, the weaknesses of the legislative process, the anti-social hours and conditions in which much parliamentary work is carried on, the lack of meaningful and honest debate in a remorselessly adversarial system, the reactionary and archaic parliamentary culture. All these unreformed aspects of the British parliamentary system undermine the legitimacy of the wider democratic process. Most continue to be defended by far too many MPs.

These defects exist within a wider network of constitutional discredit. The shortcomings of central government are sustained by a system disabled by the concession of all power to a sovereign but in many ways impotent Parliament. The absence of an enforceable charter of fundamental liberties means that power is increasingly centralised at Whitehall and with ministers. Local government is bled of significance. European decision-making is almost wholly unaccountable.

The 'great ghost' of the elusive British constitution has reduced democracy to a haunted house. No wonder sensible people prefer more wholesome ways of spending their lives.

Yet there is also a more amorphous circle of discredit, which is much less easy to define precisely. Even if every one of the constitutional reforms which so many now support were put into practice, and even if every progressive measure for modernising the parliamentary process were adapted, there is still no certainty that our lives would feel or be more democratic in practice or on a day-to-day basis. Obviously such reforms would help, both directly and by encouraging a change of mood. But unless our politics and our civil life search for, find and develop a whole series of much more effective ways of consulting and testing their plans, policies and theories, both politics and democracy itself will remain élite and minority concerns. The challenge is therefore primarily cultural. It is about finding new ways of overturning the conventional wisdoms about the relevance of politics. It is above all about sustainable participation.

Lack of participation is the greatest single defect of the existing British democratic system. Not surprisingly, it is one to which those who *do* participate are least likely to be sensitive. 'If I can, why can't they?' is the reaction. But as the numbers involved in political or civic activity gradually dwindle, this defect cannot be ignored much longer, and it cannot be rectified by simply urging people to get off their backsides. That is why participation must be sustainable. We need to look for meaningful ways of ensuring that people continue to be involved in civic life after the first flush of enthusiasm has worn off.

Any conventional wisdom is by definition both right and wrong at the same time. It is right in so far as it is wise. But it is wrong to the extent that it is merely conventional. The current fashion for disparaging the relevance of politics and democracy may be a factually correct description of how lots of people feel. But it is wrong to be indifferent to the implications. If people are unmoved by the politics they are offered and cynical about democracy as it actually exists, then the whole network of life choices is gradually invaded and infected. We ought to do something about these reprimands, not wallow in them. Either way, this is undeniably one of the most genuinely pressing questions of our time. It is not a marginal question of interest only to the political class – although that is undeniably how it often appears. It is not an esoteric argument about political systems or the balance of constitutional power. It is a question of how people relate to the society of which they are part. It is a question of whether people can have minds of their own. A democratic society in which people either have no actual power or feel that they have no power is neither an effective democracy nor a strong society. Its immune systems are unable to function. It is vulnerable to all kinds of internal subversions and external assaults, whether they come from its rulers in the form of corruption and injustice or from outside as populist challenges.

Significantly, some public figures seem to be increasingly aware of some of the problems, though they put it in different ways, blaming different factors. Some say that political institutions are not as respected as they once appear to have been (as Michael Portillo argued in a much-noticed speech in January), or that politicians are failing to relate to the lives of ordinary people (the subject of Paddy Ashdown's forthcoming book, *Beyond Westminster*), or that political argument is couched in language and in terms of antagonisms which seem increasingly irrelevant to the real world (a favourite Tony Blair theme), while others believe that party politics itself is in terminal decline (the view of the former *Marxism Today* editor, Martin Jacques). Even John Major, in his speeches which try to conjure up a vision of a lost age of English contentment, is responding to the challenge. The problem is that none of them seems very sure how to solve the problem (or in some cases whether even to bother).

Nevertheless, even to recognise that there is a problem is an important breakthrough. Britain has been so complacent and so self-congratulatory for so long about the vitality and propriety of its civic and public life that it has taken a long time even to reach this stage of generalised unease. However, having at last done so, there is a paradoxical danger that we may unrealistically demand a too instant solution to these historic problems. This questioning of the legitimacy of our systems of public life is in no sense confined to Britain. We face our own distinct version of a challenge which affects others. The reinvention of democracy is a global challenge. We should not underestimate the extent to which, in Britain and in many other societies, we are all still in the very early stages of struggling to come to terms with the consequences of changes which we do not yet fully understand.

It is important to recognise the context. At first glance it seems indisputable that the 1990s are a decade in which democracy has triumphed throughout the world, especially when viewed from the West after the collapse of Soviet communism and the rapid spread of democratic systems in Africa. At second glance it is rather less simple; what about China or the Middle East? Didn't people think very much the same after the defeat of fascism in 1945 as well? Isn't democracy simply too loose a term, covering a multitude of sins, miracles and evasions?

All these provisos are true, and important. Nevertheless, after 1989 it is still even more true — and important to repeat — that democracy appears to have achieved an astonishing historical victory (especially astonishing to historians) over all other forms of government. Everybody now professes to believe in it.

For a brief moment — embodied in Francis Fukuyama's book *The End of History* — it seemed as if we had suddenly stumbled upon a state of global grace. But it did not last long. And even though the profound instincts and mindsets of the Cold War are largely obsolete, it is now universally obvious that they have blinded us to other fissures in society. The moment of apparent triumph has been replaced by a set of powerful fears about race, nationality, poverty, environmental change and cultural well-being, with which the political system barely engages and to which it certainly offers few answers. The celebration has produced a hangover, the uncomfortable awareness that this triumphant and one-and-only legitimate system isn't actually working very well at all. Neither at the international nor the national level does the democratic system appear capable of solving our problems, in particular our economic and social problems. Nor does it seem very obviously responsive to people's general concerns. It is remote from popular life, dominated by cliques and susceptible to financial and corrupt influences. It doesn't seem to work and it doesn't seem to be very democratic either.

So at one and the same time we live in societies in which democracy is celebrated as the universally appropriate form of government and in which almost every particular form of democracy is regarded as at best defective and at worst discredited. Similar tensions exist, though in extremely different forms, in Russia, South Africa, Britain and almost anywhere else you care to choose. You might think that universality of the problem and its intensity in particular countries might provoke a response among all nationalities, if only on grounds of self-interest. But if Britain is typical, the response is far too shallow and far too late for comfort.

Democracy faces a historic challenge of renewal if it is not to fall victim to less tolerant but more effective means of satisfying the needs of the people. That democracy is discredited in practice, if not in theory, is hardly open to doubt. Polls show that the British place freedom easily at the top of the list of institutions and characteristics which they most value – far above the royal family, for example. But a Gallup poll a year ago finally confirmed what so many have believed for so long – that pride in Britain and confidence in British institutions have eroded by spectacular degrees within little more than a generation. This crisis has not been caused by politics and political institutions alone. But without new politics and new political institutions it is hard to see how such confidence can be re-created.

The process was well under way long before John Major became prime minister. It is almost twenty years since Lord Hailsham coined the phrase 'elective dictatorship' to describe what he believed was the unconstrained power of the then Labour government. Hailsham suddenly went quiet on the subject as soon as he and his party were returned to office in 1979, but as the Thatcher years gathered momentum, many observers (and not merely the government's opponents) began to echo and adapt his call. The flowering of interest in citizenship and constitutional reform embodied in the launch of Charter 88 more than five years ago was a direct response to the widely perceived strength and power of government under Thatcher.

This needs to be stressed because of the very different political atmosphere in which the present debate about the so-called 'democratic deficit' is now taking place compared with that in which it began during the 1980s. The weakness of Major's period in office has greatly accelerated the trend towards disaffection. But it began in a very different form – as a reaction against the Thatcher government's strength. Major's failure to achieve the goals he set out in the 1992 election – especially in economic policy – has completed a process of civic alienation which even Thatcherism at its most aggressively triumphalist could not provoke.

Even the Conservatives' opponents ought to be concerned that they have failed to carry out their most central aims, especially in such generally favourable circumstances. Even after fifteen years of government and even though utterly committed throughout that time to a clear policy goal of wholesale reduction of taxation, the Conservatives are back where they started on public spending. That is not merely a party failure, but a civic failure. If a party which had the means, motive and opportunity to carry out the policies most precious to it cannot succeed in doing what it sought, then what price the chances of a government which doesn't know what it wants to do? And in that case what point is there in the political process at all? Compared with such lessons, the sexual and business perils of Major's ministers and backbenchers seem the trivial epiphenomena that they really are.

In the past, political parties were able to carry the burden and responsibility of democratic participation. They were the continuation of politics after the polls closed. But today they no longer play that role. The mass party – always something of a seasonal phenomenon – has withered as the professionalisation of politics has prospered. The media have replaced the parties as the forum of everyday discourse, but without supplying any means for the consumption of ideas and images to be translated into ideas, let alone action. The electronic media in particular have invaded and massively extended our ability to consume ideas, but without giving us much more in the way of participation than the occasional phone-in poll at 38p a time. Nor is it true, as is sometimes claimed, that single-issue campaigns or groups – from Live Aid to Greenpeace to CND – have taken up the slack. As Tony Wright has put it, they are more interested in direct debits than direct democracy.

There is a very serious danger that if we fail to rejuvenate our political system from the bottom up, we will be handing it over to those who own and control the mass media. American politics is already showing the possibility, with a candidate like Ross Perot able to buy his way into politics, and the emergence of film star politicians. The burgeoning strength of Silvio Berlusconi's right-wing campaign in Italy shows how it can happen in Europe too.

Our democratic culture needs to be spiced up. Changing the constitution and reforming Parliament would undoubtedly create a tremendous opportunity for renewal, as well as being important changes in themselves. But there will still be a need for fresh and imaginative innovation. Fixed-term parliaments, with more regular general elections, would help to dilute the sense of mid-term meaninglessness. Rolling elections – in which, for example, half the parliament was elected every two years – could help politics to be more responsive. Greater use of referendums, including consultative referendums, might help to refresh the process too. There is no doubt that the peaceful constitutional revolution in Italy has been sustained by the importance of plebiscites, petitioning and public campaigning. Technology can play its part, taking up Ross Perot's ideas to allow citizens to register their views through interactive telecommunications from the home. Around these explicit civic reforms, we also need to inculcate a pluralist culture of participation, encouraging shops, restaurants, pubs, schools, churches and every other arena in which people are likely to meet and converse to look for ways in which they can extend their civic purpose. We should treat the customer as a citizen, not just vice versa.

Maybe we should relax. If government cannot change anything, then why worry how we are governed? Perhaps we will all be happier doing aerobics, playing golf and occasionally checking our bank statements to see that the donations which now constitute a large part of many people's political activity are all in order. Perhaps, paradoxically, this would be true democracy – a 'typically British' pragmatic solution of the kind beloved by so many of even our best thinkers, in which we create a workable, working society in our own image in a fit of absence of mind. But it's a cheerless prospect for all that, and not much to show for ten centuries of intellectual investigation. The perils of such a philosophy are becoming frighteningly obvious. Democracy won't be fixed on the sticky-tape stall. •

P.S.

There is no arguing with what Martin Kettle said about the decay of our political system and the general contempt in which politics is now held in his fascinating essay on democracy. But why did my heart sink halfway through? I'm afraid it was at the words: 'Lack of participation is the single greatest defect of the existing British democratic system.'

The world is divided into two: those who want to participate – to meet and talk and vote – and the rest of us. We are the ones who, when we hear the words 'participatory democracy', reach for our drinks. The phrase is almost as lowering as the idea which the government tried to launch not long ago, 'the active citizen'.

All this has something to do with Sidney Webb's distinction between the As and the Bs: 'The As are artists, aristocrats and anarchists, the Bs are businessmen, bureaucrats and busybodies. (And I,' the Fabian economist added disarmingly, if obtusely, 'am a B.') Bs are the ones who like participating – by going to meetings – while As are the ones who don't.

A few years ago a biography of the Oxford don Enid Starkie was reviewed for the *Guardian* by Richard Cobb. The biographer had done her best for her subject, he said, but kept letting the truth slip through. At one point it was revealed that 'Enid Starkie actually enjoyed attending college meetings, which is,' Professor Cobb went on, 'I think the worst single thing I have ever heard of any human being.'

Without ever having attended a college meeting, I know what he meant. For most of my life I lived in London, and I did normal grown-up things, like attend editorial conferences (the *Evening Standard*'s were held at 8.20 am, not a time of day for any social activity whatsoever).

Now I live 100 miles from the Fleet Street and Farringdon Road, and in moments of dejection all I have to do is remind myself that I'm not in a newspaper office, and not in a meeting.

This is non-participatory and selfish and probably short-sighted. As unions and parties and clubs have found, if those who ought to turn up at meetings don't, then those who do turn up get their way, but there we are. Of course our present system is hopeless and most people feel they don't belong to it and it does nothing for them. But is it really impossible to devise another answer, participatory democracy without participation, as it were?

One way of looking at our present discontents is Colonel Gaddafi's slogan – surely the most terrible of this terrible century – 'Committees everywhere!' Against that is what may be the single most profound line of political criticism ever uttered.

As Oscar Wilde said, 'The trouble with socialism is that it will take too many evenings.' •

Geoffrey Wheatcroft
10 March 1994

Simon Hoggart
9 February 1994

Major's pay-off line has them roaring

I t was one of those times when you realise why this government is so uniquely unpopular. By that I do not mean especially hated, so much as unpopular in a quite different way from others in the past.

The question to the Prime Minister seemed easy enough. Lynne Jones (Lab., Sellyoak) pointed out that John Cahill would receive some £10 million when he quits as chairman of British Aerospace in April after only two years. She asked: 'How can this be justified?'

There are all sorts of simple answers. You can mumble about regretting such high payments (Mr Major has in the past), or you could even claim that Mr Cahill is worth every penny if he put more than £10 million on the value of the company. But he did not.

'It is not a matter for me,' he said crossly. The Labour benches erupted in anger – false anger, to be sure, but anger which represented their sense of what the country might well be feeling. They shouted and booed and jeered, and someone lowered the moral tone by yelling 'You pillock!' They made so much noise that Betty Boothroyd had to wait for what seemed like an age before she even tried to shut them up.

Then Angela Eagle (Lab., Wallasey), who is rapidly becoming an effective parliamentary operator, rose: 'If you do not believe that a £10 million pay-off for somebody who has just sold our last remaining car industry to foreign competitors is not a matter for you, could you please explain precisely what is a matter for you?'

The Prime Minister merely asked what intervention and control Labour would propose. Technically, I suppose, he is right. British Aerospace could pay Mr Cahill the contents of Fort Knox every week of his life unto death, and it would be none of the Prime Minister's business. But does he really imagine the country feels the same way?

A word now about the late Stephen Milligan. He was a former colleague of mine, being Washington correspondent of the *Sunday Times* while I did the same job for the *Observer*. I liked him because he was agreeable, thoughtful and well informed, so that I read his articles with interest but also some anxiety. He knew an awful lot, and often showed me up. His private life was a mess, but that was pretty common among British hacks in Washington at the time – the late David Blundy overlapped with him for a while.

Then Milligan became an MP, and it was sad to watch the man I had known turn into an ambitious mountaineer on the lower slopes of what passes for power in this country. In private he worked hard for his constituents, and can probably claim the credit for the government's change of mind over British Rail pensions. He represented more BR pensioners than any other MP and appears to have prevented a scheme by which the Treasury would have legally purloined a lot of their money.

In public, however, he was an obsessive loyalist, always ready with a glutinous question for the Prime Minister or a burst of fake rage against an opposition which failed to recognise the government's multitudinous achievements. Many MPs behave like that, but few are as clever as Milligan and so few cause as much regret. It is not a Faustian deal; their souls are not extorted, but somehow go into hiding.

The last thing I wrote about him was rude, and of course I now regret that. But he was a politician, and in some respects he was lost before he died. •

Simon Hoggart
2 February 1994

....

Triviality breeds content for MPs

MPs often accuse journalists of trivialising the great political issues. I reply that we have to, otherwise we would mislead our readers and abandon the sacred trust to depict MPs as they really are.

Take yesterday. Several times a month the Prime Minister has to face everything MPs can throw at him: jeers, abuse, cheap jokes, barbed questions and snarling contempt. Mr Major's problem is that these days it comes from the Tory side.

No wonder that, as he arrived yesterday, Labour MPs mockingly waved goodbye with their order papers. Consider what has been said about him in the past four days alone: 'serious errors' (Norman Tebbit), 'pathetic' (Norman Lamont), 'like a moronic baby' (George Walden) and 'six feet of throbbing manhood' (Edwina Currie). No – wrong quote, sorry – what she actually said was 'the worst speaker in the Cabinet', a mini-scoop you will find in Hatchards' *Book News*.

John Smith asked him about the Rover/BMW deal and wanted to know whether it was now a definition of success for a British company to be taken over by a foreign competitor.

Mr Major launched into a list of foreign companies owned here, including Jack Daniels, which apparently belongs to Grand Met. He did not, however, explain why those lovably gnarled old Tennessee whiskey-makers you see in the ads should be any more pleased at having their lives run by pin-striped accountants in Ruislip than British car-makers are at seeing their futures decided in Bavaria.

Mr Smith deduced from 'that rambling answer' that the British government was less solicitous of the national interest than the Germans, French or Italians.

Mr Major began: 'I deduce from that pre-prepared second question ... ' and the Labour benches went into uproar. At last! A quite majestically trivial topic for them to enjoy. Everyone knows that Prime Minister's Question Time has all the relaxed spontaneity of a sumo wrestling bout. For Mr Major to imply otherwise offered a rich seam to mine.

'Reading, reading!' they bellowed – reading being, curiously, an offence against etiquette at Question Time.

'He may not like the fact, but we know he has all three of his questions written out,' the Prime Minister continued, peering at his file of papers.

'Reading, reading!' they yelled back.

Everyone was enjoying it all so much that when Paddy Ashdown rose to raise the question of Tuzla Airport, there were groans. This doesn't mean MPs are unconcerned about starving children in Bosnia; it's just not as entertaining as shouting silly things at the other side.

Luckily the fun started up again soon. On Monday a Tory minister, Alistair Burt, had called Donald Dewar, Labour's social security spokesman, 'shifty'. This is one of those generic descriptions which apply to almost every politician and so for that reason are regarded as unparliamentary. Mr Burt got away with it at the time, because the Speaker had misheard him.

Cornered yesterday, Mr Burt decided to come clean and admit what he had said. 'The honourable member is not shifty,' he said. 'We have the warmest possible relationship.'

In these days of bed-sharing and gastronomic tours of France, that was enough to set the Labour benches off again. They roared and hooted with delight, until the place rumbled as if a small earthquake had occurred. What scientists call a seismic shifty, I suppose. •

Abroad
Barbara Ehrenreich
14 May 1994

Letter from Key West: the etiquette for unzipping the fly

By now every schoolchild in America can recite the story. Paula Jones, a former employee of the state of Arkansas, says she was summoned one evening to Governor Clinton's hotel room. Expecting perhaps to be consulted on industrial policy, Jones instead found the governor in an affectionate mood. After venturing a few brief verbal preliminaries, the governor unzipped his flies and – so Jones alleges – dropped his trousers.

Possibly the story was invented simply to embarrass the President as he struggled to execute another of his celebrated high-wire Haiti flip-flops. But common sense tells us that no woman could have made this up. In the female fantasy version, there is champagne, some urgent whispering about line-item budgets or the balance of trade with Missouri, perhaps a discreet back rub in the manner of Virginia's ex-governor Robb. Certainly no self-respecting woman could invent a scenario in which her seducer abruptly lays bare his genitals and offers an exciting come-on along the lines of 'Hey, babe, wanna test drive this beauty?'

But let the pundits debate the truth of Jones's accusations. The true patriot should be more concerned, if not fully alarmed, about the President's social and sexual skills. How, for example, did he ever lure Hillary into his vast, French-fry-scented embrace? One pictures young Bill stalking her through the law-school library stacks, then – flash! – leaping out from behind Property or Torts, naked member enticingly in hand. Admittedly, Bill has spent much of his adult life living in mansions, which are a notoriously poor place to meet friendly young women. His approach would have been more suave, one suspects, if he had spent more time in female-rich environments such as tenements, welfare offices or feminist book shops. No wonder that, when faced with an empty hotel bed, he could think of no option but to order up a companion through room service. But, Bill, there is no reason for every romantic encounter to end in press conferences and bizarre tabloid stories. In the interests of national security and certainly dignity, here are a few tips for an upgraded, scandal-free social life.

First, never proceed directly to the genitals, insistent as these organs may be. Surely you are familiar with the notion of 'foreplay', and if not, the Surgeon

General would gladly fill you in. The purpose of the preliminaries is to give the whole thing a vaguely consensual air and thus diminish the grounds for prosecution. For example, it is smart to have a few topics of common interest to discuss before the time comes for the unzipping of flies. Hillary's 1,400-page health proposal has been known to put many people in the mood for bed. Or you could develop some new interests and conversational themes – Bosnia has often been suggested.

Second, it is unwise to use the constabulary to gather up potential lady friends. Jones claims to have been fetched to the governor's boudoir by a state trooper in the course of his duties. This is bad form. Many women respond poorly to uniformed pimps and prefer, as John F. Kennedy knew, to use the Mafia as a middleman.

Third, don't be so cheap. Even a low-wage clerical worker deserves some refreshments before settling down to fellate an important public official. Take-out from McDonald's will not do unless the lady in question is under fifteen: and forget about Hillary's cookies.

In fact, it would probably be wise to dump Hillary, as your advisers have been urging for reasons of their own. Few women relish a hotel-room quickie with the husband of a world-powerful woman – even when he refers to her, as Gennifer Flowers reported in her 1992 *Hustler* interview, as 'Hilla the Hun'. True, Hillary is bound to fight back in embarrassing ways. But remember that it is you who controls the courts, and capital punishment is a snap in Arkansas.

Imagine a Hillary-less future! Whitewater would float away like poultry-scum on an Arkansas stream, and fresh candidates for first lady would be beating down your hotel-room doors. •

Barbara Ehrenreich
25 June 1994

Thanks be to the O J show

Some day my grandchildren will gather around and ask where I was and what I was doing when I learned of O J Simpson's escape from the police. I will gnaw reflectively on the handle of my cane and tell them that I was watching the big basketball game, like any good citizen, since I had taken that to be the event *du jour*. See, in those days, I will have to explain, we periodically had some event *du jour* – a war, a penisectomy, a figure-skater run amok – just to see if everyone was paying attention. And woe to the distracted or derelict citizen who could not pass the follow-up quiz, administered by selected neighbours: 'Hey, whaddya think of them Knicks?' or 'So O J – think he did it, huh?'

So I had been watching the game, trying to guess what would be on the next morning's quiz, when suddenly the screen was taken over by O J's getaway car gliding along empty freeways, pursued by a flock of press helicopters. Suspecting that some typical post-nuclear-holocaust action film had drifted in from another channel, I frantically clicked the remote. But O J was everywhere and inescapable, supposedly sitting in the back seat with a gun to his head, though possibly it was a cellular phone or even a cordless shaver.

At first I was so clueless I confused O J with Jackie O – and in fact there is a certain resemblance. Struggling to explain the historic importance of O J, the newspeople kept coming up with same content-free terms they had applied to Jackie O – 'grace', 'role model' and 'bone structure'. In short, O J, like the nebulous J O, is famous principally for being a celebrity. He played football at one point, but is best known for the Hertz commercial in which he vaults over airport counters and mounds of fellow passengers in his eagerness to rent a car.

Thus the chase theme was wonderfully appropriate, as the anchorpersons' voice-overs kept reminding us. And was this not the primal experience of late capitalism – senseless, undirected, flight? The excitement mounted as O J's car approached the LA airport: maybe he would leap out and offer a live replay of the famed Hertz commercial, only this time going from car to plane. Never before had we seen all the possible genres – news, sports, docudramas and commercials – merge in such a brilliant conflation.

It was overwhelming to be 'participating', as Peter Jennings put it, in the making of a major media event. A local LA reporter broke down, choking and hanging his head, while an anchorman's voice murmured apologetically about 'the stress we've been through'. Thousands of Angelenos were shown massing along the freeways, exhibiting all the emotions appropriate to a double murder followed by a slow-motion car chase. They sobbed, embraced each other, chanted encouragement to O J, swilled beer, and thought of good places to loot. Everywhere, Americans felt themselves caught up in the kind of vast maudlin seizure that sometimes leads us to folly and war.

In those days, I'll explain to the grandkids, we were starved of any sort of tribal experience. We lived, each shut up in our single-family homes, yearning for an outbreak of communal drumming and dancing or perhaps a spectacular blood sacrifice. Hence the necessity of these events *du jour* to uplift us from the trivial and the personal into the plane of the historic and transcendent. In this, O J was wildly successful, achieving ratings that rivalled the Gulf war. He even won the newsperson's ultimate accolade: 'He brought us together.'

And that's what it was all about – synchronisation. Everyone watching the same thing at the same time, saying the same dumb things, guzzling the same brand of beer. We really didn't care what inspired them, so deeply did we crave these collective highs. Give us a war, we would cry – a shuttle blowing up, an assassination, a run-away rental-car spokesman!

At which the grandchildren will no doubt shake their heads in wonder, throw a few more twigs on the campfire, and hunker down on the ground for the night. •

Tim Radford
18 November 1993

Inside the forbidden forests

After the explosion at Chernobyl, the rumour spread through the Ukraine: red wine was a radiation antidote. At one of the research centres inside the thirty-kilometre exclusion zone around Chernobyl last week, there was a variant prescription. You take a bottle of dry red wine, and put two drops into a glass of vodka. Drink it. Repeat the dose. When the wine bottle is empty, radiation will no longer be a problem.

Welcome to the zone. The Russians call it the 'zone of alienation'. Welcome to the people who have worked in it. The Ukrainians call them the 'liquidators'. Welcome to 9,000 square kilometres of astonishing pine and birch and oak forest, fields, pasture, orchards, villages, swamps, braided rivers and reservoir. Welcome to a riverbank littered with ships that will never sail again, to fields of helicopters that nobody dares fly, fleets of buses that brought in the firefighters but can never leave the zone.

Welcome to Pripyat, ghost town, with ghostly high-rise housing in which no one will ever be at home again. Welcome to smaller, prettier Chernobyl itself, with apple trees in almost every garden, which should have celebrated its eight-hundredth anniversary this year. Welcome to tiny settlements, the fields around them scraped clean but the snow-fenced gardens now so overgrown with trees that they have started to invade the barns and homesteads.

Hello and goodbye to the tiny village of Lelev, soon to be dismantled, when anybody can work out how to do it without sending up showers of radiocaesium, and only after archaeologists have collected specimens of country crafts, unique to the region, still in the houses. Welcome to 450 hectares of ground that was once forest but which had been irradiated so fiercely that every pine tree died. Welcome to tumuli that shroud a billion cubic metres of soil, buildings, trees, road surfacing, all of which had to be buried in the zone. And then the bulldozers that interred them also had to be buried. And perhaps even the bulldozers that buried the bulldozers.

The explosion at reactor No 4 in the first hours of 26 April 1986 was the worst man-made peacetime catastrophe the world has yet seen. The blast drove the reactor floor four metres into the ground, the core heated to 3,000°C and the plume soared a mile into the air, dusting central Europe, Scandinavia and Britain with caesium 137 and other radionuclides. Radioactive iodine (which gets into the thyroid gland), cerium, caesium, zirconium, niobium and ruthenium, along with americium, strontium 90 (which gets into the bones) and plutonium (which gets into the lungs), showered over a huge area of the Ukraine, Belarus and the Bryansk region of Russia. Some 45,000 people from the town of Pripyat, nearest the reactor, were evacuated almost thirty-six hours later. Altogether 130,000 people were moved out, never to return.

The reactor had to be encased in walls six metres thick; it is now called the sarcophagus. The concrete hasn't cracked, say the Ukrainians, but they have a plan anyway to seal it in another structure. The former Soviet Union established a thirty-kilometre zone around the reactor, and within that zone fenced off a second, ten-kilometre zone around the nuclear power plant. Ukrainian scientists say it, European scientists say it: people will probably move back into the thirty-kilometre zone one day. But it is quite possible that nobody will ever live inside the ten-kilometre zone again.

And yet reactors No 1 and No 3 at Chernobyl are providing power and a repair team is at work on reactor No 2, damaged by a different, accidental fire in the turbine hall. Workers commute from outside the zone, two weeks on, two weeks off. More than 6,000 people work in the zone. There are shifts of scientists inside the sarcophagus, twenty-four hours a day, seven days a week. There are policemen, drivers, agricultural researchers, radiation biologists, nuclear experts, epidemiologists. There are cooks, secretaries, receptionists, bartenders and barbers. There are foresters, managing the forests because there is so much remnant radioactive material stuck to the bark and incorporated in the leaves that even a forest fire could be another disaster. There is even a special research centre and hotel complex for visiting experts and politicians. And there are old people – at the last count, 762 – who have moved back because they don't want to live anywhere else, and a priest, Father Feodor, seventy-nine, who moved back with them.

And there are criminals and outlaws, hiding in the woods, living off the stocks of food left behind. Three of them – all army deserters – were found by a team of hunters from the Institute of Zoology, there to cull deer and wild boar. They were doing this to study 'the transport of radionuclides in biological material' and also to compare them with the small group of cows found more than a year after the blast, still alive, but with blood immune system and reproductive disorders.

The cows are still alive and cared for in an institute. They have had calves, and even their calves have had calves, say the Ukrainian spokesmen. There are no obvious ill effects, no somatic disorders passed down through the generations. The same is true, they say, of the human population. But not of the arboreal guardians of the zone. Just outside Pripyat is a row of neglected greenhouses, which have been heated for the last seven years because there was nobody to turn off the water, or repair the pipe joints when they burst, so that steam and boiling water spray over the broken panes.

Right next to them is a little plantation of baby pines. They were grown from seed taken from the notorious 'red forest' killed by sixty grays of radiation (never mind what a gray is, but about four would kill a man). The baby pines are being monitored by Professor Nikolai Arkhipov, a veteran of the only-now-admitted reactor accident at Kyshtym, near Cheliabinsk in the Urals, in 1957. Almost all of them have damage to some of their chromosomes. Some of them branch in a surprising way, fifteen or sixteen times instead of the usual four or five. Some of them have needles that grow not pointing towards the sun, but towards the ground. Some have needles which are unusually thick and twisted.

Nobody has to twist the facts of Chernobyl. One by one the Ukrainian, Belarus and Russian health chiefs recite their litanies of loss. The figures are on an unimaginable scale. Some 23 per cent of the land of Belarus is contaminated, and on that land live 20 per cent of the population. More than 250,000 hectares of farmland have been closed down; 130,000 have had to be resettled.

Childhood thyroid cancer – rare everywhere – is ninety times the levels before 1986. There will be 140 cases of thyroid cancer every year (and the tumours, scientists note, have so far been 'large' and 'aggressive'). Breast cancer is on the increase; so are disorders of the blood circulation. Almost 2 million people in 3,331 towns and villages need 'special attention'. The republic needs 'clean' food, diagnostic equipment, radiation instruments and rehabilitation centres, and will need to spend $400–500 million between now and 1995.

The Ukrainians tell a similar story: 190 people have acute radiation sickness; 20,000 have lost the capacity to work; there are 130,000 evacuees; there are 1.5 million children whose thyroid glands received radiation doses. Only about 28 per cent of the 'liquidators' – more than 180,000 were involved in the clean-up – could be considered healthy. There are people with respiratory disease, heart troubles and nervous system disorders. There are increased digestive problems, tonsillitis, anaemia and stress. There is an increase in suicide. There are children with 'Chernobyl syndrome'.

The Russians, too, tell of 2.6 million people in 7,608 contaminated towns; of a 25 per cent increase in tumours; of a 50 per cent increase in cardiovascular disorders; of locomotor apparatus diseases. And of huge, unbearable costs. The Ukrainians have a ministry for Chernobyl affairs, and claim 3 per cent of the gross domestic product is spent on the zone and its poisoned people – a cost that could rise to 15 per cent.

Into all this, blinking a little in surprise – some of the diseases cited have never before been linked with radiation – are the Europeans. A delegation led by two Euro-parliamentarians, Dr Rolf Linkohr and Dr Gordon Adam (Northumbria) and backed by a team of epidemiologists, cancer experts, radiation biologists, engineers and bureaucrats have to make sense of all this. There is the sound of clashing agendas. In Kiev I spent $1 on a cup of tea and a bottle of mineral water and received 20,000 Ukrainian units of currency as change. The foundering economies of Ukraine and Belarus republics are in pursuit of dollars. The European team, which has somehow conjured several million Ecus out of a squeezed budget, are determined to help, but not to get involved in inter-republic clashes or to underwrite political battles. They want to push on with a £10 million framework for research and co-operation begun in 1991: to take the measure of consequences to human health and the environment; to work out the best ways to mitigate the consequences; to improve emergency management. It means years of painstaking, scrupulous work with health statistics, with the monitoring of water, ground and animal and plant tissues; the examination of leaf-litter and mushrooms; it means working backwards to try to reconstruct the dose that firefighters, liquidators, schoolchildren and nuclear workers got, and then mapping their progress for decades. It means buying equipment and training scientists. It means strengthening local health services and educating bureaucrats.

Dr Jaak Sinnaeve, of the Brussels science directorate's radiation protection research unit, says the money will go to projects in which scientists from the three republics co-operate both with each other and with European research institutions. Herbert Allgeier, a Eurocrat chief whose concern is with energy, is anxious that the facts of nuclear safety and nuclear disaster are established clearly. If the nuclear industry is to have any future – and he has no axe to grind – then it had better demonstrate that it understands exactly what an accident of this order actually means in decades to come.

But other members of the party do believe in a nuclear future, for the time being at least: the power stations are there, and the world needs energy; the dangers of low-level radiation are more perceived than actual; public attitudes are based on irrational fear rather than a calculation of costs and benefits; fossil fuels will run out; there is the carbon dioxide question, and so on.

And so on. The Euro investment in research will answer a lot of questions, but leave the biggest ones unresolved. There will be extra deaths from cancer in years to come, but since 30 per cent of the population is likely to die from cancer anyway, who will be able to say which died from radiation from reactor No 4? Nobody is in serious doubt about childhood thyroid cancers in Belarus and Ukraine, although with care many children should survive. The accident at Chernobyl seems to have cost a certain forty-two lives so far, including three in the blast itself and twenty-eight within two months. A helicopter pilot – the first dowsing of the fire with sand, dolomite and boron was done by leaning out of the helicopter and throwing the stuff down the plume – died three years later. Seven more firefighters have died, and three children with thyroid cancer. But the other reactors still burn, because Ukraine needs the energy.

And so inside the zone, and in the corridors of power in Kiev and in Brussels, there is a consensus: the accident was a catastrophe, but also somehow contained. One scientist says the radionuclides buried in more than 800 sites in the zone are 'safe': there is no evidence that the toxins will leak into the water table. But the soil around Chernobyl is a light, sandy podsol. The land is flat, the rivers are full, the Kiev reservoir is huge. There has already been one forest fire, and flooding. One document by the Pripyat Research and Industrial Association at Chernobyl says that strontium 90 levels several metres from the tumuli are 500 times above the acceptable.

Scientists refer to the zone as a 'unique laboratory' and scientists from twenty-eight nations have worked there. But it is difficult to feel objective about it. Here is a landscape so contaminated by its only heavy industry that it has been turned inside out: used as its own graveyard, buried within itself. Most of the iodine 131 disappeared long ago. In another twenty years, the strontium 90 will have fallen to half its original burden. In another twenty years, half of the caesium 137 will have disintegrated.

But 24,000 years from now – if the zone's keepers are right, and the stuff is safely interred, and hasn't leaked into the River Dnieper – half of the plutonium 239 buried in it will still be there. •

Pass Notes

29 June 1994   Carlo Maria Martini

Age: Sixty-seven.

Appearance: Robert de Niro playing a radical priest in a Martin Scorsese film (*Papal Bull*).

Job: Archbishop of Milan.

Cardinal virtues: Campaigned against corruption in high places and, as Italy's leading Jesuit, has acted as a counterweight to the authority of the Pope.

So he and the Pope don't get on? Very different worldviews. The Pope is ultra-conservative; Martini is about as left-wing as you can be in the Church without being excommunicated.

What is Martini's attitude to women priests? Jesuitical. He says there can be 'no women priests until the next millennium'.

But the millennium is only six years away: Exactly.

Why is he in the news? He isn't, yet. But he will be next month when he pays a personal visit to the Archbishop of Canterbury.

Is that significant? It could be if Martini, who is committed to dialogue between churches, becomes Pope.

Is that likely? Precedent says no – there has never been a Jesuit Pope. But smart Catholic money is backing him, and smart Catholics would adore his liberal, sophisticated, intellectual presence at the head of the Church.

Is he intelligent? Is the Pope a ... sorry! His cleverness knows no bounds. He speaks eleven languages, is an acknowledged authority on the Bible and has written almost fifty books.

A veritable Cartland of Catholicism. He can't find much time for anything else? You'd be surprised. He was dubbed 'Cardinal Clean' for his battle against corruption. He fights for the rights of the homeless, the unemployed and immigrants; organises lectures to explain the role of the Church to children in Milan; and assiduously cultivates the media.

Sounds perfect to take the Papacy into the twenty-first century: Indeed. But many of the present hierarchy rather enjoy living in the fifteenth century.

And they have their own ideas about who should be Pope? The name of Cardinal Biffi of Bologna is on every traditionalist's lips.

An arch-conservative presumably? Biffi in name, Biffi in nature. He led a campaign to abolish the music of Mozart and Schubert from the Mass; tried to prove the Turin Shroud was genuine; and is virulently anti-women's ordination.

So who do you think will win? Our half-million lire is on Martini. But of course, no one's infallible.

Not to be confused with: Carlo Maria Giulini; Super Mario; a combination of gin or vodka and vermouth.

Do say: Cardinal Martini.

Don't say: Martini, Cardinal?

Most likely to say: 'Blessed are the rich – provided they are generous.'

Least likely to say: 'Doesn't Baggio have an amazing left foot?'

Jonathan Steele
31 May 1994

Solzhenitsyn slides into his place in Russia's pantheon

In the climax to Alexander Solzhenitsyn's bravura performance at the technical university here, Russia's most famous exile said yesterday: 'I am the spiritual heir of the millions of Russian intellectuals who were murdered by Stalin, and I had no moral choice but to come home to work for them.'

His speech to almost 1,000 students and faculty was the high point of the first four days of his return after twenty years of exile. With his passionate delivery and driving moral conviction, he captivated his audience with language and ideas not heard in public in Russia for years.

They mark him out from all the other émigrés who have returned – often only for brief visits – since the collapse of communism. Mr Solzhenitsyn made it clear he was here to stay.

The writer was stung by a questioner who complained he had given up literature for journalism and politics.

'I have seventy-five years behind me. I've fulfilled all the literary tasks I set myself,' he said. 'I've written ten volumes and they're unknown in this country. I thought I would come back to a Russia which had read me, but only the older generation knows me. They remember something about an Ivan Denisovich. But the rest don't know me because our publishing scene has changed, and it's more profitable to produce detective stories and sex books.'

Gesticulating, he said: 'Writers have rarely stood outside political life. When 60 million people were repressed, when the best minds could not be politicians, philosophers or publicists because they were all killed – why wasn't I killed? Because I was just a student of physics – I am guilty before them.

'I am their heir. I have to work for them. I'm obliged to help Russia with my experience, advice, and influence, not knowing why or what result it will have.'

His voice dropped as he concluded: 'I've matured enough to try.' The hall erupted in applause.

It was hard to believe that this man had never spoken to a Russian crowd before his first evening back in Russia last week, when he read a short statement to a street meeting. In his twenty years as a writer before he was exiled, he lived in the dissident's enforced solitude under Stalinism. Two decades of seclusion in the United States followed.

At one moment he broke down and could not finish his sentence. Asked what he had enjoyed most since last week, when he began his slow journey to Moscow, to meet Russians of all walks of life and listen to their views, he said: 'It's amazing that everyone around me is speaking Russian, everyone, and so many sincere people.

'Yesterday I was in a remote village, there were old people with such impoverished, poisoned lives. It was impossible to talk to them without... ' He gulped, and his voice faded as he lowered his eyes, his sentence suspended.

In the ninety-minute session, Mr Solzhenitsyn covered many of his favourite themes: the West's moral decadence, the need for Russians to build democracy from below, the flourishing country they had before the Bolsheviks imposed communism, the need for the communists to repent publicly and for the worst offenders to be put on trial as the Nazis were at Nuremberg.

He complained at how Western evangelists were invading Russian television because they could buy time while the Orthodox church, 'plundered by seventy years of repression', could not.

He urged students not to fall into the trap of worshipping money now that capitalism had reached Russia, because although people in the West had everything material, 'something is missing'.

To a young woman who asked what Russians should call each other now that 'comrade' was discredited, he said 'Mister' was out because it was a word peasants used for their rulers. 'Citizen' was also inappropriate, 'because we're not yet citizens; we have no civil society,' he said.

When a professor of architecture compared Mr Solzhenitsyn to Tolstoy, who had switched to politics in his last two decades of life, he was riled: 'In a normal country people can get on and do their own thing, scientists get on with science, philosophers with thinking, and writers with their work.

'In Vermont I had wonderful conditions, better than anything Tolstoy ever had. For eighteen years I sat and worked. I have produced twenty-two volumes of collected works and more will come out after I am dead. I could have stayed there peacefully and in great happiness. But it would have been running away from my duty not to have come back. I could not escape our people's pain.

'I didn't come here because this country is flourishing and I wanted to join in, or because people were calling me a prophet. I don't need that. I came because of my conscience. It would have been unconscionable to sit and search for new literary genres and elegance of style so that someone in the twenty-first century could work out what I have achieved.'

His audience loved him, with good reason. •

Chris McGreal
12 March 1994

Staring death in the face and blind to all error

Even cowering beside a wounded comrade and a dead one, Alwyn Walfaardt still thought his incursion, with thousands of other white right-wingers, into Bophuthatswana was no mistake.

He probably had no time to change his mind in the moments before a black policeman did what none of the whites terrorising the homeland's capital had thought possible: he raised his automatic rifle and shot Connie Uys through the chest.

Then he turned on Mr Walfaardt. The bullet went through the back of his head, sending shock spasms through his body.

A Reuter photographer heard the wounded extremists crying: 'Please God, help us.' Then the shots rang out.

From the black crowd a voice cried: 'Are you sorry now?' The taunt was followed by the *coup de grâce*.

Hostility arose within only a few hours of attempts by gun-toting whites to run the black homeland.

Alwyn Walfaardt travelled from the northern Transvaal in a blue Mercedes in response to a call from the Afrikaner Volksfront (AVF).

More than 2,000 AVF supporters gathered at the air force base in Mmabatho, evidently with the co-operation of senior officers, some of them white.

At dawn hundreds rode into town to 'defend' the city, or cruise its streets. But some decided to make a stand for an Afrikaner homeland, a Volkstaat.

Blacks were chased from around the government complex. At least two people were shot at random in the leg. Word spread. The township seethed.

But the khaki-clad thugs with shotguns on their knees and ammunition belts slung across their shoulders had gravely misjudged the homeland's army.

Soldier after soldier poured scorn on President Lucas Mangope. Almost in the same breath they attacked the whites. The AVF, with its disdain for normal contact with ordinary black people, did not understand the rising resentment.

The army's patience broke shortly before midday. Armoured personnel carriers moved across Mmabatho and Mafikeng, rounding up the right-wingers. Some could not believe it. Others latched on quickly. Their guns were suddenly buried from sight. Terror sprang to their faces.

They were herded from Bophuthatswana like goats. Alwyn Walfaardt's car was in a convoy under the army's eye. As it passed through Mafikeng someone threw rocks that were met with pistol shots. Mr Walfaardt said someone in another car fired, although he too had a pistol in his hand. Either way, he paid the price.

A Bophuthatswana soldier hit the Mercedes with a burst of machine-gun fire. The only right-winger wearing neo-fascist insignia was killed instantly.

Lying next to the car, Connie Uys grimaced from a bullet wound. Mr Walfaardt's bearded face was pressed in to the dirt for fifteen minutes or more as he justified his incursion. 'No, no, it wasn't a mistake to come. We came because the Afrikaner Volksfront asked us to come,' he said. But still he pleaded: 'Get someone to help us.'

The policeman who shot him showed no great pleasure or pain. Why he did it was not explained.

As word of the killing spread, some Bophuthatswanans marvelled at such audacity against the *boere*. Others feared the consequences. •

Gary Younge
27 April 1994
....
The black knight

' I cannot sell my birthright. Only free men can negotiate. I will return.' So said Nelson Mandela in a message to the people of Soweto in 1985, responding to an offer of conditional release from prison from South Africa's former president, P. W. Botha.

Nine years later he has returned and negotiated, and today exercises his birthright as the world's most famous first-time voter. I have followed Mandela for the past five weeks on the final stretch of his long march to the South African presidency, watching him address rallies and press conferences, on walkabouts and official ceremonies.

To call it his 'election campaign' might confuse it with the limp affairs we are subjected to in Britain, where people in sharp suits or shoulderpads convince themselves they are getting audiences worked up over tax bands and EC employment legislation. Mandela's campaign has been more like a series of political orgasms, each rally a passionate climax offering a brief, heady release from deep-seated frustrations.

Thousands of people, squashed in cattle trucks or minibuses, will travel more than 100 miles and wait for hours in the shelter of a ramshackle stadium just for a glimpse of Mandela. Some, who do not have access to a television, will only have seen his face on posters and leaflets.

His arrival is signalled by the campaign song, 'Sekunjalo Ke Nako' (Now is the Time). Jean Paul Gaultier would call it Afrotrash – lowest common denominator lyrics, part Xhosa, part Zulu, part English, with an irritating tune that will keep you humming for the rest of the day. None of which bothers the crowd. They all, from the old and toothless to the young and barefoot, dance along until they spot the first car of his cavalcade. The sighting generates a rush of energy through the crowd. Women ululate and children cheer. All wave their flags and placards intensely, creating first ripples and then waves of excitement that roll on a sea of black, gold and green.

Mandela has returned… on the back of an open truck. He stands tall, straight and dignified; the black knight on the white horse, slayer of apartheid and harbinger of majority rule. With a mischievous grin on his face and his fist punching the air. He will insist on doing a lap of honour, even if one has not been planned, so that no one will go home disappointed.

If it is just the excitement and atmosphere you have come for, it is best to leave now. By the time he has taken his place on the stage the orgasm is over. The local ANC official who has been charged with giving Mandela a brief introduction – as if he needed one – is eager to cut himself a slice of the glory. He will keep going until the microphone is wrested from his hands.

And by the time Mandela rises to speak, after the prayer has been read and 'Viva ANC' chanted countless times, the momentum is gone and the crowd worn out with the waiting and excitement.

Mandela's accomplishments are many but public speaking is no longer one of them. His bodyguards will tell you that during the Rivonia and treason trials, when as a qualified lawyer he represented himself and his co-defendants, black people used to come from miles around to hear him cut the white man down to size with his sharp wit and analytical prowess. His powers of analysis are still sharp but his slow oratorical style appears laboured and stiff.

His speeches are also unimaginative. He starts off with a factual explanation of the ANC's reconstruction and development programme (RDP) – the liberation movement's answer to Roosevelt's New Deal – and then goes on to voter education. 'Take your ID and go to the polling station. When you get to the first booth you will be voting for the national parliament. Look all the way down the ballot paper until you see the ANC flag with the wheel, the spear and the assegai [the ANC emblem] and the letters ANC. What letters should you look for?'

'A...N...C,' the crowd shouts.

'Very good. And there you will see the face of a very handsome young man whose hair has been turned grey by all the worry you have given him.' Laughter. 'There you should put your cross.' He goes through exactly the same routine again, using the same joke, but explaining that this time it is for the provincial ballots.

It is all solid stuff, especially in a country where 70 per cent of the electorate have not voted before and many are illiterate. But as one onlooker pointed out: 'It is hardly Martin Luther King.'

The people are then asked to raise their fists for the ANC anthem, 'Nkosi Sikelel iAfrika' (Lord Bless Africa). And after the brief reign of silence that follows that soft, powerful song a protracted spell of chaos ensues as Mandela is bundled into his car before the crowd can penetrate the lines of ANC marshals.

For at least half an hour after his departure, the road to the motorway is lined with supporters punching the air and shouting 'Viva' at every vehicle that passes. By this time Mandela will have been whisked away at high speed to the next venue either by road or air. If he is flying, the ANC hires a different helicopter every time. Using the same one, his security men say, would make him an easy terrorist target.

In his personal affairs Mandela is a stickler for punctuality, but on the campaign trail he is invariably late. Those close to him say it is his insistence on shaking every hand that makes it over his wall of bodyguards and a genuine desire for human contact that is largely to blame. 'He loves to talk to people and is very polite. He will tell his bodyguards off if he sees them being even the slightest bit rough with anyone,' says Barbara Masakela, the head of staff in Mandela's office.

Not all the rallies are as formulaic. In Cape Town, where the ANC stands a serious chance of losing, no punches were pulled where election kitsch was concerned. An inflatable zeppelin in ANC colours floated next to the stage and white pigeons were released along with black, gold and green balloons. Then, in what seemed like a mixture of liberation politics and karaoke, two singers led the crowd in a marathon rendition of 'Sekunjalo Ke Nako' and one verse of 'We are the World' as Mandela danced his way on to the stage.

In Umlazi, Natal, he bored a crowd rigid by taking more than half an hour to read out the new constitutional rights he had proposed to the Zulu king, Goodwill Zwelithini. But he then went on to make an emotive speech which conjured memories of the Mandela of old: 'I am the father of all of you and I love you like you were my children. It saddens me that I must leave you now. I wish I could put you all in my pocket and take you home. And when I am troubled or lonely take you out and see all your smiling faces again.'

Once, in the eastern Cape, he actually turned up on time and in Durban he turned up an hour early, made his speech to a Youth Congress and left, much to the frustration of the journalists, who arrived shortly afterwards. At another rally he told supporters to go home before they caught pneumonia when it started raining. He had only been speaking for ten minutes.

The team primarily responsible for the campaign strategy comprises six activists with varied political histories. Carl Niehaus, the main ANC spokesperson, is an Afrikaner from a very conservative working-class background. Pallo Jordan, the secretary of information and publicity, is a fierce critic of the South African Communist Party who was detained by the ANC's security department for six weeks during the early eighties as a result of internal rivalry. Gill Marcus, his deputy, spent her years in exile clipping newspapers for the ANC office in London. Barbara Masakela (sister of jazz trumpeter Hugh) became head of the department of arts and culture while in exile in Zambia. Marcel Golding, former deputy of South Africa's mineworkers union, is the bright young thing to watch among the ANC leadership. Jesse Duarte, Mandela's special assistant, is the top woman candidate in one region.

They divided the campaign into three phases. First came the People's Forums: Mandela and other senior ANC members travelled the country addressing mass rallies and answering questions. Then they spelled out the party's plans for housing, employment and education as outlined in the RDP and contrasted them with the National Party's record. In the final two weeks, they concentrated on 'reassurance', trying to make sure people felt comfortable with the change. Throughout, there has been the constant theme of voter education.

It was no accident that Mandela did not evoke painful memories from the past, such as his time in prison, the Sharpeville massacre or the Soweto uprising. For, given the ANC's assurance of victory from the outset, it was decided that the campaign would be positive.

'It would be patronising to tell black South Africans they have had a bad life under apartheid,' says Ken Modise, who is in charge of the account at the ANC's ad agency. 'Everybody knows the ANC was a highly effective liberation movement. But will it be an effective government? South Africans look to the ANC as the incumbent. We had to show people we had the wherewithal to govern.'

As well as their political roles, Duarte and Masakela look after Mandela's personal needs. 'We make sure that he has a jumper packed, that the right food has been ordered if he is staying away, and that his schedule is not too exacting,' says Masakela.

For a seventy-five-year-old, Mandela does a good job of looking after himself.

He does not drink or smoke. Nor does he eat butter, eggs, cream or anything else that would aggravate his high blood pressure. He used to get up at 4.30 every morning, a habit acquired in prison. But age has wound down his body clock, setting his alarm for 5 am. He used to jog first thing in the morning, but now that is considered too much of a security risk he uses an exercise bike. Then he has a light breakfast of fresh fruit or oatmeal with warm milk before starting work at 6.30.

He is incredibly self-contained. Ahmed Kathrada, who shared a prison cell with him for seven years, says that he and Walter Sisulu sometimes had to force him to stop reading and talk to them. They also had to stop him jogging around the cell at 4.30 in the morning while they were trying to sleep. Nowadays the little relaxation time he does get he spends watching sport, especially boxing, and reading biographies.

He rarely goes to bed after 10 pm but during the campaign his days have been getting longer. By the end of last month, when he contracted laryngitis, there was concern that he was being pushed too hard. He was taken off the trail and out of the public eye for a week to recuperate.

The very fact that Mandela could do this a month before polling day illustrates how much the election has been a sideshow, with events in KwaZulu/Natal and the numerous efforts at mediation often dominating the political agenda. The situation has turned him into something of a Jekyll and Hyde politician. One minute he is campaigning and calling de Klerk 'weak and indecisive', the leader of a party that is still racist and guilty of collusion with the Third Force. The next he is negotiating and de Klerk has become a man of integrity, someone Mandela can do business with. This was most obvious during last week's TV debate. After an hour of sometimes very heated discussion, Mandela offered his hand to de Klerk, saying he was a man he could trust.

And de Klerk is not the only one with whom he blows hot and cold. Two weeks ago at a rally in Soweto he ridiculed King Goodwill Zwelithini for having rejected an offer that would have given him the same rights and privileges as Queen Elizabeth II. A week later in Umlazi he made a deferential speech in which he claimed to be the king's faithful subject.

These contradictions are partly due to his ambiguous position during the transitional process. For some time now he has been both the de facto leader of the country and the leader of the opposition. De Klerk cannot make any major decisions without his consent, yet Mandela has no say over the day-to-day running of the country. It is an inversion of the dilemma most politicians are used to – he has power without office.

Come his inauguration on 10 May that excuse will no longer hold. During the last two weeks of the campaign there has been some hint of what a President

Mandela will look like when he has no one else to blame. At the rallies in Umlazi and Cape Town he told supporters to scale down mass action and to 'settle for industrial peace' whenever possible in order to give the government of national unity the chance to implement the RDP: 'Mass action won us the vote but now we have the vote we must work together to rebuild our country.'

Both times the audience fell silent, fearing the worst. Could Mandela, in the name of pragmatism and national unity, follow the example of so many other African leaders and put the interests of foreign investors before those of his own supporters?

Maybe. The explanation can be found partly in his background. Born into the Tembu royal family, he was a descendant of a lineage that can be traced back twenty generations to the fifteenth century. At times he still exudes the regal, almost imperious, nature of a man convinced he is genetically equipped to rule.

A freedom fighter he was, but he has never been a revolutionary in the sense that it is commonly understood. If anything he is quite conservative. During the early sixties, while the rest of Africa's freedom fighters were embracing socialism or developing their own brand of pan-Africanism, Mandela was singing the praises of his country's former colonial power. 'I have great respect for British political institutions and for the country's system of justice. I regard the British parliament as the most democratic in the world,' he told Pretoria Supreme Court during the Rivonia trial.

There is also a paternalistic side to his character which has come to the fore at times in the campaign. During two rallies in Bophuthatswana, a 'homeland' whose former ruler was ousted in a popular uprising last month, he called those who looted at the time 'a disgrace to the ANC'. He gave stern advice to children to go to school and stop 'taking advantage of the chaos', and also insisted that the young respect their tribal chiefs, even if they collaborated with the apartheid regime.

In one area where there was an internal dispute in the ANC regional office, he slammed those who waved dissenting banners from the crowd, saying they 'were not worthy to be called his comrade', and ordered them to explain their grievances to him in front of the rest of the stadium. They came forward, apologised for any embarrassment and then explained their problem. He listened patiently, accepted their apology and said that even though they had not gone about things the right way they were 'worthy to be called his comrade' after all.

Consensus-building is Mandela's stock in trade. He is not an ideologue but a 'One Nation' democrat of the centre-left. To his reckoning, almost any question, from the establishment of a Volkstaat (Afrikaner homeland) to the involvement of the IMF in policy-making, is worth considering, so long as it will not undermine his efforts to push ahead with national reconciliation.

Sources in the ANC say that his role as president will be largely confined to healing the wounds of apartheid, with the party's vice-president getting his fingers dirty in the stuff of day-to-day politics. But if his new role earns him the title of Father of the Nation, it is due in no small part to his undying devotion to the ANC, which has come before everything else in his life.

The strain of his political activism destroyed his first marriage to Eveline Ntoko Mase, with whom he had three children. And it is commonly believed that his separation from Winnie was the result of pressure from the ANC, which regarded her court convictions and radical political stance as a liability. Asked if he thought Mandela would like to be reconciled with Winnie, Archbishop Desmond Tutu says: 'He doesn't say anything straight out but I suspect that he wouldn't want to do anything that was detrimental to the party or to the cause.'

Winnie says that ever since he joined the leadership of the ANC he has never really had a life of his own. 'The moment he stepped out of prison he was national property and it was as if we were lucky to get ten minutes of his time for the family. I think the family is still waiting for him. Psychologically he hasn't come out of prison, in the sense that now he is back for the people. It has really been a continuation of the kind of life where the family didn't have access to him.'

Not many people do have access to Nelson Mandela. His friends say that even though they cannot imagine him doing anything else, his nature sits uneasily with the restraints of high office. He would like to spend more time with his grandchildren, to travel and to read, but simply does not have the time.

Take the ANC away from Mandela and you are left with a very warm and generous but lonely man who spent last Christmas on his own on a small island in the West Indies. A man who rarely has time to speak to his friends and even then only by telephone.

Take Mandela away from the ANC and you strip the organisation of its greatest asset at the most crucial time in its history. One of the few men capable of helping it complete the transition from clandestine resistance movement to open party of government. •

Rian Malan
28 April 1994

South African election diary: making history through a haze

Friday, 22 April

Terror and ecstasy, ecstasy and terror, thus we oscillate, endlessly. Today, for the first time in many years, only one dead body was found on our blood-drenched streets, and police suspect that it might actually be suicide. A strange, trance-like calm has descended on Jo'burg, as if we are all drugged and stunned by the enormity of what is unfolding. The security forces are on standby. Jabbering, stressed casualties are besieging their shrinks, and chemists are running out of Valium. Elsewhere, these would be the symptoms of a crisis. In South Africa, they constitute the elements of a possible miracle.

Saturday

A strange vision besets me. I sit down at my machine, and try to distil it from the following tangle of facts. (1) In 1980 or thereabouts archaeologists digging in a cave at Klasies River in the Eastern Cape unearthed some bones that turned out to be the oldest human remnants ever found. This is but one of several discoveries indicating that fully modern humans first materialised within a radius of, say, 700 miles of my home town. (2) In 1987 or thereabouts, microbiologist A. Wilson of the University of California concluded, on the basis of DNA studies, that every living person carries a gene which first occurred in a woman who lived somewhere in southern Africa about 142,000 years ago – a date which accords quite closely with the estimated age of the Klasies River remains.

Wilson's so-called Eve Theory has since been conclusively refuted and triumphantly vindicated on several occasions, but no matter; I am less concerned with the scientific validity than the mythic conclusions it suggests. To wit: (1) All men are truly brothers. (2) All men are South African, rendering our present drama literally universal. (3) If this is where our species evolved, it is also the place where the dragon's teeth of ethnocentricity were first sown. It is therefore (4) entirely appropriate that we should be the first humans to transcend the scourge and embrace one another in an explosion of light that awes and blinds the world.

God, what foolishness is this? I gave up hope for this country long ago, on the grounds that it was irrational to do otherwise. And yet, this is a precondition for resurrection. All miracles are preceded by utter hopelessness. Not so?

Sunday 9.50 am

I am wrestling with my silly Eve Theory when a giant explosion rents the air. The white right has detonated a bomb downtown, killing or injuring at least a hundred. They are trying to provoke blacks into butchering some whites in retaliation, thus triggering a cycle of racial violence which ends in Armageddon. I am suddenly beset by terrible misgivings. Hands sweat, guts churn. I pace the floor, hug virtual strangers at random; I shall fear no evil, for thou art with me.

Sunday evening

Go to see *Schindler's List*, an appalling choice in this state. Ten years ago, Spielberg's film would have set me to searching my own Boer soul for traces of the virus that drove the Germans to commit the unthinkable. Now I find myself identifying with the Jews. For is this not what we pale natives are soon to be – a powerless minority, valued for our cleverness, envied for our wealth and profoundly resented for holding ourselves aloof from the masses?

Monday

Mentioned my Boer Jews of Africa insight on Australian radio chat show, drawing stern reprimand from Helen Suzman, who accused me of paranoiac exaggeration. Touché? Stepped out of the studio to hear that bombs are going off everywhere, ten in a single morning. The city is seething with paranoia – rumours flying, sirens screaming, people fleeing from unseen dangers, while ashen cops tiptoe around potential car bombs. Time to get out of here. Head for the freeway and out into the countryside, where tranquillity reigns.

Around sunset, I pass a black minibus taxi with giant sign on its back window: 'Let's build a great nation.' I hoot. The driver hoots back. All his passengers smile and wave. A good omen. Begin to feel better. A full moon hangs high in the windscreen. They're playing Dollar Brand on the radio, a music from the long lost simple times. I get all choked up, like a sentimental fuck-up.

Tuesday 7 am

Breakfast in the penthouse of the Royal Hotel, Durban's finest, having crashed out on couch in American TV network's lavish suite. Hacks galore, cellular phones on every table, they seem vaguely disappointed by the absence of violence. Three weeks ago, the army was moving tanks into Natal. ANC leaders were visiting newspaper editors and posing the following question: 'Are you willing to look the other way for a month or two while we use ruthless force to crush the Inkatha menace?' And now, just look; nothing to shoot save a lone Indian, casting his net in the calm blue shadows of Durban Bay.

The polls open in an hour for special voting. Even as we nibble at smoked salmon, the hot lame and aged are dragging themselves down sad dirt roads towards a rendezvous with destiny. For many, disappointment awaits. Some polling stations are mysteriously bereft of officials. Others have no fluorescent ink or no ballot papers. The radio tells a tragic story of an ancient Zulu trundled through the night on a wheelbarrow to draw the 'X' before he dies, only to find no mobile polling station at the appointed spot and nobody to explain its absence.

11 am

Head off to Independent Electoral Commission HQ to pursue enquiries and walk into brewing riot. Angry crown is besieging lobby. Police on hand, looking strained. Crowd closes in on lone journalist, voicing loud grievances. They are election monitors, as distinct from official election observers. The former are expected to volunteer while the latter are handsomely paid, a discrepancy which leaves the monitors desperately unhappy. After all, the government have spent the best part of a billion rand on this election, and Mrs Mildred Mngadi of Umlazi wants her share, which is why she and her comrades held IEC officials hostage last night for four hours. 'These people are greedy for money,' she shouts. 'Where's all the money?'

Where indeed? I went inside but didn't see any – just haggard IEC officials strung out from lack of sleep, struggling heroically to prevent the exercise from turning into a shambles.

Midday

Lunch at downtown coffee shop with R. W. Johnson of Oxford University, seasoned South African prognosticator. Professor Johnson is fairly sanguine, predicting that Natal will wind up under the governance of an ANC–Inkatha coalition. I tell him the only joke yet to have emerged from this edgy election. Two terrified nuns drive into surging crowd of black men with cultural weapons. 'What shall we do?' cries one nun. 'Show them your cross,' says nun two. So nun one rolls down her window and shouts, 'Get out of the way, you bloody black bastards.'

So yeah, a bit off colour, but I had to get it off my chest. Such jokes might become forbidden in a day or two.

2 pm

Pull in to Inkatha office on Umgeni Road in search of shambles anecdotes. A curious sight awaits – only one Zulu at work in the nerve centre of the pathologically Zulu organisation. Phones jangle simultaneously – disgruntled Inkathas calling from phone boxes to complain of real and imagined violations. The ANC is intimidating people. The ANC is bussing Xhosas across the border to vote in Zulu land. The local polling station has yet to open, or worse yet, the polling station is in an ANC stronghold, where Inkathas dare not tread. And worst of all there are no Inkatha stickers on the ballot papers in several locations. Heart sinks. What if Inkatha refuses to accept the outcome on the grounds of apparently widespread bureaucratic cock-ups? It's funny, in an unfunny way. We were so worried about bombs, guns, looting and chaos that it never occurred to any of us that the true threat to free elections might be African-style confusion and inefficiency.

6 pm

An IEC spokesman assures the media that the glitches have been exaggerated and that the process has been running smoothly. Yours truly pushes for greater clarity, only to be accused of waging cross-examination. Oh dear. Last week Archbishop Tutu was on my case, and now the ANC's Dikgang Moseneke has it in for me. Will my name wind up on the enemy's list of ethno-fascist traitors.

9 pm

Too nervous to eat. Feel drunk and drugged without drinking.

Midnight

The old flag comes down, while a trumpeter blows the last post and Boer choirs sing the last national anthem. Go to bed, but can't sleep.

Wednesday 4 am

A great chattering in the hotel corridors as a media army departs to witness Mandela voting at nearby Groutville. I watch the ceremony on TV. A bomb goes off at Jan Smuts airport. Twenty-two million people put on their shoes and set off for the polling stations. The hour has come. I must soon follow suit.

And so we come to the end of history in South Africa and I wind up in someone else's hotel room, alone, save for the man in the mirror with tears streaming down his face. What's he crying for? Can't really say, and won't try to baffle you with glib pieties about apartheid's many martyrs. I think he's crying for his lost innocence, for the heart that always willed this, and the brain that said it could never be.

Curious people we Boers, born into a fortress of racial paranoia, and brought up to believe that Africa's a place where only the strong survive; where a white man stripped of his guns and power is as good as dead. In our hearts, we still suspect this is true, especially when we contemplate the bloody chaos north of our borders, and its replication in the seething of black townships on our doorstep. The fear remains as strong as ever, and yet here we go, participating in an election we are certain to lose.

We have come under withering pressure to be sure, but I'm an Afrikaner so allow me this. We go down with colours flying, our surrender is an act of courage and an expression of our faith in the fact that this is the only way to become truly African. 'We must give ourselves into the arms of the Great African Mother,' said the great Boer poet Breytenbach, and 'trust that she will not drop us.' Trusting is difficult, trusting is dangerous, but here we go, here we go off into the African unknown. •

David Beresford
11 May 1994

Glitterati's procession watches fairy-tale ending

I t was a fairy-tale ending, which suited the strange story of Nelson Mandela, the herdsboy who became a convict and then the president.

The moment for which he seems to have been born seventy-five years ago finally arrived when, with the sun shining on the Bible in front of him and tons of bullet-proof glass protecting his back, he began the incantation:

'In the presence of those assembled here, and in full realisation of the high calling I assume as president in the service of the Republic of South Africa ... '

It was 12.16 pm when he started speaking, which was a little embarrassing, because he was meant to become the president in the morning.

But by the time the clock-tower had signalled the noonday hour with the Westminster chimes of a colonial past, the dignitaries assembled from around the globe were beginning to get used to the element of informality.

It was a day of contrasts, encapsulated in the setting; the grandiose Union

Buildings – neo-classical in style, a mix of Italian and English Renaissance with a dash of Cape Dutch – hacked into the African hillside of Meinjeskop.

When Sir Herbert Baker designed the building early this century, it was intended to be a symbol of unity, marking the coming together of the British colonies and the defeated Boer republics – its two wings representing an equal marriage between English and Afrikaans. But for all that, it has never hosted a union like yesterday's.

Winnie Mandela was among the first of the glitterati to arrive, resplendent in a long, green silk dress – a creation that her personal publicist had boasted would 'astonish South Africa'.

It was a poignant instant, as the woman for whom the occasion should have been her crowning moment was gestured towards the seats of lesser dignitaries. But, in response to some unseen summons, she suddenly materialised with her family on the podium.

The television announcer, a note of disapproval in his voice, assured the country that the one-time Mother of the Nation did not belong there, and would shortly be returning to her proper place. But Mrs Mandela was unexpectedly led to a position nine seats away from the leather-covered throne awaiting her estranged husband.

Yasser Arafat was another early arrival, bustling to the thirteenth row demanded by protocol of a not quite head of state. A clutch of overweight bodyguards in grey suits glared at the barrels of telephoto lenses hanging dangerously from a photographers' rampart over the head of their charge.

The Duke of Edinburgh, clutching a Panama hat, came striding up the stairs trailed by a Foreign Office entourage. He seemed bemused as he was corralled off into a corner in the fourth row.

But as Al Gore, Hillary Clinton, Ron Brown, Jesse Jackson and the rest of the United States contingent were crowded through to the same row, their bodyguards glared indignantly with the realisation that the world's leaders had not been allocated enough chairs to go round.

Enthusiastic chants of 'Castro, Castro' from South African Communist Party MPs heralded the grandest-looking figure of the day. The Cuban leader looked even grander bereft of cigar and forage cap, his uniform and silver hair sparkling imposingly in the sun.

And so the procession continued and a game of musical chairs went on ... Ex-King Constantine, Jerry Rawlings, Mary Robinson, Boutros Boutros-Ghali, Kenneth Kaunda, the Prince of Asturias, Danielle Mitterrand, Joaquim Chissano, Benazir Bhutto, Sam Nujoma, Prince Willem Alexander of Orange, Mário Soares, Julius Nyerere.

The Zulu monarch, King Goodwill Zwelithini, overlooked on the left

Austin

SO, WHAT'S NEW?

NIXON LYING IN STATE

embankment, whisked front-right. Fidel, landing up deliciously close to the Americans on the right embankment, whisked to safer ground front-left.

Up on the podium, meanwhile, the outgoing president and incoming second deputy-president, F. W. de Klerk, had arrived to the first round of international applause – a celebration of the simple comment he had made as he emerged from his car: 'We have achieved what we set out to achieve.'

He was followed by the waving first deputy-president, Thabo Mbeki, before a roar from some 50,000 people gathered on the lawns below announced the arrival of the one-time herdboy.

Mr Mandela had a party-going air about him as the security force generals led him up the stairs to meet the chief justice. He beamed with paternal pride as he walked past his daughter, Princess Zeni Dhlamini – who is married into the Swazi royal family and standing in as First Lady.

Praise singers – an African hybrid of poet laureate and court jester – held the microphones in a paroxysm of adulation. Then, one hour and eight minutes later than scheduled, the clock ticked on to the historic moment.

'... I, Nelson Rolihlahla Mandela, do hereby swear to be faithful to the Republic of South Africa, and to solemnly and sincerely promise at all times...

'Our daily deeds as South Africans must produce an actual South African reality that will reinforce humanity's belief in justice, strengthen its confidence in the nobility of the human soul and sustain all our hopes for a glorious life for all,' Mr Mandela said.

Towards the end of his inaugural speech, the 4,000 assembled VIPs rose spontaneously to their feet for an ovation in a moment of genuine emotion as President Mandela declared: 'Never, never and never again shall it be that this beautiful land will again experience the oppression of one by another and suffer the indignity of being the skunk of the world.'

As the cheering died away, Mr Mandela's personal aide, Barbara Masekela – the sister of the jazz trumpeter Hugh, and yesterday's mistress of ceremonies – looked momentarily lost.

But the generals seized the lead, moving to the heavily armoured glass at the back of the podium and staring pointedly at the distant hills of the Muckleneuk Ridge.

Out of the silence grew a thunder, as over the hills came helicopter gunships, jet trainers, supersonic fighters and aerobatic squadrons trailing the colours of the new South African flag in dedication to their first black, and surely greatest, commander-in-chief. •

Leader
11 May 1994

An epic to live in the memory

I f it had been an epic of a movie, directed perhaps by Richard Attenborough, then yesterday's amazing carnival high on a hill above Pretoria would have been a final scene to live in the memory. Spectacle on the grandest scale as the world, in its fancy dress, came to pay court. Symbolism of touching, joyous simplicity as the races of a nation once malevolently divided mingled in celebration. And a true hero at the centre, a man twenty-seven years imprisoned, now president of his nation — and preaching reconciliation with a fervent sincerity that somehow reaches to his core. A great leader, however you choose to define those words.

Such an opening paragraph is usually designed to begin the next with a 'but' or 'however'. Those will come; but not yet. For the story of the four years since Nelson Mandela's release *is* an inspirational one. After the Cold War, we in the developed, cynical West may have lost our bearings. But that same collapse made yesterday possible and gradually, within one pariah country, produced a transition of power that puts us all to shame. Hard politics and a moral imperative combined. These have been the years of living dangerously, the days and weeks where the enterprise seemed impossible, doomed imminently to end in desperate bloodshed. But a force has carried them through. Some of that force belongs to South African society itself. Some also — from white and from black — has crucially depended on the men at the helm. South Africa, in the crucible, has been a land well blessed.

The 'buts', as they come, are mild and muted. It would, yesterday, have been more conventionally neat, more movie appropriate, if Nelson Mandela's story had ended there. He is seventy-five and stiffly frail; he has never governed anything; he has been locked away from the world for nearly three decades. It defies experience to believe that the next five years can rival the memory of the five years past. He is already, uneasily, having to juggle the factions in a move-ment made to split. The secondary issues of influence and power within the white community involve real land, real wealth, real privilege, and will be bitterly fought. The promises of the campaign cannot all be kept. From the cynical West we may easily prophesy doom and disillusion.

But – a 'but' to temper the 'buts'. The coming of true democracy to South Africa has not arrived on some magic carpet of misty idealism. It has been battled over interminably by dogged politicians. The people, if they have watched, know what it will be like. They have reflected, in fear or anticipation, on the country they must somehow build together. And they saw their joint future, grandi-loquently defined, on the hill over Pretoria yesterday – a ceremony which told them where, with patience, they might go.

Now the cameras depart and, at last, there is a new life to be made quietly together. Hang out no flags. It will be damnably difficult. Yet the three last words of President Mandela yesterday are more than mere words. God Bless Africa. If this can be made to work, if whites who stay can join with blacks of gathering skill, then there is something to be built beyond one country, for a region and maybe for a desperate continent. The next story starts today. God Bless Africa. •

Leader
19 March 1994
....

Death on the road marked Whitewater

The full juggernaut is on the road. Grand juries, House committees, a special prosecutor – and now, inevitably, Congressional hearings. The Whitewater juggernaut, made in Washington, and ploughing full tilt down the old Watergate freeway. Why is it that this righteous, heaving quest for truth makes the heart sink rather than the spirits leap?

America, said David Gergen when he joined the Clinton lifeboat, 'desperately needs a successful presidency'. That must be right. The renewal of democracy depends on the hope, and sometimes the delivery, of something better; and the history of the Oval Office over a full thirty years is a history of failure, scandal and disillusion. Only Ronald Reagan, through that span, served two full terms. Perhaps Bill Clinton could turn the tide? A new man from a new generation and the traditional party of change, elected on a mandate of reform just as the upswing in the economy began to make the impossible seem possible again. He made a halting start, then gathered speed. As the year turned there was a clear sense of popularity and prosperity accreting: re-election began to look a good bet and, with it, a continuity to change.

Now all bets are off. The President is busy with what he calls 'the people's business' – beaming as Muslims and Croats sign in the White House, cancelling his last announcement on Ireland – but the business that preoccupies too many of the people is Whitewater, a morass of deals done long ago in Arkansas and contemporary mysteries from the world where aides and Treasury officials intersect. Nobody, as yet, has produced a scrap of evidence that the President did anything wrong. Attempts to define the nature of a possible offence are complex essays rather than simple charges on a sheet. But the juggernaut is rolling, absorbing time and energy, sapping the beginnings of confidence.

This is thoroughly bad news; and dismaying in its lack of proportionality. At the core, we are discussing two kinds of systems malfunction. The American system of government – taking its cue from a land where litigation sprouts like corn cobs – cannot do anything swiftly or simply. It insists on a special prosecutor *and* a Congressional investigation, legal belt and political braces, so that inquiries tumble over each in cash-rich confusion. And the weight of energy thrown at the problem is yet again likely to turn to exhausted irrelevance as the years drag by. The Irangate special prosecutor, remember, finally pronounced long after those he was investigating had retired from office, disgorging his findings to a world that had moved on and lost interest. Stagnation, whilst the files pile as high as an elephant's eye.

But there is also a systemic lack of common sense which somehow contrives to bury the point of what's happening in numbing detail. That point is easily made. American presidents have to come from somewhere and have done something. They do not inherit, when they win office, a fine-tuned machine awaiting their orders. They have to bring their machine men with them. In modern circumstances, Democratic presidents are Southerners, able to tack together a coalition of interests which can outweigh Republican Sun Belt strength. Sophisticated East Coast men from big cities don't get nominated because they can't deliver the South. So you get, as your president, a peanut farmer from Georgia – or the governor of a disregarded, dirt-poor Southern state. And they bring their chums to Washington. These are not bad people; they are the shooting business or legal stars of their community. The electorate, with its manifest distaste for Washington, has effectively summoned them from the sticks. And then, far from home and the way things were done there, the system brings them down. Bert Lance or Webster Hubbell are dismembered by distant events in a Southern town that, if they'd not come to Washington, might never have risen to bite them. The way you operate in Little Rock – a tiny place with a tiny establishment, all living in each other's pockets – is not the way you *can* operate in Washington. Crookery, of course, is crookery anywhere. But so much of the current trouble seems as yet the imposition of big city ways on a very small town. In New York or Chicago it might be sinister that X knows Y and Y knows Z; but in Arkansas they all belong to the same country club, because that's the only one worth belonging to.

The good old boys, in short, have appalling adjustment problems: the problems of culture and size. They have never before had to try running something as vast and complex as this. Seventeen months on, they still haven't found a new ambassador for India, and crucial desks remain unfilled in all the big departments of state. Twelve years of Democratic defeats, moreover, leave an aching void of inexperience. Little Rock was parish council stuff, where the state governor was paid less than a British Member of Parliament. How do you set about building cohesion and recruiting talent from across the nation? The feudings and the sense of chaos are endemic – and virtually preordained.

Here is a critical part of the Whitewater equation. What Bill and Hillary did or didn't do in the Little Rock of the early eighties needs isolating and examining in an Arkansas context. But small crisis has been turned into great drama by the appearance of contemporary cover-up, and that is a fuel lighting constant fires. Common sense, at this point, would apply logic and posit that organisations which can cover things up must be organised efficiently enough to spot things going wrong in the first place. Nothing in Bill Clinton's initial year hints at such efficiency; all the evidence, to the contrary, speaks of an embryo government struggling to find who was sitting at the next desk and the way to the executive rest room. His men couldn't organise a haircut on an airport runway, let alone a conspiracy. And yet that defence – a plea of inexperience and ineptitude – is the one argument that governments, like emperors without clothes, dare not make. They can realise their mistake, as they have; they can promise candour by the bucketload. But too late: the creaking show is on the road of hearings and prosecutions.

Whitewater might be welcome and proportionate, in sum, if it hinted at systematic malignity, if it threatened to reveal something rotten in the state of America. But that is not the case, and may never be so. What it shows so far, in fact, is something much more worrying: a system of elections and governance (gridlocked by the constitution) that stacks the scales of failure high.

Bill Clinton went the long, democratic road. He came from obscurity. He got elected. He was what the people wanted. They wanted healthcare reform. They wanted success. But they have willed the ends without willing the means. Washington chews up big men from big states like California. It was the wit and experience of Jim Baker that rescued Ronald Reagan. But small men from small states cannot count on such luck. They wander into a land of wolves without a map, and soon they are lost.

This is the curse of Whitewater. It is not yet fatal. It may ebb and flow as sharply as Hillary Clinton's popularity. But, at best, it is dragging distraction – feeding cynicism, rendering ever more remote the prospect of health reform, which in turn will mean more cynicism on the 1996 day-of-election reckoning.

The wonder of modern America is that a country of such resource and such energy can time and again contemplate a failed government, revile it, move on – and miss the larger picture, the deeper reasons for failure. This week, by chance, the same Congress that voted for Whitewater hearings decided to spruce up its own image by staging a few Oxford Union-style debates for the C-Span TV cameras, with Oxford chaps there to tell them how it's done. Put on a show, change the scenery. But Americans never pause to ask themselves *why* things are going so wrong, why government is so despised. Alas, here we go again. •

Ed Vulliamy
30 March 1994

Italy's tawdry pleasure palace

The Italians have delivered their verdict as to what kind of country they want to emerge from the most remarkable political tumult in post-war Western Europe.

A hurricane of scandals exposed their society as rotten to the core, and brought the country to the threshold of sweeping reforms – an opportunity to carve out a role as the laboratory for a new politics in the new continent. But the Italians looked over the edge and did not like what they saw.

This election was a battle between two different Italys: the country's effervescent, liberal side, and the new, self-centred materialism. In the event, the Italians opted for the latter.

Italy has voted itself into the hands of a precarious three-way alliance between multi-media tycoon Silvio Berlusconi, neo-fascist leader Gianfranco Fini, and wayward rebel Umberto Bossi, leader of the Northern League.

The first major business venture by Berlusconi, victor of the battle for Italy's soul, was the construction of a dream housing estate on the edge of Milan, imaginatively christened Milano 2. It became a temple of an emergent Italy, some of the most sought-after housing in the financial capital.

There, people wake up in the morning in houses built by Berlusconi and switch on soap operas broadcast by Berlusconi's awful television channels, punctuated by advertisements sold by Berlusconi to himself. They may then go and buy groceries from a supermarket owned by Berlusconi. The highlight of the week would be a trip to admire the wizardry of football champions AC Milan, owned by Silvio Berlusconi. It was in Milano 2 that the term 'Berlusconi-ism' entered the vocabulary.

Berlusconi is likely to be prime minister before long, and as victor of the election he would be fully entitled to take the office. But in no modern country could the head of government conceivably enjoy such hegemony over everyday society. This victory has no parallel. The Italians have decided that they want to turn their country into one big aspirant Milano 2.

It would be wrong to see Berlusconi as a Big Brother who controls society through soccer spectaculars and the bevvy of semi-naked dancing lovelies on the box each evening. We are closer to Huxley than to Orwell: Berlusconi has been elevated to power by popular consent. His victory is comparable to that of Margaret Thatcher's in 1983, an expression of a social flavour prevalent among the people that wished her to lead them. The new Italy has found the natural man for the job.

Berlusconi and his vulgar commercial empire epitomise many of the more cogent changes in post-economic-boom Italy; his electoral base bulges among the young; he is a model for a particular way of life and aspirations.

That way of life was put backstage by the 'Tangentopoli' scandals – Kickback City. The spectacle of an entire political class being put under criminal invest-igation brought rival values to the fore: a magistrature, known for its radicals, and frustrated for two generations, was rampant in pursuit of the truth; the talk was of change, justice and renewal.

But Berlusconi's election puts a brake on the spring-clean of society. Among the crowds which shrieked 'thieves' at the politicians and businessmen as they were sped through prison gates were many who had themselves gained from the system. With yesterday's vote, the Italians have said that Kickback City was going too far for their liking.

Berlusconi promises economic renewal, but he would not have got into power if the old forces that stood to be condemned by Kickback City had not backed him. His Forza Italia, which did not exist until two months ago, is a curious mix of Berlusconi's own commercial apparatchiks and a simple transfer of allegiances by members of the old Socialist Party, led by Berlusconi's life-long friend, the disgraced Bettino Craxi. Berlusconi's membership of the murky P2 Masonic Lodge has been carefully forgotten.

But it is not Berlusconi alone who represents the Italy that will host the summit of the G7 in Naples this summer. Gianfranco Fini, leader of the neo-fascist MSI, delivered the South for Berlusconi. Until a few months ago, he was an insignificant player, surrounded by posses of Nazi-saluting bravoes and old ladies and gentlemen who remembered 'better' times. As fascists, the MSI was excluded from the political club which ran the old regime, and became an opposition right-wing. Its enthusiasm for Kickback City helps to give Berlusconi's victory an apparently revolutionary edge.

But, by yesterday, Fini was already being treated as a serious government politician, which indeed he now is – shrewd, intelligent and now triumphant. He was the first to nominate Berlusconi as prime minister.

Fini knows no life outside his movement. He grew up in communist Bologna, surrounded by ultra-left students, whom he loathed. He went to work on the MSI's newspaper, *Italian Century*, in the days when it had few pretensions towards real politics except the resurrection of Il Duce's order.

But the furtive Fini had wider aspirations than his grander predecessors, Giorgio Almirante and Pino Rauti, and at the end of last year he moved suddenly and stylishly into the vacuum left by the collapse of the southern Christian Democrats. He narrowly missed victory in the Rome mayoral elections, and his sidekick, Alessandra Mussolini, nearly pulled off the same triumph in Naples.

Within weeks, Fini was paying homage to the victims of Nazi occupation, and insisting that fascism was a 'closed chapter in history'. He formed the National Alliance, which expanded the MSI to offer Berlusconi's party the ingredients it needed to win: conservatism in the South, the religious vote except for a few liberal Catholics, and the angry youth, which saw fascism as the best way of opposing the old corrupt order.

In Umberto Bossi, Berlusconi has a far more complex and unreliable ally. Bossi's rebellion, which started in Lombardy and spread across the North, introduced a post-modern politics into the fray. The Northern League is a stubborn, relatively clean movement in a constituency socially similar to Fini's in the South, but with very different motives.

The League mobilised popular discontent under an authoritarian but forcefully free market; an anti-ideological, anti-establishment and now it emerges anti-fascist assembly around the single issue of protecting the North's wealth from corrupt politicians who spent it on securing votes in the Mafia-ridden South.

Bossi is a swashbuckling demagogue – a former leftist militant and public official, and a wonderful public speaker, he is utterly unpredictable. His single-mindedness is at present Berlusconi's biggest headache. After delivering more than 100 seats for Berlusconi, he is now insisting on a veto against Berlusconi's premiership and against the presence of Fini in any coalition government.

If the alliance holds together, Italy will have emerged from years of tumult with what amounts to a new republic. It is a political transition from a system which negated democracy for fifty years to something more confident and decisive, but which is equally dependent on servility and, above all, on a complete absence of political imagination. This would be the government of the Fininvest television empire, a facile deluge of tawdry entertainment allied to the culture of intolerance.

It remains to be seen whether this new palace, built around the fantasy-land of Berlusconi's TV pleasure dome, will be taken seriously by the Europe to which Italy thinks it belongs. •

Alan Rusbridger
9 April 1994
Media moguls

In the end Ted and Jane never did make it. New Delhi had been waiting all week for the Turner and Fonda show to hit town, but ultimately it was the technology that did for them. Ted's personal Gulf Stream Four blew a reverse thrust while taxi-ing to take off from Canton – the previous leg of his eight-nation 'goodwill' tour.

In normal circumstances Turner Broadcasting System, Inc. – valued at $2.5 billion (roughly the GNP of, say, Nepal) – is well geared to dealing with such minor inconveniences of life as a troublesome reverse thrust. A new Gulf Stream Four was chartered from Singapore, and word was sent to New Delhi that Ted and Jane's goodwill visit to Mahatma Gandhi's memorial would be postponed from Thursday to Friday morning.

But along came a new problem: Ted and Jane learned that the Cantonese authorities were being less obliging than they might have been and would not allow Ted's new Gulf Stream Four to land. Word was sent to Delhi to move the Gandhi picture thing to Friday night.

CNN's Indian bureau chief, Ashis Ray, gallantly stood in for Ted at a lunch at the luxury Oberoi Hotel on the Friday, but it was a sad affair: only forty of the original 200 VIPs turned up. Even the CNN watches they were given at the end of the meal didn't seem to cheer them up much.

But the atmosphere was probably better than back at the White Swan Hotel in Canton, where matters were not improving. Ted's top men found the only way to get out of Canton was to charter a catamaran to take the party to Hong Kong. But now there was a further complication: Ted was feeling ill. The Gandhi picture opportunity was rescheduled for Saturday, with a proviso that it might slip to Sunday. Unhappily, the Indian daily papers began to develop twinklings of scepticism about the entire venture. Front-page stories began to appear to the effect that Ted was sulking because the Indian government wasn't going to play ball with him.

On Friday night the axe finally fell: the trip was off. Ted was too ill to make it; nursed by Jane, he was heading off back to Atlanta. It was a bad blow for CNN. It was a terrible blow for Major J. S. Kohli, president of the Cable Association of India. He had, he told the *Pioneer*, ordered his wife back from holidaying with her daughters in Goa to watch him shaking hands with Ted. 'It is a once-in-a-lifetime opportunity, and I wanted my wife to be by my side during that great moment.

'Now,' he added dismally, 'I can only rub my hands in disappointment.'

Rubbing their hands in satisfaction at these events across town were executives at the Indian headquarters of Star TV, whose own boss, Rupert Murdoch, experienced no such problems with his reverse thrusts when he had dropped by for a week-long visit to Delhi just a fortnight earlier. He kept all his appointments, attended all his lunches, gave numerous interviews and made a big impression all round. 'He had India eating out of his hand,' said Tavleen Singh, a leading columnist with the *Indian Express*. 'It was like the visit of a head of state. I think Douglas Hurd was here at the same time, but no one noticed.'

Murdoch was at his most charming. He had, he said, come to realise that the West 'no longer has a monopoly on knowledge'. He himself was an old-fashioned Calvinist. His papers had a strong set of moral values. There was more sex in the *Daily Telegraph* than in the *Sun*. India was going to take its place as one of the great nations of the world. He had a very good relationship with the BBC. He had read with amusement Indian papers describing him as a big media mogul. This was rubbish. 'I am just a little ant,' he said. Indeed, in the future broadcasting would be so diverse that it would be impossible for any company to dominate the world's media – 'or even be significantly large'. This was a startlingly modest assertion from a man with a company currently valued at about $7.5 billion (or roughly the GNP of, say, Oman).

Murdoch checked out of Room 651 – the presidential suite – of the Taj Mahal Hotel on the morning of 20 February. By the same evening the room had another occupant: Kerry Packer.

The current fashionability of Delhi as a stopover for retiring media moguls dates back to the events of last summer, when Mr Murdoch was holidaying with his family on a yacht in the Mediterranean. Where other dads might toy with a bucket and spade or go for a dip and a snorkel, Murdoch decided he would use the week to clinch a deal that had been on his mind for some time.

As ever, private jets play a part in the story. Murdoch ordered a News Corp plane to fetch the owner of Star TV, Richard Li, from London, and fly him to Corsica, whence he was to join him for a family lunch prepared by his novelist wife, Anna.

By the end of lunch Murdoch had parted with $525 million in return for a 63 per cent stake in Star TV. The deal gave him access to five channels beamed at 2.5 billion people in fifty countries from Jordan to Japan – more than two thirds of the world's population. It was a deal which dwarfed the potential of all four domestic American TV stations put together. His new audience accounted for 40 per cent of the world's TV sets and included seven of the ten fastest-growing economies in the world.

It was not a bad lunch's work.

But then Murdoch made an uncharacteristic mistake. Defending his newly acquired global influence, he coined a phrase that would return to haunt him: satellite television would, he said, 'be an unambiguous threat to totalitarian regimes everywhere'.

The phrase played well in liberal Western democracies, but acted as something of a reverse thrust in totalitarian regimes. China, its government already out-raged by a BBC documentary about Mao's sex life, promptly passed a law banning citizens from owning satellite dishes. Malaysia and Saudi Arabia have imposed similar restrictions. Others have threatened the same. With one stroke of Li Peng's pen, Murdoch had been denied free access to around 40 per cent of his intended audience for Star TV. The Chinese market had been growing at a frenetic pace. In just ten months last year, an extra 26 million Chinese house-holds had been hooked up to satellite TV.

Asked about this setback by an Indian journalist, Murdoch said: 'We certainly intend to do everything we can to resolve any difficulties with the government of China.' A week later he unambiguously threw the BBC off the Star satellite over China. Meanwhile, India had suddenly become a rather more important part of his equation.

To appreciate the full surreality of the New Media World Order, it is not necessary to travel far from New Delhi. Drive for an hour out of town and stop in any of the villages and try to work out what century you are in.

There is electricity here, though it is a haphazard affair liable to regular breaks of hours, even days. In the smaller villages one or two people will own a rundown car, but there are not many other symptoms of twentieth-century life. The farms are worked by bullocks. Open drains run down the middle of mud-floored alleys that divide the houses, and down which stroll women hiding their faces with veils. At dusk young children walk back from the fields bearing cow pats on their heads for use as fuel. Once darkness falls villagers stretch out to sleep on beds outside their houses.

Many people round these parts earn no more than five to ten rupees a day – let us say a maximum of 20p. The better-off ones might make £12 a month. Their homes are by and large free of possessions, apart from the basics of bed, table, chairs and cooking utensils. In terms of development, it is as an average English village might have been shortly before the Industrial Revolution.

On the evening we dropped by one such village, Khansa, the air was filled with the singing of a group of four- and five-year-olds who had gathered, as they do every Tuesday, around the temple of the monkey god, Hanuman.

We went to the house of Yogbal Sharma, who owns a van and a transport business. He has recently erected a dish on his house, just off one such alley with its bullocks and open drains, and can now receive the effluence of Star TV.

Inside, the family were clustered around the set, which was in the bedroom. In order to keep the electrical load to the minimum, the lighting was limited to one 20-watt bulb. Almost invisible in this gloom, Mr Sharma zapped proudly from channel to channel. We began with MTV, which was showing a programme called the *Headbanger's Ball*, fronted by a posturing young American DJ with a back-to-front baseball cap. The room flickered with the staccato images of pop videos. Legs, lipstick, kisses, jeans, fast cars, beaches, cafés, drink, waterfalls: white faces, black faces, but not many brown faces.

A touch on the zapper brought us *The Bold and the Beautiful*, a sub-*Dynasty* American soap revolving around adultery, transmitted twice a day, five days a week. Zap, and suddenly the features of famed British telly-chef Keith Floyd pop up on the BBC World Service (not yet chucked off the South Asia satellite by Mr Murdoch). Zap, and we have skiing on Prime Sport (available, like MTV, all day every day). Zap, and we have a programme of an uncertain nature with Chinese subtitles. Zap, and the Sharma family have the chance to see some ads.

They are, respectively, for a perfume called Lace made by 'Yardleys of London'; for J&B Whisky; for Old Spice aftershave; and for a moisturiser called Evita.

It is a representative enough sample of Star fare. At other times of the day or night Mr Sharma's family can zap from *Neighbours* (three times a day, five days a week, the plot eight years behind Britain) to *Donahue* to *Oprah Winfrey* to *Santa Barbara* to *Baywatch* to *The Simpsons* to *Dynasty* to *LA Law*. Most deliciously, they have the opportunity to start their week, every Monday at 9 am, with *Lifestyles of the Rich and Famous*.

Outside in the streets of Khansa a cluster of older children had replaced the toddlers in singing the chants. In years to come they will have to choose whether to spend their Tuesday evenings singing songs to Hanuman or watching MTV's *Most Wanted* or *Dynasty*.

Don Atyeo, general manager of MTV, thinks he knows which way they'll leap. 'We've revolutionised the way Indian kids devote themselves to leisure,' he told the BBC recently. 'We've created a youth culture where there was simply none before.'

How does Mr Sharma, who is very far from being rich or famous, afford the wherewithal to buy his dish? The answer is that it is a business, like his transport business. Once his dish is installed he – quite legally – runs a maze of cables around the village down which he can squirt Murdochvision into another sixty houses. Pretty soon he is making a reasonable profit on his original outlay.

In another village, Bakthawarpur, on the borders of Haryana and Uttar Pradesh, another tyro cable operator, Jeet Singh, explains the typical finances. He used to run a general store before moving into cable in this rather more advanced village of 15,000 people. His dish cost him £750. The cabling and boosting equipment to link up another 140 houses cost him another £1,800. Total outlay: around £2,400. He charges each house £2 a month, bringing him an income of £280 a month, so he has covered his costs within a year.

In this fashion the dishing and cabling of India has proceeded at an astonishing rate. It is thought that there are about 100,000 operators like Mr Singh across India, and that another 2,000 try and get into the market every day, though most of them fail. A country which had 400,000 homes receiving satellite TV in January 1992 now has 8 million. That figure will continue to grow at 20 per cent a year.

For the time being, at least, Mr Murdoch doesn't begrudge Mr Singh and Mr Sharma grabbing hold of his signal for free and piping it around the villages of India. His main eye, though, is on the 200 million Indians with reasonable purchasing power and on the advertising expenditure trends. According to Alyque Padamsee, chief executive of Lintas in India, chief among these is the younger Indian who 'doesn't always want to seek parental advice now and, above all, he wants to be able to buy the things he wants to buy now, and not wait for reincarnation and perhaps enjoy them in the next life'.

The Indian TV advertising market aimed at such people is worth around £80 million today. If all goes well with the Indian economy it should grow by 20 per cent a year for the next three years.

Mr Murdoch's dream as he signed the cheque for Star TV over lunch on his yacht off Corsica was that this pattern would be repeated in country after country from Bahrain to Singapore. Just keep raining down *Dynasty* and MTV to people hungry for Western culture and bank the cheques from advertisers. It may yet turn out that way. But in the meantime India has given Murdoch a series of nasty shocks.

The first and nastiest shock is that the Indian audience is disgracefully un-grateful for the munificence showered on it from the skies. There doesn't, on all the evidence so far, appear to be a huge audience for *Dynasty*, MTV or, indeed, any programmes in English. Reliable figures are hard to come by, but it is plain that few people, in comparative terms, are watching the BBC or MTV (which Murdoch is now planning partially to replace with a home-grown version called, mysteriously, Oye-MTV). Star Plus, with its diet of soaps and chat, is doing little better, as is his fourth channel, Prime Sports.

To the astonishment of all the pundits the state TV station, Doordashan (DD) – which, pre-Star, was written off as a discredited and dull propaganda outfit – has come back from the grave with a diet of livelier programmes and wall-to-wall Hindi films. The other huge success story has been Zee TV, a Hindi-language channel on the same satellite as Star, putting out some hard-hitting current affairs programmes and yet more Hindi films. Star TV picks up about 2 per cent of the TV audience, against 87 per cent for the two DD channels and 11 per cent for Zee. The success of Zee was not lost on Murdoch. Four months ago he bought a 49.9 per cent stake in the company which owns it.

The moral he will have learned on his Delhi trip is that he must get into Hindi-language programming fast. 'The huge majority of Indians don't speak English,' says Vinod Dua, a prominent producer and presenter. 'And in any case,' pipes up an assistant, 'we prefer seeing Indian women take off their clothes to Western ones.'

But making your own local-language programming is, of course, much more expensive than eight-year-old reruns of *Neighbours*. In any case, most local TV producers doubt whether there is the programme-making expertise or infra-structure in India to churn out the 240 hours a month that a new channel would gobble up. Let alone the two Hindi channels Murdoch is now promising.

That is one big headache for Murdoch. Another is that the satellite boom is only just beginning. Between now and 1996 there are going to be another forty satellites launched over Asia. The competition between Murdoch, Turner, the BBC, Kerry Packer and various local and London-based Indian businesses even now preparing their business plans is going to be intense.

The final nasty shock for Murdoch is that very few people believe he can do in India what he did in Britain – encode the signal and make people pay to watch. Indians are used to receiving their television free, and it is doubtful (a) whether sufficient people can be persuaded to pay for what Murdoch will offer and (b) whether – with a ramshackle network of back-street cable operators – any system would be enforceable. 'Remember,' says Rajat Sharma, the Jeremy Paxman of Zee TV, 'this is a country where, out of 800 million citizens, the government can only persuade 7 million to pay income tax. If the mighty government of India can't collect, what chance does Murdoch have?'

His views are echoed by Rajesh Mehra, of Shyam, the largest satellite dish manufacturers in India: 'We told Star from day one: "When it comes down to people paying, sorry, forget it."'

The problems Murdoch faces are, then, immense. India is a country of eighteen official languages and about 1,700 dialects; of four main castes and thousands of subcastes; of five main religions; a country where only 35 per cent of the population is literate in any real terms; where half the population exists on 10p a day or less. If only it were as simple as bombarding them with Oprah Winfrey and buying up the Premier League football . . .

But let us suppose that Murdoch succeeds – just as he succeeded, eventually, with Fox in America and Sky in Britain. What will be the effect on India and, eventually, the other 1.9 billion inhabitants in what is beguilingly called the 'footprint' of his satellite? Can any culture survive the Murdoch experience intact? Can it survive without being coarsened? Without its indigenous newspapers, TV and films coarsening themselves in order to compete and stay alive? Without that working through into other institutions in national life? Without instilling in the entire subcontinent a consumerist thirst such as it has never known?

And would that make enough of them richer and happier? And would we, in the already conquered offshoots of the Murdoch empire, be happy if a consumer-driven engine of growth did roar into action in India? Mark Tully calculates in one of his books that the average Indian's annual consumption of commercial energy is the equivalent of 210 kilograms of oil. If each Indian began to consume the same amount of energy as the average Briton (3,756 kilograms) that would mean the world having to find an extra 3,190 million tonnes of oil each year.

The first thing to be said is that there are plenty of young and progressive Indians who welcome Murdoch and the effect they think he will have on India. Rajat Sharma of Zee TV is one of them. His programme, *Aap ki Adalat*, in which he puts politicians and other prominent people in the dock, draws audiences of nearly 50 million and brings him a daily mailbag of 1,200 fan letters. It would, he says, all have been impossible without satellite TV: 'If we didn't have these outside influences, we'd still have only one TV station completely dependent on the government of the day. Without Star TV we were nowhere. Murdoch is not only welcome, he is necessary.'

Vinod Dua agrees: 'We haven't got the money or the experience to reform Indian television ourselves.' But what if a Dutch pornographer decided to follow in Murdoch's steps? 'That would be great,' he answers without hesitation. 'This country is so sexually repressed. Porn's better than the vicarious sexual hypocrisy you get with people watching MTV and pretending it's the music they're interested in.'

Such people dismiss any talk of cultural imperialism. 'We've assimilated the Moguls and the English and numerous other influences and we've stayed just the same lazy bums,' says Dua. 'Murdoch's no problem.'

'How do you stop him?' asks Sharma. 'The signal's there, and India is a democratic society. I'm not saying we're being raped and we must enjoy it. We're not being raped. If my culture is so weak that it can be invaded by a satellite channel then I don't want it.'

Other TV professionals and business people relish the challenge of fighting Murdoch off – of proving the culture is too strong and complex for him. 'It's much too complacent just to sit back and let Mr Murdoch and Ted Turner in and say they've got such deep pockets we'd better tune into their stations,' says Malavika Singh, a leading magazine editor and programme-maker who has assembled a business plan for five channels of her own.

'You can't stop it, but you can counter it. Because other cultures have succumbed to Murdoch, it doesn't mean India will be the same. America is a 200-year-old culture, drawn from a wide variety of people. India is a 5,000-year-old culture and it's not going to take the shit.'

A frequently voiced argument is that the domestic film and TV industry is itself already so vulgar that it would be hard for Murdoch to cheapen it further. This is a persuasive argument to anyone who has seen the genre of recently released videos, in which every scene is sponsored by an advertiser who is given the bottom third of the screen to promote his product.

Bhaskar Ghose, the top civil servant in charge of broadcasting, put the official line to the BBC: 'It's being talked about in terms of a threat to Indian culture. Actually, there will be an alternative in perception and taste and so on. But then you can't really stop it. Change can't be stopped by anyone at all.'

Come back to one of the villages to see how things are changing. Sitting just off the main street drinking sweet tea is Ram Phal, the fifty-year-old head of

Bakthawarpur, with its 15,000 inhabitants and 140 satellite households. He has, he says, already noticed a lowering of standards on other channels as they try to compete with satellite TV. 'Indian films used to have a theme. Now it's all violence, disruption and sex. They are useless, meaningless, aimless films. At the end you ask, what was it all about? Nothing. But young people are interested in them. Old films were family films you could all sit together and watch. Now you never know when you will have to leap up to hide the screen. And the ads! When you see something you want, it is natural for you to try to achieve it. But no matter how hard you work, you will never achieve the things you see on these ads. What effect will that have on life? Young people will forget religion when they see this glamorous life. They already don't go to temple so often.'

The fear of the social disruption that global television could cause in rural India (where 75 per cent of the population still lives) unites politicians from left and right.

On the left is George Fernandes, a former Janata Dal minister who has persistently campaigned for a boycott of Pepsi Cola. 'Once upon a time I used to think that Western television and advertising would create in people an anger and revulsion and that, in the process, it would help the radical movement. I thought you would gain benefit from showing people the life that was denied them. Now I just feel that people treat the ads as just another form of entertainment. The Indian middle classes of today are being overwhelmed by an escapist culture, and they are the ones who create the culture for the rest of society. When some lady called – is her name Samantha Fox? – came to perform in Delhi, I know for a fact the élite of the élite chartered planes from Bombay, Calcutta, Bangalore and Madras to flock to see her. They would have done the same for Michael Jackson had he come.

'The thing that depresses me is that television could be such an educative force for good in a country where adult literacy is so low. But instead of dissemination of ideas we get the vulgarisation of our culture and the commercialisation of every aspect of human life.'

The problem, Fernandes argues, is that the official Doordashan news is still rigidly censored by the government and thus lacks all credibility. 'Unless DD can be made credible, all our anger against foreign media is not going to be of any use. An idea can only be fought by a superior idea. The French can see the dangers: that's why they took a stand on cultural issues in GATT. The Japanese are very aware of it, so why not us? If the Americans can threaten trade sanctions against us, as they are over cloth, then we can say to them back: "We're not going to allow your stuff in. We will not allow our culture to be assaulted."'

But how? How do you stop the stuff when it drops freely from the skies? The answer, according to Swami Agnivesh, a social activist prominent in the fight against child labour, is a punitive tax on dishes. 'I would put a £2,000 tax on all dish antennae,' he says. 'The very, very rich could still buy them, but they are, in any case, Westernised. Doordashan was a bit boring, but it was educative and serious. It was not as tendentious and vulgar as it has now become. It is now so cheap and vulgar. Nothing is being given to the illiterate and the poor to empower them, to tell them about laws which have been passed but of which they are ignorant. It is a great loss to families.

'I fear democracy will be subverted, and family structures. The only social security India has is the family – economic and psychological and emotional. If you break that up India is in deep trouble. One of our great values has been a sort of contentment in life. I don't mean to romanticise poverty or glorify want, but that contentment was better than the discontent you feel with your own life when you watch glamorous Western lives on television.'

The columnist Tavleen Singh wants to see all restrictions on Indian TV stations lifted immediately so that they can compete on equal terms with the satellite barons. 'But I fear it's too late. People who say Indian culture is strong enough to withstand Murdoch are talking bullshit. India is exactly like any other country except we have a lot of poor people and we speak a lot of languages.

'In some of the villages we're talking about dragging people into the twenty-first century from the sixteenth century. We're showing them stuff that will blow their minds. They don't know why this stuff they're seeing on television is unaffordable. All they've ever had in the village bazaar has been the bare necessities.'

Jaswant Singh, a senior MP of the nationalist BJP, agrees: 'The effect could be horrifying. There is this craving for a magical world. Villagers ask, "What is this world where tables groan under the weight of food, where kids throw tantrums because they're spoiled?" To me it is self-evident that the consequences will be dire.'

The official response to this kind of debate has been a muddled tragi-comedy. The government is even now deciding whether to allow Ted Turner to form some kind of partnership with DD. This is at least a more structured approach than its attempt last year to fill five new urban DD channels with programmes from private production companies on a first-come, first-served basis – an original procedure which led to fist fights among producers sleeping on pavements for five days before the bids were due in.

The Censor Board has meanwhile been driven into a fury of indecision about how to react to the kind of public backlash there is to the generally perceived lowering of standards on TV and in recent films. The Board met in emergency session to discuss a song released last week, 'Sexy Sexy Sexy', which contrived to use that same word 118 times. After much deliberation the Revising Committee ruled that the song could be released – with one proviso: the word 'sexy' must be changed to 'baby'.

The Board allowed through one song, alluringly entitled 'What is under the Blouse?', but ordered alterations to another Western derivative which ran: 'My shirt is sexy, my pants are sexy, my father is sexy, my mother is sexy'. The Board's ruling was that the first two mentions of the word were admissible, but that the latter two implied an incestuous relationship. They were duly cut.

For Murdoch and Turner, India will be the greatest challenge of their commercial ingenuity, cultural flexibility and long-term vision, and a huge strain on their resources. As Turner succinctly put it to an audience of broadcasters in Hong Kong: 'We could all lose our buns out here.'

The prize for succeeding could be intoxicatingly large. The multinationals eyeing up India and China – and all other countries east of Suez – as future markets need a medium to convince the people that, by tomorrow, they need a whole range of products that, only yesterday, they had never heard of. The medium is Murdoch.

What will become of India in the process? That is not Murdoch's problem. 'We don't represent anything,' he told one interviewer in Delhi. 'We are only bringing in technology here.'

One of India's leading advertising executives, Santosh Ballal, put it rather more pithily to Mark Tully: 'We create the lifestyles, we create the aspirations. Whether the viewer achieves the aspirations is his problem, not mine.' •

Barbara Ehrenreich
5 March 1994

The trouble with Hillary

Critics of Hillary are generally a low-minded, paranoid lot. I cannot believe, for example, that she suffocated her mother-in-law with a pillow in order to win sympathy for the President during the pre-Christmas flurry of sex accusations. Nor is it likely that she dragged presidential aide Vince Foster out to that lonely park, shot him with an antique pistol, and then stole his files on Whitewatergate.

I, in fact, am one of the millions of American women who used her lipstick to cross out 'William H.' and write in 'HILLARY' before pulling the lever in the voting booth.

My infatuation with Hillary lasted for weeks, if not months. When the Republicans denounced her as a male-devouring lesbian communist, my heart leapt at the prospect of having one in the White House at last. Nothing she did dismayed me, not even the solid turquoise jacket-and-turtleneck combinations.

So it is with sorrow that I must finally announce I've had it with Hillary. The last straw was an anecdote related by Lani Guinier, Clinton's rudely discarded nominee for civil-rights chief.

As Guinier tells it in the *New York Times*, the two former pals ran into each other during last year's frenzied right-wing attack on Guinier. Hillary 'breezed by me with a casual "Hi, Kiddo".' Then she paused, turned back towards the battered Guinier and 'to no one in particular, announced, "I'm 30 minutes late to a lunch."'

I'm all for punctuality in alimentary matters, but what kind of a sister is this? My mind reeled back to the first sign of trouble between Hillary and me, having to do with her curious relationship with banks. Questioned during the campaign, Hillary had snapped that 'all lawyers work for banks'.

Now a bank, as far as I can see, is a building so blandly furnished that passers-by are lulled into leaving their money in it, which money is then passed along to various gamblers in suits. Thus the Madison bank, which is central to the Whitewatergate scandal and was at one point represented by Hillary, collected the savings of elderly Arkansans in order to finance dubious real-estate ventures and possibly Clinton gubernatorial campaigns.

This would seem to be a case of a bank working for a lawyer. But there do exist lawyers – generally too scruffily dressed to be admitted to a Little Rock country club – who work for things other than banks, like civil rights, for example. And some even work *against* banks.

Then there is her health reform plan. One hesitates to speak ill of the dead, but at this point the Clinton plan's only supporters are a few masochistically inclined labour leaders who so enjoyed their flogging with Nafta that they are lusting to be beaten with health.

The worst of it is not that the plan makes neuroanatomy look simple by comparison and that it can only be read by the terminally amusement-deprived. The worst of it is not even that the plan's real beneficiaries would be the nation's six largest insurance companies. And insurance companies, we note, are much like banks – soothingly bland institutions for the upward redistribution of wealth.

No, the worst of it is a pattern of health-related mendacity on Hillary's part. She portrays herself as a fearless populist, battling against 'special interests' and even the 'insurance industry'. But the only part of the insurance industry that opposes her plan consists of the small-time companies her plan would eliminate, and they've never been much for campaign contributions anyway.

Told by a member of her health task force that a majority of Americans would prefer a government-run plan that eliminates the parasitical insurers, Hillary reportedly said: 'Now tell me something interesting.'

Well, tell us something interesting, Hillary. Whatever happened to that fresh-faced anti-war activist and advocate for little children? Because next time, much as it may pain me, I'm voting for Bill. •

David Hirst
13 December 1993

Close to the edge

No one has ever doubted PLO Chairman Yasser Arafat's capacity to inspire devotion, his dedication, indefatigability — or personal courage in supreme emergency or mortal danger. It was with the born leader's perfect sang-froid that he took control when, in April last year, his plane ran out of fuel in a sandstorm over the Libyan desert. As his pilot, a faithful retainer since the age of twelve, brought down the aircraft at just the angle to guarantee the death of all those in the cockpit while ensuring the best possible chance for those gathered in the rear, Arafat organised his colleagues for the impact; and, after it, he diligently tended to those more badly injured than himself.

But even as it revealed the best in the one-time guerrilla commander, did this escape simultaneously exacerbate the worst in him too? Arafat developed a bloodclot in the brain. He likes to say that the Jordanian surgeons who operated on him inserted a computer in its place. Indeed, it is a favourite quip of his, much used nowadays on Western officials impressed by his command of facts and figures. But, at his Tunis headquarters, it has become a tired, conceited pleasantry that begs the insistent question: did that crash really do further damage to faculties already going awry?

'I asked him at the time,' said a resigned member of the PLO Executive Committee, 'what God had told him on the other side. For we hoped it had made him think of those he might have left behind, of delegating authority, of reviving the Palestinian democracy he always boasted about, but which, in truth, he was emptying of its content. The opposite happened; more than ever he thinks only of himself.'

Egotism. No one doubts that, of all his infirmities, this was ever the chief. Now it is wreaking havoc as never before. If it is only doing so, as yet, on his innermost circles of power, it is liable, before long, to make itself felt on the whole cause he embodies, on all those – Israel, the Western powers as well as the Palestinians – who like to think an Arab-Israeli settlement is finally at hand.

One has heard elsewhere, in Beirut, Amman, Jerusalem, that something is amiss in Tunis, but it does not take long, upon actually setting foot here, and penetrating the Arafat establishment, to sense that things are even worse than one imagined. 'I feel as if I've walked into a madhouse,' I told an acquaintance from Arafat's Beirut of the seventies. 'Well,' rejoined this now eminent person, 'that isn't surprising, because you have. The proof is that last week we boycotted a meeting of the EC [Executive Committee]. Yet we're the most patient of people. It takes a lot to make us explode.'

This is not just an EC member speaking, one of twelve of the original eighteen who, since the Oslo accord, still serve on that highest decision-making body. He is one of the much smaller minority who worked strenuously, unknown to the rest, to conclude it. Indeed, the outrage comes first of all from those excluded. It is they who feel most betrayed; they fear that Arafat is both undermining all their handiwork and that, in the latest excess of his indomitable egotism, he wants to put them, the very architects of the agreement, aside so that he alone can run the show, bask in the unfamiliar sunshine of international favour – and, this week, the honour of a call on John Major at 10 Downing Street.

For Mr Palestine pays his first visit to Britain tomorrow, a notable but bittersweet event in that Palestinians still regard Britain, Zionism's first imperial sponsor, as the original cause of all their woes. Ever the most peripatetic of leaders, Arafat's schedule, since 13 September, has been especially hectic. Paris, Bonn, the Scandinavian capitals – throughout Europe the grizzled, sixty-four-year-old former 'terrorist' is a fêted guest. Occasionally, he takes his young new wife, Suha, with him. When he does, that is laden for Palestinians with a significance it cannot have for Europeans unfamiliar with the effect this most unexpected of marriages had on his own people.

For was that, rather than the plane crash, the true catalyst of his increasingly bizarre pathology? His oldest and closest colleagues, survivors, like him, of twenty, thirty years of bloody struggle, daily ask such questions. Indeed, it is from them that most of the opinions in this article come. And they do not have to be extracted. They tumble forth in the tones – exasperated, lugubrious, fatalistic – of men nearing their wits' ends. Spend half an hour sipping Turkish coffee in any of a dozen demoralised PLO offices in the suburbs of Menza or Mutuelle Ville and you are almost sure to be regaled with, or overhear a telephone conversation about, the latest antics on 58 Yagorta Street. That is the two-storey villa where the Arafats live and work, and whence the 'president' of Palestine-to-be hardly emerges except when he is on his way, in a cavalcade of black limousines, to the airport and the latest of his lightning foreign tours.

'It is a tragi-comedy, I really don't know whether to laugh or cry,' lamented the head of one bureau, putting down the receiver upon learning of yet another committee their boss has just set up, probably without its members' knowledge. Is this another Gaddafi in the making, he wonders out loud, with his 'committees everywhere', the celebrated formula for the highest form of government yet known to man? Or is it Idi Amin – as yet without the bloodshed? Or the Emperor Bokassa? And Suha? To whom, he wonders, should he liken her? To Jihan, bejewelled, ambitious young wife of that other great Middle East peacemaker, Anwar Sadat, or to Imelda Marcos? Or perhaps it should be Hillary Clinton, since Palestine's First Lady has let it be known that when – or should one now say if? – Tunis moves to Jericho, she rather fancies taking charge of her people's health.

Arafat's autocratic ways have always been latent. 'They were like a little dot,' recalls an EC member who resigned in 1974, 'which have grown inch by inch, foot by foot, yard by yard, till they have taken over everything.' It mattered less before 13 September. But now, said an EC member, 'we are no longer underground, no longer in Fakhani [his Beirut headquarters], we are on the way to the homeland. He is not running guerrilla operations, he is dealing with a whole society, the building of a state.' Money, and the control of it, most obsesses him at the moment. 'For him,' said a critic, 'power comes from two things: "security" and cash. He has mastered the first. But he won't feel safe till he controls the second.'

The first Arafat mastered quite simply because that is a domain where no one even thinks of challenging him. The men who will run his police forces in Gaza and Jericho are quintessentially his own; it is no accident that most of his policemen will be over fifty. And despite his insistence on 'democracy and yet more democracy', he is consciously modelling his 'security' on that of the Arab regimes he despises.

He is still having to fight on the financial front – if only because it is others' money on which he is counting. He insists on heading the Palestine Council for Construction and Development, in defiance of Palestinian businessmen and economists, and the international donors. 'He just loves collecting chairman-ships,' said an adviser, 'like others collect stamps. And everyone knows that once he is chairman of something, he runs it on his own. Half the donors' money will go on recurrent expenditures, and that will provide the liquid cash that he wants to spend as he pleases, accountable to no one. It is for patronage, not personal corruption – there is none of that in him. It is sheer love of power, the need to know he is boss.

'But the amazing thing is that he wants to handle all the projects too. He receives some Palestinian economist from Europe – an economist, mind you, not an engineer – and grandly announces: "Dr... I want you to build me an airport here or a cement factory there." He thinks he knows everything, from fishing in Gaza to potash on the Dead Sea. He loves detail. But his idea of economics is still what it was when he was running Fakhani: money in his pocket, or under his bed, and a pen to sign cheques with.' He seems to have little grasp of concept or process. When, the adviser recalls, he told him that setting up a Palestine Central Bank would not be quite as simple as he thought, he grew charac-teristically petulant. 'I shall issue a decree when I get to Jericho,' he asserted, 'and it will be valid for all the Occupied Territories.' Told that this would be politically, constitutionally impossible, he exploded: 'That is an Israeli reading.' Most of his advisers wonder what on earth they are for.

And that is only half of the story. His wife looms large in the other. The least being said of her is that she is a public relations calamity. Even the self-effacing Abu Mazen, chief architect of the Oslo accord, flatly refused to let Arafat take her to the White House signing. But she did go to Paris, where her mother, Raymonda, lives. 'You know how the French are about protocol,' said an aide. 'The Quai d'Orsay must have spent a week preparing that banquet. So you can imagine what we felt like when Suha showed up, not just with her mother, but her father, uncle, two sisters – and one of these with her French boyfriend!' Then she went shopping with Mrs Kashoggi, wife of the billionaire Saudi tycoon. 'I can see her now,' the aide went on, 'boarding the plane with all her Louis Feraud packages. Can you imagine what our Gazan refugees would think if they knew about it?' Not to mention all those PLO employees in Tunis, some of them weeks behind on their already meagre salaries, who already do know about it?

As for the Chairman himself, he was engaged in more serious business. Of the petitioners assembled in the lobby of the Crillon Hotel the aide says, 'You could tell what they were like just by looking at them, their neckties, their hairstyles. They could smell easy contracts. And he received them, one by one, till three in the morning.' It is the same here in Tunis, where he recently set up a six-member 'economic committee', none of whom is an economist, for the only discernible purpose of bypassing his official Council. 'Look at this,' said the aide. 'I just got it today.' He produced a fax from a Palestinian businessman perplexed about a certain gentleman touting himself as agent for development projects, giving the Arafats' home as his telephone number – and a bank in Liechtenstein for the payment of commissions.

The despair in the Arafat entourage is not without self-criticism however. 'We talk about the international balance of power, about Arab weakness and decay,' said one. 'All that is true. But the fault is in us too. Arafat is a reflection of ourselves, of all our weaknesses, contradictions, personal and factional interests. He knows us all and uses us all.'

'I have no doubt,' said an EC member, 'that he really is paranoid, and the more threatened he feels the more he has to dominate.' Yet the truth is that no real threat exists; no one around him even thinks of deposing him. All know that he is indispensable, that, in a very real sense, he *is* the peace process. And no one wants to destroy that.

'He has gradually built a situation,' he went on, 'where, as with a Saddam or an Assad, everything will collapse without him, or at least he has created in us the very real fear that it will. But even Assad does not bother himself with economics. If our man had his way he would be everything from President ... ' – and he struggled for an expression adequate to his meaning – 'to ticket-collector on every bus in Palestine. We are trapped. We thought that with this agreement, however limited, we would begin to realise our dream. But the dream is becoming a nightmare. We need him – but we have to oppose him at the same time. But when we do that he blackmails us' – blackmails them, he meant, with their knowledge of his own indispensability.

And not only them. The Europeans vigorously opposed his chairmanship of the Council, seeing in this the same dangers of politicisation, mismanagement and unaccountability as Palestinian economists themselves. But last week they caved in. 'He must,' said one, 'have told them: "You will be responsible for the collapse of the talks, for the impoverishment of my people."'

Yet it is blackmail from a position of fundamental weakness, tactical gain at the expense of long-term strategy. Just look, his critics say, at his negotiating method, in detail and general design. Why, they ask, does he leave it to the last moment to name his team to the PLO-Israeli committees, thus ensuring they are completely unprepared? Why does he appoint people who can't even speak English? The answer, they say, is that he actually wants them to fail, so he can then step in himself, with a grand display of his own indispensability, his unique ability to take the high statesmanlike decisions over his underlings' heads. That, they fear, is the true import of his summit with Prime Minister Yitzhak Rabin in Cairo. 'Rabin has him where he wants him,' said one. 'He knows that, for

Arafat, the channel – himself – is more important than the substance' – in other words, that it is a trade-off, the bartering away of Palestine for the aggrandisement of Mr Palestine.

But how much more can Arafat cede? In addressing this question, his intimates, till then apt to be so vehement, tend at last to become hushed and furtive in their contemplation of the seemingly unthinkable; they do not actually volunteer the dreadful word 'treason', but nor, as a legitimate line of speculation, do they indignantly reject it either. They do not hide their fears about where, in degrading obedience to the imperatives of political survival, the path that Arafat, the boundless egotist, has chosen could eventually lead him. They do not deny that the more ground he gives, the more Palestinians will oppose him; and the harsher he would then have to be in his own defence.

Under the accord, elections are supposed to take place nine months after the start of Israeli withdrawal. 'We don't hear him talking much about them,' said an EC member. 'I fear that he will become a dictator.' But Arafat could become 'a weak dictator' whom only the Zionist enemy itself could prop up. And there would be a further price for that.

It is with a kind of disbelieving fascination that Arafat's lifetime companions watch their leader, an intimate still, yet a more and more remote one, as he takes each new step down what seems to be his predetermined course. They do not cease to wonder which, of three events, most impels him. Was it his transfiguration on the White House lawn, his elevation from 'terrorist' to world statesman, and the inexorable logic which, as for Sadat before him, flows from it? Or something more sinister? That 'strange and dangerous marriage', as one called it; or the consequences of that aeroplane crash? Whichever it might be, they have no doubt that Mr Palestine is heading at an accelerating pace towards glory – though what glory, they ask, lies in the caricature of Palestine the Israelis will ever allow him to preside over? – or perdition. 'One thing is sure,' said one disillusioned servant of what used to be called the Palestine Revolution as he left Tunis, perhaps for the last time, 'nothing can change him now, not even if the Holy Ghost came down in person'. •

Derek Brown
14 December 1993

A quiet day in Jericho

Many years ago, a distinguished BBC television reporter going about his work in Northern Ireland was mildly assaulted with an umbrella by an old lady. When he inquired what was troubling her, she indignantly complained: 'You... you... you're filming things that aren't happening!'

It was just like that in Jericho yesterday. Nothing was happening. We knew for a fact that nothing was happening, or was going to happen. But we filmed it anyway, and took pictures of it, and notes. Even when things did happen, in a very small way, they were recorded in a very big one.

Thus it was that when ten youths marched along the main street chanting patriotic slogans, they were preceded by eleven lenses. There were, it is true, occasions when Palestinians outnumbered journalists, but they were rare.

The three most interviewed Jerichoans performed heroic deeds of comment and analysis, aided by hardly any information. For the optimistic view, one turned to Adnan Hammad, Jericho organiser of Feda, the Palestine Democratic Union. 'The price of peace is more than the price of the intifada [uprising]. We always knew that,' he said bravely.

He forecast the imminent posting of Palestinian policemen in the town, and said that the Israeli forces were already shipping out their equipment.

For a more downbeat view, there was Abdel-Karim Sider, head of the PLO headquarters, which is in fact a single room in a disused lock-up shop. The office was closed yesterday in protest against the delay in implementing the accord, but Mr Sider amiably did his stuff on the pavement outside.

The Jericho people, he said scores of times, were deeply shocked. And disappointed. And yes, the delay would encourage the Islamic and other groups opposed to the accord.

On the shuttered shop front, a hand-lettered sign appeared: PLO OFFICE CLOSED BECAUSE ISRAEL DO NOT WANT PEACE. A little later 'DO' was corrected to 'DOES', and 'BECAUSE' was amended to 'BEACAUSE'.

The third of Jericho's most voluble sons, manager Rajai Abdo of the Hisham Palace Hotel, continued to decant his measured, fluent English into the world's microphones. His is essentially the voice of devout but moderate Islam, and between interviews he obligingly permitted himself to be filmed offering *namaaz*, or prayers, on the lobby floor.

Mr Abdo leans to the optimistic school. He was not disappointed by latest developments, he said. Which was rather decent, considering he has negotiated a £50,000 a year deal for the PLO to take over his crumbling hotel for its new headquarters, and has yet to get their signature on the lease.

Outside in the main market square, the knots of Jerichoans finally tired of ogling the outside broadcast unit, the satellite earth station, the massed video cameras and Nikons, and the glint of sunlight on cheap pens, and performed the much-loved local ritual of the truly shambolic demonstration.

Led by a raucous chap with a megaphone, they formed into groups of as many as twenty, and roamed around the square chanting and breaking into atrociously off-key song. There was sudden delirium in the meejah ranks as Israeli soldiers briefly, politely and rather stupidly intervened.

But – and this could be the story of Jericho's collective life – it did not develop into anything. Even when a few new PLO bodyguards arrived, fresh from training in Jordan, there was but a flicker of excitement. Everyone knew they were not coming to take over, but to sit and wait, just like everybody else, for something to happen. •

John Vidal
20 April 1994

Bottom line

Alas poor Michael Fay, contemplating his about-to-be-shredded posterior in a Singapore prison yard for trashing Japanese cars. Had he been privileged to receive a good British private education, the eighteen-year-old Yank would know that each of his six strokes would be his passport to schoolboy credibility, to be spoken of in awe by lesser mortals, something to set him up for life. ('Isn't that …? 'Yes … do you know …?') And, to boot, it will be an education in itself.

Fay will receive six of Singapore's best – little worse than that meted out in slim bamboo to most members of the British Cabinet at some point in their schooling. It will mean dropping his troos – no great problem for a young Englishman – excruciating temporary pain (he may, indeed, faint) but he should know, this will turn within minutes to deep satisfaction that so many people will have taken immense pleasure in his 'punishment'. A well-wealed bottom, he will find, is much to be admired in many quarters.

More importantly he may discover that his thrashing is his entry to the world of deception. Like most British public school boys, he will never forget the face of a flogger feigning distaste when it's perfectly plain he is loving it; the sham handshake at the end to signify that there are no hard feelings when in fact the 'troublemaker' is marked out for life; the cheery grins of contemporaries which really mean everything from 'poor bastard' to 'serve you right'. His ritual refusal to let anyone know that it hurt will be particularly illuminating in later years.

Were he but British, Fay would know, too, that there is an excellent market for beatings. Depending on the colour of his thrashed skin (none left: brill; red: excellent; purple: acceptable; green, yellow and brown: pot-poor), a young Englishman knows he can sell personal glimpses of a ravaged bot for at least ten fags/three pots of marmalade/an illicit book/video etc. With 100 boys in a house, this is not to be sniffed at, Michael.

The combination of a really good thrashing with advance publicity, a smart agent (an excitable fourth former is usually best) and a decent 'crime' should guarantee spectacular popularity for a while. Giving glimpses of his bottom to masters could lead to almost anything. He should know that most public school masters get very excited by such events.

Fay's problem is that the crime is really too right-on for maximum advantage to be gained (how much better than mildly wasting a few aerials would it have been to have stolen and wrecked the cars at 90 mph, been with a Singapore chief of police's wife, etc). But Fay is American, where the hysteria factor is important. With the country divided over the future of his bottom, Fay will surely clean up. He may never buy a Honda but his certainty that physical punishment is deeply futile will be highly developed. •

The media village

Kevin Kelly
20 June 1994

Caught in the net

According to a survey of US newspapers, the journalistic use of the term 'information superhighway' has ramped up from zero a year ago to several hundreds per month now. Indeed, it or its hip contraction, 'the I-way', is now everyday headline material. Yet nobody using it knows exactly what it means. So journalists call me.

I work at *Wired*, an American magazine about the social culture growing up around the prototypes of this I-way. I live on the Internet, and I hang out with Silicon Valley visionaries. At *Wired* we track the big powers such as the cable and telephone conglomerates, and the wistful experiments of hackers and dedicated hobbyists. We are watching to see how the 'street' uses this emerging techno-logy.

Everyone wants to know what the I-way will be like. Everyone in book pub-lishing, television-making, newspaper selling, telephone providing and satellite broadcasting wants to know how this will affect their livelihood. Could some expert please tell them what to back, what to expect? But there is an expert vacuum. The entire package is still in testing. So they call me, an editor of a magazine that proclaims: 'The future of media and information technology is whatever we want to make it, and we are deciding right now.'

I have extracted three clues as to what the I-way will really be like from observing ways ordinary citizens use the scraps of digital technology now trick-ling in.

The first clue is: Follow the free. In the three decades that digital technology has been around, many of the most profitable businesses got going by exploiting services or products originally given away free.

Software – the economic engine keeping America going these days – was often thrown in for free with the first computers. Many personal computer utilities began life as giveaways shared with friends and later grew into million-dollar industries. This trajectory will be all the more prevalent on the I-way because of its deep populist base. It's natural that really useful stuff will first be shared before it is sold.

Keep an eye on certain things served up for free on the Internet. FAQs – succinct answers to 'Frequently Asked Questions' on almost any subject written by passionate and knowledgeable amateurs. MUDs – multiple-user games offering detailed descriptions of characters and worlds created by the users; open ended, and addictive. Mosaic – an easy way to travel through a zillion documents, reading the footnote to the footnote; this is the first working part for the library of libraries. CU-SeeMe – a continuous live video feed from a remote camera, feeding your home monitor the current scene in Soho, or the level of the coffee pot down the hall.

The second clue is let the copies breed. Whatever it is that we are constructing by connecting everything to everything, we know the big thing will copy effortlessly. The I-way is a gigantic copy machine. It is a law of the digital realm: anything digital will be copied, and anything copied once will fill the universe. Further, every effort to restrict copying is doomed to failure. Copy-protection schemes in software were abandoned because they didn't work. In the US Supreme Court, home tapers of satellite TV shows won the right to copy copyrighted material in their homes. Controlling copies is futile. This presents a problem for all holders of intellectual property who adhere to the notion of copyright – such as Hollywood moguls and authors. Copyright law as we know it will be dead in fifty years. A legal system that shifts its focus from the 'copy' to the 'use' must take its place, letting copies proliferate, and tracking only how and when an item is used. Copy this article, please! But when the article is displayed to others for a fee, or quoted in another piece, a few pennies will then be deducted from the user's account. Encryption schemes can protect the privacy of these transactions.

The third clue is that it's a new literary space, man. Just as our thought shapes technology, technology shapes our thought. The technology of language and knowledge particularly shapes what we can think. A blackboard encourages repeated modification, casual thinking, spontaneity. A quill pen demands care, attention to grammar, tidiness, controlled thinking. A printed page solicits rewritten drafts, proofing, introspection, editing.

Each medium may be thought of as a literary space. The space of knowledge in ancient times was a dynamic oral tradition. By the grammar of rhetoric, knowledge was structured as poetry and dialogue – subject to interruption, questioning and parenthetical diversions. The space of early writing was likewise flexible. Texts were amended by readers, revised by disciples. When scripts moved to the printed page, the ideas they represented became monumental and fixed. Gone was the role of the reader in forming the text. The unalterable progression of ideas across pages in a book gave the work an impressive authority – 'authority' and 'author' deriving from a common root. Modernity has centred on the fixed authority of the printed text.

One possible predecessor to the I-way is the Internet. This links several million personal computers around the world. No one knows exactly how many; no one controls the Internet; no one is in charge. The Internet is the largest functioning anarchy in the world. Every day hundreds of millions of messages are passed without the benefit of a central authority. Every day millions of words are added and build an immense distributed document, one that is under eternal construction, constant flux.

The result is far different from a printed book, or even a chat around a table. The text is a sane conversation with millions of participants. Thoughts tend towards the experimental idea, the quip, the global perspective, the interdisciplinary synthesis, and the uninhibited, often emotional, response. I-way thought is modular, non-linear, malleable, co-operative. Many participants prefer Internet writing to book writing as it is conversational, frank and communicative, rather than precise and overwritten.

The job of readers of printed text was to find the canonical truth in texts. Net distributed text supplies a new role for readers – every reader co-determines the meaning of a text. This relationship is the fundamental idea of post-modern literary criticism, in which there is no canon. The truth of a work changes with each reading. In order to decipher a text it must be viewed as idea threads, some owned by the author, some by the reader and others by the greater context of the author's time.

It is no coincidence that the post-modernists arose as the networks formed. In the last half-century a uniform mass market has collapsed into a network of small niches as a result of the information tide. An aggregation of fragments is the only kind of whole we now have. The fragmentation in business markets, of social mores, of spiritual beliefs, of ethnicity and of truth itself is the mark of this era. Our society is a working pandemonium of fragments. That's almost the definition of the network many hope the I-way becomes.

The I-way will rearrange the writing space of the printed book into a new writing space larger and more complex than ink on paper. The instrumentation of our lives can be seen as part of that 'writing space'. As data from weather sensors, demographic surveys, cash registers, all the millions of electronic information generators pour their words into the Net, they enlarge the writing space of our times. Their information becomes part of what we know, part of our meaning. Their digitised bits form the new literary space we think in, which includes not only a rejuvenated interest in letterwriting, but also the syntax of

MTV, the structure of asynchronous conversations, the logic of fragmented ideas. •

Clancy Sigal
19 May 1994

Connections from Essex to Sarajevo

Second only to getting high on LSD in the sixties, and once having lunch at Warner Brothers with Liz Taylor, is the turn-on of joining the Internet e-mail system. Timothy Leary might recognise the symptoms. The same urgent blood-rush, cosmic euphoria and gratifying sense of communicating with the centre of the earth where repose the ancient, forgotten gods of personal encounter.

Truly, the 'global village' of cyberspace (cyber as in controlled even though it isn't and space as in we can't quite figure out where it is) has a heady frontier freedom that is remarkably democratic if you don't mind brushing elbows with the unseen post-pubescent sixth-formers who seem to dominate the 'network of networks' that includes e-mail, newsgroups, Usenet, threads, forums, local bulletin boards, affinity groups and the flame-out artists who specialise in joyful adolescent invective.

The Internet is no place for a serious, responsible, sober adult who has left his or her childhood behind. Mix *Star Wars* with *84 Charing Cross Road* – Anne Bancroft and Anthony Hopkins passionately exchanging letters for years without ever meeting – and you get the idea. The Internet's fibre-optic emotions are its equivalent of safe sex. That is its genius, and its limitation.

I hate technology. It's a constant surprise that my telephone doesn't burn up in my hands, my computer explode in smoke and my automobile disintegrate every time I switch on the ignition. Similarly, it is a miracle, rivalling Our Lady of Fatima and Manchester City winning a cup final that by a single keystroke I can be hurtled, as in H. G. Wells's time machine, to Emir in Sarajevo, Amanda in London, Steve in Missouri and Dave in Essex. (Keep Dave in mind – he is my greatest social gaffe on e-mail.)

It depends on whether you were the sort of kid who liked having pen pals.

Now, imagine a universe of pen pals most of whom are trainspotters in spirit if not in fact. If you cringe at the prospect, the Internet is not for you. If, however, you are a true democrat with a taste for electronic anarchy, you'll have an absolute whizz-ball.

At the moment, the Internet dominates me rather than I it. Happily, I spend insomniac hours chattering away to Judy in San Francisco (about movies and books), Gay in New York (multiple orgasms and post-feminist ideology), James in Beverly Hills (the existence of God), Richard in Santa Barbara (where did we go wrong in the New Left?), Sherri Lee in Palo Alto (how to organise Bosnia protests), Fatih in Sarajevo (how to survive on three hours of water every third day), and so on.

Collecting dust, along with my unanswered 'snail-mail', are a new but uncompleted novel and a couple of screenplays capable of earning me a fortune; which I ignore. Who cares about riches when the unseen, unknown but gorgeously accessible Arla Mae Nudelman, residence unknown, and I can engage in friendly, even flirtatious, banter without the slightest danger of real-time involvement. We hope.

You want to be careful about Internet intimacy. I'm sure there are hundreds of babies who owe their existence to some accidental coupling on the information superhighway.

It's only a short step, in theory and I suspect also in practice, from banging out inconsequential 3 am messages to Mary Jo in New York or Kitty in Salt Lake, to actually wangling a date. Is it my fantasy that Internet is alive not only with the sound of epistolary music but also the moans and sighs of 20 million Francescas and Roberts – the sexually frustrated heroine and priapic hero of *The Bridges of Madison County*.

The Internet serves an exploding population of PC users. In Los Angeles county alone there are a million personal computers, half of them with modems. The possibilities are endless – and can make you crazy. But also you can do hard-core political or humanitarian work on e-mail. Internet, at least for now, when governments and commercial cybersalesmen have yet to figure out how to screw it up, is an ideal venue for dissidents. And electronic Scarlet Pimpernels. I am actively involved with shadowy others in Croatia, Berlin, New York and Pennsylvania, via e-mail, in smuggling someone out of Sarajevo under Serb guns. The logistics of rescue, which might take weeks or months by snail-mail, get done in minutes on the Internet.

But there's no shirking Dave of Essex, either. Dave is my greatest failure and challenge. Homesick for England, where I lived and rioted for more than thirty years, I posted a pitiful message on 'alt.politics.british', one of the Internet's nearly 9,000 so-called newsgroups, asking for a pen pal to keep me up on the latest UK gossip. Dave replied with lofty twaddle about proportional representation and some sneers at Old Leftists (that is, over twenty-five).

Something snapped in me. I replied with a half-berserk 'flame' parentally admonishing Essex Dave for his ignorance of the heroic sacrifices of previous generations of CND, Labour Party and New Left activists. Picture it: a seasoned if slightly burned-out veteran of the punch-up squares – Red Lion, Grosvenor and Trafalgar – screaming at poor, bookish, zit-faced (as I imagined him) Dave, whose only real crime is that, like so many newsgroup contributors, he is callow, opinionated and (presumably) sex-starved. Like me at his age.

I'm sorry I scared him off. Next time, I'll try, I really will, to keep a lid on my larger emotions and get with the true, prankish spirit of e-mail newsgroups. To whit: a cyberspace friend recently wandered on to 'rec.pets.birds', and the first item she read was: 'Do birds masturbate[*sic*]?' •

Martin Woollacott
9 February 1994

The search for sleaze which demeans Western societies

W hy is it that at a time when tolerance or understanding of different sexual preferences is supposedly greater than ever before there should be such a fearsome taste for stories of sexual irregularity in the Anglo-Saxon world? Whether it is a question of Bill Clinton's dalliances, Tim Yeo's illegitimate child, Lorena Bobbitt's attack on her husband, Vince Foster's relationship with Mrs Clinton, Michael Jackson's alleged abuse of children, Gillian Taylforth's indecency case, Jane Brown's lesbianism, and now the circumstances of Stephen Milligan's death, the appetite for it seems voracious.

But is it truly an appetite for sexual gossip and scandal, or an appetite for something different and very much worse? What we seem to be creating in the press and on television in Britain and North America is not a theatre of sex but a theatre of cruelty. In it, the sexual 'offence' is secondary to the delight taken in the embarrassment or pain inflicted on a public figure, or on an ordinary person transformed into a public figure by the media. It is this which links these sexual cases with others where the offence is criminal, with the pursuit of the royal family, and with the harassing of politicians on charges of neither sexual irregularity nor criminality but incompetence or weakness. What is developing is a search-and-destroy journalism which probes for weakness and then moves in to hunt and harass. Any sort of lumber from the jumbled cupboard of our confused modern morality will do as an excuse.

Why say that there is more here to explain than the perennial human interest in sexual matters and morals, and the natural impulse of the press to cater for it? First, it would be hard to argue that any clear morality links these cases together. They constitute a very mixed bag, ranging from affairs of the heart through the cruder kinds of adultery, the use of prostitutes, mainstream homosexuality, public indecency, sexual maiming, and thence to child abuse. Different men and women would, these days, draw their moral lines at very different places along this spectrum.

It could be argued, perhaps, that because many people do not feel confident any longer about making clear judgements on sexual behaviour between adults, much of the dammed-up need to condemn has focused with additional force on behaviour that hurts children, whether it is child abuse itself or the irresponsible kind of single parenthood that is a favourite target of certain kinds of politicians. It is also true that many heterosexuals are worried about what has happened to marriage, and that the breakdown of the marriages of the well known has an interest arising from that. Yet these distinctions do not seem to be much reflected in the kind and amount of publicity generated by different cases. This appears to be much more a function of the eminence and the general vulnerability of the man or woman concerned.

It would also be hard to argue, secondly, that readers and viewers are these days deriving much of a sexual charge from reading these accounts. The time when sexually explicit material was so rare that the court reports of the *Daily Telegraph* or the outraged 'crusades' of American and British tabloids were staple reading for adolescents of all ages has long gone. We are much more widely exposed to representations of all kinds of sexuality and much less capable of being titillated by news reporting.

If it isn't, in the main, moral concern, and if it isn't sexual interest in the narrow sense, what is it? The standard line on these matters used to be that Anglo-Saxons have a peculiarly neurotic preoccupation with sex and sexual morality. This accounts for that irritating perennial, the story about perplexed Frenchmen and Germans who cannot understand why British and American politicians are in trouble if discovered to have mistresses. The idea that powerful men are entitled to an especially large 'share' of women, or, indeed, that powerful men are in some way lacking if they do not take it, is of course well established on both sides of the Channel and of the Atlantic. It is equally repugnant to sensible people in all countries, and is irrelevant to the argument over press treatment of scandal. If the continental press does take a different line, it is because of different privacy laws and perhaps because the idea of journalism as a hunt for victims is less established there.

A hundred years ago Mark Twain, himself a journalist, spoke of 'a press which is licensed to say any infamous thing it chooses about a private or a public man' while 'the public opinion which should hold it in bounds has itself degraded to its own level'. In those days the allegations which the American gutter press hurled at politicians were generally of corruption or sometimes, as Twain said in another piece, of wife-beating or bigamy. But the hunting impulse was there. In the intervening years the Anglo-Saxon press first got much better, but has since got worse. How much worse we are in the process of finding out.

The old problem of the Anglo-Saxon press with stories of sexual scandal was indeed one of prurience masquerading as puritanism. Writer and reader alike pretended to be outraged in order to be titillated, or, perhaps, were both. The new problem is one of sadism masquerading as entertainment. At the centre of the sort of popular exposure which is becoming a regular feature in Anglo-Saxon countries is an element of cruelty, delight in seeing a person twist in the wind. The blurring of the line between fiction and reality for which modern television, film-making and the popular press has undoubtedly been responsible plays a contributory part here. There is arguably a level at which people no longer fully understand, for instance, the difference between a terrible personal crisis for Gillian Taylforth as a character in *EastEnders* and a crisis for her in her real life.

We like to see them love and laugh and we like to see them cry; sometimes we even like to see them die. The victimisation of politicians, entertainers, members of the royal family, and of ordinary people like Jane Brown ought to be seen as an issue in itself, entirely separate from the question of whether they have or have not done anything wrong, worrying or morally dubious. That is a matter for them and ought occasionally also to be a matter for the press. But the evidence is mounting that we are becoming addicted to stories which damage and sometimes ruin people's lives and that it is the ruination rather than the stories which we are being conditioned to enjoy. •

Barry Norman
25 April 1994

Gotcha! Well, perhaps not

have just been told that my daughter Samantha is an actress. This came as a surprise to me, as indeed it did to her, because we both thought she was a television presenter and interviewer. Mind you, it was an even bigger surprise to learn that I had single-handedly destroyed her acting career in its infancy.

It was the *Sun* – what else? – that revealed all this to us and it makes a kind of sense (the *Sun*'s kind of sense) because if she weren't an actress how could I be 'a reel rat' – a pun, geddit? – who had 'blasted her debut movie'?

As a favour to a friend, Samantha appeared, briefly, in a film called *White Angel*. She played a TV presenter and interviewer doing a spot of presenting and interviewing. Playing herself, if you like – not, as I know, an easy task unless you are trained in acting, which she isn't – and she did it so well that on *Film 94* I announced that she was the best thing in a rather poor movie.

Enter the *Sun* in the shape of one Peter Willis, a jovial, chuckling cove, who phoned Sam to ask her what it was like to be praised on TV by her father. She said she was delighted by my compliment, explained carefully how and why she had come to be in the film and added that, regretfully because friends were involved, she rather shared my opinion of it. Then Willis phoned me, still jovial and chuckling. I told him the compliment was genuine and explained carefully how and why she had come to be in the film.

Not much of a story there. Father and daughter in accord? Forget it.

Ah, but what if Sam were not a TV presenter and interviewer? What if she were really an ambitious young actress, whose job prospects had vanished because her own father had so savaged her 'debut' movie that nobody would go to see it?

Wouldn't that, said the jovial, chuckling Willis, mean the end of a promising career? Well, Sam said, if I were an actress – which, of course, I'm not – I suppose that might possibly be the case.

And so the trap was sprung. Sam not only became an actress, she became a 'disappointed' actress, 'furious' with her 'acid-tongued' father. And as for me, well, the headline said it all: 'Dad's A Reel Rat'.

Indeed Sam was furious – not with me, with jovial, chuckling Willis. Never mind, I said, it's only the *Sun*. Let it rest.

But, of course, it didn't rest. The next day it rose up and lied again, summoning one of its Rottweiler columnists, Anne Diamond, to sink her gums into me. Yes, *that* Anne Diamond, the one who, a few years ago, was herself vilified by the tabloid press.

This time I was 'reel mean' – it presumably takes a lot of repetition before a pun can sink into the consciousness of a *Sun* reader. She had never, said Anne Diamond portentously, 'seen such patronising, self-important spite spoken by a father publicly about his own daughter'.

Pardon? What patronising, self-important spite? I never heard myself uttering it and neither did Samantha. All I said was that my daughter's performance was the best thing in the film. In *Sun*-speak this amounts to spite and self-importance?

Well, yes, I suppose it does if the *Sun* wants it to. In a paper that has no commitment to accuracy anything goes. It was, after all, the *Sun* which had me, earlier this year, badly shaken up by a knife-wielding thief outside the BBC TV Centre – a frightful incident which, I'm sure, would have left me badly shaken if only I'd been there.

Never mind. It may not be true, but at least it's exclusive and that applies equally to the latest episodes. Why let a few facts get in the way of a chance to stir up animosity between father and daughter? •

Catherine Bennett
28 March 1994
....
Restless country that Gerry built

This is a fine time to be Gerry Anderson. In the last five weeks he has been transformed from a popular regional name into a focus of national lamentation. Once he chatted blithely on Radio Ulster. Now he hosts an hour-long programme every weekday afternoon on Radio 4. *Anderson Country* has become the most reviled radio programme for years.

The first edition had barely ended before Radio 4 listeners began to utter faint cries of pain and disgust. By the end of its first week enough complaints had arrived at the BBC's duty office for an item on *Feedback*, Radio 4's weekly forum for listeners' opinions. Letters poured in, those abusing *Anderson Country* outnumbering favourable ones by 100 to one. By the third week *Feedback*'s presenter, Chris Dunkley, was begging for letters on other subjects. Listeners responded furiously. Why shouldn't they complain? The programme was 'patronising', 'tabloid radio', 'fatuous', 'amateurish', 'an insult to the intelligence'. Last Friday Dunkley reported: 'The cascade of ordure continues to stream down … ' So far there have been no more than ten letters in favour and 'several hundreds' in protest.

Are they justified? Sharon Banoff, editor of *Anderson Country*, offers the Radio 4 executive's traditional explanation – that their audience will complain 'if you move anything, let alone invent something… Any tiny alteration to *their* agenda and *their* programming and *their* schedule – they don't like it'. But *Anderson Country* is not a tiny alteration and both reviews and anecdotal reports suggest that it has dismayed an audience far larger than that small, sad group who pass their time perforating sheets of Basildon Bond with angry strokes of green biro. At the stroke of three o'clock some of Radio 4's most loyal and indulgent listeners now rush for the off-knob before Anderson can recite his customary ungrammatical, nonsensical introduction: 'Welcome to *Anderson Country*, where every day is not like the rest.'

The programme's critics object that it is, in fact, mortifyingly consistent: a rattly concoction of disconnected features, voices and phone calls, loosely strung together by Anderson's astonishing flow of clichés, puns and fatuities.

Emerging from his studio, Anderson is a natty figure in a cream suit and burgundy shoes, the picture of jaunty insouciance. At the mention of *Feedback* he grins and winks. 'It's easy to come here and be ignored.' Why does he think they're so angry? 'I think that people see me as being one of the first barbarians to come over the gates at Radio 4.' Is he? 'I'm a Radio 4 listener.' He likes the drama best: 'I'm not too keen on the discussive [*sic*] element of it, I get a bit bored with that sometimes when you get two or three experts and they waffle on for ever.'

He thinks critics of his own programme should 'loosen up a little ... It's more access, you know, because perhaps sometimes people do feel that Radio 4 is aloof, and they feel as if the ordinary John, the ordinary nine-to-fiver, might feel as if it's beyond him, above him, and it's not really, it shouldn't be.'

A former guitar player in rock bands, Anderson has been presenting award-winning radio shows in Ireland since 1981, typically a blend of music, phone-ins and his own personality. 'The type of programme I used to do was very much flow of consciousness and never had any planning of any kind, it was purely off the top of my head.' *Anderson Country*, which he scripts himself each day, is different – the result of months of research and discussion at Radio 4. 'It's an attempt to respond to a time of day in the schedule when we are not performing very well,' says Michael Green, Controller of Radio 4. 'It's an attempt to address that by trying something new. It actually trades in Radio 4 fare – there's nothing there that isn't part of what we normally do, is there?'

In a way, he's right. Radio 4 has discussions on serious matters, and so does *Anderson Country*. The difference is that on *Anderson Country* they often sound on the verge of some gross embarrassment, lapse of taste, or complete disintegration. More often than is comfortable, Anderson's guests seem more attentive to the discussion than their host, and more articulate. There is nothing wrong with asking an interviewee: 'When did the old bubble burst?' but when the interviewee repeats the question back in crushingly satirical tones, it does not make for easy listening.

And that, after all, is the point of *Anderson Country*. 'People at three o'clock in the afternoon find it difficult to listen to those programmes they've got to listen to very hard,' claims Banoff. 'There are a few listeners who just want to sit down and listen, but there's this whole other audience, and they haven't, because they've been turned off by the amount of dedication they've got to give to that, so we've got to address them.' Is the answer really to dilute the mixture with trivia? 'I just don't think this watering-down thing is right,' she argues. 'I think the word is accessible – overused as it might be – we really need accessible broadcasting.'

So droll, accessible items are dotted throughout. Guests learn to play the didgeridoo, sing Mongolian chant or speak in a Geordie accent. Occasionally the two styles are unhappily combined, and a silly subject is treated seriously: was the woman who had a funny feeling in a haunted house *really* in the presence of 'spirits of a non-alcoholic nature'? Invariably there is a regional story. This story need not be of any consequence to anyone outside the region, so long as it *is* regional, with accents to prove it. So reporters rove around what Anderson calls 'this fair land' – to Grimsby to ask residents about the pervasive smell of fish, to Sheffield to hear gripes about the bus service.

Anderson Country is the most egregious example so far of Radio 4's compliance with John Birt's injunction to 'broaden its base', to reach beyond the ABC1s, those wretches who have had the impudence to become educated and self- supporting. This accounts not only for the dogged regionalism, but the desire to 'give people a voice' – the non-accessible term for a phone-in.

The hour is duly punctuated by Anderson's pleas for people to dial 071-765-5540. They say things like 'time's a great healer' or 'I feel disappointed and resentful'. 'Access' seems to mean having less interesting people on than would ever appear if they were edited, selected or paid.

'Isn't that being a wee bit élitist?' Anderson says. What does he mean by élitist? 'I think possibly maybe people who don't really like to hear ordinary people speaking on Radio 4, just don't like ordinary people.'

But shouldn't radio try to present something slightly better than ordinary?

'From a personal point of view it wouldn't annoy me in the slightest

Anderson speak

Oh to be young again! There was a time when people knew where they were, the sun came up, stayed up for a while, then it went down again, certain things remained constant, like the ground between your feet, or so it seemed at one time ...

Shelley ... If I'm allowed to be Irish for a moment, I'd have to say that if he were alive today he'd be turning in his grave.

Isn't it important to realise what is important and what isn't, it's all subjective, isn't it, really?

Do you think in any way that hubbies have become scapegoats for what's perceived as the general breakdown in society and the family?

On now to something completely different. Now this weekend the Loch Ness monster, funnily enough, has been caught with its pants down ...

to hear somebody coming on Radio 4 talking about something, even if they hadn't got anything interesting to say,' Anderson remarks. 'At least they were saying what they felt.' Such receptiveness has its risks. 'John from Dorset' recently tricked his way on to air, then asked: 'I wonder why it is that a programme like yours is being allowed on the radio, because it has such a low standard.' 'I thought we were talking about driving in America,' Anderson protested, as 'John' was efficiently de-accessed.

You would need a heart of stone not to feel some sympathy for Anderson. His irrepressible jocularity and fund of homely wisdom would no doubt delight another audience, but they could not be better calculated to alarm regular listeners to Radio 4, particularly when forced upon them daily, and especially amid growing suspicion that the network is to be systematically lobotomised. Surely this is an experiment which failed? Michael Green accepts the programme needs improvement, but insists that it's a fixture. 'Oh, it's part of the fabric of the network, this would be as important to the network as *Woman's Hour* in the morning.' In fact, he says, he's had 'quite a lot of letters from people who say they love it'. How many? 'I've probably had a dozen.'

Accessible Mr Anderson is also confident that listeners will be converted. 'Every time I've done something new I've been condemned from a height,' he says. 'But for some reason, and I've noticed this, I seem to grow on people like a wart.' •

Richard Neville
23 March 1994

It's a mad, mad multi-media world

Now that the world fits into a satellite dish, hideous new ailments are striking down baby boomers in their prime. Media Alzheimer's Disease (MAD) is one of the quirkiest, and scariest, with the potential to slash profits in publishing, TV, cinema and the entertainment industry.

It starts small, as in my case, with the breaking of a lifelong habit of reading the morning newspaper. Later, it can progress to a terminal disinclination to see any of the top ten movies, *Larry King Live* or boot up the modem. It's a cruel, embarrassing forgetfulness to consume the media, which targets former fanatics, and is not susceptible to drugs, electro-therapy or counselling.

At first, you tell yourself it doesn't matter, or that it's a temporary aberration. In my case, two factors combined to trigger the onset. Work pressure put time at a premium, so I started losing my grip on party political nuances in Tasmania, and felt hazy about the who's who of gangster rap.

Worse was to come. One Thursday, I failed to buy the morning newspaper. OK there are mitigating circumstances – it's now so vile, it isn't worth the loose change. Like most media, it's plunged downmarket. But one needs to stay in touch. Cruel contagion – instead of a guilty, rudderless ignorance sapping my spirit, a cheeky flood of euphoria filled up Thursday afternoon: an incredible lightness of being.

A week later it happened again, only this time for two days. Somewhere a child had been tortured to death for three weeks by his father, and I was now appraised of the details. A girl was probably suing her mother for forcing a breast into her mouth as a baby, instead of the preferred option, a bottle, and its significance would never be expounded for my benefit.

Eventually, a friend will spot the warning signs of media forgetfulness, and rub the victim's face in it. 'Ho, ho, so you didn't twig to the stock market rumble in Tokyo?' Then comes denial, or a feeble excuse: 'Hey, what's the point of all this information, if I can't act on it?' Perhaps a soppy, new age rationalisation: 'Maybe it's better to play snakes & ladders with the kids than plough through the *Modern Review*.'

If MAD was confined to the print scene, the patient could still muddle through. Mainstream magazines are now so trashy and predictable – produced by Ph.D. graduates and gifted littérateurs vying to part dollars from dopes – that one glance at a billboard fuels a year of dinner party chitchat. Alas, MAD is multi-media.

One sultry afternoon at the cinema, I finally lost my marbles. For a stint of movie reviewing, I was obliged to see two blockbusters in a day. During the second one, *Silver*, a bolt from the blue hit home. 'What am I doing here?' Sure, I wanted to see thingamejig naked and wrapped around a pole, like everyone else, but at the cost of a whole afternoon, plus parking fee?

Instead of unravelling the intricacies of the plot, I worried about the billions of hours that Hollywood had stolen from humanity's life. Millions have convinced themselves of the vital importance of spending decades in dark halls, held sway by the fantasies of strangers. Philosophers, from Heraclitus to the Hindus, have argued that human existence is a veil of illusion and the purpose of life is to strip it away. Movies are an illusion within an illusion.

Perhaps it all started with *Battleship Potemkin*. Seeing it for the first time hurled us into the thick of history. It saved us from reading books, learning the language or travelling on the Trans-Siberian Express. Ever since, on a subliminal level, millions now imagine that *Batman Three* could be an updated *Potemkin*.

It takes about forty years to lose heart. In the days before I was afflicted with MAD, and hired the odd tape, I was amazed by the bombardment of trailers –

excerpts from sixty-eight features that no one would want to see in a lifetime, not even on fast forward. Where now are these tapes – seething in landfills?

Next stop, cyberspace. It's interactive, global, sexually safe. After the intro razzle-dazzle of a million minds flashing on the Mac, the mastering of electronic hieroglyphs, the fabulous download of hospital floor plans from Norway, you suddenly wonder why it's 4 am and you're still in pyjamas, eight days later. Farewell Internet.

I joined MAD Anonymous. One woman recounted how she had let the virus into her home, by subscribing to the *New Yorker*. It landed on her doorstep week after week, in a polyurethane sheath, until she could no longer keep track. The magazines piled up the stairs and spread into bathroom and bedroom, accusingly, like a bulk order of condoms never enjoyed. She dealt with her guilt by denial – shunning all printed matter, even the blue-chip guides to restaurants in Paris.

Is there a cure? Scientists and medical schools are working around the clock, funded by media magnates. Shielded from celebrity gossip, CNN and the latest opinion polls, sufferers represent a tragic throwback to a bygone era. Everyday they can be seen feeding the birds, staring at sunsets, strolling through botanical gardens, playing with stray children and reciting Wordsworth in cafés – the new underclass, spawned by media overkill. •

David Mellor
18 March 1994

The diet of worms

I awoke on Tuesday morning to the satisfying crunching sound of dog eating dog, as the *Guardian* savaged the hosts of Murdoch for their role in the downfall of Sir Peter Harding. It has been a particular sadness to those of us who care about a free press, and don't really want privacy legislation, that the broadsheets have been so reluctant to condemn the excesses of the tabloids, even while gargantuan portions of prurience have been served up on a daily basis, liberally sauced with all the cant that the *Guardian* rightly found so sick-making.

The tabloid journalist as Ethics Man is too ludicrous a spectacle to avoid the keen eyes of broadsheet editorial writers for ever. After all, it was a sign of weakness and not of strength that so many broadsheet editors, who are privately as disgusted by the behaviour of the tabloids as the rest of us, have for so long felt unable to break ranks because of their fear that they will thereby be aiding and abetting those who want to curb press freedoms. But it is the hallmark of a free profession that it has not only the right but the duty to condemn back-sliders. In truth, the unwillingness of serious newspapers and their proprietors to do this has damaged the cause of a free press in this country, as has the steady stream of inane procrastination from their flexible friend, the Press Complaints Commission.

The packaging of the Peter Harding story was the work of Max Clifford, a sleazeball's sleazeball if ever there was one. He has masterminded the whole thing, and I daresay in typical style has invented some of this sorry tale's tastier titbits. I don't believe for a moment Peter Harding discussed defence secrets between the sheets. This sounds to me like pure Clifford, who will, in time-honoured fashion, have assembled a menu of juicy details, some true, a lot not, and offered them à la carte to slobbering tabloid executives to choose whichever dishes they want, on the understanding of course that the more they take the more it costs.

In my own case, for instance, we now know from Antonia de Sancha's interview with Julia Langdon in the *Guardian* that all the stuff about the Chelsea strip and the toes was made up by Clifford, who sought to persuade her to go further and claim she had become pregnant and miscarried. The football shirt wasn't even a new invention – he tried to sell the same story about Derek Hatton, only in that case the guilty team was Everton.

It's a sad comment on the tabloids that neither the *Sun*, who paid lots of money for these lies, well knowing they were not true, nor the others, who have lovingly perpetuated these myths, chose to make any mention of de Sancha's admission. In such a fashion are their readers' opinions and attitudes cynically manipulated, and thereby tabloid journalists, whose whole lives have become dedicated to condemning others, escape condemnation themselves.

At the time my life became intertwined with Clifford – an act of folly for which, by the way, I blame no one but myself – I was naive enough to imagine, given that at least one set of tapes apparently exists of Clifford laying out his menu of lies and exaggerations and their price, that another tabloid might wish to expose what he was up to. Oh no, I was told, Clifford's too valuable. He might be selling us a story next week. Silly old me, I should have known that in the circulation war, anything goes.

But I'm in danger of spending too much time on Clifford. I should recall some sage advice I was given at the Foreign Office – never get into a pissing competition with a skunk. Besides, Clifford himself doesn't really matter. What matters is that so debased have the standards of the tabloid press become, so great their feeding frenzy for sleaze, that they are happy to be putty in Clifford's hands, falling over themselves to buy his stories even though they know full well many of the gory details have been invented.

The only basis on which the press can claim to be entitled to reveal these things is that they occupy the moral high ground, and are calling upon others to join them there. But by their dealings with Clifford they show that they do not. They have touched pitch, and have been defiled, not once, but regularly, indeed so often that they are now little more than an organised hypocrisy. And that, dear reader, is why the *Guardian* should speak out more often. •

Matthew Engel
20 December 1993

Strong, thick and glossy

Chaps: still in doubt about what the little lady wants for Christmas? Let me try to help. After a long session with a couple of dozen different women's magazines, it has become clear to me – unless all these publishers have got it very wrong – that women are all only interested in one thing.

It is a well-known fact that men do not think about sex the whole time, certainly not during moments of extreme professional stress or the last minutes of extra time of the FA Cup Final. Women though ...

Recent researchers show that more than 10 per cent of these magazines' readers are men, though it does not mean they actually go into a shop, as I had to do, and buy an armful of this stuff – it's so embarrassing.

The January edition of *Cosmopolitan*, which sells nearly half a million copies, reached the shops last week. The main feature is entitled 'Cock-eyed optimists: How men feel about SEXUAL rejection'. This replaced the December issue – main feature: 'Coming this Christmas! How SEX feels after a long dry spell'. The word SEX and its derivatives appear in capital letters on *Cosmopolitan* covers, perhaps to distinguish SEX from a and the, the only words that appear anything like as often.

But sex is everywhere. *Marie Claire*, generally regarded as the thinking woman's magazine, had the word on its cover eight times out of twelve in 1993. The subject, if not the word, infests even the fashion pages of what one thought of as staid old *Woman's Journal*: 'Dresses men want to take off'. After a while you start to imagine it. When the headline 'Man of many parts' pops up in *Woman's Weekly*, it comes as a surprise to discover it's merely a profile of actor David Jason, who thinks there's a great deal of rudeness on TV.

Not only on TV. 'I like to dress up and talk dirty,' says Susan, a twenty-four-year-old marketing assistant. 'I get off on seeing him literally buckled at the knees with excitement without me undoing so much as a button. It's a huge turn-on.' This is from a piece on masturbation in *Company* (indeed, on masturbation in company), 'Magazine of the Year'.

Susan is swiftly followed by Annabel, a twenty-seven-year-old aerobics instructor: 'Sometimes I can't resist giving him a hand.' *New Woman*, in its January feature, 'Disaster Sex', is slightly more specific about its informants. 'When he dropped his trousers I saw that his penis was minute, even when fully erect,' reports air hostess Marion, twenty-four. Now, I have been in this business a long time. I know that in these difficult

Weeklies		
Woman's Own/IPC	48p	715,327
Woman/IPC	48p	715,120
Woman's Weekly/IPC	44p	783,974
My Weekly/D C Thompson	40p	439,329
Woman's Realm/IPC	48p	367,947
Monthlies		
Cosmopolitan/Nat Mags	£1.80	477,437
Marie Claire/Euro Mags	£1.80	313,866
New Woman/Hach EMAP	£1.70	269,372
Company/Nat Mags	£1.60	250,343
Woman's Journal/IPC	£1.80	151,332
For Women/Portland	£2.95	145,032
Bite/Ann Summers	£1.95	75,000

All figures are ABC Jan–June 1993 except for *Woman's Weekly* (March–June), *For Women* (Jul–Dec 1992) and *Bite* (publisher's estimate). Figures given only for those publications mentioned in the copy.

situations a measure of anonymity helps people talk about very personal and perhaps distressing matters. I also know that no journalist would dream of making up anything like this. Other people, though, might have nasty, suspicious minds.

There is a belief that there is a difference between the allegedly 'young' magazines like *Cosmopolitan* and the 'middle-aged' weeklies like *Woman*, *Woman's Own* and *Woman's Realm*. But when you realise that *Cosmopolitan* has been going twenty years the difference between young and middle-aged gets blurred, especially when you can read in the weeklies: 'Why do so many men turn to stripping?' (*Woman*); 'I slept with my boss at the office party' (*Woman's Own*); and 'I had sex with Santa' (*Woman's Realm*). Well, competition must be pretty hot, since they are all owned by the same company, IPC, and produced from the same tower block.

So how big a step is it to what are called the 'top shelf' magazines which specialise in full-frontal male nudity? In the January issue of *For Women* 'photographer Jess Esposito captures the heart and soul of Enrique, part little boy lost, part Puerto Rican fighting machine'. He may or may not have captured Enrique's heart and soul but he has captured his willy in some detail. Meanwhile, *Bite* magazine contains the result of its 'BIG Penis Survey' on a page with pictures of nine penises, the Leaning Tower of Pisa, Concorde, a banana and a sausage.

This was supposed to be a growth area (oh, go on, titter) of publishing. But it was reported last week that three of the top-shelfers – *Women on Top*, *Women Only* and *Ludus* – had closed down, perhaps because it is true what they say and women find the sight of the penis, on its own, absurd rather than erotic; perhaps because women find it difficult to reach the newsagent's top shelf; or perhaps because it cannot be easy to run an overtly pornographic women's magazine when the supposedly respectable ones have 'Coming This Christmas!' and 'Cock-eyed Optimists!' all over the front cover.

There are publications for males that are every bit as obsessed with sex but they are not the 'men's magazines', they are the ones that everyone knows are merely aids to masturbation. Is this obsession with sex really what defines womanhood?

Few women's weeklies or monthlies can be trusted to stay away from the subjects that used to be called taboo and are now compulsory. But it does still appear to be true that while *Cosmopolitan* will tell you how to have an orgasm, *Woman's Weekly* will tell you how to knit one. And then there is *My Weekly*, 'the magazine for women everywhere': 'As they talked, their faces were turned to each other, inches apart, and now those faces made the small yet vast journey that ended when their lips were touching.'

Isn't that nice? It is the conclusion of a story billed as fiction. Now, as the other magazines would ask, did he dress up and talk dirty? How many orgasms did she have? Did she masturbate him? And did it look like a banana or a sausage? •

Arts, books, culture

Nancy Banks-Smith

30 June 1994

Coronation tales of soap, sex and secrets

'**O**ops, where am I going?' were Prince Charles's first words in *Charles: The Private Man, The Public Role* and it came, rather appropriately, after *Coronation Street*, inheriting its audience.

It was a lively night in Coronation Street. 'The months of lying and cheating take their toll on Des as he finally finds the courage, with the help of a few drinks, to confess all.' Des, for those who have difficulty keeping up, is simultaneously involved with two barmaids. The daffy, delicious and deceived Raquel and Tanya, the wicked other woman.

Any resemblance between the two story lines is entirely coincidental as the prince – Jonathan Dimbleby always referred to him as the prince – pointed out, going into quite a prolonged splutter. 'Just look at the level of intrusion, persistent, endless carping, pontificating, criticising, examining, inventing, the soap opera… ' This was apropos the strain on 'people who marry into my family and are simply not trained for it'.

He spoke over the sad strings of a memorial concert for Lady Fermoy at which the black-lashed princess, her grand-daughter, sat heavy-eyed like a panda who has rejected a peculiarly unsuitable mate.

Charles: The Private Man, The Public Role was, like its title, far too long. It would have been too long for the Prince of Peace descending in His glory. Beside me I heard the sibilant insistence of Lord Deedes: 'I want to be away by shix.' This was an afternoon preview, arranged like King George V's death, to catch the daily papers.

You can sympathise with Charles's persistent, endless carping criticism of the media, though, after a couple of hours, you did feel trapped at some dreadful dinner party at which the prince was saying again: 'As I see it'.

Every remark, however heartfelt, was qualified by a diffident disclaimer. 'It seems to me' or 'I think' or 'For what it's worth', as in 'It's stark raving madness,

I think. Let's use it instead of moaning about it, that's the way I look at it' (on scrapping the royal yacht, *Britannia*); 'I don't see why it should be an impediment. That's the way I look at it' (on the breakdown of his marriage); 'We're all actually aiming for the same goal, I think. The pattern of the divine which is, I think, in all of us' (on religion). If all the hesitations, qualifications and polite disclaimers had been edited out, the programme would have been half an hour shorter. But it would not have been the same prince. This one had more hesitations than Prince Hamlet.

He seems a prime candidate for his own Prince's Trust, which, as Phil Collins said, was to 'get some of their self-esteem and confidence back'. If a question cut too deep, as when asked about his marriage or if he expects to become king, he answered on the defensive crest of a blustery laugh. That there is a hurt is obvious. He told Dimbleby about offering to become governor-general of Australia if all the political parties wished it. They did not. 'What,' he said, 'are you supposed to think when you are told you're not wanted?'

Dimbleby summed up: 'The prince is not unduly given to looking on the bright side.' A scene which caused an immediate ripple in the audience was Phil Collins singing 'Always look on the bright side of life' at a Prince's Trust course. The youngsters from nowhere danced. The prince only moved his lips. •

Edward Pearce
19 February 1994

BBC builds new house of Eliot on traditional foundations

Middlemarch is over, Bulstrode has taken flight, transformed from canting elder to victim! Lydgate has settled for a mediocre comfortableness once a horror to him and now a spar, and Dorothea, upon whom one wanted to urge irregular, unsanctified and decently endowed union, has done her high thing for Ladislaw, deeply unlikeable as played here, either through subtle intention or the unbanishable smirk of the young actor clearly being groomed for something on the strength of what the trade calls good bones.

There is a purist view deploring classic serials: high-thinking *Brooksides* or alternately, in the obtuse view of the anti-literacy educators, expensive élitism. The intelligent reservation is that you never can convey in the most sensitive, most *nuancé* and conservative production, the refinements of the original narrative. Now I would settle at any time to have Judi Dench read me the unabridged text of *Middlemarch*. But realistically, what we got was very good indeed. It was indeed very conservative, as such things must be if we are not to suffer from Pountney's Complaint, belief that *Macbeth* needs green blood and Charles Manson to make its point. Andrew Davies, who adapted it and who could be summed up as 'left-wing and keen on sex', was very restrained. Presented with my friend Dobbs's novels, which are politically Tory and sexually speaking only *comme ci*, he turned out something very enjoyable which showed the Tories as a fascist conspiracy and, sexually, was at least *comme ça*. But here he let the nineteenth-century radical Marian Evans say her own statement, and as to sex, only intimated what Declan Donnelan, say, would have picked out in spotlights.

Middlemarch worked because everybody involved sat at the knee of the good and wise woman who wrote the best English novels of the century, and worked with old-fashioned respect to convey her through a different medium. We should be grateful at the trouble taken to transform Stamford, a lovely town anyway, into a credible early nineteenth-century place. That isn't kitsch or sentimentality; it is an attempt to achieve the feel of the times and make a central Eliot point, that the limping present attached to the antique past exercises great attraction, and that those like Lydgate pulling against it will have their work cut out. Things as they are, as depicted by stagecoaches and earth roads, constitute a major character in the book.

This production benefited from some very fine acting. I can take or leave the *jeunes premiers* – one handsome young actor schooled in significant silences, insolent stares and ungorgeous pouts is much like another – and I can always do without Stephen Moore, who bawled here as he bawls at the National. But Peter Jeffrey, who had always seemed good BBC – steady, sensible and professional but not special – pulled off in Bulstrode the acting of his life, playing both the façade and the man behind it, rigid implacable authority and anxiety and real conscience struggling on a slope. He slowly dissolved in the last two episodes from first to second with wonderful sensitivity.

Patrick Malahide as Casaubon *zerstreuter Professor* observer of chivalric punctilio with perfect insensibility... and a very unhappy man, grasped all this, especially the last. Malahide understood that there is a small place for Casaubon in Eliot's heart. Juliet Aubrey, quite apart from being delectably beautiful, something I hope we are still allowed to say, is a major find. There has been some hesitation over her. There is nothing to hesitate about. Asked to start in the deep end with the heroine furthest from the butter and honey norm, a clever girl with a high liberal conscience, someone whose youth is incidental to her grave purpose where it is not a hindrance to it, Miss Aubrey met the complexities head on and won, with a Dorothea – especially in the last scenes with Rosamund, another fine performance – convincingly good, but not too good to be true.

At the pinnacle of a very fine cast stood, of course, Robert Hardy. Those people will appreciate Hardy best who saw him long since in another Eliot adaptation, *Daniel Deronda*, a point that has gone pretty well unremarked. He was there the dreadful Mr Grandcourt, aristocratic without grace, rich, confident, command-ing, greedy, contemptuous, speaking the accent of a caste – consonant-drop-ping, auxiliary verb not agreeing. 'No point in waitin'. She don't care for you' – with the carelessness of massive psychological strength, a winning side mightily indifferent to any rules.

To set that recollection against Brooke of Tipton – selfish but meekly selfish, rummaging fearfully about life – that not uncommon thing, the valetudinarian, the practitioner of a half-cock hedonism that nevertheless leaves him happy – is to establish a gulf. Only a special actor could bridge it; and Hardy, for all that he (or his agent) has wasted years of his alpha talent on mediocre commercial roles, is very special. There is no fashionable young actor sunning in the hype who has Hardy's scope. And scope is the word. For me he is up there with McKellen, Gambon and Michael Bryant.

But the acting apart, what about the enterprise? My reaction is uncompli-cated. We live in a disculturing world. Rupert Murdoch twists one end of the rope and Doug McAvoy for the 'professionals' of an under-lettered teaching profession twists the other. Gameboy does everything else. Maybe far more copies of *Middlemarch* have been bought than will be read, but some will be read (the book every novice should start with is *Silas Marner* – short, warm, heartlift-ing). What matters is that Mr Birt should be persuaded, as he may well be, that the classic serial, the 'costume drama' as the smarties call it, is a national asset, something which Britain's formidable reserves of first-class acting can make to get up and dance.

We are fighting to keep high culture above water, to keep it known. The best dramatisation in the world will never be as good as a great book, though for an inferior and frankly windbagging writer like Trollope, it may be salvation.

But even for the best, it is two things: for some a way *to* the book, for others, all they will know of it. Not wise, when you need it, to quibble about the consistency of rain •

Pass Notes

15 April 1994   Albert Camus

Age: Born 1913. Died 1960.
Appearance: Fifties film star.
Status: Novelist and philosopher.
Why is he in the news? His latest novel, *Le Premier Homme*, has just appeared.
A little tardy? His family objected to parts of the highly autobiographical book, and there were problems deciphering the text.
Some autobiography please: Born into a poor settler family in Algeria, his father was killed in the First World War, and he was brought up by his grandmother, who used to belt him with a dried ligament of bull's neck. Was variously an actor, teacher, journalist and playwright. Fought for the French resistance. Died in a car crash.
Wasn't he Sartre's mate? They met in Paris in 1943 and set up a left-wing magazine, *Combat*. Joined the café-going existentialist group, but in 1952 he and Sartre fell out.

Over unpaid bills at Les Deux Magots? Don't be absurd. Sartre hated Camus's *L'Homme Revolté*, which rejected communism, while Jean-Paul was trying to arrange a marriage between existentialism and Marxism.
What was Camus's view? The revolutionary can never be absolutely right and the fatal dialectic of power idealism leads to murder and oppression.
Could you sum up his philosophy in two words? Nihilism and absurdity.
That's three words: Don't quibble.
Was he unreadable? Not at all. His novels *L'Etranger* and *La Peste* won him the Nobel Prize for Literature in 1957 and produced a generation of angst-ridden students.
What inspired Camus's philosophy? His impoverished upbringing, life in a settler community but perhaps most of all football.
You're joking? No. He once said: 'All that I know most surely about morality and the obligations of man, I know from football.'
You're not confusing him with Paul Gascoigne? No.
What was he? Dignified centre-half; cultivated outside-left? A goalkeeper, actually, like all literary greats.
Now I know you're joking: The evidence is irrefutable. Yevtushenko was a very fine goalkeeper; Nabokov was a rather shakier custodian ('I was less the keeper of a soccer goal than the keeper of a secret'); and Roy Hattersley was no mean performer.
But did keeping goal really contribute to Camus's art? You bet. 'I quickly learned that the ball never came to you where you expected it,' he explained. 'This helped me in life.' His *Myth of Sisyphus*, about a man condemned to forever roll a large football-like stone up a hill, could be seen as a paean to the goalkeeper's lot.
Not to be confused with (or by): Camus cognac.
Most likely to say: *'Je croisen la justice mais je défendrais ma mère avant la justice.'*
Least likely to say: *'Eh, Jean-Paul, où est Cantona?'*

Will Self
5 February 1994

Junking the image

There were two cultural revolutions in the sixties. Both appeared to involve the overthrow of established orthodoxies, both were spearheaded by almost mythic figures, and both of them had undertaken long marches. But whereas the Orient had a Great Helmsman, we in the Occident merely had a Great Junksman.

The Great Helmsman has been in his grave for over a decade, but defying the exigencies of the toxified body, the Great Junksman is still with us, and celebrates his eightieth birthday today.

During *his* long march William Burroughs went south from New York City, fleeing a federal rap for forging morphine prescriptions. In New Orleans in the late forties he marshalled his revolutionary cadres: Jack Kerouac, Neil Cassady and Allen Ginsberg; before fleeting still further south to Mexico City, this time on the run from a marijuana possession rap. In Mexico City Burroughs accidentally shot dead his common-law wife, Joan Vollmer Burroughs, and while on bail once more skipped the country, this time headed for South America.

From South America to Tangier, from Tangier to Paris, from Paris to London, and then eventually back to New York in the early eighties. In his absence Burroughs's magnum opus, *The Naked Lunch*, the arcane text which became the little red book of our spurious cultural revolution, had been published. Initially it was only available in samizdat form, courtesy of a Chicago-based alternative magazine, *The Big Table*, which, appropriately enough, self-destructed after the issues that carried *The Naked Lunch*. But latterly the Olympia Press in Paris brought this explosive text out in book form. The rest, of course, is history.

These are the bare bones of Burroughs's long march. Put down in this fashion they already take on the lineaments of some biblical tale. Burroughs's mark of Cain was homosexuality and drug addiction. And his 'sin' was both destructive and creative. He himself has written (in the foreword to his autobiographical novel, *Queer*) that were it not for the accidental shooting of his wife, he doesn't believe he would have become a writer.

Why did the Great Junksman survive, while so many of his confrères fell by the wayside? What specific qualities have allowed him to become that rarest of things: a legend in his own lifetime? But perhaps more pertinently, what does the Burroughs myth have to tell us about our attitudes towards the creative writer in the late twentieth century?

I think it tells us this: that ours is an era in which the idea and practice of decadence – in the Nietzschean sense – has never been more clearly realised. And that far from representing a dissolution of nineteenth century Romanticism, the high Modernism of the mid-twentieth century, of which Burroughs is one of the last surviving avatars, has both compounded and enhanced the public image of the creative artist as deeply self-destructive, highly egotistic, plangently amoral, and, of course, the nadir of anomy.

This is why the cultural revolution of the sixties has been shown up to be so spurious. This is why the avant-garde has never been deader than now. This is why there is no meaningful input from youth into the cultural mainstream.

A friend of mine once said: 'When I was fifteen I read *Junky*, when I was sixteen I was a junkie.' I could say the same of myself. My form prize in the lower sixth at Christ's College, Finchley, was *The Naked Lunch*. As far as I was concerned, Burroughs demonstrated that you could have it all: live outside the law, get stoned the whole time, and still be hailed by Norman Mailer as: 'the only living American writer conceivably possessed of genius'. When I awoke from this delusion, aged twenty, diagnosed by a psychiatrist as a 'borderline personality', and with a heroin habit, I was appalled to discover that I wasn't a famous underground writer. Indeed, far from being a writer at all, I was simply underground.

Of course, it would be simplistic to regard this as a casual relationship. No responsibility for my delusion can be laid at the feet of Burroughs. He is blameless. He never claimed any suzerainty over the burgeoning cultural revolution of the sixties. In fact, he was appalled by the sloppiness and lack of tone displayed by the counter-culture as early as 1952, when he was resident in Mexico City and saw the first wave of Beats follow in his wake.

The idea of the pernicious druggie writer spawning a generation of emulators far antedates Burroughs. De Quincey was accused of having just such a dangerous influence after the publication of *Confessions of an English Opium Eater* in 1822. In the years that followed there were a number of deaths of young men from opium overdoses that were laid at his feet.

The truth is that books like *Junky* and De Quincey's *Confessions* no more create drug addicts than video nasties engender prepubescent murderers. Rather, culture, in this wider sense, is a hall of mirrors in which cause and effect endlessly reciprocate one another in a diminuendo that tends ineluctably towards the trivial.

Thus it is that in the heroin subculture – a crepuscular zone which I feel some authority to talk about – the Great Junksman is known of, and talismanically invoked as a guarantor of the validity of the addict lifestyle, even by those who have never read a single line of Burroughs's works. By the same token, the image of the artist that the Great Junksman represents has now pullulated into the realm of popular culture. His true heirs are not junky writers at all, but pop musicians who fry their brains with LSD and cocaine, ecstatic teenagers who gibber at acid house raves, and urban crack-heads who dance to a different drum machine.

The status of 'drugs' as panapathanogenic – inherently evil or nasty – is something that artists, such as Burroughs, and the law enforcement agencies he would affect to despise, have conspired in creating. One man's creative meat is another's social poison, but both parties in some strange way wish to keep it that way. It was Burroughs himself who, in the preface to *Naked Lunch*, drew his readers' attention to the fact that there was something inherently 'profane' about opiates, in contrast to other kinds of drugs.

But this is false. The fact of the matter is that the self-destructive image of the artist, and the failure of occidental culture to develop meaningful and valid drug rituals, are two sides of the same coin. It always puzzled me that I was unable to sort cause and effect out in this fashion. The reason was that while I understood the above intuitively, I was still in a very important way an apparatchik of the Great Junksman.

I, like him, came to believe – as many addicts do – in the reality of a magical world of hidden forces. I, like him, came to writing as a function of a dialectic of illness and recovery. The heightened sensitivity of heroin withdrawal produces a ghastly reactive sensitivity, which in turn calls forth a stream of grossly sentimental imagery, an imaginative correlative to the spontaneous and joyless orgasms experienced by the kicking addict. This is the origin of De Quincey's *Suspira De Profundis* and Coleridge's *The Pains of Sleep*, just as much as it is of Burroughs's *Nova Express* and Cocteau's *Opium*. It follows that the nineteenth and twentieth centuries form a dyad. And in both, some of the finest creative minds have traded the coin of their own self-realisation for the noxious draught of notoriety. The Great Junksman's perverse and – given his own femicide – macabre obsession with the 'right to bear arms', his affected militant homosexuality and consequent misogynism; his – and our – confabulation of an image that owes as much to the facts of his fiction as to the fictions of his fact. All of these reach a peculiar apogee in this one perverse fact: he is eighty and alive whereas by all rights he should be long gone.

By saying this I mean no disrespect. I merely wish to point up the paradox of this anti-establishment establishmentarian. This sometime junkie with a ribbon in his buttonhole that shows he is a member of the American Academy of Arts and Letters; this bohemian exile who lives in Andy Hardy, small-town America; this 'hombre invisible', who has become so terribly visible. If the Burroughs story tells us anything, it is that we are in a pretty pass. We desperately need a new image of the creative artist with which to replace this tired old *pas de deux*. At the moment we circle round creative genius like hicks visiting a freak show. And this is, of course, the attitude that has spawned an industry of literary biography which threatens to overtopple fiction itself.

So, let us use this anniversary not to celebrate and further garnish the legend of the Great Junksman, but instead to re-examine the continuing relevance of his alter-ego's great fictions; his superb, hard-edged satirical visions of cancerous capitalism and addictive consumerism; his elegiac and poetic invocations of sadness and dislocation; his enormous fertility of ideas and imagery. And let us say: rest in peace, Bill Burroughs – may you live to celebrate many more birthdays; but a pox on the Great Junksman – let's topple his monumental statues and move forward on our own long march towards some more spiritually valid conception of the writer's role. •

Andrew Clements
23 November 1993
••
An eye of the afterlife

'**G**limpses of the beyond' seems the most useful translation of the title of Olivier Messiaen's final work. Like virtually the whole of Messiaen's output, *Eclairs sur l'au-dela* ..., first heard in New York a year ago, six months after the composer's death, is a meditation upon the mysteries of God and a celebration of his religious certainty, and like so much of the music of his final years, it is designed to operate on the most expansive scale.

Messiaen's 1983 opera, *St Francis of Assisi*, is one precursor, another is the 1970s masterpiece *Des canyons aux étoiles*. But in this last work the scope is much narrower, and Messiaen's eyes are much more firmly fixed on the afterlife. Where *Des canyons* found the room to celebrate the natural beauties of the world (the landscape of Utah in particular) as well as God, *Eclairs sur l'au-dela* ... is aimed always towards what Yvonne Loriod Messiaen calls 'the Beyond and the heavenly Jerusalem'. Birds sing throughout the work – Messiaen enters a final clutch of new Australasian species in his catalogue – but only as heavenly musicians, not to evoke a precise sense of place.

There are eleven movements, lasting about seventy minutes. The score calls for a vast orchestra – a huge battery of percussion, multiple woodwind (ten flutes, eight clarinets) and brass, a standard complement of strings. But the full forces are rarely unleashed; Messiaen extracts specific colours and instrumental groups for each movement, defines distinct sound worlds, so the perspective is constantly switched and refocused. Biblical epigraphs adorn each movement, ranging across Testaments Old and New as well as the Apocrypha, though most are culled from Revelation; in late Messiaen the Apocalypse was always just around the corner.

Though the tenth movement recapitulates many of the earlier ideas, and the last movement, 'Christ, Light of Paradise', offers a final serene striving towards the celestial light, there is, typically, no sense of a large-scale symphonic structure, no long-range musical goal; each edifice is self-contained, a votive offering that hangs in its own musical space, slowly turning.

The range of invention is prodigious, as rich and vivid as anything Messiaen wrote. There is no sense of late-work spareness; the music is always direct and economical. Dense monolithic textures dominate some movements, highly variegated, abruptly sectional music is used for others.

The whole celebration pivots about a rapt string meditation in the fifth, 'Abide in Love', which seems to be a distant descendant of a similar moment in the *Turangalîla Symphony*. Now, though, it is clothed in harmonies that are less saccharine, more rarefied.

Most extraordinary of all are 'And God Will Wipe Away Every Tear from Their Eyes', seventh in the sequence, and a jewel-like invention around a Wagnerian horn call, a xylophone rattle and a flute singing the song of a blackbird, and number nine, 'Birds of the Trees of Life', which spins an intricate woodwind web from the songs of twenty-five birds, with cymbals and triangle haloed about them.

Such moments seem as precious as anything Messiaen ever wrote. In his some of his earlier massive works Messiaen tested his audiences' religious credibility to destruction, but in *Eclairs* there is never any feeling that disbelief has to be forcibly suspended. The music unfolds with total conviction; the pacing, the incidents, the musical structure all seem utterly comprehensive.

In every sense it is the consummation that Messiaen would most devoutly have wished, and Sunday's faultless Barbican performance by Nagano and the LSO provided the kind of commitment worthy of the work. •

Jenny Turner
18 June 1994
....
Preacher woman

J eanette Winterson lives in a fantasy world. That much we all know for
sure. She lives in a tall, grand, flat-fronted house from which she seldom
stirs, among rich, dark surfaces, cats, and a coven of eager, loyal women
who soundlessly cater to the writer's every humdrum need. She is completely
convinced that she is the only living writer in this country worth reading: 'No
one working in the English language now comes close to my exuberance, my
passion, my fidelity to words,' as she recently told the *Sunday Times*. How do we
know these things? Because we have read them in the papers. So whose fantasy
is this? Winterson's, or ours, or a mixture of the two?

When I arrived on Winterson's doorstep, I knew exactly what to expect. The
door, I had read, would be opened by Margaret – Peggy – Reynolds, Winterson's
girlfriend of the last five years; as indeed it was. We would then enter a
resplendent library-cum-parlour, lined with antiquarian-looking books. As indeed we did. Then Winterson herself came forward, short, sturdy-looking,
wreathed in smiles. There ensued a few minutes of that eh-dear-yes-dear banter
couples often indulge in when they want to impress on a third party how happy
in their togetherness they are. Reynolds then retired, leaving Winterson to get
on with the job of talking to me.

Jeanette Winterson uses words in a very particular way. As she talks, she seems
to see the image she is describing, as if on a screen, ahead of her and a little to
one side. It is as if she is both writing and reading her own private autocue, all
at once. Early on in our conversation, she started comparing the experience of
reading her latest novel, *Art & Lies*, to what it is like to enter a big house you
have never been inside before: 'What are these rooms, where does this staircase
lead?' As she was talking, I actually saw this house, shadowy and mysterious,
transmitted on to a private screen of my own.

This is a preacher's trick, a trick of times before television, times when the
spoken word was used to carry not soundbites but pictures. The successful
preacher is the one who can plant not a phrase or joke but a whole image inside
a congregation's mind. As fans of the semi-autobiographical *Oranges are Not the
Only Fruit* (1985) will know, long before she turned to novel-writing, the young
Jeanette had some success as an evangelical preacher. There was no television in
her parents' house, and there is no television in her house either. There is no need
for one. Jeanette Winterson can throw words and images round her parlour
perfectly well on her own.

Jeanette Winterson's sentences, unlike most people's, come out of her mouth well formed and whole. She seldom uses slang, or ums and ers, or even standard short-cuts like 'didn't' or 'got to' or 'each other'. No, she will say 'did not' and 'I must' and 'one another' instead. She has a terrific voice, with a Lancashire accent which she will shamelessly thicken at moments of high tension: 'Ah moost seh,' she said when I asked about her coven, 'Ah did laff when Ah heard about that.' And she has a fine line in aphorism. Viz: 'Praise and blame are much the same for the writer. One is better for your vanity, but neither gets you much further with your work.' ...

'Words are very powerful things,' Jeanette Winterson tells me. 'Because they can become realities. If you are absolutely convinced something is going to happen to you, then very often it does, though not in a straightforward way.'

You don't really believe that? 'Yes, Yes, I do.' We had been talking about cancer. Winterson believes that if you worry endlessly about cancer, you will end up getting it. More specifically, we had been talking about Winterson's last novel, *Written on the Body* (1992), in which Louise, the beloved whose charms form the book's erotic focus, is discovered to have an untreatable cancer attacking her from inside. Had Winterson been drawn to this image by any personal encounters with the disease? No, her interest in cancer came only from her 'recognition of it as a potent modern terror'.

But then, shortly after the book was published – 'You tend to write yourself into the future very often' – she did get to know a woman whose disease was in many ways like that of Louise. This woman, in common, says Winterson, with many others who wrote her letters, found *Written on the Body* to be 'a very positive and healing book'. And this woman, I am glad to say, is apparently now well. Is there a causal connection between these two things? Winterson, I must stress, was not so foolish as to say there was outright. But you'll get, if you pardon the pun, the picture. Jeanette Winterson's relationship to language is not exactly the same as yours or mine. She imagines a thing, a concept, a relationship; she puts it into simple and striking words. Then, for as long as she is talking, that is her reality. Whatever she says, logical or not so, interesting or banal, is for the duration of its utterance felt completely to pertain.

Jeanette Winterson has a reputation among gossips for being controlling and manipulative, a consummate practitioner of phoney polite-society charm. But really, such words do not give a fair impression of how exactly it is that the Winterson charm works. She really likes talking, with the infectious self-admiration of the practised raconteuse. She does her charming like she can't help it and, as the occasional overkill suggests – 'You'll understand, you're serious' (Do I? Am I? How would she know?) – she probably finds it as difficult to stop.

I'm telling you stories. Trust me, as the narrator of *The Passion* teases us more than once. Put like that and face to face, it would surely be churlish to refuse.

Jeanette Winterson's most impressive story so far is still the one she has woven out of her own life and literary career. She was born in 1959, and grew up in Accrington, Lancashire, the adopted daughter and only child of evangelical parents who hoped she would grow up to become a missionary for their fringe Pentecostalist church. But then, as *Oranges* relates, the teenage Winterson found herself steadily drawn to books other than the Bible, and to falling in love with girls. She left her parents' house at fifteen, after which she studied to win a place at St Catherine's College, Oxford, working to support herself all the while. 'Mrs Winterson', as Jeanette always refers to the mighty woman whose portrait is at the centre of her novel, died three years ago. Her daughter wasn't at her deathbed.

After university, Winterson went to London to seek her fortune, trying, and failing to knuckle down in, a series of vaguely alternative-culture, graduate-type McJobs. Then *Oranges* happened, then *The Passion* and *Sexing the Cherry*, all very popular novels which also received great critical acclaim. By 1990, when *Oranges* was serialised for TV, Winterson had become a wealthy woman, and an icon. How did the BBC trail *Oranges* in the days leading up to its transmission? By showing Winterson herself, talking admiringly about her own work. Winterson's personal presence was used to guarantee the quality of what we were about to see.

But as the 1990s wore on, the Winterson effect very suddenly wore off. An interview with the *Guardian* revealed Winterson ensconced like a queen bee, surrounded by willing drones in her swanky house: 'My women friends and my lover and everybody who works for me ... really believe in what I do and they want to enable me to do it, in a way that is very unselfish.' A nation gawped. Then, in *Written on the Body*, Winterson's normally fastidious prose style was revealed *in flagrante*, with pages and pages of stuff about how 'You are the winged horse Pegasus who would not be trained. Strain under me' and such like. At its best, this very puzzling book evoked Marvell and the Song of Songs in a modern context. At its worst, it reeked of solipsistic, arty-erotica cheese. Reviewers almost unanimously hated it, some of them regretfully, others with an unbecoming glee.

Winterson explains this hatred with reference to 'hidden agendas' and a lack of 'serious critical engagement' among British book-reviewers. This is not fair. Several of *WOB*'s reviewers were very sensitive to the book's aims and critically engaged with its content – but they still ended up hating the book none the less.

At the end of 1992, the *Telegraph* asked her to name her rave read of the year. 'My own,' Winterson replied, 'is this year's most profound and profoundly misunderstood book.' The next year, she told another paper about her exuberance, her passion, and her fidelity to words. She says that partly she was being camp, because the questions were so stupid, 'and camp perhaps isn't understood in the hallowed portals of literary London'. But she was also being honest: 'I take the standards of written work seriously, and I don't believe that other people do.'

Also, she never normally answers her own phone, but for some reason on the exuberance-and-passion occasion she found herself picking it up, 'and I got this nerd from *The Times* and I have such a short fuse, I immediately got into a fury. I really must learn some Zen about that.' ...

'I'm a loner. I just don't need the outside world,' JW said to me more than once. This is how she likes to see herself: Jeanette the loner, all on her ownsome with her books and her cats. But Winterson always seems unable to resist the pull of an audience, any chance to talk about herself and, of course, to talk about her work. After *Oranges* won the Whitbread Prize for Best First Novel in 1985, Pandora marketed its big discovery to the media thus: *If you want to interview this talented, ambidextrous vegetarian* ... The middle 1980s were a time of much cuddly-feminist winsomeness. But even so, all this cats and vegetarianism seemed unusually eager to please.

After *Oranges*, Winterson quickly wrote and published a second book, a genre-comic novel called *Boating for Beginners*. Straight after that, again besting the conventions of the time, she starred in her very own workout book, called *Fit for the Future: For Women Who Want to Live Well*. Neither is ever mentioned on her official biographies these days. Is she embarrassed about them? 'No, no, no! People often forget that I've been paying my own way since I was sixteen. I don't see anything embarrassing about earning money if it's money that you need. And I didn't want to get involved with a newspaper ... ' Actually, she did precisely 'get involved with a newspaper'. She wrote screeds and screeds for Nigella Lawson at the *Sunday Times*, and she wrote a fair amount for the *Guardian*. 'Nigella is a woman of great intergrity,' JW tells me, in a Miss Jean Brodie way, when I point this inconsistency out. 'I always did it in the expectation of stopping as soon as I could afford to. And as soon as I could, I did.

'How many working-class girls from Accrington end up here? This is not done through apathy ... I didn't get here today because I had rich parents; I got here by working.' JW, as you can see is 'not political as such' but 'more interested in values'. Which is to say, her political ideas are as woolly, ill-thought-out and frankly boring, as are most people's. The only difference is that hers are expressed with an unusual gusto and conviction. People do not tell her to shut up and throw a cushion at her quite as often as perhaps they ought.

She says she blames the decline of the church for many of society's present problems: 'Whatever you think of the church, it does provide a coherence. It is better to have a framework to fight against than no framework at all ... ' And she gets enormously het up over the notion, which seems to have only just occurred to her, that children growing up on her street in a posh part of north London 'cannot play out'. 'We are living in a society in which kids can't play on the streets! That's new, it seems to me, and that's really terrible!'

Winterson is proud of her wealth, not so much for what it is materially as for what it seems to prove about her formidable Protestant spirit. She 'swanked' (a JW word) a little about having taught herself Italian, reading Calvino for starters in order to learn to read Dante in the end. She managed to mention that she also reads music, and Latin and Greek, 'being a good Classics girl'.

She is adamant that being very rich matters to her not at all. She would give away everything rather than lose 'the liberty which I prize over all things'. This sort of thing is easily said by the wealthy. But I am pretty sure that she believes it, while she's saying it at least.

In *Art & Lies*, her fifth novel, Jeanette Winterson brings together 'three voices ... in a single place in a single day'. So runs the magnificently pedagogical Jeanette Winterson blurb – 'Handel, Picasso, Sappho, each separate through the structure of their language, all united through the structure of the book'. Winterson is proud of her new novel's extremely decentred and deconstructed, plot-free, character-free narrative method. 'There's nothing worse than the writer who learns to do something and then goes on doing it because it's comfortable and safe,' she bracingly explains. 'It is a gift of wings, and you learn to trust yourself, that you will not fall – or if you do, that you will just swoop up again.'

Yet *Art & Lies* is strewn, as reviewers observed of its predecessor, with passages which read like they have been torn straight out of rant-packed notebooks. For instance: 'I fear the executive zombies, the shop zombies, the Church zombies, the writerly zombies, all mouthing platitudes, the language of the dead.' Or again: 'Roll up! Roll up! Art for all, tuppence a peep. No previous experience necessary. Every man his own connoisseur. Popular culture, that's art, isn't it? ... Clock culture. Stuff me until I burst and make an installation out of the purée. Art? Don't be silly. The contemplative life? I have a lunch appointment. How long will it take?'

Around literary London, Jeanette Winterson is famous for having had, in her past, 'many, many' – her words – girlfriends. For instance, she had a famous affair with her former literary agent, Pat Kavanagh, then and now also the wife of Julian Barnes. This is one of the reasons why she now agents her own work, with a company, Great Moments Ltd, which is run from her house. This is also possibly why she is gossiped about with a ferocity that has to be heard to be believed. 'A lot of literary-type people really seem to have it in for you,' I mentioned, as you do, at one point in our conversation. 'I know that.' Why? 'I don't know that.' A little later, she says, 'You know in *Oranges*, where Mrs Winterson flings all the crockery at the wall? I used to be like that with my girlfriends. It's very exciting, that violent emotion. But it must, eventually, be renounced.'

JW has now been going out with Margaret Reynolds for the last five years. Contrary to the popular belief that Winterson 'keeps her chained in the kitchen, bringing me piles and piles of rump steak'. Reynolds actually holds down three jobs of her own. She lectures in Women's Studies at Birmingham University. She works as a presenter for Radio 3. And she edits books, including recently, and controversially, *The Penguin Book of Lesbian Short Stories*, which included Winterson as 'the leader of her literary generation'. Reynolds, says Winterson, will redo her timetable to make sure she is on hand if ever, as today, there are to be strangers in the house. She makes the tea and hangs around in the background, on hand lest Winterson get into trouble or find herself shouting at a 'wazzock'.

As Winterson has said before, *Written on the Body* was very much written with Margaret Reynolds in mind. 'I was in love,' she says, 'and I wanted to be absolutely precise about my feelings, to find inside myself the emotional extravagance to stay in one place this time.' Reynolds, like Louise in the novel, has creamy skin and flaming dark-red hair.

Out of the two of them, Reynolds reads, says Winterson, 'everything' that comes out: new theories of gender and sexuality, the new queer aesthetics, all that trendy, academic stuff. Winterson herself claims to read nothing written later than Virginia Woolf – or Louis MacNeice, who is her favourite literary critic. Yet lesbian critics have noticed close affinities between Winterson's recent writing and that of sexually dissident avant-garde. 'She takes a word, straps it on, penetrates me hard. The word inside me, I become it. The word slots my belly, my belly slots the word. New meanings expand from my thighs', goes one of the Sappho parts of *Art & Lies*. Winterson swears that she never ever reads any examples of the current fashion for gender-transcending lesbian porn. And Peggy never tells her about it either. 'Often I say, do I need to know about this, Peggy? And she says, no dear, you don't. And I say, are your sure? And she says, you've already done it ...'

When Reynolds comes in she broadly concurs with this. Although she did slip her girlfriend a few facts about castrati which have been worked into the text of *Art & Lies*, towards the end. She herself is currently working on a study of the castrato. Though, 'as usual', Jeanette's book is already out and her piece is still nowhere near finished.

All the time I was sitting in Winterson's library, I was desperately hoping to see some of the other women who make up her famous ménage. As none presented themselves, I had eventually to ask. 'We have two assistants. One comes in to do the general typing; the other one deals with the business side of things. They are *really* keen on my work, but then, it's a very intimate kind of job ... And there's a cleaner as well, and I don't think she needs – no, I suppose she is quite loyal to me as well ... ' Does she pay them? 'Of course I pay them! I pay them extremely well!' One doesn't like to think of a coven of women devoting themselves to the art of another for no glory and no pay. Yet when I heard that Winterson runs her household in much the same way that many other wealthy women run theirs, it seemed like a little bit of excitement had passed irredeemably out of the world.

The minute I got home from the Jeanette Winterson job, heads started poking round my door and the phone started ringing from old pals. So what was she like? Was she as mad as they say she is? Did I like her? When I said she wasn't mad, and that yes, I liked her very much, the heads started shaking and there was a sound of tutting from down the line. Hadn't I just allowed myself to be charmed? Yes, of course I allowed myself to be charmed. Did she flirt with me? No, I don't think so. Of course she wanted to make me like her. That was necessary and sensible, given that I was interviewing her for a newspaper. Wasn't she really arrogant? No. Arrogant behaviour is rude and dismissive. Winterson was courteous to a fault.

So did meeting up with Winterson make me more sympathetic than I had been to her books? Yes and no. As Winterton says, 'The writer chooses her own antecedents.' Winterson has chosen herself the Bible, the poets of the English Renaissance and Virgina Woolf, and she simply does not relate to anybody that comes any later than that. Such apparent hubris is common among serious artists. It inspires them to be ambitious and it spurs them on. In telling us the barefaced truth about what she is thinking of as she writes, Winterson is thus, in a very good way, teaching us how to read.

Yet, although Winterson is convinced of its newness, *Art & Lies* is actually a very old-fashioned book. It reads as if it could have come out ten or fifteen years ago. Its experimentalism, its very title, is reminiscent of what Kathy Acker did to the novel in the 1980s, to great underground acclaim but without lasting mainstream success. The rapt, involuted texture of many passages within it might well appear impressive if they were coming from the pen of a clever twenty-one-year-old fresh out of some fashionable art college. But it seems strangely retrograde from a woman of thirty-five who already has three big mainstream hit novels under her belt.

'My belief,' Virginia Woolf wrote in 1928, 'is that if we live for another century or so ... then the opportunity will come and the dead poet who was Shakespeare's sister will put on the body which she has so often laid down ... ' Is Jeanette Winterson the Shakespeare's sister, 'man-womanly, and conversely woman-manly', that Virginia Woolf was thinking of? That would certainly be a pretty wonderful fantasy to have.

Can Winterson in her writing make a fantasy like this one real? Of course she can – for as long as she can make her readers believe it. *I'm telling you stories. Trust me.* What you read as a conventional literary tease could also be taken as commanding, or as an eager, almost urgent, request. •

Deyan Sudjic
2 June 1994

Landmark for the information age

There is no clearer insight into Britain's schizophrenic confusion about contemporary architecture than the confrontation now taking shape under the windows of the Department of the Environment's Westminster offices. In the red corner are the headquarters of Channel 4, designed by Richard Rogers. In the blue corner is King George Square, two blocks of which its developers, at least, eagerly claim will be luxury flats, designed in illiterate neo-classical style by nobody in particular.

The former is the television station's nod in the direction of civic duty. The latter is a purely commercial attempt to help pay for that nod. To ensure that the station's decision to build its own headquarters didn't have the same disastrous consequences as ITN's foray into property development, when its Norman Foster-designed building cost the company its financial independence, Channel 4 sold off half the site to a housebuilder.

Every compromise has a cost, however. And in this case, the cost is the glaring mismatch between the architectural quality of the opposite sides of the square. On one side is Roger's first major building in central London since the Lloyd's building. On the other is a wedding-cake slab of stodgy post-modernism, a throwback to the darkest days of the 1980s. And the two clearly have nothing but contempt for each other. Yet here they are, inextricably intertwined, each determinedly spoiling the view for the other.

From the windows of their penthouse offices, the Channel 4 top brass look out over the crass attempts of St George's Square to look classy. And, conversely, on the other side of the square, the kind of people attracted by the lure of exclusive luxury, King George style, are going to have to put up with the provocative sight of the Rogers flying saucer from their twee little windows.

Had it wanted to push its commitment to good architecture a little further, Channel 4 might have insisted on an architect of its own choice for the rest of the site. But it didn't – a curious oversight, given the swashbuckling determination of the station to fly in the face of conventional wisdom, and build a distinctive HQ for itself just at the moment that the full horror of the balance sheet meltdown at ITN, caused by an unwise venture into property, was becoming clear.

By the time Channel 4's Michael Grade went looking for an architect to design him a new headquarters, London's property market, still muzzy from being pumped full of steroids in the 1980s, had gone over the edge of a cliff. If he had been ready for a daily commute to dockland, and signed up the station for a couple of floors at Canary Wharf, a pathetically grateful Olympia and York no doubt would have thrown in gold-plated taps, five rent-free years and a fleet of limousines to shuttle executives back and forth to lunch in Charlotte Street. Any of a dozen developments, from reclaimed toxic waste dumps around Heathrow to the empty towers of London Wall, desperate to stave off creditors, would have done anything to secure a TV station as a tenant.

As Thames and London Weekend both demonstrated, from a functional point of view a television station can be accommodated perfectly well in an off-the-peg office tower. In Channel 4's case, the technical requirements shaping its building are minimal. No elaborate collection of studios, no large-scale transmitting capability: the station is in essence a publishing house. What it needs most of are offices for its commissioning editors and its advertising-space sales force.

But Channel 4 wanted something that looked special. And that was as much to do with establishing itself as a force in its own right, emerging from the grip of ITV, as it was with moving out of its scattered rented offices in Fitzrovia. It started looking for a central London site and determined to use its own architect. To that end it held an architectural competition for the design, with a short-list that included both James Stirling and Richard Rogers. The latter won on the basis of a design that said 'modern', 'progressive'.

Depending on your point of view, it was a gesture that could be seen as a civilised investment in the future of the city, or else naked egotism. The truth is that, like most of the best things about big cities, it is the product of a mixture of both impulses.

Rogers's design is a Savile Row suit for Channel 4, not an off-the-peg number.

As soon as you see the building, it tells you at once that it could be nothing else but a television station. It's got its transmitting mast, a high-tech steeple, painted precisely the same shade of rusty red as the Golden Gate Bridge, as a tribute to the great age of engineering, to announce loud and clear that this is a building that is in the business of broadcasting. Yet, of course, just like the dummy wireless mast which occupies pride of place on the roof of the original Broadcasting House as a conspicuous symbol of its determination to let nation speak peace unto nation, so Channel 4's mast doesn't actually do anything except act as a landmark — the architectural equivalent of one of those giant neon cowboys outside casinos on the Las Vegas strip. The original drawings show it festooned with dishes. But these have shrunk to a couple of television aerials and what looks like a domestic Sky dish.

Rogers is an architect whose career so far has been dominated by a couple of giant projects, rather than measured in a steady stream of more modest designs. The Pompidou Centre and Lloyd's were hugely ambitious buildings that took the architect's ideas to an extreme. Channel 4 represents a departure from that pattern. It's designed to a budget, it has to function in commercial terms and it offers the architect not that much to go on in terms of functional demands to make the building anything other than a simple rectangle.

Roger's response has been to create an altogether sleeker skin for the building. If the Lloyd's building was a mainframe computer, Channel 4 is more like an elegant piece of consumer electronics, as far ahead of its predecessor as a compact disc player upstaging an ancient component system turntable. Where Lloyd's was a muscular celebration of the clanking, whirring machine age, Channel 4, with its matt silver skin, belongs to the pared-down era of beeping electronics and anorexic plastics.

Rogers has used two devices to give an identity to the rectangular office spaces that form the building's two street fronts. There is the mast, with its accompanying battery of see-through glass lifts, a Rogers trademark familiar from Lloyd's. And there is the entrance atrium, finished in a spectacular piece of look-no-hands architectural bravado in frameless glass that cascades down from the roof like a waterfall. It forms a glass hinge to the two rectangular blocks, and is echoed in its semicircular form by the restaurant block flying saucer which sweeps out into the square at the other side of the building.

This is the first time that Rogers has actually managed to build a building with a strong circular element, though it is an idea that has been cropping up in his designs for some time, and will dominate the next building that his office is due to complete, the European Court in Strasbourg. Curiously, it provides another echo of the shape that many television stations have taken, from the old ORTF in Paris, to the BBC's television centre, where the circle was used as a signal for a brave new world.

This is not going to be a Rogers landmark in the Pompidou tradition. It attempts what is in many ways the harder task of making architecture out of the meagre ingredients of conventional office life. And it is to the credit of Rogers, and of Channel 4, that it manages to offer so much both to its workforce and to London in the attempt.

Even if it does worry some of its neighbours. •

Anne Karpf
17 February 1994

My mother's story

I felt nervous going to see *Schindler's List* with my mother, but for which of us I wasn't sure. I worried about how she'd react to Steven Spielberg's re-creation of Plaszow, the concentration camp where she spent ten months before being taken to Auschwitz. But also about how I would: Plaszow and its commandant, Amon Goeth, were part of the mythology of my childhood. It was all accurate, she said, the camp, the kapos (the Jewish police), the selections, and it made her choke. But 'the faces were all Polish faces, not Jewish'. There can't be enough young Jewish faces to be found in Poland any more.

Ralph Fiennes's Goeth was chilling, but the real Goeth was more sadistic: 'He'd call his large dog "Man", and human beings "dogs". He'd say, "Man, eat the dog" and the dog would tear someone to pieces. We were terrified every minute.'

It was Goeth's birthday on 9 December, 1943, the day my mother arrived in Plaszow with her sister and two other Jewish friends to be shot, after being caught trying to escape from Poland on false papers. The kapos, knowing that Goeth was a music lover, told him that a distinguished pianist had arrived. She was summoned to play.

'A hairdresser did my hair, and they took me past screaming inmates to the villa. There was a party, uniformed German officers, women in evening dresses, Goeth in a white dinner jacket, drinking and food. I was so frightened, and I hadn't played for so many years because of the war that my fingers were almost stiff.' She played Chopin's C Sharp Minor (Posthumous) Nocturne; when she'd finished he declared, '*Sie soll leben*' (She shall live). 'Not without my sister,' she insisted. Goeth commuted the four women's death sentence, recalling her often to play for him.

After the war, Natalia Karp (she dropped the 'f' in her professional name) moved to London and resumed her career, playing at a concert for Schindler (whom she never met in Plaszow) in 1967 when he received the Martin Buber Prize.

Unlike Claude Lanzmann, the director of *Shoah*, who regards the Holocaust as unfilmable, she thinks it right that *Schindler's List* was made. My own feelings are more ambivalent: I found the film eloquent and distressing. This wasn't the banality but the cinematography of evil. The film is black and white with many memorable scenes: a Jew is killed in the white snow and his blood turns the snow black. The swift camera, the skilful editing – which is it that absorbs us, the filmic achievement or the events it describes? Lanzmann's nine-hour *Shoah* was the definitive film about the Holocaust because, by eschewing archive footage, he acknowledged that those images no longer retain their power to shock but now resonate with familiarity instead.

Spielberg has animated the images honourably, but the imperatives of the Hollywood movie still obtain. The scene when Schindler leaves his factory at the end of the war is soapy; the soaring violins place the film in a genre from which it's tried to escape.

But the Hollywood movie must be redemptive, so when the Schindler Jews go into the gas chamber and Spielberg's camera follows them, they cannot die: first Schindler, and now Spielberg, saves them.

And by the film's end, we know far more about Schindler and Goeth than about any Jew. The Jews remain a clump. We've learned nothing of the differences between them, though survivors testify to the importance wealth, for example, played in helping you survive.

My mother and I also both felt angry at the relative lack of interest in Plaszow before now, as if only an American film could confer reality on it. At the same time the film is deeply moving and engrossing, and has given me concrete images in which to place my mother's story; and whatever its flaws with the spread of Holocaust revisionism, *Schindler's List* isn't just a fine film but also a necessary one.

Plaszow to me has always signified survival, but after the screening I learned that my uncle Milek was shot there. As Lanzmann said, the Holocaust had no happy endings •

Sebastian Faulks
20 January 1994
······························
Rock of sages

f you had picked up a *Daily Mirror* ten years ago and seen that Keith
Waterhouse was writing a column in it, you might have been amazed that
the man who wrote *Billy Liar* was still around. It would have been like
finding Gilbert Harding on the leader page of *The Times*.

But Keith Waterhouse long ago passed the stage of being a 'survivor'. He
glided through the incarnations marked 'anachronism' and 'dinosaur' before
officially being declared a 'monument'. He is sixty-five next month, still at it,
and now past classification; he just goes on and on.

He has written more than fifty books, plays and scripts, as well as a twice-
weekly newspaper column since 1970. His monument status has granted him
immunity from the usual critical fire.

He has ruminated at length about Yorkshire trams and bread-and-dripping
but has escaped the derision aimed at fellow 'professional' Yorkshiremen such as
Roy Hattersley and Michael Parkinson. His tales of shopgirls Sharon and Tracey,
who say 'sorr-ee' and do their nails at the perfumery counter, are not considered
out of date or patronising; on the contrary, they have become, according to his
publisher at least, 'a national institution'.

He has joined the Garrick Club and written more articles than anyone in
England about the decline of grammar and literacy but has never been touched
by the tweed-underpants mockery normally aimed at old fogey musings. His
heavy-handed parodies of European Community proceedings (his German dele-
gate is called Mr Bratwurst; Waterhouse is keen on Funny Names) are gathered
into anthologies and reprinted in A-format popular paperback.

His play about his old friend, *Jeffrey Bernard is Unwell*, which is opening in
Dublin this week after long runs in London, has probably rendered Waterhouse
permanently untouchable: Bernard has been so fashionable for so long that
people associated with him are beyond criticism. And it helps that it is also a very
successful play.

Only a monument could have his newspaper style-book (a collection of grammatical and technical advice to *Mirror* journalists) published in Penguin. Only a
major monument could get away with a book called *The Theory and Practice of
Lunch*. The actual quality of Waterhouse's output is, like that of most writers,
variable. Highlights include his and Willis Hall's superb adaptations of Eduardo
de Filippo's plays – *Saturday, Sunday, Monday* and *Filumena;* their screenplay for

Whistle Down the Wind; Waterhouse's solo novel *Billy Liar* (1959) and his new book *City Lights*. Lowlights would include his liverish 1988 novel, *Our Song*.

Last weekend the *Sunday Times* disclosed that Waterhouse's former secretary and lover, Jean Leyland, is taking him to an industrial tribunal for unfair dismissal. 'He was a monster to live with and work for,' she told the *Sunday Times* in a classic Fleet Street 'outburst'. She claims that Waterhouse had twice made her have an abortion because he thought a small child in the house would spoil his writing routine. And there are further complaints about his alleged meanness and the personal demands he made of her.

However, Waterhouse has not yet chosen to put his side of what is certain to be a complicated story. It is his answering machine, with Miss Leyland's undismissed voice still inviting the messages, that is taking the brunt of Fleet Street's inquiries.

Waterhouse is very vague about his personal life. He cannot remember when he married either of his two wives or how long the marriages lasted. The first one went the way of most Northern journalists' marriages, according to him, because he was 'out on the piss in London'. The second one, to fellow journalist Stella Bingham, went wrong, he thought, because they got married; things had been fine when they just lived together. According to Jean Leyland, the fact that he started his affair with her a few weeks before marrying Bingham may have had something to do with it.

Keith Waterhouse was speaking in the dark sitting-room of his Earl's Court house. He is a smallish, softly spoken man. His famous spaniel's-ears hairstyle, disappointingly, had just been trimmed. It was a Thursday morning and he was chatting through the idle hour before lunch. His writing routine would not easily admit a noisy child.

Wednesday and Sunday are put aside for the *Mail* column, which leaves only three days for plays, novels, screenplays and the rest. It's quite a tight routine – unless, of course, he works seven days a week? He looked startled: 'Oh, yes, I work seven days.' Four hours' concentrated work in the morning is enough to keep up with the game; it is followed by lunch and some less exacting stuff in the afternoon.

At the weekends he goes to a flat with a conservatory and walled garden in Bath. For twenty years it was Brighton but he was driven out of his flat in an art deco building by noisy foreign language students who, he half-admiringly admits, were even more loutish than English yobs. He was sorry to leave Brighton. He 'took a shine' to it when *Billy Liar*, the play, opened there, even though the audience booed. 'They didn't like the language. There were too many bloodys.'

All writers live a double life, in that they simultaneously experience something and examine it to see whether it is usable in some form. Waterhouse can barely blow his nose without wondering if there is a paragraph in it. He was once mugged in Dallas and 'even as I was running down the street with these three young men chasing me I was working on the intro'.

In that morning's *Mail* column the lead item was a cod press release from Number 10 on the back-to-basics theme. Among its Funny Names were Mr Albert Blobs and his niece Miss Fifi Golightly; a new minister, Mr Charles Clump; and a junior minister in the Department of String, Mr Rupert Plonk. Waterhouse likes pretend statements and press reports, particularly from the Northern town of 'Clogthorpe' with its mayor, Councillor Enoch Bulge.

The second item that day was about vehicle exhaust emissions. Waterhouse wondered whether Mrs Bottomley would ever pursue motorists with the same 'messianic zeal' as smokers. Waterhouse is too good a writer to use clichés but, in his dedication to the workmanlike idiom, he often comes close to them.

Waterhouse was lured to the *Daily Mail* by Sir David English in 1986, when he put it about that he was unhappy with Robert Maxwell, his proprietor at the *Mirror*. His column transferred unchanged. 'There was no political problem. I'm less and less interested in mainstream politics. I find that they less and less have the solutions to anything. The column has always been more social than political.'

Pressed on this, he described himself as a former tin-roof tabernacle radical, which seemed to close that line of questioning.

The column is always gentle, clear and pertinent, but before you even pause to wonder whether it is anything more – like funny, or trenchant, or original – you should know that, as far as Waterhouse can remember, every single paper in Fleet Street, except the *Express*, has tried to buy it at some time in the last ten years. It has won almost as many prizes as admirers and is regarded by many newspaper professionals as the definitive column. The world is divided between people who, when they see a newspaper item on the Association for the Annihilation of the Aberrant Apostrophe, settle down for a good chuckle and those who hurriedly turn the page. But – as all Fleet Street editors except Sir Nicholas Lloyd appear to know – there are many, many more of the former.

Waterhouse's first job was as a feature writer on the *Daily Mirror*. During a newspaper strike he wrote his first novel, *There is a Happy Land*, about childhood. 'I just bunged it off to a publisher. It never occurred to me it would be turned down. In fact it was once but I was sure this was a mistake.' It was well received and, with one child and another on the way, he rashly went freelance. It turned out fine. He had started a new novel called *The Young Man's Magnificat*, a 'pretentious, stream-of-consciousness' thing which he mercifully left in a taxi. 'I began again in a more workmanlike way.' He called it *Billy Liar*, and it made him famous.

Willis Hall, an old friend from Leeds, told him there was a play in it, so they wrote that too, and that also went fine. 'We offered it to Albert Finney and he said yes, and he did it.'

It was a great time to be young in London but to be a Northerner was best of all. 'There were artists and writers coming in by the trainload. There was so much energy. You could sell the film rights to a train ticket.' Waterhouse, John Braine, Stan Barstow, Alan Sillitoe and Willis Hall were taken in a taxi to see J. B. Priestley in his Albany rooms. Priestley drew long and hard on his pipe and said: 'I hear you're angry young men. Well, let me tell you something. I were angry before any of you were born.'

It all came so easily that even now Waterhouse looks surprised when asked about the different disciplines. Not only did journalism, fiction and plays come with equal facility, he never felt pushed to choose between them. 'I always wanted to be what I've become, a journeyman writer. I was very influenced by Bennett and Priestley, who could turn their hands to anything. I never had any sort of programme at all.'

So it was a 'Why Oh Why' column for the *Mirror* in the morning and a script conference with Alfred Hitchcock and Paul Newman in the afternoon. 'I was very blessed in not acquiring self-doubt until very late in life. I'm a great believer in innocence. In those days I would have written an opera if someone had asked me.'

Is there any kind of writing, then, that he cannot do? There was a long pause before he said in his quiet, mumbling voice: 'I haven't tried any verse since I was about twenty. And I find short stories rather difficult. I've only written about a dozen.' But have any novel reviewers tried to patronise him because he also wrote journalism? 'No. They've always assessed the novels as being by a novelist.' And did any bull-necked types at the newsdesk sneer at him for writing fiction? 'No, Because I was good at my job. I could do anything.'

He appears not to have had any failures at all. A play called *Say Who You Are* ran for only three weeks on Broadway, but it had already run for two years in London, so the failure was relative. The book he is proudest of is the novel *Maggie Muggins*. 'All my women friends say they sympathise with the main character. I spent days travelling on the tube just being this woman. It works very well.' His favourite play is *Celebration* (1961), a 'slice of life, with a wedding and a funeral. It's the only properly Northern thing I've done. *Billy Liar* could have been set in Cardiff.'

His new book, *City Lights* (published by Hodder in March), is also properly Northern. It is about the Leeds in which Keith Waterhouse grew up in poverty in the 1930s and 1940s. He has used the story of his own childhood to evoke the lost sooty towns of aldermen, trams and Victorian offices let out to detective agencies and ratty businesses that got exposed by the *Sunday Pictorial*. It brings out the best in him: a story of genuine hardship; subversive humour and self-mockery (the names have their own resonance, with no need to be made Funny); a clear, unaffected style; and his real passions for education and urban architecture.

And so to lunch, a daunting meal to take with someone who has written a book on the theory and practice of it. The chosen restaurant was a seen-better-days Soho joint with red plush seats and a three-bar electric heater that grilled our trouser legs. Most of the items on the menu have drawings of flames beside them, indicating that they would be flambéed at your table. A bit of theory and practice there, for sure ... But no. Waterhouse has the same thing every time: the haddock. He handed back the wine list. 'Why are you giving that to me? The house white's fine.'

He left almost all the haddock and would have no dessert or brandy. After a grumble about the clingfilm on the cheese, he had a small nob of Emmenthal with white bread. The end. A man who can write a book on the theory and practice of that is probably a magic realist manqué.

Waterhouse reads all the other columnists, he explained in the course of lunch. 'Alan Watkins – the *Observer* should never have let him go. Craig Brown in the *Sunday Times*, though I've no interest in food writing. Anything gossipy like McKay or Worsthorne. Levin's still pretty readable. Bill Deedes – he has the art of readability. Rees Mogg, but he seems to be ... consistently wrong. The *Standard* has brightened up considerably – it makes you feel you're in on something. The *Telegraph*'s my favourite for news.'

The breaking up of Fleet Street was, he thought, more significant than it looked. 'El Vino's was a job exchange, as well as a place for gossip and news. Now it's full of bankers. The only time I go there is after a memorial service at St Bride's. The doors burst open and a large group of red-faced men burst in and throw down a huge amount of gin, saying, "It's what he would have wanted"'.

The British press on the whole, he thinks, is good and variable. 'A press that is a constant irritant is a good idea, and I like the brashness and cheekiness of the old *Mirror* at its best. Kelvin MacKenzie may be raving mad but he has a kind of genius, that fellow.'

On the debit side is the loss of literacy, even in the 'qualities', and even in headlines. 'Whose sorry now?' was a recent favourite. A heavy weekend supplement this autumn gave its whole front page to the headline 'Feminists didn't used to look like this'.

This loss is irreversible, Waterhouse thought, but his interest in it led to him working for the Kingman Committee on the Teaching of English Language in 1987–8. What annoys him most is that teachers withhold what they know of grammar because they think the children will not be able to handle it. The teachers' knowledge may not be great though: in the course of working for Kingman he discovered that one in four secondary school English teachers has no qualification beyond O-level.

After lunch Waterhouse went off to stir another of the innumerable pots he keeps simmering. In the evening it will be a big vodka martini and some more wine; the next morning the yellow pad, the Adler typewriter and the Woolworth's (USA) university notebooks. His main worry at that moment was that Jeffrey Bernard would peg out at the Dublin opening. The play itself is too workmanlike to do anything so unprofessional. •

Catherine Bennett
9 December 1993

Darling, you were wonderful

Michael Gambon has short legs and dwells in Forest Hill. Fiona Shaw treasures a lump of Irish bog wood and flourishes in Primrose Hill. Amanda Donohoe once had an affair with a married man and believes that life is a journey. One recent weekend these and other shreds of information were stitched into interviews and spun out over pages of newspaper supplements. By now they have been snipped out and folded away in cuttings libraries from which they will, in time, be retrieved in order to plump out future interviews and profiles of the same actors. Before long, some interviewer or other will place a tape recorder beside Amanda Donohoe, check that the red light is burning and – desperate for something to ask – say, 'Amanda, uh, that thing you once said about having an affair with a married man, I mean, you haven't had one since, have you ... ?'

Why are actors and actresses interviewed so much? Like most of us, few of them have new ideas worth hearing, any power to speak of, a home life of unusual interest, or particular brilliancy of expression. They differ in being better known, better looking, and in having an unusual job. That job requires them to pronounce words written by other people. Yet we are constantly after them for words of their own. Wrong end of the stick, what?

Why on earth should we want to know what they have to say? There is no reason why they should be any more intriguing than, say, a teacher or a plumber. A gift for recitation is not, as Samuel Johnson noticed, any guarantee of social talent. 'Pritchard, in common life, was a vulgar ideot,' he remarked of one actress. 'She would talk of her *gownd*: but when she appeared upon the stage, seemed to be inspired by gentility and understanding.'

These days Pritchard's idiocy would serve her well. The *Daily Mail* would ask for details of her gownds, her diet, or experience of adultery. She could do 'A room of My Own' in the *Observer*, 'A Day in the Life' in the *Sunday Times*, 'The Questionnaire' in the *Guardian*, 'My Perfect Weekend' in *The Times*, 'Me and My God' in the *Sunday Telegraph*, 'Me and My Health' in the *Standard*, and 'Feuds Corner' – Johnson vs. Pritchard – in the *Sunday Times* Style section. She could have done 'Me and My Mantelpiece' in the *Telegraph* Magazine had it not, tragically, been discontinued.

On radio, Pritchard could be on *Midweek*, swapping fatuities with Brian Hayes one day; the next on *Woman's Hour*, bemoaning the plight of the middle-aged actress with Jenni Murray. On television, she could enjoy Richard and Judy's homely chat, Clive Anderson's feeble mockery. Because they have recognisable faces, all actors, as a group, are included in the category marked People Worth Interviewing. This is a category mistake, resulting in misery for actors, for journalists, and for readers.

Sometimes, when they become closely identified with a character, it's hard to remember that the character belongs to the writer who invented it, not the actor. Well, that's not true actually. It's perfectly easy; we just don't bother. Whenever a powerful character strikes us, we promptly forget what's really behind it, and trot off in search of the actor who played it, as if meeting him is equivalent to meeting Inspector Morse or Travis Bickle.

When *The Silence of the Lambs* came out, for instance, we believed Sir Anthony Hopkins would offer rare insights into Thomas Harris's creation, Hannibal Lecter. How had he prepared for the role? 'Well,' he told Robert McCrum in the *Guardian*, 'I read the book.' You don't say? From start to finish? Every page? 'From the beginning, Lecter was very clear to me,' Hopkins disclosed. He decided that slicked-back hair would be crucial. Apart from this revelation, the interview dwelt, as most Hopkins interviews do, on his historic drink problem and solitary childhood.

Many actors are pleasant, accomplished, hard-working people who no doubt can, in other circumstances, make fine friends and agreeable companions. The pressure to seem interesting and original in these interviews without giving anything away or regretting it later must be a burden for them too. Why should they be expected to subject themselves to analysis by some impertinent amateur thespologist? 'When he was ten his mother remarried and his life thereafter seems to have been dominated by a need to impress his stepfather,' was Lynn Barber's diagnosis of William Hurt, after a single cream tea.

But that's exactly the kind of thing people want to read about actors, isn't it? The public don't want any more laments about the state of the British film industry, blather about Buddhism, or rollicking anecdotes about the late, great Binkie Beaumont. They want to know about personality defects, off-screen lives, dislikes, problems, money, face-lifts. Most of all, they want to know about sex. As most film stars and many stage actors are prized for their sexiness, this seems reasonable enough.

And at one time the stars were happy enough to oblige. 'The matter with me is – *I want a man!*' Tallulah Bankhead exclaimed to a journalist in 1932; 'I told you I haven't had an *affaire* for six months.' In another interview, also included in Christopher Silvester's *Penguin Book of Interviews*, Mae West spent ages showing off her boudoir and reliving her conquests to the journalist Charlotte Chandler. 'One Saturday night we were at it till four the next afternoon. A dozen rubber things. Twenty-two times. I was sorta tired. Like I always said, "It's not the men in my life, it's the life in my men."'

Fascinating, eh? They must have used them twice in those days. But try asking Daniel Day-Lewis how many rubber things he's bought recently. Try getting Emma Thompson to show you her bed, or persuading Alan Rickman to talk about the life in his girls. You wouldn't want to do that, would you? (Though you wouldn't mind if somebody else did it for you.) But that – or a genteelly diluted version – is still what journalists are expected to ask actors: 'Er, Juliet, you're playing a nymphomaniac with some rather unusual tastes – have you been able to draw on your own experiences for the role?'

That's why the attempt to discover something that is neither tedious nor already known about an overinterviewed, oversensitive celebrity who has been paid to lie since his late teens almost invariably results in an hour's floundering disappointment and professional humiliation. When they are not humdrum or sycophantic, few interviews now are free from the sense of tussle and exasperation which obviously gripped Chrissie Iley when she interviewed Meg Ryan. 'Finding out anything about Ryan is a challenge,' she despaired. 'Here, today she wants to be nobody.' Maybe a nobody is exactly what Meg Ryan is? Why not? It won't stop her being interviewed.

Money is the motor for a good deal of this nonsense. Most actors grant interviews when obliged to do so by their contracts, to get free publicity for plays or films or autobiograhies. Newspapers and magazines gladly take the copy to fill pages between advertisements. If only readers weren't interested in actors and actresses, editors would have to find something better to put there, and the celebrities could save themselves the trouble too.

For many established actors and actresses make it clear that interviews take the most grievous toll on their time and patience. If you quote something from a previous interview, they will complain bitterly about journalistic myths and misquotation. If you ask them to tell their life story anew, they sigh gustily and ask why you don't just get it off the cuts. The oddest things will offend them. I once asked Prunella Scales why she'd wanted to become an actress. A pathetic question, to be sure, but hardly below the belt. Miss Scales looked profoundly disgusted by it. 'I must say,' she said, 'that when people say at parties "Whatever made you become an actress?" I think what a rude question.'

Only visitors from *Hello!* are guaranteed a civil reception. Who would object to being asked – as was Kirstie Allie, recently pictured in eight different outfits, with her dog, baby and cook – 'You have a very solid marriage?' (absolutely); 'Did you have a happy childhood' (rather); and 'You're also mad about animals?' (indeed). For the representatives of less exalted publications, no welcome is too cold, no meeting too short, or too readily delayed. Lynn Barber was cancelled by Jeremy Irons two dozen times in three weeks before he turned up, without apology, and failed to make the wait worthwhile. 'I don't want to give a cool appraisal of Jeremy Irons, or even to be snide,' she wrote. 'I just want to boil him in oil.'

Some actors will only be interrogated in the presence of a PR or personal favourite, who helps them deflect questions or gang up on the journalist. They will rarely be seen at home, which is why so many interviews include digressions on the way the subject interacts with room service or does the honours with a hotel teapot. Immensely grand or stroppy actors may also demand to see copy for pre-publication censorship, or insist that the interviewer signs a gagging form, the better to present the public with a false, untarnished image.

Publicising *Indecent Proposal*, Demi Moore, that willing belly-flasher, threatened journalists with immediate termination of their interviews if anyone asked a personal question. They dutifully recorded her plaints about international stardom: 'As a young woman, you're taken less seriously because got a greater cross to bear.' As an older woman, Vanessa Redgrave passes on her cross in the shape of a contract which not only forbids journalists to ask questions 'relating either to Miss Redgrave's private life or political views and activities', but also prohibits editorial comment on these sacred subjects. So the best you can expect from a Redgrave interview is a nice balance between banal observation – Miss Redgrave's eyes are allowed to be blue, her name famous – and the actress's remarks on her theatrical technique: 'It's not pretending,' she confided to Megan Tresidder. 'Acting is not about acting.'

Well, what *is* it about? Assuming we really want to know the answer, acting is a safe subject, and one on which actors are unarguably authoritative. But there is little novelty here. 'Are you, Sir, one of those enthusiasts who believe yourself transformed into the very character you represent?' Johnson asked Kemble in 1783. Kemble replied that he was not. 'To be sure not, Sir,' Johnson said, 'the thing is impossible. And if Garrick really believed himself to be that monster, Richard the Third, he deserved to be hanged every time he performed it.'

Nowadays actors still tend to divide into those who say they act instinctively, a process which cannot easily be described, or methodically, which takes a fearfully long time to explain and might be better placed in an actors' trade paper or drama students' manual. Jeff Goldblum is noted for being methodical. Before acting in *The Fly*, it is often said, he imprisoned a fly in a plastic bag and watched it buzz about, while intuiting its feelings. Acting a human being in *Deep Cover*, he sought veracity in a shooting lesson with an ex-policeman: 'He said I was the best natural shot he had ever seen.'

Sabine Durrant of the *Independent* discovered a more amusing side to Goldblum when she had the good fortune to excite him sexually. 'Are your toenails red?' he quested. 'Let me see them. Just quickly. OK, from a distance, but not too quickly then. Oh, so you have beautiful feet.'

For less pedally gifted journalists, the majority of actor interviews decline into a flat-footed tour of semi-private areas of life which are personal without actually being revealing. Childhood, God, Urine Drinking, Being a Woman and Personal Growth are all subjects which may inspire a long, transcribable monologue, without awkwardness for either party. They are simply insupportably dull to read. Lewis Duder, a journalist, encouraged Fiona Shaw to soliloquise on the meaning of life. 'I am aware that this is a little blip in eternity,' she told him, 'and I want to know that I was here. I often think I may miss the point by the very act of trying to know that I was here. The fellow stacking turf in Connemara may know, much more fundamentally than I do, that he is here.' Shall we go and ask him?

John Malkovich defined to Minty Clinch his sense of being driven: 'Being driven means that anything I do has to be as good as I can make it, however limited that may be in any given instance.' Kenneth Branagh blurted out his Hamletian angst to William Leith: 'You're suddenly faced with all the old cobblers about who am I and what am I doing here, and of course in my case the assumption that something dreadful is going to happen.'

Maybe we're stupidly persistent in asking them the wrong things? It's hard to say. In interviews with non-actors there are usually worthwhile questions to ask.

With actors, you don't even know what you want to know. Naturally I used conscientiously to ask myself, what would a reader of this piece *want* me to ask? Now that I've seen the *Observer* Magazine's 'questionnaire with a difference', in which readers send in their own posers, I realise this too was a waste of time. Offered Anthony Hopkins, readers asked questions perfectly calculated to elicit a bland or evasive answer. Who are your heroes? they were agog to know. Hopkins said no one especially. What is your best asset as an actor? Hopkins had no idea. Perhaps they should send in multiple-choice forms, or concentrate on simple questions? How many false teeth have you got? What's your favourite make of jam?

If actors acted in interviews, something entertaining might come of them. Why can't they think of their invisible audience – lie a little, do different voices, carry on being larger than life? They would do well to study party pieces by Sir Ralph Richardson, who disappeared behind a magnificent show of eccentricity, wild reminiscence and free-associating epigrams. Kenneth Tynan described a meeting over Richardson's special cocktails, in which the actor remembered a pet ferret he had washed regularly in Lux flakes, mused about the economical nature of God ('Wastes nothing') and gossiped about his colleagues: 'Don't you think Peter Hall has something *Germanic* about him? I hope he doesn't get Germanic with the Willie Douglas-Home play, because if he does we shall all go down with the Titanic ... or the Teutonic.'

Today we have Amanda Donohoe twittering, 'It's *painful* being me.' We have Helen Mirren interviewed twice in one day, and showing the strain. 'I've been an actress for quite a long time,' she divulged to the *Daily Telegraph*. The *Independent*'s interviewer asked if she'd ever been to a garden party at Buckingham Palace: 'No, no and I'm sure I never will. I'm a famous anti-monarchist.' A 'rare interview', as Michael Gambon's was advertised in the *Sunday Telegraph*, will not necessarily be more enlightening. Here were some top tips for getting into character: 'Is he fat or thin? Lace-up shoes or slip-ons?' So that's how it's done!

It may be objected that these quotes are taken out of context. So they are. But actor interviews are all about wrong contexts. Actors belong on stage, not in interviews. If we must feature them in newspapers, let it be in pictures, as big, as glamorous, as retouched as you like. But not another word please. Enough. Mum's the word. The rest is silence. Or else. •

James Wood
4 January 1994

Fatherhood in its funday best

The Man Who Loved Children
by Christina Stead (Flamingo, £7.99)

For a critic to look back upon Christina Stead's great novel *The Man Who Loved Children* is to risk being turned into a pillar of salt. For the reviewer, this book is as great a reproach to carelessness and sin as any biblical city in flames. It was published in 1940, in America (its author was an Australian, at that time living in Washington). A few discerning readers, like Randall Jarrell, and later Elizabeth Hardwick, kept its reputation afloat. But the reviewers of the day did not think enough of it to keep it in print. There are letters, written by Stead's always loyal husband during the 1950s and early 1960s, begging influential critics to recommend the novel to publishing houses. It was not published in this country until 1965, buoyed by its American reprinting in the previous year. It is now available in this handsome new Flamingo edition, as well as in Penguin Modern Classics.

Both versions reprint, as a long introduction, Randall Jarrell's essay about the novel, 'An Unread Book'. One of the truest things in Jarrell's marvellous criticism is his observation of just how literary this novel makes others seem. It is sometimes a little wild, a little repetitive, a little overwritten, but it comes at you in such a rush of life that none of this matters. It is one of those novels which you can't believe was not written in a day; that the writing of it is not somehow coterminous with the reading of it. So powerful is its material that it has the feeling of something not invented but revealed, with Christina Stead its hapless Mohammed.

The man who gives the book its title is Sam Pollitt – a great, monstrously lovable and childish patriarch, who lives in Washington with his crushed wife, Henny, and his gang of loyal children (six in all). Sam is a self-taught biologist, a sanctimonious zealot (he disapproves of tobacco and alcohol) and a tiresome but brilliant monologuist. It is clear that he has ruined Henny's life. He is the very model – how brilliantly Stead captures this – of the kind of man for whom fatherhood was invented. He is a brilliant father and a terrible husband because the children exist for him and his wife exists for his children. A child himself, he forgives and forgets easily. How he loves his children, and how they love him back! He is a great storyteller, an inventor of projects, always on the move round the house with his swarm of children. He speaks to them in a magical invented language which they adore (it drives Henny to despair – 'talk, talk, talk, boring me, filling my ears with talk').

An index of Stead's absolute faith in her material – and her faith in our interest in its every intimacy – is that she boldly reproduces Sam's childish language: Sunday is always 'Sunday-funday', porridge is 'pog', Sam calls himself 'Sam-the Bold', their aunt Bonnie is always 'Bonniferous', his eldest daughter, Louie, is always 'Looloo' or 'Looloo-girl' or 'loogoobrious'; and poor, maddened Henny is always 'mothering'. Few writers have captured so perfectly the awful vanity of patriarchy – its luxurious, idle tyranny; its joyful, lively, sentimental smugness. 'You are myself,' Sam tells his daughter Louie; 'I know you cannot go astray.' And few writers have captured so well the irresponsible, forgetful joy of the child. Great misery surrounds the Pollitt children: every night Sam and Henny argue and fight to the death in the kitchen. They hate each other, and are locked into one of the most miserable marriages in fiction. Upstairs, lying in their beds, the children dimly hear this, and then fall asleep. Yet the next morning begins afresh – for Sam, who is a child, and his children, everything is forgotten and erased. Only Henny (and increasingly, Louie) smoulders. When Sam returns from nine months away in Singapore, he is disappointed that his children have not carried out any of the jobs (he is a great one for jobs) with which he entrusted them; indeed, his children seem almost to have forgotton about their own father. Brought to book, they are suddenly miserable: 'In all the wild, vacant months that had past, like a stupid, shouting, windy holiday, they had never given one thought to their father's schemes and ideas.'

Angela Carter's intelligent essay on Christina Stead, attached to this edition, is worth having; but her insistence on the lack of poetry in Stead's style is surely wrong. Stead is not a self-conscious stylist; but she is an instinctive poet. Her prose has a great rushing beauty. Many of her most lyrical moments occur when in a quick phrase she pieces a truth – as when a woman is described as 'his soft, scuttling wife', or when the Pollitt children, crowding round a large, set table, are described thus: 'they kept swallowing and looking at the glassware'.

The Man Who Loved Children is a great novel because it is such a fine example of the novelist's capacity to make us see. We see Sam Pollitt in all his oppressive love; we know his type, we have all encountered him in the world. Yet the world cannot offer a Sam Pollitt as vivid, as real, as terrible as Stead's fictional creation. Or, it should be said, as lovable. Angela Carter refers to Stead's 'pitiless' eye; but it is because Stead sees Sam Pollitt with love – albeit a kind of vengeful love – and not just with pitilessness that we are able to see him as monstrous, yet also able, to understand why his children love him. The books enjoins us to love him too, and this may be its greatest achievement: we become the novel's willing children. •

Tony Tanner
12 April 1994

Boor with a big heart

John Steinbeck: A Biography
by Jay Parini (Heinemann, £20.00)

When I first arrived in Cambridge in 1955, feeling rather lost and disoriented, I holed up in my room for a couple of days and read a long novel – *The Grapes of Wrath*. In my adolescent years I had read, with pleasure, many books by Steinbeck, and I suppose I reached for a familiar author as some sort of solace. The book moved me, as whom would it not. But the fact remains that I have never read another work by Steinbeck since then, and do not imagine I ever will. Am I implying that a taste for Steinbeck is an adolescent taste, that he is himself an adolescent writer? I suppose I am. Is this unfair? Jay Parini thinks it is, and uses his – extremely long – biography to make the case for Steinbeck as a major, serious writer, still popular with the world at large (*The Grapes of Wrath* still sells 50,000 copies a year, and most of his many books are, apparently, still in print) but unjustly done down and neglected by nasty, superior, élitist academics and critics.

The life itself comes across as a rather typical life of a successful American writer – recounted, I may say, in as much detail as anyone could conceivably want. Steinbeck was born in 1902 in California, which remained for him 'a kind of imperfect Eden' and is the site and setting of his best work. He had a puritanical, ambitious mother, while his father was a rather feeble, failed businessman (as a result, he never thought his work was good enough, due to mother, and always worried about his manliness and financial insecurity, thanks to Dad – the psychology of this book is of the simplest). With his bulbous nose and huge ears he always thought himself ugly, and compensated by bragging of unlikely sexual exploits and occasional outbursts of boorish behaviour. He was no good at university and left Stanford without a degree. He spent some years on the road, doing various kinds of manual labour, and it was here ('everything good is on the highway,' said Emerson) that he met many of the characters and types who people his best work – 'bindlestiffs' (itinerant ranch hands), migrant workers, hoboes, poor Mexicans, winos, the unemployed, Dust Bowl refugees, broken men, lost souls like George and Lennie (in *Of Mice and Men*), men who, in his own words, have 'no families, no money and no ambitions beyond food, drink, and contentment' – in general, the overlooked and the discarded (whom Pynchon calls the 'praeterite') who were growing very numerous as the American

Dream turned particularly sour during the Depression years. He resolved to become a dedicated writer in 1925, a year which saw publications by Hemingway, Scott Fitzgerald, Dos Passos, Sinclair Lewis, Sherwood Anderson, Willa Cather, Dreiser – i.e. being a novelist looked like going for 'an heroic profession'. He became obsessed with marine biology at the Marine Station in Monterey, and lived a shambly sort of bohemian life, with lots of wine, jazz, and all-night talks about the meaning of everything. Success was not very long in coming, and when it came, it came in spades. He became a phenomenally best-selling author all over the world – equally successful films were made of his books, and the money poured in. He had trouble handling the success; got into an uneasy relationship with booze; had two bad marriages and showed himself to be a poor husband, and not much of a father (a third marriage, however, seems to have been happy to the end). He went to report the Second World War and sent back powerful dispatches (as Gore Vidal said, he had the instinct of a journalist – a very good one). He received the Nobel Prize when he was long past his best, but was still fêted everywhere he went all over Europe. He hobnobbed with presidents, and the man who had been treated as a dangerous revolutionary after *The Grapes of Wrath* (right-wing groups like the Associated Farmers vowed to 'get him', while the book was banned by the school boards of many states) ended up defending Lyndon Johnson's Vietnam War (his pusillanimous behaviour during the McCarthy hearings also did him no credit, while it is unpleasant to learn that he was against the release of Ezra Pound from St Elizabeth's Hospital). He died in 1968, knowing himself to be 'a worked-over claim', and long out of fashion with those aforementioned élitist academics and critics. It all seems par for a certain kind of course.

But Parini wants to promote him to the pantheon of major modern writers. I appreciate the generosity of his intentions, but cannot assent to the nature of the claims he makes. He damages his case by ill-considered overpromoting. Conceding Steinbeck's 'naive magniloquence', his sentimentality and romanticisim, he nevertheless compares parts of his works to, variously, Conrad, Joyce, T. S. Eliot (ludicrously), Frost, as well as the more obvious Norris and D. H. Lawrence (from both of whose work he 'borrowed'). When Steinbeck starts to dictate work, we are solemnly reminded that Milton, Henry James, and Borges did the same. More, he is championed as 'a founding father of modern ecological thinking' and, even less plausibly, 'an early feminist'. And try this. With extraordinary candour, Steinbeck acknowledged the radically subjective nature of reality – or the reality that one can construct in language: 'We knew that what we would see and record and construct would be warped, as all knowledge patterns are warped, first, by the collective pressure and stream of our time and race, second by the thrust of our individual personalities.' Here Steinbeck is saying very little that contemporary theorists of language, history, and philosophy, from Foucault and Derrida to Stanley Greenblatt, haven't 'discovered'. Nevertheless, it's interesting that he was there ahead of them all, insisting on the tainted and contingent nature of truth.

After Steinbeck, it's a wonder they all bothered! At times, reading this book, I found myself looking rather more curiously at Parini than at Steinbeck.

By any standards, Steinbeck was not a very intelligent writer ('thought is the evasion of feeling,' says one of his characters). He had a big, sentimental heart and lots of sympathy for the underdog, and in *The Grapes of Wrath* he wrote, as Malcolm Cowley very exactly said, 'a great angry book, like *Uncle Tom's Cabin*'. He read a few books on evolution and adaptation, and, fatally as I think, some Jung (there seems to be nothing more corrosive of the intelligence than taking Jung seriously), and studied lots of marine life. As a result, he decided that 'man is a double thing – a group animal and at the same time an individual'. He developed his 'theory' of 'the phalanx' – collective group behaviour when men act, I'm afraid, at the behest of the collective unconscious. As a result, he often deals, as Edmund Wilson noted, 'with the lower animals or with human beings so rudimentary that they are on the animal level'. But Steinbeck did not really want to be a documentary realist writer. His first novel was *Cup of Gold*, a romantic quest story, based on quasi-historical legend. Steinbeck was obsessed all his life by Malory and the Arthurian stories (he spent a period in Somerset, writing with quill pens, to get nearer to the feeling of Camelot!), and he was always drawn to knightly quests, mediaevalism, Druidic rite magic, old chants, 'heroism', and so on. 'My people must be an over-essence of people,' he said in a revealingly meaningless aspiration. He is always straining for the 'big' ('over-big'?) book. The titles aim high – *In Dubious Battle* (Milton), *The Moon is Down*, *The Winter of Our Discontent* (Shakespeare, of course), and so on. Worse, he is always trying to turn his material into allegory or parable or mytho-whatever, packing it with embarrassingly obtrusive Christian or Arthurian symbolism. His first agent, Mavis McIntosh, advised him: 'avoid unnecessary oddities ... curb tendencies to write quasi-poetic and pseudo-philosophical passages'; his first wife advised: 'stay with the detail'. He should have listened to the women. •

Elaine Feinstein
12 April 1994

Comrade Pushkin's myth

Strolls with Pushkin
by Abram Tertz [Andrei Sinyavsky] (Yale University Press, £17.95)

I n Andrei Sinyavsky's short story *Pkhentz* (which was published in the West under the pseudonym Abram Tertz just before Sinyavsky's trial for 'anti-Soviet agitation' in 1966), the sole survivor from the spaceship of another planet crashlands in Moscow.

The unhappy alien's attempts to make sense of Soviet life, and the sad absurdity of his efforts to find some private place to bathe his spiracles, has a surreal resonance, and Sinyavsky himself has acknowledged it as a metaphor for a writer in a totalitarian society.

Sinyavsky is certainly a brave man. Until his arrest in 1965, he was a young teacher at Moscow's prestigious Gorky Institute of World Literature. There he wrote brilliantly on the poetry of Boris Pasternak, though *Dr Zhivago*, and the poems at the end of that novel, were still under ban; in 1960 he was, with Yuli Daniel, a pallbearer at Pasternak's funeral. Disillusioned by attempts to recruit him as a KGB agent, and by the unjust arrest of his father, he began to write stories and criticism that he knew would be unacceptable to the Soviet regime, allowing them to be published in the West. In choosing the name Abram Tertz for his pseudonym, Sinyavsky had in mind the outlaw hero of an underworld ballad of the Moldovanka, the thieves' quarter of Odessa, written about by Isaac Babel; he particularly relished the Jewish freebooter associations of the name.

These publications led to Sinyavsky's sentence of seven years in the Dubrovlag Camp in Mordovia, and it was there that *Strolls with Pushkin* was written, and smuggled out in letters to his wife.

Unlike his earlier, ironical *What is Socialist Realism?*, Sinyavsky's *Strolls with Pushkin* may not seem an obvious source of controversy, yet when it was published in the Soviet Union, at the height of glasnost, there were Russian critics who compared Sinyavsky's disrespect with that of Salman Rushdie. The introduction to the present volume offers Western readers some help in understanding why this should be. In no country of the West, of course, is literature accorded so high a place as that occupied by poetry in Russia. And Pushkin is incontestably Russia's national poet, not only by reason of his accessibility and popularity, but in the purity of his lyricism and the generations of Russian genius – Gogol, Dostoevsky, Akhmatova, Tsvetaeva – who have so saluted him. Yet

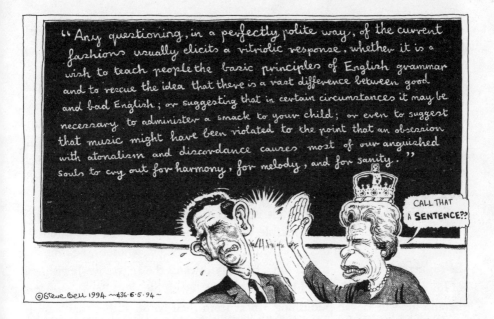

the Russian attitude to Pushkin is touched with another reverence than, say, our English love of Shakespeare. As the hero-victim of authority, he was politically useful both to the Soviet regime and to those who opposed that regime in their turn.

The Pushkin myth itself was begun in the nineteenth century, and proved enormously evocative. Pushkin had friends among the Decembrist opposition to the Tsar, though he was not directly involved in their plot; there were rumours that his own fatal duel was engineered by the Tsar himself. What with Pushkin's love for his peasant nanny, and his affection for the common people and their folk-tales, it was easy enough to present Pushkin as a saintly example of a Revolutionary poet. On the other hand, since the Tsar had exercised a personal censorship over everything Pushkin wrote, those living under a later tyranny could make use of him as a martyr figure comparable to those who suffered under the ogres of the Soviet regime. Anyone who has ever stood in Pushkin's last apartment on the Moika canal, preserved exactly as it was when he went out to fight his fatal duel, will be tempted to feel the power of one myth or the other. Pushkin has become an icon.

It is Sinyavsky's intention to remove these political robes, and return to Pushkin his legitimate power as an artist. He adapts an impudent lightness in doing so, using labour camp slang, and allowing the narrative to take the most casual shape. For all his impatience with the tired clichés of the Pushkin cult, no one could doubt his responsiveness to Pushkin's use of language.

Nevertheless, he aroused virulent criticism, not only in the Soviet Union but among the emigration. Solzhenitsyn, for instance, described Sinyavsky's 'childish playfulness' as sacrilegious in relation to the sacred person of the poet, insisting that an attack on Pushkin is an attack on all authority.

Some time in 1978 I visited Andrei Sinyavsky in Fontenay aux Roses, just outside Paris, where he had been living since his exile from the Soviet Union in 1973. Bearded like a gnome, he lived with his formidable wife in a house marvellously piled with books and papers. Russians often take exile hard, but Sinyavsky seemed perky enough, though his wife spoke of the homesickness which had led her to return rashly on her own to Moscow without any guaranteed exit visa. She was fortunate to make a second escape.

Sinyavsky agreed they both felt isolated in Paris, though he regarded that isolation as an entirely honourable position, since he disliked the intensely fraught, angry world of more chauvinist groups of writers, whose anti-Semitism, he suggested, led them to feel some hostility towards the aggressive Jewishness of his pseudonym. (It should be said he is not Jewish himself.) For this reason, he and his wife began publishing *Syntax* from their house, rather than simply contributing to the longer-established émigré magazines.

Now that the Soviet regime has fallen, and its literary tenets are fast disappearing into history, perhaps it is hardly surprising Sinyavsky is still in trouble. For all his obstinacy, his stance has never been precisely political. And in his insistence on aesthetic judgement, we have something to learn from him. Even if *Strolls with Pushkin*, written more than a quarter of a century ago, will hardly shock Western readers, who are only too accustomed to think of a poet as a 'A goldbricker. A deadbeat'. Sinyavsky's attack on the philistinism of political correctness surely remains relevant. •

Sex: war and peace

Catherine Bennett
28 May 1994

....

A prophet and porn

She was in Berlin. The sun was beating down upon the Institute for Advanced Study, a little mansion in a verdant suburb where Catherine MacKinnon has been working all year, on leave from her main job, teaching constitutional law at the University of Michigan's Law School. MacKinnon is a law professor working on the cutting edge of feminism, whose latest book, *Only Words*, caused a certain commotion in literary New York. If she is known here it is usually as the friend and collaborator of Andrea Dworkin, the critic of sexual intercourse, whose picture, once seen, is never forgotten. Both Dworkin and MacKinnon think that relations between the sexes are monstrously polluted by the existence of pornography. Being American, they also believe that the ills of the world can be cured by repeated doses of idealistic legislation, and have duly concocted a law together to eradicate pornography, in the same spirit that alcohol was once prohibited in their country. So far their statute has been thrown out by a succession of judges, lastly in the Supreme Court, but the two have not given up. Far from it.

Rising from her seat in a cool, polished reading room, MacKinnon greeted me without warmth, as if normal courtesies might be somehow compromising. Her appearance was sleek: rust silk matching shirt and trousers, a deeply fringed tan suede jacket, swirled-up silvery hair fastened with a silver pin, dangly earrings, a couple of showy rings. Unlike Dworkin, whose wild aspect immediately signifies that you are in the presence of the untoward, MacKinnon's smartness suggests a more conventional interest in things like texture, colour, harmony. Camille Paglia's description of MacKinnon – 'a fierce gargoyle of American Gothic' with 'witchy tumbleweed hair' – seems, aside from a certain keen flintiness, somewhat unkind.

MacKinnon led the way into the glaring heat, past groups of jolly academics eating their lunch and drinking wine, out to a bench on a small lawn. It was 1.30. Oddly for a modern American, she seemed not to mind the sun beating full on her face, and as the hours went by, she showed herself curiously indifferent to thirst, heat, sweat – the usual sensations of a human body being progressively dehydrated. From time to time we'd switch benches, but the sun merely came at us from a different angle. It would have been more comfortable inside the Institute – indeed, after four hours of exposure a dark, rat-infested cellar would have looked inviting – but MacKinnon avoids close contact with journalists. Almost her first words – both unexpected and rather lowering in the circumstances – were: 'I don't do personal interviews.' So, if MacKinnon sometimes seems as hard to fathom as Hamlet was to T. S. Eliot – 'dominated by an emotion which is inexpressible because it is in *excess* of the facts as they appear' – the mystery is unavoidable. MacKinnon resents personal questions as 'a way not to face the analysis in any way at all'.

If this was a blow, her physical endurance might have been expected. Jeffrey Masson, the former analyst and reformed womaniser who is now MacKinnon's sweetheart, told *New York* magazine: 'She will sit for sixteen hours and not eat or drink unless I say, "Kitty, you've got to drink!"' Living with MacKinnon, he said, was like 'living with God'. He once made a shrine to her in the dashboard of his Subaru, featuring a photograph, fragments of driftwood and seagrass. 'She is the greatest mind at work in the world today.'

Catharine MacKinnon brooks no argument. That's the polite way of putting it. Perhaps I should have been warned by the way she had me screened as a potential interviewer? It seemed a little odd. She's well enough known in the States, but it's not as if she's Madonna or Prince, Thomas Pynchon or J. D. Salinger. Her latest book, *Only Words*, which comes out here on 6 June will be MacKinnon's first major publication in this country. So, not having realised that MacKinnon believes the media will peddle any lie or smear it deems necessary for the defence of pornography, I naively asked for an interview. Had I understood then how suspicious she is of all criticism, how mortified and inflamed by dissent, had I imagined that she would virtually accuse me of self-serving, self-censorship – 'as a writer for a mainstream media outlet there are certain very real constraints on you' – I would probably not have bothered. There is very little point in arguing with somebody who treats all disagreement as an affront. Indeed, had *she* known that I would argue with her, I don't thinks she would have agreed either. MacKinnon will not enter into public debate with women who contradict her from a feminist position, considering such encounters 'the pornographers' latest strategy'.

Before the interview could be arranged, MacKinnon did her best to establish to her own satisfaction that I was not, at least overtly, a pornographers' stooge. She asked to see some of my work. Aiming to please, I sent her an article I'd written about the implications of rape in Bosnia. Apparently I passed this preliminary exam, but Professor MacKinnon wanted more. She had heard that once, years ago, I'd interviewed Andrea Dworkin herself. MacKinnon told her British publicist that interviews with Dworkin are a kind of 'litmus test'. So that was dug up too. She did not take exception to it. I had proved myself fit to speak to her.

Jeffrey Masson's weakness for gurus is well known, but MacKinnon inspires worship in many quarters. 'I think she's an intellectual giant of the century,' says Dr Catherine Itzin, of the University of Bradford, a woman who would pass the litmus test with flying colours. She has collaborated with MacKinnon, and seen her lecture to adoring academics in America. 'She just *shone*, out and above every one of them, and not only that, she was regarded as being *exceptional*, and as the real leader, the pioneer of exceptional work.' Itzin sounds quite overcome.

Her report is confirmed by Katie Roiphe, who described MacKinnon's astonishing hold on scholarly audiences in *The Morning After*, her account of how American feminist orthodoxies have infected life on campus. Roiphe saw MacKinnon speak at Princetown. 'The politics professor who introduces her says that reading Catharine MacKinnon was the closest she'd ever come to a religious experience,' Roiphe writes, recalling the subsequent performance – the sweeping allusions to Hitler, lynching and to slavery, the tumbling hair, the fire and brimstone. 'Many people emerge from her lectures using religious language – "she's a prophet" – and it's no wonder.'

It isn't. After four hours in her company, I too felt that I'd been in the presence of the paranormal. Interviewing MacKinnon is not like questioning just one person; it's strangely like encountering a whole host of personalities: a fussy Jesuit, a cranky despot, a stroppy schoolgirl, an irascible tutor, a ferocious aunt, and an adroit legal wrangler – which, of course, she is. The Jesuit quibbled and disputed meanings: 'I am construing the term victim'; 'now you will note what I have *not* said'. The despot made lurid claims: 'the media discovered the lie they could sell about the book'. The schoolgirl threw in 'really dumb', 'get real'. The tutor reprimanded me for my 'sloppy thinking'. The aunt said, 'Well, I will decide when you can have it and when you can't.' The lawyer kept the grounds of our argument shifting so fast that it was almost impossible to keep a foothold. One moment we would be discussing the evidence that pornography causes harm, the next we were mired in the question of whether Ted Bundy, the late mass murderer, could reasonably be called a liar. Even now, I don't understand how God, or one of the century's most gigantic minds – whichever you prefer – could have sat in front of me defending the credibility of a conman and sadistic killer of at least eighteen women, claiming that he was subjected to 'media gang rape' because of his claim that violent pornography inspired his crimes . (Bundy also blamed a malignant being which slowly took him over.)

As an interviewer I've had my difficulties in the past, from the icy petulance of Bette Davis to the physical threats of a fraudulent car dealer, but none of them compared to the bruising, hostile, intimidating ordeal that was interviewing Catharine MacKinnon. She dictates and she bullies; she is suspicious and secretive; she personalises but will not be personalised; she cannot understand how you can read her book and not accept every word as gospel. If she's written it, what more is there to say? But she's a casuist, too: if it serves her, she'll dispute her own words. If she chooses, she'll redefine a word altogether, like Humpty Dumpty telling Alice, 'When *I* use a word it means just what I choose it to mean – neither more nor less.' If you don't accept her terms, she has nothing to say to you, except that you're wrong. 'I mean it's so stupid to have to argue about this obvious stuff, I'm sorry to say,' she says, when I challenge one of her claims. If an inquiry irritates or bothers her, she may act bored, refuse to answer – 'I'm not talking to you about it' – or simply swat it aside. 'What I'm interested in doing and what I am actually doing is working to end male supremacy, and that's that.'

A few facts are available. Catharine MacKinnon is forty-seven years old, of Scottish descent, the daughter of a Republican judge who once offered the legal opinion that sexual activity at work is 'legal and expectable'. She was raised on a farm in Minnesota. Like her mother and grandmother, she graduated from Smith College. She worked in a lawyers' collective, and began writing and agitating on issues relating to sex inequality. For years she toured universities as a temporary professor, and achieved tenure in Michigan in 1990.

She encountered feminism in the late sixties and early seventies, the heyday of Robin Morgan and Kate Millett. She will say it has taught her 'everything I know'. Camille Paglia has identified this as a problem: 'She is someone who, because of her own private emotional turmoil, locked on to seventies-era feminism and never let go.'

MacKinnon was then at Yale, reading law, which appealed to her as an effective means of political change: 'That's where things got real, that's where things were on the line, and the real crunch came.' She objected to the way law was practised, complaining it 'had nothing whatever to do with the problem of sexual inequality as it's experienced by women'.

MacKinnon was stirred by stories she heard from women sexually harassed at work or in education who, at that time, had no legal recourse. Her solution was to create a legal claim, interpreting sexual harassment as sex discrimination. Thanks to her, this argument is now accepted by US courts; thanks to them, sexual harassment cases have become an epidemic, some of them perfectly legitimate, some surpassingly silly. 'I think the general concept that sexual harassment should be recognised as gender-based discrimination, which is against the law, is a very important contribution,' says Nadine Strossen, a professor of law at New York Law School and National President of the American Civil Liberties Union, 'but I fear she advocates applying that concept to situations where I think it's completely inappropriate. We now have cases in the United States where any sexually suggestive material has been ruled to be completely out of bounds at the workplace, on campus, in any context whatsoever. We have a situation in a college in the Midwest of an assistant professor who didn't have tenure being told to remove a picture of his own wife in a bathing suit because some of MacKinnon's followers were saying that this created a hostile and demeaning environment!'

MacKinnon hopes to do with pornography what she has done with sexual harassment: to convince the courts that it is a form of sexual discrimination. The difference lies in its alleged extent. One incident of sexual harassment does not persecute all women. But pornography, in her analysis, not only affects the individuals who make or see it, but works against every woman on the planet. In her world of male supremacists, pornography plays a crucial, active role in crushing women, by subordinating them sexually, eroticising dominance and submission. She calls it 'the power of men over women, expressed through unequal sex, sanctioned both through and prior to state power'. Even for women who never see it, for men who never see it, pornography is somehow there, 'making the world a pornographic place'. Nor can homosexuals and lesbians escape its mystical loathsome influence. 'The possession and use of a lower other is what is sexual about pornography and also what is socially defined as sex, generally speaking,' says MacKinnon. One understands that to MacKinnon all sexual contact must therefore be contaminated. In fact she has written that 'violation, conventionally penetration and intercourse, defines the paradigmatic sexual encounter'. Could she be a body-hating puritan who has spun her own feelings into a global theory? Since she won't talk about herself, there is no way of knowing. Certainly her friend Dworkin has been denouncing heterosexual intercourse for years. 'Intercourse remains a means, or the means of physiologic-ally making a woman inferior, communicating to her cell by cell her own inferior status, impressing it on her, burning it into her by shoving it into her, over and over, pushing and thrusting until she gives up and gives in ...' MacKinnon's speech is comparatively moderate, but she approvingly quotes Dworkin's char-acteristically brash and empty assertion: 'pornography is the law for women'. Not a law, not a law for all women, surely? 'Well, good for you for thinking you're beyond it,' said MacKinnon cattily.

Their proposed law, which would allow women to take pornographers to court on the grounds that pornography subordinates women, has inspired much agi-tation among American civil libertarians. There are many objections. Subordi-nation is a subjective term. Her law would not exempt works of art. Principally, though, they fear that to legislate against one form of speech (as pornography is legally defined in the US), just because what it says is repugnant, would be a dangerous precedent which would allow the state to prohibit all manner of material which might offend a disadvantaged group. Furthermore, such censorship is contrary to the First Amendment.

MacKinnon's response is her new book, *Only Words*, in which she makes a blazing attack on pornography, repeats her claims that it subordinates women, and argues that equality should sometimes come before freedom of speech. It is as hectic and hyperbolic as her conversation, full of dogmatic pronouncements and unsupported assertions. It elides distinctions both of kind and of degree.

She describes its reception as 'one of the more amazing media gang rapes of late'. 'Gang rape' is an expression she seems to use quite carelessly, casting herself and Ted Bundy as unlikely joint victims, metaphorically speaking. In fact the book received much solemn, if highly critical attention, but one reviewer, Carlin Romano, began in *The Nation* with an odious fantasy about her imagined rape by himself and by a man called Dworkin Hentoff (a composite name, fusing two well-known critics of MacKinnon: Ronald, not Andrea, obviously).

Romano's aim had been to parody one of MacKinnon's more dubious contentions – that pornography actually *is* sex, not 'only words' – men who watch a film of a gang rape are no different, in their response, from men actually watching a gang rape. But Romano's method served only to confirm all MacKinnon's claims that the media degrade and pornographise her person in order to annihilate her message. There was a terrific scrap. Subscriptions to *The Nation* were cancelled. MacKinnon wrote to the real Nat Hentoff, the *Washington Post* columnist, begging him to 'please disavow this rape of me in your name'. Hentoff chivalrously obliged. Jeffrey Masson wrote to Romano threatening: 'If there is ever anything I can do to hurt your career, I will do it.' Paradoxically, MacKinnon emerged from this ballyhoo as a figure of wounded dignity, a modern Lucrece, defended by a few gentlemen protectors. I'd say she triumphed. MacKinnon disagrees. 'They're not at all bothered by the fact that pornography is there, and is doing ten times worse to women who they don't know, who aren't real to them, and on a ten billion dollar a year scale; in fact they protect that, they defend that, but along comes somebody and breaks a literary standard, you know, and goes a little far in a magazine they think of in a different way, and all of a sudden they think it's a real outrage.'

MacKinnon's case against pornography rests on her assertion that it saturates all our lives and it is clearly a constant source of chagrin to her that we can't all feel the same. Myself, I find pornography repulsive, from Page 3 downwards, but I feel less directly threatened by it than by stray dogs, dangerous driving and 'care in the community'. The fact that I share a lot of MacKinnon's distaste but can't agree on her draconian solution simply leads to an allegation of dishonesty: 'None of your questions comes from your own perspective on it.'

When I feebly assert that my own life, and the lives of many other women, seem to be relatively unscathed by pornography, she becomes either wrathfully indignant or patronisingly doubting. 'The fact that you haven't seen it doesn't mean it isn't there,' she says. 'Women avoid it, and it isn't for us – it's designed to be, and does live, in parts of men's lives where women are not supposed to be.' So it's there, invisibly lurking, even if you don't know it. Spooky! Or perhaps just paranoid.

Is there any way of countering such a total claim? Perhaps by drawing out the implications of MacKinnon's own arguments. For example, 'Sooner or later, in one way or another, the consumers want to live out the pornography further in three dimensions. Sooner or later, in one way or another, they do,' she writes. If this were true, if most men, as she also claims, move from the consumption of soft porn to 'violent stuff', acting it out along the way, most of the soft porn consumers of the 1960s would now be drooling over and perpetrating appalling acts of bestiality, perversion and violence. Are they?

MacKinnon's shunts the onus of proof on to those who disagree with her. She is a virtuoso of the double negative. 'There is no evidence that pornography does no harm,' she remarks in her book. Challenged, herself, to provide direct evidence for her arguments, she raises the nameless spectres of women who *have* been tortured, forced, raped, even murdered to make pornography. When she supplies an identity it is often that of her client, Linda 'Lovelace' Marchiano, who was coerced into making the film *Deep Throat*. In *Only Words*, MacKinnon goes one better, conjuring up an imaginary victim who has been subjected to 1,000 years of horrendous tortures: 'Imagine that for hundreds of years your most formative traumas, your daily suffering and pain, the abuse you live through, the terror you live with, are unspeakable – not the basis of literature. You grow up with your father holding you down so that another man can make a horrible searing pain between your legs. When you are older, your husband ties you to the bed and drips hot wax on your nipples... the camera is invented and pictures are made of you while these things are being done...'

No doubt this kind of stuff had them sobbing in the aisles at Princetown, but how can this crazy conflation of centuries and subjects possibly convince as an introduction to a serious critique of pornography? Besides, rape and sexual assault are criminal already, aren't they? The victims have legal recourse. She looks at me with contempt. 'Men aren't in prison for raping prostitutes; they're in prison for raping women who can get themselves believed by prosecutors and juries and get their rape taken seriously, and these women overwhelmingly are not prostitutes.'

Are there, then, no women voluntarily working in pornography? As if it were answer enough, MacKinnon says that she addressed this question in her book. But all she does there is assert that pornography is made 'overwhelmingly by poor, desperate, homeless, pimped women who were sexually abused as children'. To me, she says she *knows* that because she's talked to 'huge quantities' of them and read about them, 'and all of them say the same thing, and so I reported on that and analysed it, and the word voluntary is an insult to them'.

So no woman could freely choose to participate in pornography. No woman would accept its existence unless she had been conditioned to do so. There is no such thing as a free woman. Protesting or not, all of us are dragged into Mac-Kinnon's dystopian world view, imprisoned inside one or the other of its two great categories.

I tell her I like being a woman. It's good fun. I don't *feel* like the victim of male supremacy. 'Well, you're under it,' MacKinnon said grimly, 'and you'll either face that or you won't.' No matter how powerful a woman, goes her great, trumping argument, no matter how powerless a man, 'he can still rape her'. Does she walk around constantly thinking that rape is in the air that she breathes? 'It is. I mean, if you keep your eyes open, you see it out there all the time. It isn't about the state of my head.'

A motley group of American feminists, from Wolf to Roiphe to Paglia, are disturbed by her fatalistic depiction of women as so many little bunny rabbits hopping around in the middle of the road, waiting for the next juggernaut to come thundering round the corner. MacKinnon's protective stance can be eerily reminiscent of a time when men insisted that women needed to be preserved from their own vulnerability. In the late nineteenth century, Nadine Strossen reminds you, women were banned from being lawyers in America because of the stress of the courtroom, including exposure to vulgar language. 'I think now we're seeing Big Sister in the place of Big Brother,' she says, 'telling us that when we think we're making certain choices for ourselves, oh we're not really thinking freely because we're not really thinking freely because we're so brainwashed by the patriarchy. And those of us who take the kind of views that I do have been told that we're victims of false consciousness, that we're not true women.'

If a woman can feel this way about MacKinnon, imagine how it must feel for a man to read her tirades against their sex. Why does she lump them all together, just as men used to do with women? 'That's false,' says MacKinnon, 'and it's unfortunate that you read the book and you say that.'

Don't men ever tell her they're hurt by what she writes? 'Yeah,' she says. 'But the problem is that the men who perceive the most about what men do to women, and who actually do the least to women and are the least aggressive, are the men who never say that.' What she is saying is that no decent man could possibly disagree with her. Or in other words, if you're a man, and you read this book and you *do* object to the way it depicts men, then you're one of the men it depicts. It's a classic piece of MacKinnon either/or topsy-turviness.

Does she not believe that anyone could possibly disagree with her on intellectual grounds? 'How I measure whether a disagreement is intellectual or not is whether is responds to changes in evidence,' says MacKinnon. She means the evidence *she* claims: the 'overwhelming scientific and experimental evidence' that exposure to pornography causes actual harm. But this evidence is disputed everywhere. It's inconclusive. 'Well, listen, I've read it; you haven't, have you?' she demands. 'It doesn't take a rocket scientist to read this stuff, and they all essentially find the same thing, that's all. It's a simple, objective statement of what is there.' But they don't, and it isn't. Bill Thompson, for example, a criminologist at Reading University, has seen hundreds of these studies and drawn the opposite conclusion. 'On the contrary, they prove that soft core is good for you, because it lowers your aggression level.'

This evidence business gets painful. I am treated to more angry hand-waving, accused of 'another wave of denial'. The interview seems increasingly futile, unproductive, an exercise in female–female submission. It's easier to mumble assent, to accept her more bizarre pronouncements and check them later. Did Nat Hentoff *really*, as she claims, defend snuff movies? 'NO!' says Nat Hentoff, down the line from New York. 'All I said was, you have to first *prove* it's a snuff film before you can take it off the cinema; you can't just go around taking books and movies away unless you can prove that something illegal was done.'

Do snuff films even exist? 'Yes, and I have evidence,' MacKinnon says darkly. Why doesn't she put it in the book? 'For reasons of security.' For the same reason she will not divulge her address or telephone number. 'People attack people who oppose pornography. We've been threatened endlessly,' she says, adding that she's also wanted by white supremacists, not to mention the Serbs. The Serbs are after her because she's taken out a lawsuit against Radovan Karadic on behalf of her clients, raped Croation and Bosnian women. 'We asked for an injunction which would stop him from doing the ethnic cleansing.' Well, it's a nice idea. 'It's a good idea, and we could enforce it as well.'

Stopping ethnic cleansing is perhaps a small matter compared with her task of revolutionising relations between the sexes. What will sex be like in her ideal world? We can't even imagine: 'If you don't have an equal context in which to answer that question, you're not going to know, are you?' But won't some physical factors, such the tendency of men to be bigger than women always have some implications for their relations, however unfortunate? 'I really don't think so, no, and actually the size differential, I think, is a consequence of men raised under male dominance systematically selecting for women of a size they can more easily dominate, and it comes to have an average biological effect.' Mac-Kinnon has thought it all out. 'I think it's completely bogus, in fact. I also think it's mind rot.'

Mind rot. 'Well, it's just part of the bigotry everyone is taught in order to keep women in their place, and with sex, we're supposed to enjoy it on top of it, and I guess, given the alternatives, lots of people apparently do.'

In the vision of equality that concludes her book she pictures a world where 'sex between people and things, human beings and pieces of paper, real men and unreal women, will be a turn-off'. I take it she means that equality will stamp out the disgusting practice of masturbating in response to a graphic stimulus. 'Well, yeah, um, I think that it's a hierarchy in itself,' she explains. 'In other words, it's a person over a thing, and you're the person, and it, i.e. she is the thing, and the idea that that relation is in itself a sexy thing is sort of the core of this on a certain level, and it seems to me that if sex is something that is not that, that it involves equality, then this will not be a quintessential act.' So – stop it.

With all their faults, men are at least preferable to bits of paper. Catharine MacKinnon's choice of Jeffrey Masson, who once told Janet Malcolm that he'd slept with nearly 1,000 women, must be one of the most improbable matches in history. At the risk of being personal, I ask her if it's true she's engaged to him. 'Probably,' she allows. Well, it's a lovely engagement ring. 'Oh thanks,' she says, in a sudden, heart-warming flash of civility. 'Yeah, it really is a nice thing, it's an alexandrite, it changes colour, it's very amazing.' She holds out her hand to show me, the way engaged women do in old films. 'See, here it's teal blue, a blue green, then under artificial light it's distinctly and completely a red purple – that's its range, all the way from one to the other.'

Would it be permissible to ask how marriage fits into a world where equal relations between the sexes are impossible? 'I think I'm not going to talk about that part.' Not even in principle? 'That more or less is my personal life.' She has, however, said this to *New York* magazine. 'We do our best. He's not a man, and I'm not a woman.' Stripped of its spurious negatives, this might seem to translate as, 'He's a man and I'm a woman.' But two negatives don't make a positive, do they? •

Pass Notes

7 March 1994   Sister Wendy Beckett

Age: Sixty-four.

Appearance: George Formby cameo in *Nuns on the Run*.

Nickname: 'One-Take Wendy'.

Occupation: Bride of Christ, living in spartan Porta-kabin in grounds of Carmelite convent in Norfolk; part-time art critic and TV presenter.

Has she been seduced again into roving all-expenses-paid from art gallery to art gallery, staying in plush hotels, and lunching journalists at the Ritz? Only with great reluctance. Her BBC2 series *Sister Wendy's Grand Tour* starts tonight.

So how much can a top nun expect to make from a gig like that? Apparently her agent argued her fee up this time from £1,200 to £10,000.

Why is she in demand? She says it's just 'novelty value', and the BBC loves eccentric presenters. But she does have a knack for the soundbite, praising a Stanley Spencer nude's 'lovely and fluffy' pubic hair, observing of Botticelli's *Venus* that 'you can't imagine her doing the washing up'.

How is the rated by other art critics? Views are mixed. The late Peter Fuller encouraged her to write for his magazine *Modern Painters*; others see her approach as setting criticism back 150 years. Germaine Greer scoffed at the spectacle of a virgin discussing sexuality in art.

What does Wendy say? 'You don't have to experience things to understand them. Look at Jane Austen – she was a virgin!'

Is she a feminist? Consider the evidence. She went out and got a job because she was finding life wholly devoted to her somewhat distant 'husband' less than fulfilling. She favours women priests. Her début book was *Contemporary Women Painters*. She insists on being called 'Sister'. Looks like she qualifies.

Unfruitful conversational ice-breakers: 'Liam Neeson – is he a hunk or what?'; 'Where would *you* play Le Tissier?'; '*Absolutely Fabulous* has really gone off the boil, hasn't it?'

Fruitful conversational ice-breakers: 'You must identify closely with Juliana of Norwich?'; Is Cindy Sherman's work narcissistic, or a satire on narcissism?'; 'Another kir, Wendy?'

Parallels with *The Word* presenter Huffty: Shaved head; doesn't sleep with men; not wild about Guns N' Roses.

Merchandising opportunities overlooked by BBC: Bendy Wendy dolls; Sindy's New Look micro-habits; Jasper Conran wimples; robot Sister Wendy gallery guides; Carmelite Culture Key Notes.

Not to be confused with: Samuel Beckett; Margaret Beckett; Thomas à Becket; Trevor Nunn; Julie Andrews; Whoopi Goldberg.

Least likely to say: 'Yo, dudes, poker in my trailer after we rap?'

Most likely to say: 'Now, Damien Hirst's *Dead Moose with Gangrene 43* – here I must confess to being just a *tiny* bit disappointed.'

Suzanne Moore

25 February 1994
....
Sloth about the house

I am intrigued by the prospect of a 'Newish Man'. It is not a phrase I had
heard until last week. I know full well that New Man is old hat and long ago
disappeared into the mists of media myth from whence he came. I know too
that New Lad was but a trend-spotters' flash in the pan. But Newish Man? The
term has been invented by experts at Mintel 'to capture the one-fifth minority
of Britain's male population who are only just beginning to see the sexual egali-
tarian light'. This turns out to be a guy who doesn't share equally the household
tasks but takes responsibility for just one job around the house.

Well, big deal. Newish Man, puny offspring of the peculiar liaison between
fantasy New Man and clapped-out Oldish Man – is this vague entity really what
we have to settle for? Apparently, yes. Unless of course we divorce him. Mintel
researcher Angela Hughes is quoted as saying: 'This total selfishness is often
what prompts women to divorce.' Half of married men were happy to admit they
are 'sloths' who have far more leisure time on their hands than their wives.

Given the choice between a newish man, a sloth and a selfish pig, it's really no
wonder that home is where the heartache is. Or that one of the biggest factors
in women saying no to sex with their partners is their tiredness. It takes a lot of
energy to work part-time and go home and service a sloth, yet increasingly this
is how women are expected to live. If I sound impatient, it's because I am. It's
one thing to read that attitudes 'to the roles of the sexes are too deeply ingrained
to be rewritten in a single generation'. It's another to watch sensible women
vacuuming under their boyfriends' feet as they sit pretending not to notice what
is going on.

If work patterns, as I wrote last week, are changing to demand a more flexible
approach to work, then clearly this flexibility also has to be transferred to the
home. Reports this week have been full of how men are facing an age of insecurity, how uncertain and vulnerable they are. A quarter of them are living on their
own, due mainly to marriage breakdown. The word bachelor has bounded back
into our vocabulary – though I have never heard anyone use the word except as
code for being gay.

'This Newish Man deserves some sympathy,' we have been told. What a hard
time men are having of late, the poor, confused things. No longer assured as
breadwinners, weekend fathers, unsure as to what demands women are making
on them, these bachelor boys are now reduced to having to look after themselves.
Can you believe it – grown men having to work microwaves?

As you can tell, my sympathy is limited. If you look at the statistics, we are all having a hard time, but it is still women who are doing the double shift of working both inside and outside the home. The issue does not seem to me to be one of men's inability to shake off social conditioning but men's refusal to give up a good deal. This is about power. And those who have someone to shop and cook and clean for them will always have more power than those who don't.

Female disgruntlement at this situation reflects their powerlessness as, more often than not, it is only manifested through individual 'nagging'. There is no pressure group powered by exhausted women with dusters, no lobbying of MPs on the issue; indeed, it is hard to imagine a less 'sexy' topic in media terms. And this is because, as was pointed out a long, long time ago, housework is largely perceived as a private issue. Something that takes place between mutually con-senting or, as it turns out, not so consenting adults. Campaigns such as Wages for Housework were formed to make the point that domestic labour is a form of unpaid work. There were long and tedious debates among feminists in the seventies about how domestic labour oiled the wheels of capitalist exploitation. But we still carried on doing the dishes.

During the eighties, while you could get thousands of women to sit in the mud at Greenham Common or march on the streets in protest at the sale of porno-graphy in newsagents, housework remained something to be swept under the carpet. Yet I would bet that if you gave most women a choice about what on a daily basis would most affect the quality of their lives – the banning of porn or the men in their lives taking more responsibility for the domestic routine – they would plump for the latter.

Apart from the inestimable time 'nagging' must take up, the average woman has fifteen hours a week fewer than her partner because she is busy with 'essential activities'. Hardly fair. However, the survey also shows what odd ideas we have about men in that we think it's strange if they have to live alone and look after themselves.

Some of this, of course, is not men's fault at all. In the past, women have had an enormous amount invested in maintaining the mystique of housework: after all, if they were being kept to do it, they had to make out it involved some mysterious skill. Indeed it wasn't until I left home that I realised there was nothing particularly intellectually taxing about washing up, going to the laun-derette or even cooking. The dull truth dawned: it wasn't hard to do but it was very hard to keep doing it over and over again.

But just as women gained a scrap of self-respect from knowing how to be very good at doing these boring jobs, so men have gained an enormous amount of freedom from either never learning how to do them, not noticing that they need to be done in the first place or, the old favourite, doing them so badly that they are never asked again.

I remember once, when interviewing Paula Yates, she told me that after ten years of living with Saint Bob, he asked her if they had a washing machine. This charming anecdote may relegate him to the sub-sloth category but even Bob must have realised, the times they are a'changing. His kind must eventually go the way of Nanette Newman, who is to be replaced in the Fairy Liquid ads by what we can only presume will be a specimen of Newish Man.

For Newish Man apparently believes in women's 'right to work' (gee, thanks); some are even 'happy cookers', preferring to entertain rather than do the every-day cooking. Some can even iron their own shirts. All this in a week in which this very paper asked Are Men the Real Victims? Victims, maybe, but still victims on to a pretty good thing, if you ask me.

Somehow I suspect the results of this latest survey will be quickly forgotten. Instead we will have to put up with more guff about how difficult it is for men to change and more speculation as to What Women Really Want, as though we haven't been telling everyone for years. The answer to the question What Do Women Want strikes me as neither abstract nor mystical. It is, as my friend Deborah says: 'Six hours of cunnilingus a week and someone who wipes down the worktops after washing up. I want someone who can do both jobs properly.' Now surely even Newish Man can get his head round this one. •

Sally Weale
8 January 1994

I do, I do, take you and you

> There once was an old man of Lyme,
> Who married three wives at a time.
> When asked 'Why the third?'
> He replied, 'One's absurd!
> And bigamy, sir, is a crime!'

The English poet and critic William Cosmo Monkhouse penned his limerick on the merits of multiple marriage almost a century ago. The old man of Lyme was indeed right – bigamy, the act of marrying a person while still legally hitched to another, was a crime. And although adultery today has gained a certain social acceptance – many of Tim Yeo's critics this week stressed that their concern was with 'hypocritical' ministerial rhetoric rather than with the act itself – bigamy remains taboo, an act that is still considered a felony.

'Bigamy,' in Erica Jong's celebrated definition, 'is having one husband too many. Monogamy is the same.' But the difference is the seven-year jail sentence that may await you for the former. Bigamy first became a criminal offence in 1603. And even today, under Section 57 of the Offences Against the Person Act 1861, those caught face the threat of imprisonment.

In 1992 throughout England and Wales 32 bigamists were cautioned, and a further 12 were convicted in court. An offence is more likely to go to court if there are aggravating factors – if it is habitual or involves deception to extract money. Take the case of Victor Harris, a Reading solicitor jailed last October for three years. He had two wives and a girlfriend, but it was the fraud and theft charges totalling £280,000 that earned him the heavy sentence. Then there was the case of Pat Jackson, Britain's only known habitual female bigamist, who has served three separate jail terms. At the last count this so-called 'Bigamy Queen' was on her tenth husband.

Last year Stuart Freeman and his two wives, Pauline and Lynne, became the latest of a string of bigamy cases to attract attention. The newspapers were dazzled by the case because of the breathtaking scale of deceit involved. To the stupefaction of the police, the court and the women he married, the kindly, self-effacing electrical contractor (described by one as 'a perfect husband') had managed to lead a flawless double life for over eight years. He had kept both wives in separate homes without either suspecting the other's existence.

He would spend half the week with Pauline, whom he married at Chesterfield register office in 1967, and their two now grown-up sons, in their three-bedroomed detached house in Eckington, near Sheffield. The rest of the week he spent in Bootle, Cumbria, with Lynne, with whom he sealed the knot in 1989 at Moid register office, North Wales, after a long live-in relationship. The Eckington Freemans were an ordinary, likeable couple, who enjoyed barbecues, gardening and walking their dogs. The Bootle Freemans were similarly unremarkable, leading lives as unexceptional as those of any of their neighbours.

Each of the wives believed Stuart was working on a contract when he was away. He made few slip-ups. When he did, he swiftly covered his tracks, a consummate liar after years of practice. On one occasion he dropped off Pauline, a nurse, for a night shift and made a two-hour journey to spend the night with Lynne, who was then living in Morecambe. He returned the next morning to collect Pauline but was caught speeding in Morecambe. When the summons arrived she demanded an explanation. The police got the date wrong, her husband lied.

Lynne, an administrator at Sellafield, was also puzzled from time to time by her oft-absent husband. How come he had that deep, Mediterranean tan, when he had been away on a week's contract in Bradford? It was only later, after a note-swapping session on the telephone with Pauline, that the jigsaw began to fit together. He had in fact been holidaying with his first family in Ibiza.

So accomplished was Stuart at duping his wives that his double life might have continued undiscovered to this day had he not been made redundant last January. He still had two households to support, two mortgages to pay, and a large petrol bill to meet as he journeyed up and down the country. To keep his head above water he stole his second wife's credit card. He mounted up a £1,600 bill before being caught using it in a Whitehaven supermarket. The police investigated and he was forced to reveal the truth to both women.

Stuart was given a year's probation after admitting fifty-seven credit-card offences. At a separate hearing last October he was unexpectedly sentenced to three months in prison for bigamy. He served six weeks, during which time he wrote a journal to try to help him sort out his own feelings. Two weeks before his release he decided he wanted to go back to Lynne.

'Eight years is a long, long time to do what I did and get away with it. My biggest regret is that I ever allowed the thing to escalate in the first place,' he said this week, in his first interview since his release. 'Perhaps I was weak. I was in that situation. I had to cope with it the best way I could. It's just that I didn't want to hurt anybody. I didn't want to hurt anybody. I didn't realise at the time I would eventually hurt people even more.

'I met Lynne quite by accident. We just got talking in this pub one night and we arranged to meet the next day. The relationship developed very quickly. We just fell head over heels for each other. I never set out for it to be that way. All the time I had been working away before I was never unfaithful and I never went looking for a relationship of any description.

'On our second meeting Lynne made it quite clear she would never go out with a married man, but by that time I realised I wanted her.' He told her he was divorced; the relationship took off almost immediately. Within six weeks he had moved in to the small Morecambe hotel she ran.

'Once I had told the first lie by saying that I was not married, the lies just escalated. One weekend I approached Pauline and asked her as a matter of interest how she would feel if I had found someone else. She was so emotional about it, I made light of the whole thing. She had done absolutely nothing wrong. I couldn't bear to hurt her. I still cared for her very deeply.

'Human nature being what it is, as no problem arose and everybody was happy, including myself. I couldn't find any reason to end either of the relationships.

'Even when I was in Morecambe with Lynne, I still used to phone Pauline every night on the way back from my shift. There were some emotional scenes. But with Lynne things just got better. They've never stopped getting better.

'There was the occasional thing that cropped up but nothing I couldn't lie my way out of. I had gone past the stage of being able to tell either one or the other the truth.'

After a couple of years, Lynne, a divorcee with two children, began to bring up the subject of marriage. For a while Stuart, now forty-seven, put it off; then in 1989, when they moved to an idyllic country cottage in the North Welsh village of Pontybodkin, it came up again. This time Lynne was adamant.

The date was set, the ring was bought. At the last minute the register office cancelled because of an overbooking. Saved by the hand of fate. A few days later, however, the office called back offering a slot the next day. Stuart was not there to consult and Lynne agreed. The next morning she put on the flowery suit she had bought in Penrith specially for the ceremony and they set off.

'As I was going to the register office I was racking my brains thinking, "What am I going to do"?' Stuart recalls. 'When we got there and they were asking me for all my details, I gave them a complete load of rubbish. I thought, "All right, I'm going to go through with it, but there's no way this can be legitimate because I've given them false information. I lied about my father's name and my date of birth. But Lynne was so happy, there was no way I could spoil her day. I was so desperate. It was the only way I could convince myself that everything would be all right".'

Everything was all right, for four years anyway. When the truth finally had to be confronted it was almost a relief. 'That's when the remorse came, when I started to feel the guilt and the hurt I had caused. For about three days I just lay on my bed. I couldn't eat, sleep or do anything. I don't think a person can go any lower than I did. I felt as though I wanted people to punish me as much as they could to try to cope with the guilt I was feeling.'

Lynne and Pauline were shattered. They both threw Stuart's clothes out of their houses and dumped all his possessions. 'I think I hated him then,' says Lynne, now forty-five. 'He had made me into a mistress. That's the one thing I hated. The marriage was a charade. I feel cheated for weeks after it happened.

'At that time I didn't want him back at all. I changed my mind when he was in prison. I knew I couldn't live without him. He was always the perfect husband, very kind, very understanding. That's why it happened. Because he wouldn't be unkind.'

Stuart is now back with Lynne and they are trying to rebuild their lives. She still wears his wedding ring; she is still called Mrs Freeman. 'It's hard to un-think being married. We'll do it again. Not a big church wedding, just a register office – a bit like *déjà vu*. But we won't rush into anything.'

Stuart's task now is to explain to his distraught first wife, his disgusted sons, who have cut him off, his bewildered mother, and the world, *why*. The answer is in the final words of his journal: 'Many will say I did it so I could have two women. They are wrong. Women may say I was weak and selfish. They too are wrong. Dual personality? No. A romantic womaniser? No. The reason is not as deep or profound as one might think. I simply loved two women in entirely different ways and could not hurt either.' •

Richard Neville
26 January 1994

·····

Bush blazes that inflamed the sex war

After twenty-five years of being battered by Women's Lib, the Australian male was a pathetic figure as he lurched into the new year. Fat, sedentary, ashamed and clumsy, he had lost his way – in the boudoir, in the office, in the locker room. (Female reporters asserted their right to enter footballers' dressing rooms.) Even sensitive guys were a mess; the ones who could mash carrots, make a stab at finding the G-spot and burst into tears when they couldn't find a parking space.

From the frontlines of social changes, women cited statistics to demonstrate their oppression, dumped the kids with 'dad' and dashed off for urgent meetings with yoga teachers, Tibetan llamas and hair colourists. Then the bushfires came.

The Missus got very quiet. We were holidaying by the sea, 400 kilometers south of our home in the Blue Mountains, when the fires hit the headlines. I was mopping the floor, flipping the pancakes and wondering if I should put my hair in rollers, when the call came through from the houseminder. 'Nothing to worry about,' came a tense voice. 'Funnels of black smoke on the horizon.'

That night, as I polished the bedroom mirrors and ironed the linen, I assured my wife it would take more than a few flames encircling our isolated home for me to abandon the family holiday, rush back and leave her alone with two children, her mother, several friends and supportive neighbours.

By Saturday morning, the fires had worsened. The houseminder had fled, the road to the mountains was closed, 'except to residents', and the 'Little Woman' started to worry about her photos, especially the ones of old boyfriends. 'I'll rescue them,' I said, jumping into her mother's delightful two-seater runabout, as 'My Better Half' – get this! – packed me a hearty lunch and a Thermos of coffee. Six hours later, after inching through police road blocks, I was zooming along the Great Western highway, wondering why all the traffic headed the other way, tugging trailers of furniture. Sirens blared, the sky was pink and ash blotted the windscreen. Maybe the whole state was on fire? On ABC radio, everything was normal. The *Coming Out Show* carried an in-depth report from the inner city on radical feminist Arabic poetry.

That night I slept alone, circled by a distant ring of burning cliffs. In the morning, my helpmate called from the resort to say that nearly a 100 houses had been lost overnight, and the experts advised homeowners to stay put and fight the inferno, but could I please first evacuate the wardrobe and pack her china? I put on big boots, a hard hat and plastic goggles. By nightfall, the house was fortified and my consort's bric-à-brac was stacked in the runabout. Just as I was about to take a breather, a gang of men in bright yellow overalls burst into the room and asked to borrow the tea towels. A mountain men's group? Pointing to a rapidly approaching sheet of flame, they wrapped the towels around their faces – as did I, feeling like a Lone Ranger, though not alone.

From then on, it was the whirr of water pumps, the screech of saws, the crackle of singed eucalyptuses. Soot tarred our flesh, smoke got in our eyes. We spat, we cursed, we lit a few fires of our own – strategic backburns – and we aimed our big long nozzles at the shimmering furs and flaring bush. A cock crowed, hoses spurted, intercoms crackled. Black-jacketed brigade captains with petrol torches melted into the thicket. The sun rose like a scarlet moon. The ground was black, the air was hot and a few ancient stumps blazed near the front door. The heavy machines and their minders moved on, but fire stalked the house from all directions.

Over the next four days, side by side with various local mates, I battled renegade blazes with wet sacks, shovels and a chain saw. I grew fond of my tea towel and catnapped in my boots. When winds gusted, Victorian tankers and their beefy crew arrived to stop the 'spotting', a term I hadn't heard since birth classes. Another worry was 'crowning' (flames soaring through tree tops), a word which also recalled the drama of parturition.

When the last tankers left, myself and a sequence of 'buddies' resumed hand-to-hand combat, as army helicopters criss-crossed the sky and flare-ups persisted. There was no time to answer the phone, wash our faces or rustle up a quiche. I barely slept for a week, and never felt better. All of us felt the same, even the ones who had attended classes in breast-feeding. None of us had seen a woman for – oh, months – and managed to refrain from expressing our sense of loss. A firefighter later reported his wife had shaved her legs, put on a dress and begged him not to wash off the soot. Then came the mopping-up, more fun than mopping. A neighbour, an apron-clad wimp who hosts the local playgroup, pleaded, 'Let's start our own fire brigade.' Us blokes scratched our designs for a scarf in the smouldering soil with flaming sticks.

When the Missus finally made it home, I was sprawled on the parquetry gnawing charred kangeroo tail, wearing nothing but a Lone Ranger tea towel. 'Chuck me a beer,' I snarled, burping. That was two weeks ago, and she is still under sedation. •

Suzanne Moore
17 June 1994

Taking the law into our own fists

I realise that cuffing is too good for them and I am out of sync on this one. Not many people may have bothered to vote in the European elections but they could be bothered to respond to every phone-in and opinion poll going on the case of Constable Steve Guscott, who was fined £100 for clipping a 'teenage tearaway' round the ear. Guscott has been overwhelmed by support from Texas, Sweden and Germany. Cash donations have been made and flowers sent to his wife.

If only John Major clouted a few delinquent ministers now and again, perhaps he could be this popular. Heroic even ... However much we might understand this policeman's actions, though, to excuse them is something else altogether. The man lost his temper. He hit a fourteen-year-old. To turn him into a model back-to-basics bobby is seriously misguided. Do you really want the police to go round beating up juveniles? Does that make you sleep more soundly in your bed at night?

According to every poll, it does. It is only because, according to the *Sun*, 'despite fifteen years of so-called Tory rule, the country is run by *Guardian* readers' and we have a 'soft-sentence society'.

All this is pretty desperate, as I imagine PC Guscott was when he struck the boy involved. It is a result of fear, of frustration and a sense that if our kids are out of control, then someone – if not parents and teachers – will have to take charge. The nation feels emotional about this and what we are seeing is an emotional rather than a rational reaction. No wonder, then, that talk of rights seems a load of bunkum to the catch-'em-and-clout-'em brigade.

Let's be realistic here, though. We are not talking about a collection of village bobbies who have known the children and their parents all their lives. We are talking about a modern police force which now argues that it is necessary to be armed. While I have sympathy for PC Guscott, I would like to ask his supporters a few questions, because surely if we are going to start salivating over the beating of children, let's do it properly, let's set some guidelines. How do you feel about public cuffings? How do you feel about equal opportunities in the clip round the ear stakes? Should the police hit girls as well as boys? Should it be done in the station or on the beat? Should parents be notified before or after? Before the officers concerned administer their short, sharp shocks, should they inquire about age? In other words, does size matter? Is eleven too young for a bloody nose? Perhaps police cars could carry around those measures they use in theme-park rides. Any youngster over and above a certain height would be liable for a clip round the ear.

It's a jolly business, all this. We make the beating of children sound so cosy – a clip, a clout, a box round the ears. No mention of blood, bruises and broken noses. But then, we make no mention of children either. Instead there are only those aliens – yobbos, tearaways, thugs and hooligans. They have no respect for the law and so we ask the law to somehow beat it back into them.

These boys – and it is mostly boys we are talking about here – are undoubtedly a menace. It is true that threatening them with physical violence works. Not, unfortunately, for very long or for everyone. I know. I used to work with adolescents in care. At sixteen, most of them had a string of offences to their name. Some of the male staff could get them to tidy their rooms or whatever by intimidating them. As a form of discipline, this was effective for about twenty minutes. It is that limited. And if these kids responded only to physical threats, how were the female staff supposed to deal with them?

A clip round the ear may make the person who did it feel better but let's not mistake that for a long-term solution to crime. If I thought it were that simple, I'd be out there with the coppers thumping every other suspect. Even *Sun* writers have to admit, begrudgingly, that this is not the way forward.

The law and order lobby has become synonymous with calls for tougher sentencing and harsher treatment of criminals. But there is another law and order lobby that is concerned with what is workable, what stops reoffending, what makes the difference between the wayward kids who spend a life in and out of prison and those who don't. It's easy enough, as you go around giving teenagers bleeding noses, to caricature my position as that of a bleeding-heart liberal. Yet it is also the position of a pragmatist who wants punishment that cuts down crime rather than punishment born of frustration. So if you call me a liberal again, I'll clout you one. •

Miscellany

Armando Iannuci

16 June 1994

Politics, paper bags and nasal penetration

few weeks ago I stood face to face with an Eminent Figure. He's a very
important man, and much in the public eye, but I cannot for the life of
me remember a single word he said, because I spent all my time mesmer-
ised by his nasal hair. It was a stunning tress, a single long, silken strand which
grew conventionally out of one nostril but which then, unconventionally,
swerved horizontally away from the nose and across the cheek for at least several
centimetres. I'm afraid I'm prevented from saying who he was since ultimately
I get quite a lot of work out of him, but I do assure you he is Very Eminent.

I spent the rest of that evening wondering why no one in this man's office ever
told him how ridiculous he looked (and this figure must have an office of at least
thirty staff, he's so Eminent) or, if they felt unable to tell him directly, why none
of his staff dropped him helpful hints. It wouldn't have taken much effort to
write into his Appointments Diary anonymous prompters like 'Gooseberry Face'
or 'You've got a big nasal hair growing across your head', but if they did, then
clearly he didn't take the point.

The interesting thing is that over the last year or so this Important Man has
had quite a bad press (I really wish I could tell you who he is, but disclosure
would probably ruin me) and I think I can see now how it happened: it's not
through anything he's done, but is a result of the awkward impression he's given
journalists who have met him, including myself (although I have the decency not
to name him). Unable to take him seriously in the flesh, and hair, they then rush
back to their laptops and slag him off on to a hard disk.

The big question I want to ask them is this: what effect has embarrassing facial
hair had on the course of history? If Richard Nixon had not forgotten to shave
one fateful day in 1959, he would not have looked like Boris Karloff on his
televised presidential debates with John Kennedy; Kennedy would not have
been elected or shot in the head; Jackie Kennedy would not have had to take her
suit to the cleaners; and Lee Harvey Oswald would probably today be a fat
video-store owner in Denver, Colorado.

Students of British politics may well be asking the same sort of question thirty years from now, since it's obvious the current race for the leadership of the Labour Party all boils down to hair. In the lead is the media favourite, Tony Blair, a smooth-shaven man with a baby's bottom for a head. Lagging far behind is Robin Cook, who, though acknowledged as the best parliamentary operator around, is felt to be massively handicapped by being the only man in the House of Commons to look as if an escaped animal has just sat on his face.

Image is everything, substance is chaff (though it amazes me that no one has yet paused to consider the implications of having a prime minister called Tony). Presentability is the only topic on any political agenda these days, but maybe for a good reason. It could be that the outcome of many a summit has been determined by the demeanour of the statesmen present. Maybe Gorbachev managed to push through so many changes because all his opponents were too busy staring at his forehead.

What irritating accidents of the body determine our future? Does Mitterrand have a tendency to dribble, or Kohl to breathe loudly through his mouth? I've never met Douglas Hurd (which thus rules him out of the Eminent Figure conundrum you've no doubt been running in your head) so I don't know whether his face is covered in blotches, pockmarks from his adolescence, stray hairs or dried-up spit, but I'm sure if we were all shown we would arrive at a better understanding of why he has had such a limited effect on negotiation with the Chinese over Hong Kong.

If we do want to run our affairs purely on the merits of policy and by the talents of politics' practitioners, then the only foolproof method of doing so is by making it compulsory for all politicians to wear paper bags over their heads, especially in the run-up to elections. This would surely lead to the emergence of sensible debate and intelligent *Newsnights*. It may be that the paper-bag solution ought to be applied to anyone who performs a major role in the public arena; it would certainly have deflected much of the criticism received by the Important Man with the fertile face I met recently. At the very least, it's an idea he may want to consider as he makes his way every morning into his office at the BBC. •

Pass Notes

18 March 1994 New Zealand

What is it exactly? A democratic country in the South Pacific 1,000 miles south-east of Australia.

What happened to Old Zealand? You mean Aotearoa, discovered by the Polynesians around 1,000 years ago?

That's the one: It got renamed in 1642 by a Dutchman called Abel Tasman, then claimed by James Cook in 1769.

Should we be interested? Well, it is part of the Commonwealth.

How nice for them! Amazingly, this proud island race would prefer to go it alone. Jim Bolger, the prime minister, wants New Zealand to become a republic by the year 2000.

What's the hurry? So Australia won't get there first.

What's the difference between New Zealand and a natural yoghurt? One's got a live culture.

National emblem: The kiwi (pictured above). An almost blind, flightless, nocturnal bird used in making boot polish.

The myth: A steamy quagmire, populated by morose, sexually repressed Europeans and cheerful, fecund Maoris, New Zealand is surrounded by glistening white beaches, on which grand pianos are often found by beachcombers.

The reality: Two mountainous islands, inhabited by 67 million sheep and a few human servants.

A kind of paradise, right? Wrong. Suicide rates for young males are the highest in the industrialised world, crime rates are soaring and the prison population is growing by 10 per cent a year.

New Zealand's gifts to the world: Katherine Mansfield, Janet Frame, mooning and barfly jumping.

Eh? Participants wear a velcro suit, bounce on a trampoline and compete to see who can stick himself highest to a Velcro-covered wall.

Is that it? Well, they were first with the welfare state, and introduced a national health service ten years before Britain. It all got a bit pricey so Mr Bolger's national government is now dismantling it.

You've forgotten the kiwi fruit: No, I haven't.

Some eminent New Zealanders: Dame Kiri te Kanawa, Jane Campion, Bryan Gould.

Where are they now? London, Sydney, London.

You've forgotten Keri Hulme: No, I haven't.

Will we miss it when it's gone? Not unless they stop exporting green-lipped mussels and Cloudy Bay Sauvignon Blanc. They can keep the Anchor butter.

Least likely to say: Rule, Britannia.

Most likely to say: Baaa, Baaa, Baaa.

Germaine Greer
24 January 1994

....

Why the young need their single ticket to freedom

T he day I left home was the happiest day of my life. I walked away from my parents' house, along narrow suburban pavements, beside nature strips both barbered and shabby, on to the railway station and into the brightest afternoon I had ever lived. I had no baggage but a briefcase and in it nothing but a gingham nightshirt, a paperback translation of *Metamorphoses,* a hairbrush and a sample bottle of Shocking by Schiaparelli. 'A *single* ticket!' I sang at the man in the ticket office. Even now, whenever I go a-wandering, I feel the warm afterglow of that afternoon.

If I was entitled to housing I had no knowledge of the fact. I didn't even know if I was eligible for the dole, and it never occurred to me to ask. I don't suppose I thought of a home of my own so much as somewhere to live. For years I lived in other people's houses. Sometimes, keeping the fact that I was at university under my hat, I worked as a housekeeper. Sometimes, I house-sat in properties that were to be pulled down or done up or sold. More than once I came 'home' to find my few belongings dumped unceremoniously on the pavement and the locks changed. But one day I found an empty hayloft at the back of a Victorian house near the university. The tenants in the house didn't mind whether I lived there or not. They accepted my rent of fifteen shillings, although they were not the owners.

My loft was only fifteen feet by eleven, the sole access was a trap-door in the floor, and the ventilation was a half-door that opened into a tree. It was freezing, it was insecure, it was perfect.

I bought an old cast-iron woodstove, strung a rope on the gantry and lifted it in. Somehow, I manoeuvred the illegal flue through the slate roof. I used to burn the hardwood blocks that were removed as the streets of Melbourne were mac-adamised; being impregnated with tar, they burned a treat. On the stove I kept a pot of stew, bunged in the least battered vegetables I could find after the market closed, and scrag ends of this or that fowl or sheep, and six-penn'orth of bones. Dozens of people survived on stew out of that pot, probably because of the antiseptic action of the red wine that we drank by the demijohn.

Whatever my abode was, it was not fixed. The owner could have thrown me out at any time. With no running water, no electricity but a single 40-watt bulb hanging from a rafter, bare brick walls, no ceiling let alone insulation, my home was unfit for human habitation. I was living in a shed and I liked it fine.

From the outside you would never have known that anyone lived there, which is why I was not turfed out as a fire risk or a health hazard or a lunatic. If I'd been gathered up and forced to return to my parents' clean, warm house, I would have gone berserk, beaten up my warders and thrown myself under a truck. I needed that space just as it was; perhaps I felt that I had proved I could survive in a crack in the consumer society. It didn't matter to me whether people classified me as beatnik or a loony as long as I could sit with my feet in the oven of the stove reading my book until I felt sleepy, and sleeping until I felt like waking up.

My parents made no attempt to find out what had become of me. I was both glad and bitter. I told myself, as children tell themselves now, that I need fell no remorse about running away and not letting them know where I was. If they'd wanted to know, the university could have told them. What I didn't realise (because, like all teenagers, I was totally self-absorbed) was that when a child does not fit in at home, the tension is felt by everyone. It was probably better for the rest of the family that I had taken myself off. It was certainly better for me. In my parent's house I was sleepless and nervous and suffered repeated bouts of bronchitis; in my loft I had to develop a resistance to respiratory and gut infections.

Why am I telling you this? Because I'm trying to get my head around the situation of the homeless young. I can see and feel with vividness that they need their space. It is not simply a matter of putting a roof over their heads, keeping them warm and dry and well fed, as if they were hamsters. They have bought their single ticket as I did that unforgettable, wonderful afternoon, the single ticket to freedom – and terror.

When you run away from home, your life changes from being a grind and having your head jumped on every hour of the day and night, to become a grim but exhilarating adventure. For some, probably most of us, it is a necessary preliminary to knowing yourself. You don't know what you can do until you are allowed to try. You don't know what shape a day is until you are allowed to fill it by yourself.

The efficient welfare state, which ours never was, eliminates risk and therefore eliminates adventure, which young people need as much as they need oxygen. To see the world is to make your fortune; your fortune may be to become rich and famous or to be annihilated or simply to survive to be a sadder and a wiser person. For too many of our children, drugs are the only adventure, travelling inside yourself and taking risks with yourself by yourself.

The ache in my heart when I see cold children sheltering in doorways is my problem, not theirs. The answer is neither to force them to go back to living with their parents, with more ill-feeling between them than ever, nor to shelter them in regimented housing, whether prison, hostel, B&B or the Ritz.

Not long ago the adventurous young could liberate buildings and experiment with all kinds of ways of living in them, both solitary and communal. Squatting used to be the adventurous option. Changes in the law have made it virtually impossible for our children to experiment in lifestyles in order to come to an understanding of themselves and what they want.

We have cemented up too many of the cracks in the consumer society. There is no room left to be free, before agreeing to step on the treadmill of debt slavery that is 'responsible' living in the 1990s. •

Richard Gott
18 April 1994

··

Whose D-Day is it anyway?

The Prime Minister, belatedly and under pressure, has summoned the nation to a celebration. The anniversary of the Normandy landings of fifty years ago is to provide the excuse for a splendid binge – 'Major Mobilises Britain for a Huge Tribute to D-Day Heroes', as the *Daily Mail* put it so succinctly in last week's headline. Street parties have been decreed, schoolchildren will be on parade, and so too will the stars of stage and screen, particularly the heroes and heroines of the nation's favourite soap operas. *Coronation Street, Brookside* and *Eastenders* (and doubtless the cast of *Neighbours* will be enrolled to provide an evocative Anzac angle).

On D-Day itself, 6 June, according to an eager reporter from the *Daily Express*, 'Dame Vera Lynn will give a concert with Bob Hope and other stars on the QE2 as it cruises in the Channel. Everyone will be able to join in as the Kilroy Television Company, owned by *Express* columnist Robert Kilroy-Silk, broadcasts the show live on BBC1.'

The *Sun*, meanwhile, has been anxious to do its bit, calling on its 'family of 12 million readers to mark the 50th anniversary of D-Day by holding a giant street party'. A marketing insert – 'Street Party Goodies offer' – advertises hats, flags, balloons and T-shirts ('one size baggy white cotton only'), and urges prospective organisers to hurry ('don't delay, you must allow 28 days for delivery').

So that's the fun and games; everyone likes an excuse for a party and a marketing opportunity, just as they like a free handout of British Telecom shares. Bread and circuses have always been a significant part of any government's armoury (and it's hardly necessary to point out that these junkets – state-encouraged but privately funded – will take place in the week before the European elections).

But what about the serious part? Who are these celebrations actually for? What is it that we are trying to remember? What are the lessons to be rediscovered? What exactly are we *celebrating?* And if we're soberly paying tribute to the valour and sacrifice of recently dead men – the husbands, fathers and grandfathers of people still alive – should we really be celebrating at all?

Across the Channel in Normandy, more than two dozen immense war cemeteries bear witness to the human cost: among them nearly 5,000 British graves at Bayeax; 9,000 American graves at Colleville-Saint-Laurent; 3,000 Canadian graves at Bretteville-sur-Laize-Cintheaux; 12,000 German graves at Huisnes-sur-Mer – a tiny proportion of those who died in the June invasion. Street parties? Is it surprising that the British Legion expressed its surprise over the weekend at the 'light entertainment' tone of the government's commemorative plans?

The Second World War occupies a unique position in British life in the twentieth century for the simple reason that traditionally we do not much mark its defeats or victories. It was a matter-of-fact kind of war. 'Give us the tools and let us get on with the job' was an early, workaday Churchillian appeal. It was a war tacitly supported by the entire nation, yet it did not arouse national passions. These were battles fought without party division: Clement Attlee, Labour's leader, was Churchill's deputy PM; Ernest Bevin, the boss of the dockers' trade union, kept the privatised mines at work; Sir Stafford Cripps, rather to the left of Tony Benn, tried to establish a close friendship with Stalin and to give India away. It was a war in which the left, for the only prolonged moment in this century, played a major part in the life of the nation – in government and on the battlefield.

When the war ended, there was little enthusiasm for building monuments to the fallen. Their memorial was to be the creation of a better society. No attempt was made to emulate the local cenotaphs put up after 1918 in every village and hamlet in the land. Fresh names were carved on the space remaining, or simple memorial stones added to the existing structure. No special day was set aside; annual solemn remembrance of the Second World War was simply tacked on to the agenda of Armistice Day on 11 November. Old combatants, of course, have held regular reunions, but for the most part these have been private affairs, with reminiscences exchanged and memories mulled over without much wider participation. Even wives and families have often been kept in ignorance of what really happened on that latter St Crispin's Day.

The Great War, for the British, remains the most shocking – and revolutionary – event of the century, endlessly recycled even today in film and fiction and historical reportage. Stories of Gallipoli and the Western Front, in particular, still have immense emotional power. This was the time when the youthful heads of the nation's élite were cut off like Flanders' poppies and when simple farmboys were dragged from their ancestral shires to die in foreign mud. These are the ineradicable images that survive of an unbelievably foolish endeavour, symbolizing a dramatic change in our national life. They marked the end of the patrician optimism of the nineteenth century and the start of something altogether darker, a foreshadowing of the horrors ahead.

By contrast, the events of the Second World War have made less of an impact on our culture, yielding few novels, poems or art works to match the production inspired by the earlier conflict. English fiction has always stuck chiefly to the home front, leaving the war stories to the Americans. And after the early congratulatory films – *The Wooden Horse, The Dam Busters* – British film-makers looked elsewhere for inspiration, as have others. Auschwitz and Hiroshima, rather than any particular drama in the West European theatre, remain the twin significant symbols that preside over the post-1945 world. But they have acquired a global rather than a purely national significance. For most British people born since 1945, the Second World War has been tucked away, largely forgotten, into a convenient part of the subconscious.

So when we are summoned to celebrate events we have been happy to quietly digest and think about over the last fifty years, without much additional fanfare, we are obliged at least to question the motives of the sponsors. John Major (aged fourteen months in 1944), to be fair, has been reasonable and restrained as usual, and Iain Sproat, the minister in charge of the government's jamboree, has been at pains to emphasise that it will be a 'commemoration' rather than 'a celebration'. Major spoke last week in civil service prose of his determination that 'the commemoration should reach out and touch all generations, especially the children of this country, so they would understand the part D-Day plays in the tapestry of our nation'.

This, of course, sounds splendid: here is an appeal to history, woefully neglected by the Conservatives in the Thatcher era. Indeed, Mrs Thatcher herself, with little sense of the importance of the past except as a (rather minor) prop to her otherwise unobstructed view of the present, clearly shared the sharp opinion of Henry Ford that 'history is bunk' (except when she was trying to force a particularly nationalist view of the past on to the national curriculum).

But Mr Major is made of more imaginative stuff. He emphasised last week that he would like today's children, when remembering D-Day, 'to have a sense of the event, a sense that what is being commemorated is not something static in the pages of a history book but something real and remarkable – of continuing relevance to us all'. He seemed to be laying down the ground rules for a national debate, to be inviting and encouraging us to discuss the past. What, then, is the 'continuing relevance' of the Normandy landings? What part, we may fairly ask with the Prime Minister's blessing, does D-Day really play in the great tapestry of the nation's history? Is it the warp or the woof – or does it form, after fifty years, part of a seamless, meaningless, whole? And what, more generally, are the lessons that we wish to draw from our wartime experience?

Traditionally, a thumbnail history of the Second World War designed for British consumption consists of four significant dates: Dunkirk, the Battle of Britain, El Alamein and D-Day – a battle lost, two battles won and a successful invasion of Europe. These were the dramatic wartime occasions from which personal memories were created – and then passed on to subsequent generations. Yet for historians, pondering over the course of the war, the first three events – when Britain 'stood alone' – have, already begun to fall by the wayside, proving to be mostly of parochial interest solely to the British. Other participating nations – the Russians, the Americans, the Italians and, of course, the Germans and the Japanese – have over the years, put other events closer to the top of their historical agenda. Stalingrad and Pearl Harbor, in particular, mark significant turning points of the war that all can recognise.

D-Day, however, remains the one iconic happening of that war – the start of the land invasion of the heartland of Europe from the west – that unites nearly all the participants in recognition of its peculiar global significance (even if some took a pardonable national advantage: 'This is the Battle of France, and it is France's battle,' General de Gaulle announced on the BBC on the evening of 6 June 1944). The Normandy landings seemed of dramatic importance at the time, and the passage of years has not altered that judgement.

Here the difficulties begin, for D-Day is both reality and metaphor; it is a dramatic and incomparable tale of individual and collective heroism, in which the British people rightly (if undemonstratively) still take pride, but it comes tightly coupled with the sharp realisation (growing ever more obvious over the years) that the invasion of Normandy marked the beginning of a definitive (and not altogether happy) break in the life of the nation – not so much a caesura as a change of direction.

The Prime Minister himself has recognised this difficult fact. D-Day, he said, 'changed our future'. But he put the comfortable gloss on the change that is today's easy piety: the Allied landings, he said, 'laid the foundations of the peaceful and free Europe we have today'. Such a phrase might happily have been used in most years since 1945, but in 1994 – as the warplanes wheel over Gorazde and the guns blaze out over the valleys of former Yugoslavia – it does not quite seem to hit the right tone.

Over the years there have been a variety of such simple formulations, for in every decade we have had to reassess what happened, and to ask again what was the result. In 1944, of course, the single, simple, limited justification for invasion was to assist in the defeat of Hitler's Germany. There was no other agenda, no subtext, nothing hidden. It was certainly not perceived as a battle for democracy, even though there was a strong sense that this might be the start of a new period in world history. Almost all survivors of that period, when pushed to remember, reflect on the closeness of comradeship, the absence of class conflict, the hope that a better future would be constructed from wartime co-operation. And it may be that John Major, with his curious evocations of that strange forgotten England – forever amber, forever Hovis – is hoping to recover that lost land, for himself or his party.

Yet it may be that here, too, he will come unstuck. For this is dangerous ground. D-Day at one level is a stirring tale of unparalleled drama, men and machines pitted against the ocean and the enemy on a gigantic scale. But 6 June 1944, is also, for the British, one of the more problematic dates of the twentieth century. In his D-Day speech last week Major spoke in the gardens of Grosvenor Square, in the shadow of the US embassy and within sight of the statue of General Eisenhower. It was an appropriate place to be. For the real importance of D-Day, as H. P. Willmott points out in his book *The Great Crusade* (Michael Joseph, 1989), was that it 'marked the emergence of the United States as the major power in Western Europe'.

Willmott, a lecturer at Sandhurst, goes on to recall that 'the American dimension to the Normandy landing represented the first invasion of Europe from the outside world for 590 years' – since Suleiman Pasha pushed across from Turkey into the Balkans in 1354, halting (with considerable prescience) at Gallipoli. Perhaps more significantly, the American involvement 'marked the end of the period of European supremacy in the world that had existed for four centuries'. Rather than being the centre of power, Europe henceforth would be 'the object of attention of those powers that would determine her fate'.

So there is an inevitable national sadness when we remember D-Day, not just for our fallen heroes but for our lost history. For the conservative right, it represents an end to national sovereignty, and end to empire, an end to a time when we could do things on our own, the beginning of our national decline. For the liberal left it recalls opportunities lost, utopian dreams unrealised, a world made anew that went badly wrong, the exchange of our national traditions for the Anglo-American culture that we experience today.

A closer understanding of the real historical significance of D-Day, by both left and right, might help us all to understand why this year's street parties seem so out of place, and why we have been so reticent to celebrate the Normandy landings in the past. For just as Dunkirk was a defeat that we made sound like a victory, D-Day may well seem to future historians like a victory that we turned into a defeat. •

John Ezard
21 April 1994

Spam and flimflam

Human character often shows itself more clearly in parish pump affairs than in great world crises. So it is with the case of John Major and the D-Day Spam fritters disaster.

In only seven days, through a combination of right motives, wrong motives, opportunism and incoherence, he and his advisers – pre-eminently Sir Tim Bell – have brought themselves to within an inch of having to call off the only substantial event in their D-Day programme, a Family Day for 300,000 people in Hyde Park. Yet they happen to be innocent of all the sins of which the Royal British Legion and others accuse them.

Their real sin has been trying to assume the credit for other people's work. All they have managed to assume is the blame. I first spotted something amiss at the programme's launch, when like dozens of other journalists I was handed an eighty-page press release headed Commemorative Events in the UK. This bore the crests of Sir Tim and the Heritage Department.

Yet its contents were virtually identical to a *Guardian* office file I had been accumulating for more than a year. It simply relisted the sing-songs, knees-ups, museum displays, church services and other D-Day-linked shenanigans which local councils, tourist boards and voluntary groups have spent nearly two years devising.

These events – some reverent, some purely concerned with Spam fritters – are nothing to do with the Heritage Department's planning team, which started work only in December, or Sir Tim, who got the PR contract in January. Yet in their speeches Mr Major and the heritage minister, Iain Sproat, hoovered them all up into their programme: 'Over 500 events have been planned all over the UK.' Mr Major even annexed the *Sun's* mistimed call for street parties, though he did credit the paper for the idea.

Though less then honest, the attempt to pad out the government programme was understandable. Its own contribution – the family day, a memorial garden and a schools pack – would otherwise have looked desperately threadbare.

But God's punishment was immediate. Virtually all the media took the government's word and credited Mr Major for fritters, knees-ups and even street parties. The wrath of the veterans descended.

Mr Sproat has tried to deflect it by belatedly stressing the distinction between the national and local programmes. Here he fell foul of my colleague Patrick Wintour's disclosure yesterday that in March Sir Tim sent local groups a list of suggested events.

Sir Tim's staff, with £62,000 fees to justify, might well like to portray that as 'central co-ordination of events'. But by March it was too late to start organising virtually anything. All Sir Tim achieved with his list was to look busy. That instinct has been the doom of this whole small and ludicrous but instructive affair. •

Boring in the gloaming

ines on the present state of the Church of Scotland

(With apologies to William McGonagall)

Alas! The sad decline of a
God-fearing race
Is reported from Edinburgh, that
fine bonny place.
Where a panel of elders of
Scotland's church
Have decided following lengthy
research
That the reason why some of their
flock take to snoring
Is because so many of their
sermons are too boring.

Alas! Sad decline of the once
thoughtful Scots.
Whose ancestors liked little more
than to listen to lots
Of advice from their ministers
laden with gloom
Though some more enlightened
ones preferred David Hume
Who provoked his listeners to
rather more smiles
Than the grim-faced folk
preaching in St Giles.

Alas! What has become of
Scotland's good kirk
That it is now felt needful to
preach with a smirk

Because of the modern world's
congenital antipathy
To ministers whose talent for
stirring up apathy
Has nevertheless brought the
word of the Lord
To several generations of Scots,
most of them bored.

Alas! That the elders of the
General Assembly
Should feel tradition's hold to be
so trembly
That the Church of Scotland
should now have gone sour
On a style which once gloried in
being so dour
And feel that the Gospel should
now be communicated
By means which in the past
would have led them to be
excommunicated.

Alas! Rue the April day in
Nineteen Hundred and Ninety-Four
When the honourable title of
awful Scots bore
Was applied where it never has
been before
Which has made many ministers
feel very sore.
So let this proposal be shown the
kirk door
And of interesting sermons let us
hear no more.

John Vidal
12 March 1994

Take a few pigs along to the Pie in the Sky café and watch payment go bob-bob-bobbin' along

Siobhan Harpur cut someone's hair the night before last and 'earned' herself seven bobbins. She was given a note and her bobbin account was credited on a computer. It went towards 'paying' for her hall, which David Harris painted (very nicely, thank you) some weeks ago for 100 bobbins.

Meanwhile her daughter Cara earns bobbins making the tie-dyed shirts and young Kelvin spends them on lifts to concerts. The whole family could be deep in bobbin debit – it isn't, actually – but Siobhan Harpur would not particularly mind. 'Being in debit could be seen as a social favour,' she says, 'because to be in debit is to create wealth in the bobbin system.'

Siobhan is serious. She works at the National Museum for Labour History and the bobbin is a year-old but fast-growing Manchester unit of currency. You can earn them doing anything that any one of the 330 people in the Manchester local exchange trading scheme, or 'Lets', wants. You can spend them on anything they offer.

The Pie in the sky Café in Withington now takes bobbins in part exchange for meals. Otten and Skemp, solicitors, encourage them, Lyn Woolry offers her vegetarian cookery, and Mrs Bend bakes bread. 'It's a super idea,' says Bob Merrall, who tiles. ' I'm inundated with work from the scheme.'

Cashless trading via local exchange currencies is the local rage. This, some social analysts suggest, is a product of the do-it-yourself culture now rife in grassroots Britain. Whether it has something to do with the recession, or lack of confidence in authorities, is immaterial: the practical result is that Bath now has its 'olivers', Scunthorpe its 'pigs', Swindon its 'dons', and Reading (you get the idea) its 'readies'. There are 'acorns' being traded in Totnes, 'cockles' in Exmouth, and 'solents' in Southampton. Most have rough parity to sterling.

Two years ago there were five local currency schemes in Britain, but now, says Liz Shephard, co-ordinator of the national network, there are 200. Even she does not know how many are operating. The largest have more than 300 members, the smallest just a handful. A pamphlet out next week from the think-tank Demos suggests their spread could even help solve unemployment.

Those trading in what Jonathon Porrit calls 'the manic minusculism' of local currencies swear it is better than money. There is undisguised glee at the parallel economies being created (to the discreet consternation of the Inland Revenue, which is watching their development closely). There is fervour at the social possibilities, and messianic hope that, if people really catch on, local communities could wrest back some power from unaccountable banks, supermarkets, chancellors and the infernal, mysterious supranational economics system.

Fat chance, perhaps, but the theory is simple enough. To understand it, says Shephard, you should wipe crude notions such as sterling out of your mind. Lets are no more than self-help initiatives, simple non-profit-making schemes that allow people to trade their goods and skills whether or not they have money.

'The currency is simply recorded information. Since it's always available for trade, interest cannot be charged,' she says. 'Do you know hidden interest amounts to more than one third of UK spending?'

A local currency, moreover, stays local. 'It cannot leak away from a community or be used to bring imports from across the globe. It's an incentive to stop locally, use local services, and cannot be used for money-market speculation. Cash-flow problems can't exist as the supply of Lets perfectly follows the supply of goods.'

The implications, says the theorists, are enormous. In a cash-starved economy (one in five British households is severely in debt), despite the existence of wealth in the form of skills and resources, traditional exchange is hijacked by a lack of cash. With local currencies, as long as people make their goods and skills available, their exchange can just go round and round. 'The community therefore becomes richer,' says Paul Ekins, a green economist.

A good sales pitch, but does it work? 'We haven't even scratched the surface,' says Harry Turner, an art teacher from Warminster in Wiltshire. 'We've got 330 members in the scheme and are probably not even turning over in a year what the average shop does in a month. But it restores people's faith in each other, links them, helps them. It's a human way of trading skills and services.'

The scheme is called Tradelink and is growing by the day. Now three years old, it includes qualified midwives, car mechanics, carpenters, ironers, clothes repairers and electricians. Mrs Mathew offers her horse trailer for twenty-five 'links' a day. That's just about what Beverley Kenyon asks for looking after a dog for a week, or what Roger Perks will want for a week's hire of his tent.

Harry Turner was living in Lanzarote until he went to Warminster a couple of years ago and found himself in the Lets national co-ordinating office, Letslink UK, which has been besieged by 27,000 inquiries in the last year. He is hooked, and says about one sixth of his personal economy operates via links. 'The Thatcher years have taken the humanity out of doing business,' he says. 'So much trading is depersonalised now. You go to the shops and don't talk to anyone. This way you are directly exchanging your skills and goods; you are individually creating a currency.

'Because the currency is local it isn't owned by anyone. No cheques can bounce so no one gets unhappy. There's no sense in accumulating units to use as power. It's a saner, more equable way of organising an economy.' Harry feels he has understood economics for the first time in his life. Happy Harry.

Siobhan Harpur's Manchester group has attracted businesses, professionals, creative people, the unemployed. It is now one of the largest in Britain: 'People feel this loss of neighbourliness. Lets gives them a tangible way to be neighbourly. It's a way of getting to know people, but it's not just a social circle. People are trading skills and resources so there's a productive, positive relationship.' She helps organise trading meetings in local halls – 'trading usually increases immediately afterwards'.

Harry Wearts of Haverfordwest is a cabinetmaker, and runs the only school, he says, which will take seventy-five-year-olds and teach them to turn out a *chaise-longue*. There are sixty members in his Lets group, ranging from accountants and osteopaths, to the unemployed. It is growing rapidly and crosses all social classes.

'Assume I have a chair,' he says ' if you gave me a "cheque" for fifty "lets" [the Haverfordwest local currency] it could not possibly bounce. No one loses anything by the deficit incurred. It's your deficit, that's all. There's no interest charged, no fixed time to pay; the liability just sits there in a book or a computer. Lets can't be stolen or borrowed; you can't use them outside your area, so there's an inbuilt trust. It doesn't matter if you're in credit or deficit.'

Wearts, who moved to the Welsh borders ten years ago, is negotiating with the Co-Op to try and get them to buy local food produce with lets and sell it back for lets. They like the idea, but the technicalities are horrendous. He sees endless possibilities for local authorities, hard-up businesses considering laying people off, or those just starting. His grand plan is to take a vandalised local school and restore it, via the Lets economy, into a day nursery – staffed by people being paid lets. The local authority is interested.

The list of initiatives is huge. In many cities there are several groups, each with its own ethos. There is one investigating paying a farmer in local currencies to grow the vegetables they want; Wales has a Lets pub; Scottish Pensioner Power is hoping to set up six systems; the Lightmoor community on the edge of Telford managed to get the first community mortgage to build fourteen houses on the basis of their 'sweat equity'. The Manchester group has turned down a £10,000 grant, preferring to convert it to a loan and pay it back over ten years in bobbins. In Stroud, one of Britain's largest trading communities, with more than 300 members, there are architects, market traders, hairdressers, and every shade of alternative therapists.

'It's the local multiplier effect, so is a tool for local regeneration,' says Ed Mayo, director of the New Economics Foundation. He is part of a new London scheme and (there being no great rush for economists in Greenwich, London SE10) bakes bread for a local currency. 'There's a parallel with the [small is beautiful] Schumacher dictum on appropriate technology – that Third World countries have the labour resources but not the capital, so the technology needed should reflect that.

'With mass unemployment in Britain many people have the time but not the cash. Lets gives them access to things they would not otherwise have.'

A Third World in west London? Nicola Cairncross, a former fashion designer, certainly has no capital and appropriate technology for her would be a shiatsu massage, a facial and a clean flat. In the sterling world of bank managers and pay cheques, she should be slapped on the wrist for even considering them: she has just started a business and is cash-poor.

A few weeks ago she proposed the 'bello' (as in Portobello). She has been overwhelmed with people wanting to trade or just make contact. Next week the bello goes local. Anyone want to learn Spanish cooking or how to set up a record company? •

John Perkin
11 April 1994

One down, thousands more to go

Solving – and setting – crossword puzzles is a sort of intellectual jogging – it keeps the parts moving that need to be kept mobile. It can be very beneficial: some *Guardian* solvers have been centenarians; perhaps some still are. Crossword-setters, like lexicographers and orchestral conductors, also seem to be a long-lived bunch. The *Guardian* has some in their seventies, as well as some in their twenties.

The crossword was devised by Arthur Wynne, a Liverpudlian émigré to America, in 1913 and his puzzles were published in the *New York Sunday World* for ten years before the craze took on there. They were called word-crosses until a printer's error made it into 'cross word', which seemed a better idea. The first recorded use of the word is 1924.

In the US two young men just out of Harvard, Robert Simon and Lincoln Schuster, brought out a book of fifty simple puzzles. They sold three quarters of a million copies in the first year. Simon and Schuster, the publishers, have not looked back.

There was a lot of sniffery from eggheads and traditionalists – even the editor of the *Sunday World* thought crossword puzzles 'beneath a sensible man's consideration', though he continued to run them. Doctors were dubious. Some said the grids could damage your eyesight, others believed there was a risk of 'developing neurotic traits through frustration'. This was borne out when a man shot his wife when she would not help him to solve a puzzle.

Magistrates in New York ruled that crossword addicts who spent so much time on puzzles that they neglected their families should be rationed to two a day. On one occasion a dinner party refused to leave a restaurant at closing time because they were so absorbed in a book of crosswords. They landed up in court and were delighted to be jailed for ten days as it meant they could finish the puzzles undisturbed.

The first crossword to appear in a British newspaper was in November 1924 in the *Sunday Express*. It was such a success that other papers started running puzzles. Prime Minister Stanley Baldwin was said to prefer spending his time on crosswords to Cabinet meetings – they were probably those in the *Daily Telegraph*, which started in 1925. The *Manchester Guardian* followed with a weekly puzzle in 1929, and *The Times* started in 1930, giving the job of producing the first ones to Adrian Bell, who had never before solved a puzzle, let alone devised one. He had ten days' grace. He went on to produce more than 4,000 over fifty years.

The first *Guardian* puzzle gave a hint of the way clues would develop. 'A river in Russia and a gentleman in Spain' for Don is edging towards the cryptic clue. This was given a spurt by Edward Mathers (1892–1939), who took the pen-name Torquemada, after the Spanish inquisitor, when he started puzzles for the *Observer*. He found definition clueing bland and boring, and in 1926 began the series of crosswords that showed off his literary knowledge and versifying skills.

At the same time, Alistair Ferguson Ritchie (1887–1954), Afrit of the *Listener*, was developing his own brand of cryptic puzzles, followed by D. S. MacNutt (1902–71), Ximenes of the *Observer*, who codified a set of rules for crossword construction and clueing that has become the touchstone for many of today's setters. These are best summed up: 'You need not mean what you say but you must say what you mean.'

And as Pasquale of the *Guardian* (Don Manley) puts it: 'The solver who follows the structure of a clue literally should expect to discover a grammatical set of coded instructions leading to the answer. A crossword clue is rather like a mathematical sum. The symbolism must be fair to lead the solver to the correct answer.' The aim, after all, is to entertain by creating a solvable mystery, and it is done by using words deviously and often without their apparent meaning.

Every word in a clue must be examined and sentences taken to pieces. Does 'does' for instance, imply action, or does it mean cheating ('I've been done'), or does it mean female deer? Clues normally require some sort of defining element, but this can be misleading in itself – 'Scot on hill changes into middle gear' gives 'loincloths', where 'changes' indicates the anagram of 'Scot on hill', and 'middle gear' provides the definition.

Many compilers make some sort of recognition of the Ximenean canon but recognise that it can lead to heavily plodding, pasteurised puzzles. Araucaria – John Graham – thinks Ximenean fundamentalism a great mistake: 'There is no law which says we must follow his guidelines exactly.' In *One Across*, the monthly subscription crossword magazine, he set out his own attitude: 'Speaking for the ordinary compiler, I have to say that our aims are different [from those of Ximenes-type puzzles]. It is not a question of difficulty – our puzzles are no doubt easier than Ximenes's own, or his successor Azed's – but the point is that we don't normally aim to use rare words. I allow them only if the requirements of the puzzle are such that nothing else will fit (or sometimes if an exceptionally attractive clue can be had). . .'

Don Manley is a card-carrying Ximenean and his put-down of Araucaria in his *Chambers Crossword Manual* as 'a setter who shows great flair in his puzzles but who is by no means a strict Ximenean in his cluemanship' brought howls of rage from Monkey-puzzler devotees.

'Nothing short of outrageous,' snorted Hornblower in *One Across*. 'The invariable characteristic of an Araucaria puzzle is the imparting of sheer delight to the solver, manifested in an audible chuckle or an admiring shake of the head at the ingenuity of the finest mind in the business. There is usually, too, the satisfaction of actually completing it, for there is never the frustration inflicted by some other compilers when you want to kick the damn thing round the room. Nor do you ever fill in an answer without knowing why, a heinous compiling fault. There is wit and erudition lightly borne; and above all scrupulous fairness about the clueing.'

He condemns 'this nonsense from the Oxford Mafia' about Ximenean rules. 'The solver knows instinctively whether the setter has been fair or not: we don't need a Department of Ximenology to tell us.'

John Graham has been sending puzzles to the *Guardian* since 1958. Like many crossword setters, his interest was stirred in childhood. He was nine when he and his parents used to share *The Times* crossword puzzle and make up small crossword puzzles of their own involving cryptic word play. After Cambridge and wartime RAF service, he became a curate in south London, thus starting a thirty-year ministry. Long retired, he lives in a Cambridgeshire village and his puzzles emerge out of a continuous process – an idea may come to mind and lie dormant for several weeks, before germinating and bearing fruit.

Araucaria's puzzles in the *Guardian* first roused Enigmatist's interest in a new style of crossword. John Henderson started solving puzzles at the age of seven, when his parents were *aficionados* of the *Daily Mail* and *Daily Telegraph* cryptics. He compiled his first puzzle at ten and his first *Guardian* puzzle was published when he was fifteen. Now twenty-nine and a lecturer in psychology in London, he remains the paper's youngest setter.

The longest-serving contributor is Ruth Crisp (Crispa). Her first *Manchester Guardian* puzzle appeared in 1954. A former civil servant, she is still fully occupied producing puzzles from her eyrie in Westcliff-on-Sea for the *Guardian*, *The Times*, the *Daily Telegraph* and the *Financial Times*. She is one of a small band of people who produce puzzles for a living.

Another, who holds the Guinness Book of Records award for the world's most prolific compiler, is Roger Squires (Rufus) – he passed his millionth clue in 1989, and claims more than 40,000 published puzzles. He joined the Royal Navy at fifteen and started making up puzzles when time lay heavy at sea. Once a comedy-magician and actor, he now has a production line going from his home overlooking the Severn at Iron Bridge.

He could not do this without a comprehensive filing system. There are, after all, a limited number of ways of clueing a word and some repetition is almost unavoidable.

Fawley is Mike Laws, who, after classics at Cambridge and twenty years teaching, now enjoys life as a postman with time to devote to his passion for crosswords. He regards Ximenes as an 'impeccable tutor – you have to know the rules before you can bend them'.

Alec Robins, Custos, is a founder member of the Ximenean school. He regards the rules as he would regard the grammar of a language (he taught classics in Manchester for many years) – that there is a right way, and only one right way, of doing things.

Among other *Guardian* setters who have taken Ximenes on board are Frank Blakesley (Janus), a retired civil servant who started making puzzles out of boredom in 1941 while he was stationed with an artillery unit in Caithness, and Eric Burge (Quantum), of Cheltenham, was a psychics lecturer before becoming principal education officer for Gloucestershire county council.

Like Burge, Don Manley studied physics at Bristol University and they both had their first puzzles published in *Radio Times* – as did Roger Squires and Ruth Crisp. Don Manley ('the Oxford Mafia') has been in publishing for over twenty years and, as well as puzzles for the *Independent*, contributed 'advanced cryptics' to the *Listener* since 1976.

A lapsed Calvinist upbringing led Bunthorne's Robert Smithies – formerly a *Guardian* photographer, later with Granada Television – to devise for a Belloc quotation, 'I forget the name of the girl, but the wine was Gevrey-Chambertin', the eventual anagram: 'High vintage, memorable yet: but fie! for the wench, I regret, wasn't.' Bob has a good cellar.

John Young is Shed. He was born in 1959 to a crossword-loving family, his mother being a *Guardian* compiler, Audreus. He worked as a rep and tour guide in Spain, Austria and Morocco before teaching English to unemployed Dresdeners. He is now doing a Ph. D. in German history at Sheffield and living with 'his most vicious critic'.

Ken Guy (Mercury) is another who started composing puzzles in the forces, as a wireless operator in the Middle East. This came in useful when a heart attack forced him to take early retirement from banking at the age of fifty. He now sets about fifteen cryptic puzzles a month for various publications.

Bert Danher (Hendra) has been making a living from crosswords since 1977, with puzzles for the *Guardian*, *Daily Telegraph*, *Financial Times*, *Independent* and *The Times*. He, like Bunthorne, has a liking for self-defining anagrams such as 'A pure N. W. Somerset resort' for Weston-Super-Mare. He used to be a peripatetic music teacher and still plays the French horn in amateur orchestras (a recent Araucaria clue for French horn was 'cor!'). He works from the Wirral. A cousin is Paul McCartney, whose father used to tell the singer to tackle crosswords to increase his word power.

Logodaedalus is Don Putman, who took early retirement from a Royal Ordnance works in Lancashire. His first serious puzzles were published in the *Listener* and the *Birmingham Post* in the late 1960s. He now takes up to twenty hours to complete and document crosswords for the *Guardian*, much longer if the clues are written in rhyming couplets.

Michael Curl – Orlando – takes twelve hours or so to set a *Guardian* puzzle but jots down clues as they occur to him. A computer software developer in Leeds, he is among the most succinct of clue-writers.

Gordius, the Rev. David Moseley of Devon, now is the only full-time clergyman on the *Guardian* team. He began reading the *Manchester Guardian* in the 1940s while a schoolboy, progressed to solving the crossword years later and eventually to constructing them. As examples of economical clues he cites O (8,6) for 'circular letter' and B (6,6) for 'bottle opener'.

Gemini is the byline for Vincent McLachlan and Walter Reid, who met as maths masters in Belfast. 'For us, the fascination of the crossword was, and still is, its strict economical use of language allied to its essential logic.' The day could run smoothly, they say, after they had completed the 'top three' in the dailies over coffee before classes began.

Time taken to finish a puzzle depends, obviously, on how difficult it is and who is trying to solve it. There is a legend that a woman in Fiji took thirty-four years to finish a *Times* crossword but the story is spoilt by the fact that it was from an old newspaper used for packing.

Guardian puzzles go to distant places, and a reader of the *Courier-Mail* in Queensland claimed to have finished one in two minutes twenty seconds – it must have been a very easy one. A provost of Eton was said to time his egg, however, by the time it took to solve his daily puzzle, and it was presumably lightly boiled. P. G. Wodehouse reacted to this by complaining: 'To a man who has been beating his head against the wall for twenty minutes over a simple anagram, it is gall and wormwood to read a statement like that one.'

The late John Sykes, who regularly won the national crossword puzzle championships, needed about half an hour to solve puzzles by Fidelio (Tony Fontaine), compared with ten to twelve minutes for others – entries for Fidelio puzzles are generally a hundred or so, when Custos or Araucaria will bring in thousands.

Alan Clarke, the right-wing Conservative, is not your typical *Guardian* reader, but he records in January 1991: 'Time lies on my hands, I spend much of it with Alison and we do the *Guardian* crossword in the cafeteria.' On another occasion he might have come up against a *Guardian* clue, 'Lacking resolve, Tories rule badly', which produces 'irresolute'. Sometimes clues can be superbly on the ball. •

Centipede
11 March 1994
....
Didn't he do well?

Wakey, Wakey! Hello, playmates! Can you hear me, Mother? Hello, good evening and welcome. Put your hands together now, please, and let's hear it for your very own Centipede – who he? I haff vays of making you remember the catchprases of your worst nightmare. I'm going to make you an offer you can't refuse, so come on down! Are you sitting comfortably? Then I'll begin. I thengyou!

I've started, so I'll finish. Yes, Christmas has come early this year, so do not adjust your set. Pin back your lugholes, and before your very eyes, before you can say Jack Robinson, we'll have some close encounters with those strangely compelling clichés, slogans and sayings that we use all the time, and no doubt will continue to use until we are not a million miles away from the end of civilisation as we know it. Good game? Nice one, Centipede. A nice little earner too – I should cocoa! Well, I would say that, wouldn't I?

What do you think of it so far, on a scale of one to ten? Gordon Bennett, you ain't seen nothing yet! Hold the front page as we name the guilty men: the Mr Bigs of advertising, speechwriting, film screenplays and television game shows who foist upon us these awful substitutes for spontaneous thought and the exercise of our vocabularies. The buck stops there.

Unaccustomed as I am to taking a stand against anything, let us say to these hackneyed wordsmiths: thus far and no further. Not tonight, Josephine. It's a free country (although the Queen rules – OK?); we shall overcome – we shall not be moved. When the going gets tough, the tough get going. Put a sock in it, fellas. Even if every newly minted *bon mot* is in the best possible taste, it soon becomes flavour of the month. In a trice they're calling it the greatest thing since sliced bread, but the fact of the matter is it's just another nail in the coffin of life's rich pageant.

And yet, dearly beloved, 'twas ever thus. Catchphrases are not a phenomenon of the latter half of the twentieth century. There's nothing new under the sun. It's just that today there's a line for all seasons, and whole conversations can be conducted by a ritual exchange of clichés. (Anyone for tennis, by the way?) Eat your heart out, original thinking! What a way to run a language.

And now for something completely different – because, when all's said and done, what's up, Doc? Maybe it's just the way the cookie crumbles, and all is fair in love and advertising copywriting. It's just one of those things – and after all language is a living organism, constantly evolving simply because it is there, so maybe we should just suck it and see.

We may blanch now at the utterances of those who don't appear to be aware how many beans make five, but sometimes in the dim and distant we may look back through rose-coloured spectacles and look on these as the happiest days of our lives. It could be a case of who dares, wins. So good on yer, hackneyed wordsmiths of the modern era. Here's looking at you! Who loves ya, baby! More power to your elbow! May the force be with you! Break a leg!

Ah well, onwards and upwards, as the bishop said to the actress. Just when you thought it was safe to forget about the whole shooting match, a man's gotta

do what a man's gotta do — Centipede must decree which of these vapid utterances is the best, or worst, which is much the same thing. That, not to be the
economical with the truth, is the sixty-four thousand dollar question. They're all
very interesting, but stupid — or maybe it's the way I tell 'em.

Anyway, no more Mr Nice Guy. When it comes to the scores on the doors at
this particular moment in time, the one they're calling Mr Big with regard to
this one is none other than Bruce Forsyth, who is responsible for more of these
empty creations than any other living being. We'll pick a card, any card, and go
for 'Nice to see you — to see you … nice!' Catchy, meaningless, utterly vacuous
and yet deeply insidious. That'll do nicely. What say you? Am I right or am I
right? Watch this space. Hit me with a 'True, O king' or a 'You cannot be
serious', but please, not a 'No comment', Go ahead — make my day! And now:
it's goodnight from me, and it's goodnight from him. •

Martin Walker
28 February 1994

···

Major on sticky wicket with plan to cap special friendship

President Bill Clinton does not yet know this, but by this afternoon he will
be the rather baffled owner of a Surrey County Cricket Club cap. This
gift has been chosen for him personally by John Major, who is very proud
of his ingenuity, and thinks this curious bit of headgear is just the thing to cap,
as it were, the formal reconsecration of the rather sickly 'special relationship'
which Bill and John will doggedly celebrate over the next forty-eight hours.

Mr Major thinks the present of a cricket cap of his favourite county team is a
spiffing wheeze because his last such offering worked so well. When he came to
stay with the late lamented George Bush at the family summer home on the
Maine coast at Kennebunkport, Mr Major proudly handed his host a cricket bat.

You can see the way his mind works. Next time, a nice white cricketing
sweater, and then a little red leather ball, and doubtless as Mr Major dreams of
future elections won and future presidents visited, there will be a set of batting

pads and some nice white flannels. He'll have the entire White House kitted out for a test match before he's done, electorates and Tory rebels permitting.

This business of prime ministerial gifts should not be taken lightly. A great deal of diplomatic effort has gone into this week's present. The British Embassy here was asked for its thoughts on what might make a suitable token of personal esteem. Nothing too expensive, lest it embarrass the Americans, who have rather strict rules about this sort of thing. Any gift from a foreigner worth more than $225(around £150) has to go to the National Archives – which is why Mr Bush's only personal memento of Mikhail Gorbachev is some Russian Christmas tree ornaments.

Something both intimate and useful was called for, hinting at the consideration that had gone into the choice. The embassy, which knows Mr Clinton loves crosswords, thought that some British crossword books would be just right, so long as they were chosen to be neither so hard that the President would be frustrated (that lets out Ximenes), nor too easy.

One book each of the collected crosswords from the *Guardian*, *The Times*, the *Daily Telegraph* and *Sunday Express* should bracket the target nicely. Oh yes, and a Chelsea Football Club shirt for the First Daughter, Chelsea. A nice touch, so long as nobody remembers the curious habit of one of Mr Major's former ministers for wearing Chelsea soccer strip at romantic moments.

Then Mr Major intervened with his cricket cap wheeze. Consternation at the Foreign Office. Did anybody know whether Bill Clinton had ever shown the slightest interest in cricket in his Oxford days? Had he played the game? (The answer is no.) Had he ever watched it? (Yes, but only in passing, and with baffled amusement.) Had he ever expressed any opinion on our national sport? (Yes, he frequently observed that it was very boring. The kindest thing he ever said was that any game that lasted five days was unlikely to grip the American imagination.)

The question began to float: was a cricket cap quite the right thing? Had Mr Clinton ever showed any interest in any other sports that would not inspire distasteful speculation about Mr Clinton's fondness for astroturf in the back of his pick-up trucks? At this point the *Guardian* came to the rescue. Was her Majesty's government aware that Mr Clinton had played rugby at Oxford? (No.) He loved the game, playing second row forward, sometimes for the University College First XV, more often for the second team, and trained and turned out regularly for two years.

Diplomatic wheels began to churn. Could a University College rugby shirt be acquired, size extra large? Yes, from the college buttery, or from the Lyle and Scott, in Broad Street, Oxford. Doubtless one could be ordered by phone, and delivered to Downing Street in time for Mr Major to take it to Washington.

British eyes began to gleam. Mr Clinton, being an affable and considerate chap, always likes to honour people who give him T-shirts by wearing them for his morning jogs. Nothing could better symbolise the vigorous health of the special relationship than the televised image of John Major handing the President a college rugby shirt, followed by scenes of Mr Clinton's robust frame sporting the thing as he trotted round the Washington monument the next morning.

But John Major being John Major, I fear that if the Thoughtful Gifts department of the Foreign Office gets its act together and ensures that Mr Clinton is lucky enough to jog in his old college rugger shirt on Tuesday morning, he will be expected to top off the British nostalgia look with a Surrey County Cricket Club cap. We know that a passion for Monty Python remains one of the most enduring of the cultural ties binding Bill Clinton to Britain, but making him look like the man from Ministry of Silly Hats could test his good will a brim too far. •

Paul Foot
28 February 1994

A frenzy of goodness

'The homosexual way of life,' says Douglas Hogg, minister of state, out loud, in public, on *Question Time*, 'is less satisfactory.' That's the kind of ministerial statement which makes you reach for your dictionary. 'Satisfactory (adj.): satisfying expectations or needs'.

Mr Hogg, QC, is a careful man who measures his words, and it is inconceivable that he would assert something without proof. Presumably he has tried out the 'homosexual way of life' and found it satisfies his expectations and needs less than the heterosexual way of life. I think we are entitled to know the results of his findings (frequency of orgasms, etc).

Even if he can convince us with facts and figures, however, he still has a problem. Let us assume, for instance, that he is, like most people, right-handed. No doubt he could easily demonstrate that if he had to do with his left hand what he normally does with his right, life would be less satisfactory. But would that justify discriminating in law between those who commit crimes with their right hand (not guilty until eighteen) and those who commit crimes with their left (guilty at sixteen)? Most rational people would object to such a law, but it would be no less grotesque than the Sexual Offences (Discrimination) Bill just passed by the House of Commons.

Nor, for once, was the government solely to blame. Supporters of the bill included thirty-nine Labour MPs (including normally fair-minded ones like Jim Callaghan, Nigel Spearing, Bob Cryer, chief whip Derek Foster and his deputy Don Dixon). What is wrong with these people? Can't they spot the most blatant prejudice even when it stares them in the face?

One of the definitions of 'satisfactory' in my thesaurus is 'good'. Even a simple little word like that doesn't seem safe any more. It was used twice the other day at Manchester crown court by Judge Rhys Davies. He told Roy Greech of Rochdale: 'You have not only been a man of good character. You are a good man.'

What had Mr Greech done to deserve this rare judicial encomium? He'd killed his wife. In a frenzy of goodness, he had stabbed her twenty-three times with three knives, and then, when she was probably already dead, had smashed her head in with a vase and a picture frame. What made all this so good was that Mr Greech had overheard his wife fixing an outing in the country with another man. Enraged with jealousy, Greech grabbed her round the neck and tried to throttle her. She had the effrontery to seize a knife. He forced it from her and stabbed her to death. When the jury convicted Greech of manslaughter, Judge Davies let him off with a suspended sentence.

Jealous wife-killers seem recently to have become rather popular with judges, but the defence of provocation doesn't always work. The Greech case must have been read with some interest by Sara Thornton, who is in Styal prison, jailed for life in 1990 for stabbing her husband to death with a single blow. When her lawyers went to the Home Office recently with evidence of the most dreadful violence and abuse inflicted on Mrs Thornton by her husband – and the devastating effect this had on her – even the tough civil servants in the C3 'injustice' department were moved to recommend the case should go back to the Court of Appeal. Home Secretary Howard scrawled across the papers 'I am not inclined to do this' and Mrs Thornton rots in jail. Mr Howard has not only been a man of good character. He is also a good man.

A last word about judges. I see one of my heroes, Judge Prosser, was in good form at Swansea crown court last week. A jury there found a man not guilty of malicious and unlawful wounding. The judge promptly told the man: 'In my view you were guilty.' It is hard to imagine a more blatant assault on the central principle of the jury system. Generous as ever, I offer Judge Prosser a paragraph in my next column to apologise. If he doesn't, Lord Chancellor Mackay can have the space – to explain why Judge Prosser should not instantly be sacked. •

Sebastian Faulks
15 September 1994

Back to the front with Tommy

I n 1988 I was sent by a newspaper to report on the seventieth anniversary of the Armistice. I went with a party of veterans organised by the historian Lyn Macdonald, who, in the 1970s, had seen the danger that most of these old men were dying without ever having told their stories. We stayed in Bethune, in the flatlands of north-eastern France, and I remember being amazed at the passion for tea evinced by these old men. In the morning we drove to the battlefields of Neuve Chapelle and Aubers Ridge, where in 1915 the British launched their first attacks of the war.

The old man sitting next to me on the bus took my hand as he explained how it felt to be wheeled on a general service wagon over rutted ground with the two parts of your shattered leg rubbing together. When we stopped and got off, he showed me where the fire trench had been; he pointed to the German line about ninety yards distant, still marked by the indestructible concrete pillboxes.

It was on this exact spot, he said, that his best friend had been blown to pieces beside him. 'I picked them all up – none of them was bigger then a leg of mutton – and dropped them into a sandbag. I dug a hole in the ground and dropped the bag in. I marked it with a cross but they never found it.'

The following afternoon I was walking with him in one of the eerily beautiful cemeteries maintained by the War Graves Commission where the air of tranquillity given by the clean headstones and neat jars of flowers is threatened only by the terrible number of graves. Suddenly my veteran friend gave a start. He was staring at a headstone at our feet. It was marked with the name of the man he had buried: someone had found the emergency grave and buried him properly. 'Oh, I say,' he said, reunited for the first time since 1915, 'Oh, I say...'

For some time I had had the impression that the terrible scale of the Great War was something that had not been properly understood by people of my generation. Now, as I stood with the yellowish mud crawling over my shoe, I saw that it was not only larger but much more recent than I had imagined. It was not 'history', something that could be kept comfortably at bay; this man was old, but he was cogent and alive. This was the place; here we stood in the same clinging mud – he and the rest of us whose grandfathers had survived. This was his life, and to some tragic but inevitable extent it was ours too.

Later I watched a burly young Australian who had travelled all the way from Sydney to visit the battlefields. Lyn Macdonald took him to the cemetery where his grandfather lay, among furlongs, among miles of headstones, and the young man's body seem to convulse with grief and shock.

Initially the idea of that war repelled and bored me. One knew of great suffering and loss of life: that much remained from school history lessons. Yet it seemed unmanageably remote. The method of remembrance had a deadening effect: two minutes' silence on Armistice Day. More silence, more mystery to add to the self-imposed secrecy of so many of the combatants, few of whom talked of their experiences. Then there was the ambiguous poppy. Was it a lamentation or a symbol of Empire? Was it death or beauty?

In newsreels you could see Tommies with their upturned, obedient faces, shuffling at double speed to their cheery death. All that seemed to remain of their feelings was an improbable stoicism, mockingly recalled in their sentimental songs. On the mantelshelfs of old people I had seen photographs of boys in flat service caps and puttees, their faces rendered smooth by sepia, the sensations they had felt removed, distanced and forgotten. I remember thinking, it cannot have been like this.

But how to recapture or re-create what it was? The silence of the soldiers had all but buried the experience of war. Some did not speak at all for years; few talked about it openly. At the Armistice in 1918 Marshal Foch described it as a truce for twenty years. When the end of the subsequent conflict began to reveal the extent of the Nazi Holocaust, the world had something even more monstrous and perverted to remember. The existence of film and the insistent passion of worldwide Jewry made these events the touchstone of twentieth-century suffering.

So the men who had fought at the Somme and Passchendaele, who had seen extermination on a scale never before or since witnessed in war, became the victims, to some extent, of their own reticence. Because they could not, or did not care to, describe the scope of what they had seen, they became remembered half ironically. There was no museum of their holocaust, only songs and silence and quaint brown photographs.

Six years ago I wrote a novel called *The Girl at the Lion d'Or*, set in France in 1936, in the course of which I had to research the French experience of the 1914 – 18 war. *The Price if Glory* by Alistair Horne, an account of the siege of Verdun, was the book that first confirmed what I had suspected: that the scale and nature of this war were something beyond what people normally understood. In the numbers of dead and the manner in which they had died, there was something that taxed human understanding in the same way as Auschwitz.

I suppose I had read Graves and Sassoon, but hastily, a long time ago. And these were the memoirs of officers, written with degrees of protective irony and suppression. I admit to being ignorant, but I believed that even well-educated people of my generation knew equally little. I asked my contemporaries about it. They shook their heads in sorrowful respect at the names of those foul places – Ypres, Verdun – but the truth was that they did not really know what had happened. I was not alone in my ignorance.

When I returned from the first trip to the battlefields in 1988 I began to read about the war. It was not long before I came across a paradox: the First World War may be inadequately remembered, but it is extremely well documented. From the official military history to the numerous collections of private documents there is an abundance of material – from the rigorous to the useless, from the poignant to the banal. I followed a haphazard course of study, through the lists of specialist publishers, public libraries, private collections and the vast and expertly marshalled resources of the Imperial War Museum.

I attended a lecture by its director, Peter Simkins, on '1917, the Year of Endurance'. It was packed. Here was another paradox: perhaps the war was understood by few, but those who did were passionate about it. Excusing himself from talking about events on the Eastern Front or in Mesopotamia, Peter Simkins said, 'I'm a Western Front man myself', and the audience let off a stifled murmur of approval. Later he showed a rarely seen film of the Battle of Arras.

Although all this was interesting, none of it was helpful to someone contemplating a novel. If your starting point is a belief that the scale of something is almost beyond human comprehension, then you feel a sense of presumption in attempting to go where the actual participants have gone before. If you then have to grapple with the extent of documentation and amateur knowledge in an area which you believe to be under-reported, it is hard not to be discouraged.

Soon I began to handle collections of documents. Here was the actual stuff: postcards written from the front, diaries and letters whose paper was wrinkled from rain that had penetrated the roofs of inadequate dug-outs. Here at last was food for the imagination unmediated by the selection and comment of any other writer.

The raw material gave a view of a world I was sure had been forgotten. The feudal attitude of the private soldiers to their officers, for instance, was striking. They expected little from their superiors except courage under fire. Their contempt for the occasional coward is withering. The letters of condolence are frequently works of art. I remember one lamentation from a schoolmaster to the mother of a boy who had just been killed; he was the last of his beloved class to die, all that talent nurtured, trained and wasted. The teacher's private anguish almost overwhelms the politeness of his sympathy. Boys of nineteen or twenty write astonishing prose, spangled with classical allusion; private soldiers write the cool, neat hand of the elementary school.

There was no typical attitude to war. One diarist who seems almost comically keen recounts in 1917 that he is to be transferred to a training job in Canada because he has not shown sufficient enthusiasm at the front. Others lived and let live; few hated the Germans, but some emphatically did. Every man's war was different.

Even the documents were of limited use until two other things happened. The first was my discovery of the extent of the mining operations under no man's land. This was a kind of special concentrated hell, contained within the greater inferno; and it was something not much written about even by the professionals. If I was to try to re-create the experience of 1916, I felt I should at least examine some unknown aspect of it, and here was a way in.

Almost all the accounts of war stressed the strange persistence of natural life – birds, rats, dogs, cattle – even in the great bombardments and holocausts. The soldiers found it both perplexing and reassuring. In a book about mining I discovered the story of a cage of canaries that had broken underground, allowing the birds to escape. Each one had to be recaptured so that the enemy would not guess that there were mining operations in the area. One canary flew out into no man's land. Three snipers shot at it, but could not kill it. Eventually they brought up a trench mortar and bombed the bird. I did not use the story in the book, but its symbolism was suggestive.

The second development came about when I started to visit the Somme area. I looked at the great memorial at Thiepval, then wandered into the wood behind it, which had been the British headquarters on the terrible morning of 1 July 1916. The first thing I saw was a shell.

It seemed like a lucky charm. My research had been based on a kind of faith: that this war was far more recent than people seemed to understand. Now here was the proof. Later I learned that ploughing in the spring frequently yields a harvest of unexploded shells, but that did not matter: this was my shell. It was by repeated visits to the area and simple contemplation that I began to form a larger picture in my mind. I filled a little jam jar with earth from the Sunken

Road on the British frontline and kept it on my desk while I wrote in the superstitious hope it would keep my hand steady.

As the hero I took someone who was not blue-eyed and innocent like so many who died, but compromised and involuntarily experienced before the war begins. *Birdsong* is in fact not a book *about* the war; it is a love story, the story of this man's life. Three of the six main characters are women; children play a peripheral but vital part. Yet at least half the book is about the war, an attempt to re-create the physical and emotional sensations of it, on both complete and minute scales: it is an attempt to understand.

Remembrance is prompted by emotion, but becomes useless if it is mere self-indulgence. If the lamentation of the dead is to be turned into something purposeful, it takes not just compassion, but will and judgement. We have learned to endure the footage of the concentration camps, more or less at the insistence of the survivors, and we are all humbled by it. But what took place on the banks of River Ancre on 1 July 1916, when 60,000 British casualties were sustained in a single day; what took place at Arras and Passchendaele; the ripping up and evisceration of a country's youth, the fragmentation of its society, the grief of mothers, lovers and fathers, not some amorphous national sadness, but each pain, singly, multiplied – this was our holocaust, and I think it is this more than anything else that has shaped the century that in Britain, Germany, France, and even in Sarajevo, is drawing to a close. •

Catherine Bennett
10 September 1993
....
Crowned heads of the kitchen

There are more than fifty pictures of Anton Mosimann in Anton Mosimann's new cookery book. Some show him in his prime, as he is today, others reveal that he was once young. Here he sniffles wine, there he smiles in close-up. In one shot he displays his frivolous side, larking with a bottle of preserved pears. In fact there are so many pictures, and such a wealth of biographical detail, that anyone who feels daunted by his recipe for Roast Chicken with Gold Leaf (Does Sainsbury's stock it? Can you really eat it? Will my guests laugh at me?) may find it easier to prepare a Mosimann instead, for which the whole book is one comprehensive recipe.

Just take one moustache, one bow-tie, a chef's hat and a sprinkling of hair. Stir them together in a Swiss valley, leave to rise in a warm kitchen for about forty years *et voila!* – ready to serve.

What could be simpler? The real mystery about Mosimann is not what he's made of but how this amiable Swiss cook has become a Personality. Of course he's a dab hand at banging the old pots and pans, he's been Michelin double-starred, winner of the Croix de Chevalier du Merite Agricole and all that – but do we need the picture of his first car? The name of his spaniel?

Egon Ronay remembers meeting Mosimann in the mid-seventies. They were introduced by the Dorchester's chef, Eugène Käufeler, whom Mosimann was about to succeed. It was not, Ronay remembers, an event likely to generate much excitement. Hardly anyone had heard of Käufeler. Still fewer had heard of Mosimann. They were just chefs. 'It is absolutely amazing,' Ronay says. 'Until twenty years ago, even fifteen years ago, this was practically not known. Nobody knew any chefs, and even if you wrote about food you had to ask yourself, or ring up and say, what's the name of the Savoy chef? Nobody knew who was the chef at the Ritz or at the Dorchester.'

If anyone counted in restaurants in those days, it was the smarmy maître d's, the head waiters or proprietors. Chefs were just the fat geezers in the white coats, stomping around in the nether regions, chopping their fingers off or shouting about carrots. Now chefs get to be on first name terms with Lloyd Grossman. Chefs write books and marry models. Chefs are interviewed by Lynn Barber, and do fashion shoots and advertise products like cameras or Canary Wharf which have nothing to do with being a chef. Chefs have their own agents and TV series, and provide stories in gossip columns. People are polite and respectful to them because chefs are now thought to be creative and sensitive and interesting. This, thinks Nico Ladenis, the august proprietor-chef of Nico at 90 and possessor or two Michelin stars, is quite inappropriate. 'I think a chef should be asked about food, and that's it. That's his trade. He shouldn't be asked to comment on a particular make of car or a particular architecture, or whatever. They are not important people. They are not! Why should they be? They are craftsmen. Why haven't we got a cult of the carpenter or a cult of any other trade? I don't understand this.'

But in the depths of the Grosvenor House Hotel, he heartily disapproves of it. 'It's a sign of how frivolous society has become, in order to devote so much attention to food. It's part of the fashion, it's very fashionable. We haven't got better things to do than to sit down and write about food.'

Good or bad, chef-fêting seems to have started around the late seventies, after nouvelle cuisine arrived from France, where it had been identified and promoted by Henri Gault and Christian Millau in their magazine and guides. It helped that there were now food writers and colour magazines to promulgate these dainty new inventions, and a new class of affluent, non-posh eaters who hadn't had their palates ruined at public school and didn't realise it was common to comment on your food.

'Interest in grub generally, and the distaste for any sort of etiquette and pomposity around food, have shifted the spotlight on to those who actually do the work,' says Shaun Hill of the Gidleigh Park Hotel, 1993's Chef of the Year. 'Coupled with the fact that, before, you worked to a system, you worked to Escoffier's repertoire of dishes, which was largely the same, done better or worse, across the whole of Europe.

'With nouvelle cuisine coming in, it moved towards an individual look at the food and that brought the chef into bigger prominence. Because people don't go to have Chicken Chasseur, or Tournedos Rossini, they go for a specific person's idea of how to cook food.'

By 1979, Raymond Blanc, a cute, self-taught French cook, was being pictured large on news pages, having won Egon Ronay's 'Gold Plate' Restaurant of the Year award for Les Quat' Saisons in Oxford. By 1982, the Roux brothers' Le Gavroche had three Michelin stars, and they brought out their first book, *New Classic Cuisine*, the following year. 'Chefs have always been revered in my mother country,' says Albert Roux, famous not only for his food but for five cookbooks and a droll TV double-act with his brother, Michel. 'They appear on television, they're always in the newspapers, people want to know them. So it was bound, sooner or later, to catch up in England.'

Is it a good thing? Roux recites the first rule of the serious chef, an old saw of which they never tire: 'You can only be as good as the meal you cooked last night.' Then he adds: 'You've got to recook it again. It's not like a painter, when you point something and it is there for eternity. A meal is as good as the digestion will take it, and then, after that, the loo, I presume.'

Even so, Roux food has been studied, admired and talked about by people who will never have the chance or the money to ingest Albert's simple salad of lobster, frisee, diced tomato, gull's egg and pale-green herbed mayonnaise. The name of Nico Ladenis, too, has been familiar to non-diners-out since he attracted the attention of the tabloids in 1975. On the door of his restaurant in Dulwich he had replaced his menu with this haughty placard:'We have now been open for two years. We do not feel we have to produce our menu to show you how good we are. For your information, we do not serve prawn cocktails or well-done steaks ...'

The notice is reproduced in his 1987 cookery book, *My Gastronomy,* one of the first autobiography cook books, lavishly illustrated with pictures of Mr Ladenis. 'I suppose I was one of the original naughty boys, the people who were throwing tempers,' he says solemnly. 'And that might have marked the beginning of the controversy in chefs.' Was it deliberate? 'It wasn't calculated, it wasn't a designed image. I didn't think, "Oh my God, how am I going to make my mark in life?" I got fed up.'

He had demonstrated, however, that notoriety pays. In 1983, when Anthony Worrall-Thompson opened Ménage à Trois, a gimmicky nouvelle cuisine outfit serving only titchy starters and puddings, he ensured that everyone knew it was Princess Diana's favourite, and probably sole, source of nourishment. The place was perfect for anorectics. 'It was a scam,' remarks Worrell-Thompson, who still dresses in faultless wide-boy uniform – Prince of Wales check trousers, blazer, silver bracelet. 'It was very posey food. The eighties were very much when people showed off their money and wanted these temples of food around. That's when chefs came into the limelight, and there were lots of antics and prima donnas around. It was a decade of prima donnas.'

Worrell-Thompson, who would prefer to be styled simply 'A.W.T' or 'Wozza', didn't say things like, 'You're only as good as your last meal.' He got on the telephone, wrote letters, told the food writers how brilliant he was. 'Everybody thought I was a cowboy anyway, I couldn't get any worse. So I thought, 'To hell with it, I may as well push my own boat out.' And I just had this public school arrogance, being a public school boy, that probably more commoner chefs didn't really have. They were trained so they were underground, and to creep out the back door, and never be seen by customers ... I was prepared that cheffing would be a star-typed role so I pushed myself really hard. I decided that this is the way forward.'

At the height of eighties idiocy, Alastair Little, a Cambridge archaeology graduate, admired by Worrell-Thompson as a 'subtle promoter', opened a restaurant in Frith Street and called it after himself. That, he says, was an unwitting, if highly rewarding, bit of PR. The rest of it wasn't. 'I'd realised that very clearly. I'd realised that a long time ago. I've always promoted myself in some form – not consciously; I mean, most chefs can't actually walk and chew gum at the same time, you know, let alone talk.' But Little was that new kind of prodigy – a chef who was also intelligent, articulate and self-taught.

'I think that appeals to the English, because they love an amateur,' Fay Maschler says. 'I think that's one of the reasons the English embraced those people.' The day he opened, the first edition of *Elle* came out, with five pages on Alastair Little. 'That was my lionisation. There was a full colour spread on me in a Paul Smith suit.' The next week was London fashion week, and the models, buyers and journalists dutifully trotted in to push around Alastair Little food while they stared at one another. 'When we opened we were so trendy I could have just sent cardboard cutouts of the food, and they would have sniffed it and said, "Wow, great", and looked at it and sent it back, and I just threw it away.'

In 1989 chef-groupies were scrambling to Wandsworth, hoping for fresh outrage from Marco Pierre White, a remarkable cook who scowled and sulked and talked not about carrots but about his penis. Alastair Little remembers being shown nude pictures – 'Quite put me off me petit-fours, it did.'

The *Sunday Times* Magazine devoted five pages to the sweaty despotism of his kitchen, followed by coverage in the *Face*, *Arena*, *GQ*, the *Daily Mail*, everywhere. He wrote a book, *White Heat*, ornamented with Marco's image and Marco's Thorts. 'It broke boundaries,' he claims, eyeing celebrities from his special table in the Canteen, a restaurant where he appears but does not cook. 'Rather than having little pretty plates of food, mine actually took the other side. There were lots of pictures of my cooks as well as me: it shows you that the other side is not all sunshine and f***ing roses; there's a lot of dirt in there, there's a lot of blood, there's a lot of guts – Hello, Michael.' Caine, his partner in the Canteen, has just walked in. 'We were the chosen ones in Britain,' White remembers fondly. 'We were like almost the rock stars of catering: we were wild, we got away with f***ing murder, we were notorious within the profession, we all had long f***king hair – it was madness. But you know, it was something which was never to last for ever. We all grew older, we all grew wiser, the game became bigger, more money on the table.'

Now Harvey's has closed, the Canteen prospers, and White is about to open a new restaurant in the Hyde Park Hotel, with, he claims, little organised publicity. He doesn't need it.

But there, no doubt, his disquisitions on My Life as a Man will continue to titillate journalists and infuriate less modish chefs who already suspect him of debasing their profession. Some can't stop talking about him; some can't bear to talk about him; others get round it by calling him 'a pig'. Unfortunately for them, this pig can cook. 'I give back to the profession!' he announces, adopting his role as the commis' patron saint. 'I remember where I f***king came from, and why should I forget where I came from when it comes to a young boy's future, and that's right isn't it? All of these fat c***s in the Académie have forgotten. I dislike the Académie, I think they're a bunch of f***ing arseholes, except for one or two individuals, but the majority of them can jump in the f***ing Thames, because they've achieved f*** all.'

White will swear – 'on my daughter's head' – that he never sought publicity. 'I never did it purposely. The people I swore at, the press I jumped at, was all through emotions, that's all.' Then again, 'I must thank the press, because if it wasn't for the press, I would not be the man I am today, and I might not be in business today.'

For Wozza and his rivals, the recession has made self-publicity still more necessary, more competitive, perhaps more stressful. One talented chef recently sent Craig Brown a tube of KY jelly, a mirror and an obscene suggestion of where he could now put his (not particularly critical) review. Ladenis banned Fay Maschler from his restaurants. At the end of his mobile phone, Worrall-Thompson is furiously available, marketing a group of restaurants which currently serve sturdy Italian pastiche to an impoverished and increasingly fickle public. He's written a new book, *Supernosh*, he has his radio programme, his column in the *Sunday Times*, slots on Sky TV – 'Major revealed he liked cabbage, so I talked about cabbage.' It all brings people in. 'You can see them think, "Oh, there's that man from television", so it's good if people come to the restaurant because they want to see you.'

Outside Dell 'Ugo, a restaurant in Soho where he occasionally cooks, chef-victims spill, of an evening, into the gutter, fulfilling Wozza's latest ambition to feed London's café society with lentils and 'fun'. But will rocket outlast kiwi fruit? Will café society's appetite prove any more dependable than Princess Diana's? 'I hope it's going to be around. If it's not around I'll be there, on whatever the next band wagon's going to be.'

He may even have to get back inside an apron. 'I personally think this is going to be the shortest-lived phase of all phases, because it is based on pure expediency, on pure pounds, shillings and pence,' the austere, undeviating Ladenis says. 'People will hanker and eventually go back to the traditional way of eating, the French style, the correct *haute cuisine* style.

Marco Pierre White says he'll be in his new restaurant six nights a week. 'I won't let things interfere with what I actually do, which is cook' Alastair Little says. 'I think the public might actually be slightly rebelling against the celebrity chefs. They might like some recipes, and some sensible sort of stuff, but I think they're pretty sick of antics.' Little's recipe book, out next month, has almost no pictures of himself, and is called *Keep It Simple*. 'The cult of the table is coming back – and actually what we do is rather dull, isn't it? Chefs cook. They either cook, or they go round and open restaurants, like Anthony. It's not a sexy profession – we *smell* when we've finished, you know.'

So after all that, all the personality books, the interviews and the TV shows, we still need simple recipe books. Gary Rhodes, chef at The Greenhouse, whose emergent celebrity – wacky haircut, new BBC series, spin-off cookbook – is now being keenly monitored by his competitors, has decided to appeal to his audience with basics. 'Most professional chefs' books are purely written for other professional chefs, that's my theory. They're great coffee-table books for housewives, they've got Marco's book sitting there – but who's going to sit and make his stock for six hours? People don't do that any more.'

What *do* people do? They read about famous chefs but they don't cook the same food. They know about the chef's divorces and wives and sackings, but they've never eaten at their restaurants. 'It's really now carried to absurd lengths,' Ronay says, 'when chefs jump from the food column into the gossip column. That is an exaggeration which has nothing to do with good food and nothing to do with the improvement of cooking and so on. That is simply a kind of mass hysteria, really.'

Despite his absurd Cher Albert agony-cook column in the *Evening Standard*, Albert Roux thinks the cult has gone 'a bit too far. Too many chefs leave the stove to have their photograph taken.' All the same, he says, the publicity has enhanced his profession. 'It attracted young people who would have said "I don't want to go into catering." Suddenly it became respectable.' It meant you didn't have to cook all the time. 'When you're here putting in five or six days a week,' Gary Rhodes says, 'putting in sixteen hours a day, I like to be able to do something else as an interest as well. There's chefs who've worked fifteen hours a day all their lives and never do anything but that. Well, I think that's a sad lifestyle in many respects.'

Outside London, some chefs have little choice. 'I can appreciate what I'm lacking is the skill of manipulating the press, and manipulating the press obviously is the biggest thing,' admits Franco Taruschio who started The Walnut Tree, Elizabeth David's favourite restaurant, thirty years ago. But even in the hills outside Abergavenny, customers like a personality. 'I explain to my young chefs, "People are not interested in the way you cook; they're more interested in your soul, your character."'

It doesn't seem to matter that character has little to do with what goes on a plate. You can't eat a chef, however fascinating he is. But chefs have joined the band of names who float around in a circle of pure celebrity, divorced from craft, profession or achievement. They are at one with the super-models, showbiz MPs and former footballers with whom we go through the keyhole. They tell us about a day in their life, how they met, what they keep on their mantelpieces, what they wish they'd known at eighteen and what their favourite word is. And, beguiled by the power of their own names, chefs have begun to use them assiduously, endorsing and opening restaurants where they will rarely, if ever, cook – not sautéeing, but syndicating. The more restaurants they open, the more they need publicity to keep the restaurants fashionable. Who needs the *Michelin Guide*, when you can get into *Hello!*? •

Nancy Banks-Smith
4 February 1994

The dismal diary of Adrienne Mole

> Honour the worthy
> And honour the keen
> Honour her daughters
> And *honneur aux dignes*.
> ### Roedean school song

Fifty years on it strikes me that it may all have been a dreadful misunderstanding. My parents ran a boozer in Blackburn which everyone called t' new pub. Except my mother, who called it The Mill Hill Hotel, taking pains with the unaccustomed aitches.

The name may have confused the Roedean bursar into believing that, like many colonial administrators dislodged then from their rubber plantations by the Japanese, they were sitting out the war in some country hotel. Then there was the Banks-Smith. I believe the double barrelling comes from some fisherman none too sure about his father, but I do realise that Nancy Banks-Smith sounds like someone falling off a horse at Hickstead. In the hell of total war these little mistakes are easily made.

I was an only child and my parents were great believers in bettering yourself. In the quiet afternoons, when the last customer ('Na then, lads and lasses!') had hit the cobbles, my father would read my Arthur Mee's *Children's Encyclopaedia* over and over again and regale the boys in the back room with the bits he thought they would enjoy, like:

> I often wonder what the vintners buy
> One half so precious as the goods they sell.

Education, my dear Omar, that is what the vinters can buy.

Which is how, much to our mutual surprise, I found myself at Roedean, thanks to the boys in the back room whose hoarse, sweet, homesick, Irish tenors rose like smoke every evening singing that they would take you home again, Kathleen, to where your heart would feel no pain. Though, in a way, I never did go home again.

Roedean rallied, like a good hostess, without a flicker of surprise. The first thing they did was get rid of the Lancashire accent I didn't know I had. Rather *Pygmalion*, really. I had to recite poems like

It was eight bells ringing
And the gunners' lads were singing
And the ship she lay a-swinging
As they polished every gun

until I stopped hitting my 'ings' like dinner gongs. The way I speak is an interesting social curiosity. I'd change it if I could be bothered because it sounds ridiculous now. Bloody cut glass, as the boys in the back room would say. Of course, the way my parents spoke didn't change. The moment I noticed that we sounded different a little fissure grew between us, the earth shrugged and shifted. I don't think I'm imagining it. I don't believe we ever really talked to each other again.

To lose one parent may be regarded as a misfortune. To lose two looks like a first-class education.

Roedean was evacuated to the Keswick Hotel, the kind the bursar had in mind. Dame Emmeline Tanner, the headmistress, was reputed to have moved the whole school overnight from Brighton to the Lake District with a Bradshaw in one hand and a Bible in the other. She had one of those undivided bosoms popularised by Queen Mary on which her pince-nez, leaping from their perch under the stress of strong emotion, would flutter to rest.

If she was quite a nice old bird really, I don't wish to know that. She once delivered such a powerful oration on the subject of Gels Seen Buying Chips in Keswick that several blameless children had to be escorted out in floods.

The deputy head, Topsy, so called because she just growed, asked us to calculate the percentage who left sobbing. Topsy was a senior wrangler who saw everything in terms of mathematical purity. She had such a clear mind that now and then, like the disappearing rear light of a train you had just missed, I almost thought I got the hang of maths.

We were permanently, achingly hungry. The hotel was run by a couple called Ma and Pa Wivell, who were, to my mind, quite suspiciously fat. The cheers we were ordered to give for them at Christmas stuck in my throat like a pauper's pudding. On half-holidays we were detailed off to climb a mountain. There was a depressingly large choice. As Dame Emmeline wrote in the school magazine: 'On a perfect October day, forty-three girls climbed Great Gable, sixteen climbed Scafell Pike, seventy-nine climbed Helvellyn, sixteen bicycled to the Langdales (forty-six) miles and seven walked all round Derwentwater. I was obliged to go to London.'

I groaned up Helvellyn which, as Wordsworth remarked, is remote from human road or dwellin', and damn well deserves to be. On the saw-toothed ridge my packed lunch, a pork pie, fell from my frozen fingers and leaped exuberantly down the mountainside, each bound more exhilarated that the last. Topsy said that given Helvellyn was 3,113 feet high, could we calculate the time of arrival of a pork pie at the bottom. I still feel quite violently that all mountains are a great mistake and that all pies should be made square by law.

While travelling somewhere east of Suez where the best is like the worse, the maiden ladies who founded the school had come across the djibbah. They adopted this as the ideal school uniform as it disguised the growing gel at all salient points. We wore blue serge djibbahs by day and, dressing for dinner, velvet djibbahs at night. My best friend, Ros, was so tall and willowy and I was so short and fat that, when we walked up the aisle to be confirmed, the same suggestible small girls had to be escorted out sniggering. In djibbahs we looked much of a muchness.

The Outlaw was showing around this time and we heard that Howard Hughes had designed Jane Russell's bust bodice (as the school called it), on the soundest aeronautical principles. Ros and I, who felt strange stirrings under the djibbah, cut a couple of bust bodices out of the school blackout which was the occasion for another Dame Emmeline special on Gels Who Have Taken Leave of Their Senses. Though, strictly speaking, this applied more to Howard Hughes, who later went completely off his head.

Gels were expected to be clever, alert, athletic, loyal, and most seemed to be. I never seemed to get the hang of it at all. Not for a minute. Any of it. A damp diary reveals me as Adrienne Mole aged $13^3/4$.

Mon: Unpacked. Can't find fountain pen. Very unhappy about it. Prunes and junket.

Tues: Bike not arrived. Lost? Snowing.

Wed: Found bike. Lost laundry book. Felt bitter against God.

Thurs: Found laundry book. Lost brolly. Thunderstorm.

Fri: Amy shared her fish paste and everyone got diarrho. Minnie (a teacher called Minnie Ha Ha because of her resounding laugh) said she nearly polished us orl orf.

Sat: Broke my watch that had just been mended for 10s6d. Wrote bitter poem. Rattle windows! Blow O Wind! Flail your branches broken tree! Though the world be washed away What concerns it me?

Sun: Rained, snowed and hailed all the way to church. Terrible man from the United Society for Christian Literature shouted at us. Rice pudding. Lost 'crosse stick.

Lacrosse is a Red Indian game. I believe they played it with the heads of their enemies. That is how Roedean played it. I was usually put in goal on the grounds that they might go easier on someone in glasses. This was entirely fallacious.

Miscellany

They came in like Sioux, hair streaming, supporters screaming 'G squared D No. 3!' (Grit, Guts and Determination No. 3 House). I found that if I closed my eyes, I didn't scream. 'Played No. 3' says my diary. 'Lost 15–1.'

Where did they all go, those clever, alert, athletic, loyal gels? I never came across any of them again but I did meet one or two misfits who were doing rather well. It was as though kicking violently against the regime sent you into some kind of eccentric orbit.

The great thing about public school is that life comes as quite a nice surprise.

Corkscrewing on Nemesis at Alton Towers.

Picture: Don McPhee

Sporting life

Stephen Bierley
4 July 1994

Short-change final

So much power. So much impotence. Those who witnessed yesterday's men's singles final will surely not have any lasting memory of it. For here was a match with no melody, no variation of tempo and ultimately no entertainment.

It was a quite stultifyingly tedious final, the mercy being it was one of the shorter ones. By comparison the women's on Saturday was wonderfully quaint.

And what of the future of the men's game? Unless the rules and equipment are radically changed it can surely be only a matter of time before a super tall, black American from Watts or Harlem decides that basketball or American football are hard work and there are easy bucks to be made in tennis.

There is no point blaming or criticising Pete Sampras. He is a perfect product of his time and at twenty-two may return to the centre court for many a year to come. Perhaps we may grow to love him.

Goran Ivanisevic is the same age and could, theoretically, join him on the final Sunday for the remainder of the decade. But the Croat is psychologically composed of quite different stuff. There is something of the crazed poet about him.

For the most part he has kept his volatile temperament in check during the past fortnight but at two sets down yesterday afternoon the rich muttering began. Many half hoped he might suddenly erupt, for that at least could have been memorable. Instead he simply slunk away in the final set, ears flattened, tail between his legs, a thrashed hound.

The centre court crowd has a notoriously 'Come on, entertain us' attitude to its tennis. Rarely, even by Wimbledon standards, can they have made so little noise. There was never a question of becoming involved in such a match, for it was devoid of continuity – excluding the awful procession of bludgeoning serves.

On the aces count Ivanisevic won 25–17 but Sampras had a quite astonishing 90 per cent success record on points won with his first serve. It is an awesome statistic. Yet tennis – ill-served yesterday on the BBC by John Barratt's hushed tones of reverence towards Sampras – would be fooling itself if it believed this was a great performance.

There was more of a stir for the entrance of Princess Diana, clad in scarlet (red, if the latter troubles you), than anything Sampras or Ivanisevic managed collectively in the opening set. It had tie-break written large from the moment Sampras opened up the wing-ding.

Here, at least, was a little excitement, albeit on the penalty shoot-out level. Ivanisevic succumbed limply in the first and was little better in the second. He had so badly wanted to do well this time after the disappointment of his defeat against André Agassi two years ago, a final he felt he should have won. This one, by contrast, almost completely bypassed the gangling Croat.

Inevitably there will be more calls for the Wimbledon turf to be ripped up. Yet women's tennis undoubtedly benefited from the aggressively athletic game Martina Navratilova played in her prime.

On Saturday the legs had gone, and with them went the nerve. Conchita Martinez simply pummelled the ball past her as the Czech-American was stranded in nowhere land. It was, for all the nostalgia, more than a little sad. Great champions are notoriously unsure, and frequently ill-advised, about when to retire. Navratilova really should have gone earlier.

As for the whole week, the weather was wonderful, apart from a dismally bleak first Tuesday when Steffi Graf was eclipsed. The overall standard of matches was not so marvellous. Indeed, had Navratilova not reached the final, the second week would have died.

Her final Wimbledon passing, at least as far as singles is concerned, was a peculiarly SW19 occasion: all rather stiff and arch, with talk of a long-lasting love affair and tea with the Duchess. About as far removed from real life as the people who run this tournament. •

Stephen Bierley
23 June 1994

Sampras cops the long and short of it

There is much talk within tennis currently about the desperate lack of 'personalities', and most of it is total rubbish. History is being reinvented.

Connors, Nastase and McEnroe – all wonderfully talented but a collective pain in the butt – are suddenly being spoken of as if they had imbued the game with a wit and repartee of unblemished sparkle.

Poor Pete Sampras, a technician of the highest order, finds himself roundly damned as a bore and a dullard. Stung by such unfounded criticism, he has taken refuge in that last bastion of the vilified man: a pair of funny trousers.

The trouble with tennis, notably on grass, is not the lack of personalities but the chronic lack of variety. When Roscoe Tanner thundered 100mph-plus serves in the 1970s he was regarded almost as a freak. Now everybody breaks a ton, including many women.

The big arms have it. Yesterday Sampras flogged twenty-six aces past his fellow American Richey Reneberg. It was awesome but tedious. Rallies were an oasis in a desert of destruction. One, lasting fourteen strokes or so, drew tumultuous applause. Of relief.

Serve and volley, at least in modern times, has been the stuff of Wimbledon. But now, with the huge racquet heads and kryptonic technology, the serve is damn nearly all. Vortex Extender, Sledgehammer, Pump Upset, Ultra Hammer – the names say it all.

Sixty-one per cent of Sampras's serves on court 14 were not returned by Reneberg, who duly lost 6–3, 6–4, 6–2. 'Pete, was it as simple and straightforward as it looked?' 'Yes.' And, goodnight.

The most unnerving thing about Sampras's decision to wear long shorts, or short longs, is that he appears almost vulnerable. As if he were at home in a cardy and slippers. But the man is totally wired, an electric hum of concentration and application.

His mannerisms are minimal, the most obvious being a ritual, almost obsessive plucking of his racquet's strings while waiting to receive. Occasionally he flicks a forefinger across his thick black eyebrows or tugs at the shoulder of his shirt. Otherwise barely a mutter. 'Got any balls?' he asked one of the green-and-purple clad girls. It was the nearest he came to controversy.

Reneberg once won the Kuala Lumpur singles title, which sort of makes him the Jeremy Bates of American tennis. He took some extremely good points against Sampras, but the cracks in his game widened set by set as Sampras bludgeoned on.

One service break was enough for the No. 1 seed in each of the first two sets. Reneberg engineered a shockingly unexpected break of the Sampras serve in the third, but lost his own immediately before and after.

Maximum speed, maximum aces. Boring? For many the answer is an undoubted and unequivocal yes. But then others have complained bitterly about interminable rallies on hard surfaces. There is no obvious solution, and probably never will be.

Meanwhile the players are a soft target. Blame Sampras, blame Courier, blame the lot, and pray that somebody – anybody – turns up who will not think twice about swearing at all and sundry, and slagging off umpires.

Then crucify him. •

Mike Selvey
19 April 1994

....
Lara joins the greats

'**R**ecords,' as Sir Garfield Sobers said yesterday, 'are just there to be broken.' They come and they go. But this one was special; not just the most prized crown in cricket but one of the greatest individual records in sport. At 11.47 am Eastern Caribbean time Brian Lara, a diminutive left-handed batsman whom the gods have touched, became the highest-scoring batsman in Test history.

It was a moment to savour, treasure and pass on to the grandchildren. Twelve thousand people were there to witness the thunderous pull to the square-leg boundary that took him to 369 and beyond the 365 that Sobers had scored against a hapless, depleted Pakistani attack thirty-six years ago in Kingston. Many thousands more will claim to have seen Lara's innings in the fullness of time.

As the ball crossed the boundary and Lara raised his hands to the sky, a tidal wave of humanity swept across Antigua's Recreation Ground, engulfing and overpowering the constabulary ring that had been posted around the boundary and swamping the hero in the maroon hat. Others stood and danced, so much it was a wonder the stands did not collapse.

As pandemonium reigned, a distinguished, grey-haired, rather Mandela-like figure appeared from the West Indian players' balcony, made his way down the steps and with a police escort, hobbled sedately out to the middle to greet Lara. Sir Garfield St Aubrun Sobers had his own, very personal congratulations to deliver. It was in 1954 that he, as a teenager, had been introduced to Test cricket, and so fitting amid the fortieth-anniversary celebrations that have been preoccupying the islands that Lara's achievement should have rounded them off.

'I can't tell you how proud I am of his achievement,' said Sobers, who has been

Lara's idol and mentor since the first time he set eyes on the precocious young-ster. Even before the Test Sobers had been counselling, cajoling and coaxing Lara into the massive self-belief and discipline that such an achievement demands.

'The record could not have gone to a better person,' added Sobers. 'From the day I saw him I knew he had the ability, and it is a pride and joy to watch.'

So Lara becomes only the ninth person to hold this record of records in the 117 years since Charles Bannerman opened the first innings of the first Test with 165 runs. Only eleven batsmen have made more than Lara in any first-class match, and this is only his sixteenth Test and third Test century.

Lara's 766-minute innings			
Runs	Minutes	Balls	Fours
50	150	121	7
100	228	180	16
150	324	240	24
200	436	311	27
250	511	377	32
300	610	432	38
350	721	511	42
369	748	530	44
375	766	538	45

To get to his goal he had to bat longer than any West Indian before: Sobers's 365 took ten hours fourteen minutes. By the time Lara, on 375, was caught by a tumbling Jack Russell behind the stumps driving loosely and extrava-gantly at Caddick's last ball before lunch, he had been at the crease for twelve hours forty-six minutes, since the first half-hour of the match on Saturday, when Fraser and Caddick, unbelievably now it seems, had reduced West Indies to 12 for 2.

In all there had been forty-five boundaries and not the semblance of a chance, for this was as near a faultless display of batting as is possible.

Lara would acknowledge the debt he owes first of all to Jimmy Adams, with whom he added 179 for the third wicket, and to Keith Arthurton, who saw him to his double-hundred during their fourth-wicket stand of 183.

But above all he will forever regard Shivnarine Chanderpaul as a blood brother. When his nerves began to bite, it was the teenager, in only his fourth Test, who soothed him, who took the strike for a while to let Lara regroup and who was there to walk off triumphantly when Lara was out, their fifth wicket partnership worth 219, Chanderpaul's contribution an unbeaten 75.

Lara had spent an uncomfortable night on 320, but yesterday great names disappeared in a blur: one square cut saw off Graham Gooch's 333 and Brad-man's 334, a back-foot cover drive rocketed him past Hammond's 336 and Hanif's 337 and, to Lara's relief, a cover drive took him from 361, past Hutton's 364 and equal to Sobers. Then, and only then, did he know he was safe.

Had he not got out, there is no knowing whether Courtney Walsh would have declared. It was welcome respite for the bowlers, however, although after seven sessions in the field a target of 394 to avoid a follow-on represented a tough

Brian Lara kisses the Antigua wicket where he has just made 365.

Picture: Frank Baron

challenge and England failed to make the best of starts, losing Alec Stewart (24) and Mark Ramprakash (19) to Kenny Benjamin.

By the close, though, Mike Atherton and Robin Smith had rectified things with an unbroken third-wicket stand of 115, as England reached 185 for 2. Compared with what had gone before, it was small beer, but one never knows. •

WEST INDIES

First Innings (overnight 502–4)
B. C. Lara c. Russell b. Caddick	375
S. Chanderpaul not out	75
Extras (lb3, nb23)	26
Total (for 5 dec.)	593

Fall of wickets cont: 593
Did not bat: J. Murray, W.K.M. Benjamin, C.E.L. Ambrose, K.C.G. Benjamin, C.A. Walsh.
Bowling: Fraser 43–4–121–2; Caddick 47–2–8–158–3; Tufnell 39–8–110–0; Lewis 33–1–140–0; Hick 18–3–61–0.

ENGLAND

First Innings
* M.A. Atherton not out	63
A.J. Stewart c. Ambrose b. K. Benjamin	24
M.R. Ramprakash l.b.w. b. K. Benjamin	19
R.A. Smith not out	68
Extras	11
Total (for 2)	185

Fall of wickets: 40, 70.
To bat: G.A. Hick, G.P. Thorpe, R.C. Russell, C.C. Lewis, A.R. Caddick, A.R.C. Fraser, P.C.A. Tufnell.

Umpires: D. Hair and S. Bucknor.

John Mullin
11 June 1994
·····················

God's gift to the game simply born to be great

There was no thunderstorm, no midnight sun, no star above Mitchell Street. Brian Lara was born a mere mortal, much like his ten brothers and sisters. But there are those in Trinidad and Tobago who believe a god is in their midst.

Joey Carew, aged fifty-six, a former opening batsman for West Indies and Lara's mentor, is an otherwise level-headed man. But hark at this: 'Muhammad Ali, Pelé, Martin Luther King: people the Lord has charged to spread his word. Lara is one of them.'

Nobody who has coached Lara, aged twenty-five, believes they have taught him anything he would have failed to pick up for himself. Great batsman, brilliant tactician and motivator, and even an excellent wicketkeeper.

The 5ft 5in left-hander is on the way to millionaire status after his record-breaking 375 agains England in the fifth Test at Antigua and 501 not out for Warwickshire against Durham, the highest score in first-class cricket. To think he was once laughed all the way to the crease as a tiny schoolboy batting at No. 7. He turned in a century.

'It was in his genes, something in the combination of his parents,' says Carew, a surrogate father to Lara since his dad died. 'He was simply born this way.'

Lara was, though, lucky enough to be the youngest of seven boys in a family of eleven whose ages now range from twenty-three to forty-five. His father, Bunty, who succumbed to his sixth heart attack five years ago, spoiled him, says Agnes Cyrus, his elder sister.

'I remember Rudolph, my brother, made him a wooden bat and he would play around, hitting marbles and pieces of fruit. He was three years old, and he used to execute every stroke perfectly.

'When he was six, I saw an advertisement in the local paper asking for young-sters who were interested in cricket coaching at the Harvard clinic. I filled the coupon in and took him along. I bought him a little green cap, some white clothes and his first proper bat.

'I took him down for the first two Sundays, and then my father took over, wholly and solely. He never missed a practice or a match of Brian's until the day he died.

'Brian was seven when he told me he wanted to be the world's greatest cricketer, and then to be a sports master. He ate and drank the game.

'He had a tremendous feel for it. When he wasn't playing, he would sit with a piece of paper and work out fielding positions.'

Lara was a short boy, but played with older neighbours outside the family's home in Mitchell Street in Cantaro, a village outside Port of Spain in the lush Santa Cruz valley. Bunty Lara was an agricultural store manager, and although the family was large, there was always enough food on the table.

They were queueing up to recall their Brian Lara tales there yesterday. Harvey George, forty-two, was bragging about how he made the youngster cry when he bowled him out, often using an unripe orange plucked from a tree. Gavin Pegus, twenty-six, thought he was a fantastic footballer, but a sublime cricketer.

Brandon Hazell, twenty-five, was back on to Carew's theme. 'God gifted it him all. Nobody else could have made him.'

Lara was as determined boy. He was too good for the others. They would resort to cheating to get him out. It would be a joke, but he rarely saw the funny side. He would storm off into the house, taking his bat with him, so finishing the game.

He spent half-a-dozen years at Harvard under the tutelage of Hugo Day, now seventy-six, who is still convinced Lara was the most talented boy he had ever seen. But they played only friendlies at Harvard, and Lara was to struggle at first at Fatima College, one of Trinidad's best grammar schools.

With one voice, its 900 boys proclaimed the visit of the school's most famous pupil this week. Tariq Abousalen, who plays for the Fatima Under-14 team which Lara graced just over a decade ago, said: 'He is the greatest Trinidadian of all time.'

Lara's results in the 1981 entrance examination were a shade too low. He was earmarked for another school. 'Then we realised he was a cricketer,' said Mervyn Moore, the principal. Around his office were scattered old Fatima year books. One, from 1987, refers to the InterCol Cup final. Lara is at the wicket; the bowler is Dhanraj, now one of Trinidad's finest spinners. It reads: 'Lara took up where Sagar left off, punishing anything loose from bowlers and seeming to play the leg spin and googlies of Dhanraj with consummate ease.' With a four, a three and a single in an over, Lara, the captain, won the match. Fatima had lost in the final the previous two years.

'When he came here, we all thought he might be a little small to make it as a cricketer,' said Moore. 'It was something that used to frustrate him. I was once told he had burst into tears because of it.

'But his greatness soon became clear in the Under-14 Giants league. He was marvellous at pass-out, where there is no wicket and when you're out if you miss the ball. He would be in there all day.

'I remember going to Barbados in 1987 for a tournament involving schools from West Indies, Canada and England. Garfield Sobers was there. He said then that Lara was the greatest talent he had seen for a long time.

'Our team wasn't that good. But he could really motivate the boys and get the best out of each of them. He was fiercely competitive, but I never heard him shout. He just had this calm authority which everybody responded to.

'He never lorded it over anybody. I always remember him with a little smile on his face. He was well mannered. I never had to discipline him.'

Herry Ramdass, the dean of the lower form, ran the Under-14 team when Lara arrived. 'He struggled for a little while, because he was playing boys five or six inches taller. But he had a tremendous tenacity. He would bat all day in the nets without flinching.

'I remember one match against St Anthony's school. We were really up against it. He was counting the balls so that he would be batting again at the beginning of the next over. He knew exactly where the field was. He even seemed to know who was weak on what side. We won the match.

'The St Anthony's coach said he thought it was a fluke at first. But then he realised it was deliberate. He had never seen anything like it before.

'We might have pointed out a couple of things. But Brian was his own toughest critic. If he was having a problem with a particular shot he would tie a ball on a string to the nets so that it was coming in at the problem angle, and he would hit them until he had beaten his difficulty.'

Francisco Garcia was the coach of the Under-16 team. 'There was no coaching on my part with Brian. It was just a joy to umpire and watch him bat. He never seemed to hit the ball to the boundary. He just stroked it. It was a sheer delight.

'I remember reading that Bradman would practise with a stump and a golf ball or that Sobers would use a stump and tennis ball. Lara used a ruler and a marble. Can you imagine?

'He never forgets here. He always comes back to say hello. He is amiable and likes a joke. We have a saying here: to go and lime. It means to relax, have a few drinks and enjoy yourself; maybe he feels he can do that better here than in England.'

Around this time he played football for the Trinidad and Tobago Under-14 team, where he met Dwight Yorke, now with Aston Villa. Lara himself was a quick forward and loved the game.

He once badly cut his knee playing football in the street when there were roadworks. His father was furious: Lara's involvement in other sports was mainly to sharpen his cricket expertise. He liked squash, because it helped him move his feet more quickly, and table tennis because it aided his eye co-ordination.

He needed extra maths and English to get through the equivalent of his O-level examinations. But he did pass half a dozen, and could have gone on to take his A-levels. But there was a two-month youth tour to Australia, and then he won a cricketing scholarship to England.

Carew was leafing through a copy of Wisden in his office at Queen's Park Cricket Club, the site of England's ignominious 46 all out in the third Test this year. He was looking at Denis Compton's 1947 record of eighteen centuries in fifty innings.

'I don't think there are too many records which will be left standing when Lara retires. He was always going to be brilliant.'

Carew's two sons, Michael and David, were at Fatima with Lara. His home is a hike away, and so he often used to stay with the Carew family.

They would watch old cricket videos. There were sometimes furious arguments. Lara was strong-willed, but always prepared to listen, says Carew.

The quartet talked the game all the time, and it meant Lara developed faster. Carew's sons both play now for Queen's Park, where Carew, recently recovered from a heart attack, is executive manager.

'His father was a great driving force in his upbringing. He was a little spoiled as the youngest boy. His father was not a cricketer as such. But to some extent it's more important for a son to know his old man is really interested than in him being a coach.

'There was a wonderful turnout for his funeral. The entire West Indies team went. They made a great combination, Bunty and Pearl, Lara's mother. A lovely, big family which has been good for Lara.

'He never really talked to me about his father's death. I never saw him cry, but he loved his father very much. I don't know if he has bottled it up. But Bunty would have been very proud.'

Most people seem to have a favourite Lara innings. Carew was astonished by his performance against Jamaica for Trinidad this year. 'He was in with the No. 9 or No.10 batsman. They put on a stand together of 108 which turned the match. The other guy scored something like three of those runs. He astounds me. It's impossible to analyse a person who can score 501 runs. You run out of superlatives. It's just genius.'

Those who know Lara say he has barely changed. Charles Guillen, thirty-three, a friend from Fatima, says: ' If anything, the more success he achieves, the more humble he becomes.'

His sister Agnes, whose two elder boys are promising cricketers, says: 'He has mellowed out a little. He is more subdued now that he has reached where he has wanted to go. Before, he was maybe too fixed on all of that.'

But there was a hint of a chink in the armour after a recent incident in a Port of Spain nightclub. He and Yorke, a close friend, were reputedly involved in a fracas after they were picked on.

Carew chuckles, and says there are no problems with temperament. 'You wouldn't be bringing up children if they didn't get involved in the odd incident. It is sometimes hard to remember, but he is only twenty-five. I don't think he'll end up like that English footballer, the one who keeps injuring his leg.' •

Pass Notes

19 May 1994 — Ray Illingworth

Age: Sixty-one.

Appearance: Northern Premier League football manager.

Occupation: Annoying members of the Establishment; selecting the England cricket team. His first side take the field today against the might of New Zealand.

Are New Zealand mighty? No, I was being ironic. At present, they would struggle to give the Shetland Islands a game.

I see, so Ray should enjoy some sunshine? Indeed, though the capacity for English cricket to shoot itself in the foot is legendary.

Illy's a Yorkshireman, isn't he? You certainly know your cricket.

And famed for blunt speaking? As you said, he is a Yorkshireman.

What did he make of the team he inherited? Too young, not hungry or hard-working enough, preoccupied with money, too many batsmen, too few bowlers, no decent all-rounders, totally useless really.

Any new blood in the side now he's in charge? Graham Gooch.

I thought he was ancient: He is – pushing forty-one – but Illy likes old-timers. He's hoping to get Fred Trueman fit for the Tests.

You're joking? Always on the ball.

No need to be rude. Doesn't Illy think he should be more diplomatic? Diplomatic is not a word much used by the Uncle Morts back home in Pudsey. In any case, Illy thinks he's blameless: 'I've only ever offered constructive criticism. I've never slagged anyone off.'

Is that true? Ask Hick, Tufnell, Lewis, Ramprakash, Russell, Smith, Fraser. Oh, and Fletcher.

Who he? Keith 'the Gnome' Fletcher, the England manager, who has already had a ticking off from his new boss over his handling of Gooch.

Fletcher feels threatened presumably? Only in the sense that Troy felt threatened by the Greeks.

So Illy plans to be hands on? Indeed. Probably on the throats of underperforming players.

When did Illy play? In the balmy days of the sixties and seventies when a pint of Theakston's was fourpence and English cricket the best in the world.

And Illy himself? Good player, great captain, regained the Ashes in 1970–71.

How to describe him: Gruff, bluff, rough, tough, in a huff.

Not to be confused with: Geoffrey Boycott.

Definately not to be confused with: M.J.K. Smith, A.C. Smith, M.C.C. Smith, I. Zingari-Smith.

Most likely to say: 'Get that booger out of the team. He couldn't hit a barn door with a bluddy football.'

Least likely to say: 'Jolly bad luck, Hicky. Curtly's yorker is always difficult to spot.'

David Foot

7 June 1994

....

Five-ton Brian Lara rewrites every record in the book

History was made with surreal splendour in the Birmingham sunshine yesterday. Brian Lara, the West Indies' elfin genius with the Merlin wrists, off-drove the makeshift bowler John Morris at 5.30. The ball skimmed the manicured grass on its way to the fence – and Warwickshire's wondrously gifted overseas player had made the record books redundant.

There were only two balls left, according to the frantic words of his century-making partner, Keith Piper, as Lara rocked on his elegant heels for the boundary which gave him a remarkable 501 not out, the highest individual score in the records of first-class cricket.

Gently hit on the helmet by the previous delivery, Lara goaded himself into a final flourish of jaunty response as he aimed for the extra-cover area, to beat Hanif Mohammad's total of 499 at Karachi in 1958.

Warwickshire were 810 for 4. The records were by then as plentiful as the Midlanders who chased belatedly from work to watch – and journalists, dispatched by their offices from Test-match grounds and watering holes.

The biggest irony was that these two counties had failed before the start to reach agreement over a contrived contest. So Warwickshire and Lara simply kept going against Durham's depleted attack.

It seems almost disloyal to the quality of greatness in agreeing with Lara that this was still not, taken all through, one of his better innings. Edgbaston was understandably heady with the reverberations of Brummie-Caribbean cadences, at least in spirit. There has been an aura of worship for him, created in a matter of weeks since he arrived, to compound the most extraordinary frisson since Richards and Botham were savaging in tandem. Bejewelled talent like Lara's must carry any reservations with reluctance.

Yet, by his shimmering standards, he scratched at the start: shivering in Friday's cold, looking weary, as if suddenly confronted by the reality of county cricket's unrelenting pragmatism, after the convivial rum-punch ambience at home.

He should have been caught at the wicket when 18 and was bowled by a no-ball; yesterday, driving a trifle loosely for once through the off-side on 238, he grazed Cummins's fingertips as the ball went on to the boundary. That was a questionable chance; more acceptable was his fallible scoop when on 413, in the direction of square leg. The fielder misjudged badly and did not get under the ball.

There were pained expressions from the tiring, mostly unrewarded, Durham players, already regretting that they had not agreed with Warwickshire over artificial forfeitures in pursuit of a result. The fielder, slow off the blocks and – dare one say – confused subconsciously by conflicting allegiances, was the substitute Michael Burns, Warwickshire's reserve wicketkeeper.

Lara, assuming that he was out, was already racked by self-rebuke. Slowly he glanced towards square leg and the smile of relief that lit up his face was evident, even from under the helmet, at boundary distance.

He is not a batsman of flamboyant persona. There are no fancy tricks to adorn the sublime style of the little man. But the emotion emerged as he got to 400. The bat was raised in boyish joy; he embraced his partner, Piper. They are like blood brothers, rooming together, shielding each other on Friday from the cold, when the advertisement hoardings were careering in the wind.

The tentative beginnings, the occasional flaws, had all been superseded by the exquisite grandeur of his attacking strokes, which came with eager and instinctive skill. When he pulled or cross-batted, there was nothing ugly in the execution. The cover drives scorched through, evading fielders with embarrassing ease.

There can surely be few in the present game with better timing, with a greater facility to find the gaps. Durham were mutilated and one could sympathise with them. They were without Graveney (thigh), who could at least have kept going with some attempt at his normal economy, and without Saxelby (back), injured as he practised in the morning in anticipation of a coerced bowling spell.

For Warwickshire, the bit players savoured their own morsel of posterity. Piper finished on 116 himself. Earlier Penney, who for much of the time had stood at the other end rather like a uniformed attendant with innately appreciative eyes at the National Gallery, scored 44 before being taken at extra cover.

But the day belonged imperishably to Lara. 'It doesn't make me a great player,' he said afterwards with sweet, if unnecessary, diffidence. With sixty-two fours and ten sixes – and a timeless exhibition of batsmanship extending over almost eight hours – his place in the game's hallowed thoughts and almanacs was assured. •

Matthew Engel
4 May 1994
···
Death and the risk business

A bad week, everyone agrees on that: yet another boxer dead, two grand prix drivers killed, a National Hunt jockey grievously ill after being kicked in the head.

Nothing links these three sets of events except that they all fit on to the sports pages of British newspapers. Outside this country, Bradley Stone, the boxer who died fighting for a British title, might rate a paragraph in the papers, the jockey Declan Murphy not even that.

There is no pattern here, no sudden upsurge of danger: sport has not suddenly become more risky. All that has happened is that momentarily we have become aware of the perils posed by sport in general.

Seven years ago the polemicist P. J. O'Rourke wrote an essay called 'Safety Nazis', mocking modern America's neurosis about risks: 'How many lifeboat drills were held on the *Mayflower*? Where were the smoke detectors in the Lincoln family cabin?'

It touched a nerve. And since last week an American theatregoer marched up to an actress on stage and demanded that she stop smoking (and the producers then rewrote the script to ensure that she at least cut down), one may conclude that American life has now gone beyond the power of satire.

O'Rourke said it was impossible to be both safe and alive. Any parent of a child under ten – no, on reflection any parent, the fears never go away – mentally battles with this fact every day. Life itself is invariably fatal. The risk that it will be unwontedly shortened is inherent in every activity, and certainly every sporting one.

Mankind advances because there are people willing to accept those risks, and perhaps to die, in war or in peace. As an enthusiast for that suicidal diversion, the Isle of Man TT, once said to me: 'You put handrails up Everest, you'll get an icepick in your back.'

But where should the line be drawn? In motor- and horseracing and in boxing the dangers are obvious and part of the appeal. In the first two they have diminished enormously in the past twenty years – there is no comparison between the way grands prix are conducted now and the manner in which gung-ho young men of the fifties and sixties who just missed the chance to be Battle of Britain pilots would cheerily go off and kill themselves, if not on the track then in a light plane or an impromptu race on the Guildford bypass.

There is further statistical evidence that sports such as American football are getting safer: thirty killed every year in the early seventies, none at all in 1990. This is not, however, true in boxing. Indeed, some would argue that it is getting more dangerous: spectators are no longer interested in the art of self-defence; they like seeing men thumped and thumped hard.

If adults who go into the sport are aware of the risks then no one should have any power to stop them: that is what freedom means.

But there is also a particular question about whether fighters do know the risks. The frightening sight of the shambling, broken figure of Muhammad Ali, who was meant to be so smart, is a devastating reminder that in boxing it is not just the single, freakish punch that can smash a man's brain but the endless repetition of blows throughout a career.

This is not a reason for banning boxing. That would be wrong, not just because of the argument – parroted with increasing desperation by members of the fancy with each new tragedy – that it would drive the sport underground and then more people would get hurt. It is simply that in a free society consenting adults must have the right to do anything they like to each other provided they do not do it on the street and frighten the horses, a point those who write letters to this newspaper find hard to grasp.

There is, however, a serious case for ceasing to give boxing the credence and respect it gains from being treated as a regular sport, not simply because it destroys lives, but because it is no longer a believable sport.

There are seventy-eight people paraded as world champions to kid the gullible in different parts of the planet that their local boy is truly the best in some obscure weight division or other. Some elements of the British public, convinced that a posturing actor such as Chris Eubank is some kind of significant sportsman, are fooled as easily as those in less sophisticated countries.

The *Guardian* has always reported boxing with a sense of perspective. In my view, it is no longer possible to do that. It should be treated like wrestling, which in atmosphere it increasingly resembles except that wrestling kills fewer people – as a dubious entertainment and a small-time con-trick. •

David Davies
12 April 1994
....

From Mr Irascible to Master Olazabal

The fateful day came during the third round of the Tenerife Open in February, the day José-Maria Olazabal lost his temper for the umpteenth time. He threw a club, shouted at his caddie and stomped off, raging at all around him: José-Maria Irascible.

It was disgraceful behaviour and it seriously offended two people watching from the sidelines. One was Olazabal's manager, Sergio Gomez, for whom the scene was drearily familiar. The other was Gomez's wife, Maite, for whom it was the last straw.

When Olazabal finished his round he was confronted by something for which he was utterly unprepared, a furious friend. Maite Gomez told Olazabal that if he wished to behave like that he was wasting his time, and that of many others, by continuing in the game. In short, it was time he grew up.

Olazabal was stunned. He had been told the same thing many times by many people but never by a member of his exclusive inner circle, someone who had always been completely loyal and supportive. Only then did he realise that the situation was serious, that something had to be done.

That evening he resolved to try to be more relaxed on the golfcourse, to stop behaving like a boor, to give his golf a chance. That evening he went a long way towards winning the Masters title that came his way on Sunday.

Two weeks later Olazabal and Sergio Gomez were walking towards the practice ground at the Andalusian Open when they bumped into John Jacobs, the noted coach who had taught Olazabal in his teens. Jacobs was immediately coerced into a lesson and, within the space of one swing, he had analysed the fault that had plagued the Spaniard for eighteen months.

'The only problem was to find a way of telling him,' Jacobs said later.' He's not an easy guy to teach.'

Olazabal had gone two years without a win and for over a year this stubborn man had been carrying a swing fault so obvious that anyone could spot it. Yet without a regular teacher he had no one to point it out to him, certainly no one to whom he would listen.

Within an hour he was hitting shots with his driver, off the ground, to order – fading, drawing dead straight, anything. That lesson on the practice ground near Jerez, combined with his drastic dressing-down earlier in the year, was the second and last component in Sunday's triumph.

By the time he arrived in Augusta at the start of last week he had won the

Mediterranean Open, finished fourteenth in the Player's Championship and second at New Orleans. He was ready to win his first major.

'He is a changed man,' said Gomez on Sunday, 'but he had to be. Every time he played golf it was as if he were going to the slaughterhouse. When he went to Tenerife the ghosts were still there but after that third round he was like the man who says to himself, "I'll stop smoking, right now." And he did. He relaxed overnight.'

Olazabal, still only twenty-eight, brought his first ulcer on himself when he was twenty-one and has a spectacular history of sulky and stupid behaviour. After a tournament in Japan, where he lost first prize by missing a putt on the last green, he flew home from Tokyo to San Sebastian, via London and Madrid, with out a single word to Gomez. When they parted at San Sebastian Airport Olazabal finally spoke. 'See you tomorrow,' he said.

Gomez recalled caddying for Olazabal on another occasion when, after a row, he carried the clubs for forty-five holes without a word being exchanged.

But the contrast between that Olazabal and the one who won the Masters is perhaps best illustrated by an incident in the final round. Olazabal, only just on the green in two at the long fifteenth, holed from forty-five feet for an eagle. It took him two strokes ahead of Tom Lehman, his nearest challenger, and was the vital move of the final round.

His long-time (since 1986) and long-suffering caddie Dave Renwick recognised the moment and could not help but rejoice. 'I was jumping up and down as we walked to the next tee,' said Renwick, 'but Ollie said, "Hey, take it easy; we haven't won yet." For years I've been trying to tell him not to get so excited but, of course, he won't listen to me.'

But he did listen finally to Maite Gomez and he also absorbed a note left in his locker by his fellow Spaniard Severiano Ballesteros before the start of the final round. Ballesteros, his Ryder Cup partner, twice a Masters champion but not now a challenger, simply wrote: 'Go out there and be patient. Let the others get nervous. Technically I cannot tell you what to do because you are the best player in the world.'

Olazabal was patience personified in that final round. Lehman, hardly known in his home state of Minnesota, let alone America, refused to go away and for much of the round the 1987 champion Larry Mize was also in contention.

All three were at eight under after eleven holes but the short twelfth began the sorting-out process. All three were long but only Olazabal, with the most delicate of chips, got down in two more. That gave him a one-stroke lead he never really surrendered, a lead that doubled when he eagled the fifteenth. Here he hit a five-iron second 202 yards on to the green, where for one anxious moment it looked about to roll back into the greenside lake.

Lehman, who had a twenty-foot eagle chance at the same hole, dropped to his knees and beat the ground with head and hands in anguish as his putt missed by a whisker; and he went on to waste a wonderful tee shot at the short sixteenth as well, missing a four-foot putt for a birdie. 'When you see a player do things like that,' Olazabal mused afterwards, 'you think that maybe it is time for you to win.'

Lehman regained a shot at the seventeenth, where Olazabal putted poorly from off the back edge, but squandered that too by hitting an iron into a fairway bunker.

And so the boy born to play golf – he was raised in a house close to the ninth green and the practice putting green of Royal San Sebastian – had won his first major. He did it by realising that anger does not necessarily equal aggression and that no one, not even himself, knows all there is to know about the golf swing. He had gone from José-Maria Irascible to José-Maria Irresistible.

But the perfectionist streak is still within him. The morning after the glorious night before, he was up at 5 am to catch a 7 am flight to Raleigh, North Carolina, where his club manufacturers have a plant.

'Some things never change,' sighed Sergio Gomez. 'He's still not quite satisfied with the irons ...' •

Matthew Engel
31 March 1994

....

Eccentric England 'rest in pieces' with worst performance since 1887

The innocuous-sounding figure of 46, otherwise noted merely as a bus route, was tattooed permanently yesterday on whatever is left of the body of English cricket.

Forty-six? 46! England, having been reduced to 40 for eight on the fourth evening of the third Test in Port of Spain, were bowled out six runs and fourteen minutes into the fifth day. West Indies thus won a match in which England had been on top almost throughout by 147 runs, took a winning 3–0 lead in the series and secured the Wisden Trophy for the eleventh time running.

England, however, avoided by one run reproducing their worst performance. It was merely their worst performance since jubilee year – Queen Victoria's jubilee, that is. On 28 January 1887, England were bowled out for 45 by Australia in Sydney. However, on the eccentric pitches of that era, England went on to win the game. These days it is just the cricket that is eccentric.

The result yesterday was witnessed by a small crowd, mostly comprising British tourists who, after the ninth wicket fell, began singing 'Abide With Me'.

When Chris Lewis was caught at long leg to complete the match there was some dancing by West Indian supporters carrying placards reading 'Rest in Pieces'. But for the most part the last rites were administered in something close to respectful silence.

Later, the English supporters crowded in front of the scoreboard showing the full extent of the humiliation and took photographs of each other, Japanese fashion.

The England players, meanwhile, went straight back to their hotel rooms, not stopping by a consignment of champagne by the door that was chilling for the arrival of the winning team. They left their captain, Mike Atherton, behind to try and explain everything away.

Atherton was as honest and good-humoured as could have been expected in the circumstances, though there was a certain amount of head-scratching.

He praised the fast bowler Curtly Ambrose, whose awesome bowling on Tuesday night had destroyed the batting. But he denied that England's fear of him had contributed to their downfall. 'There were no negative thoughts in the dressing room beforehand. It was just a matter of showing the temperament and technique to get through it, which we didn't show.'

He said the key to facing Ambrose was not giving him a breakthrough early on. He then grinned ruefully: his own dismissal to the first ball of the innings had started the rout. 'Down to me, I suppose.'

Richie Richardson, the West Indies captain, said he thought England had become demoralised by the dropped catches that allowed his team to come back from the verge of defeat and set England 194 to win. Asked how his men would have faced Ambrose, he said: 'We would have played a few more shots.'

The tour now moves on to Grenada, where England have a four-day game before the fourth Test starts in Barbados a week tomorrow, with at least 5,000 England supporters expected to crowd the ground and the island, mopping up the sun and moping about the state of English cricket.

The most likely victim of all this is the team manager, Keith Fletcher, whose role is certain to be much reduced when the more forceful figure of Ray Illingworth moves in as chairman of selectors in the summer. Graeme Hick, once believed to be one of the best batsmen in the world but now completely nerve-racked by high-class bowling, is also in considerable jeopardy. Meanwhile, a vast number of Why Oh Why? leader page pieces can be confidently expected.

Since the collapse of school sport is probably the main structural factor behind English cricket's continual failure, every politician who has held power over the past thirty years and everyone who has been connected with education ought to bear some responsibility.

Within cricket there are increasingly loud voices suggesting that the whole domestic structure needs to be demolished. Too many mediocre players, it is now said, are earning their living from the game. It doesn't actually matter how many mediocre players there are. All England need is eleven good ones.

The lowest Test innings to date are:

26, New Zealand vs. England (Auckland) 1954–5
30, South Africa vs. England (Port Elizabeth) 1895–6
30, South Africa vs. England (Edgbaston) 1924
35, South Africa vs. England (Cape Town) 1898–9
36, Australia vs. England (Edgbaston) 1902
36, South Africa vs. Australia (Melbourne) 1931–2
42, Australia vs. England (Sydney) 1887–8
42, New Zealand vs. Australia (Wellington) 1945–6
42, India vs. England (Lord's) 1974
43, South Africa vs. England (Cape Town) 1888–9
44, Australia vs. England (The Oval) 1896
45, England vs. Australia (Sydney) 1886–7
45, South Africa vs. Australia (Melbourne) 1931–2
46, England vs. West Indies (Port of Spain) 1994
47, South Africa vs. England (Cape Town) 1888–9
47, New Zealand vs. England (Lord's) 1958

Matthew Engel
7 March 1994
....
Cobblers nobbled

Northampton 0,
Hereford 1

Somewhere Graham Greene is really good on how hope is always relative. After total despair even the smallest glint of optimism can bring an extraordinary shaft of happiness. I think it was in *The Power and the Glory*, which is not about the very bottom of the Football League. That would be in a different volume: *The Impotence and the Shame*, probably.

There was so much enthusiasm for the game at the County Ground on Saturday that the kick-off was delayed for fourteen minutes so the queues could be admitted. Then the Hotel End, the home supporters' enclosure, was declared full for the first time since Northampton were Fourth Division champions seven years ago.

It was possible to stare at the throng, cast the mind back twenty-eight years and imagine the golden days were back, that Northampton were again taking on Leeds and Arsenal on level terms and not entirely disgracing themselves. For this reverie to be effective, however, it was best not to look at the grotesque temporary structure – so small that even from the rear it was possible to smell the Deep Heat from the dressing rooms – that has replaced the main stand, nor look at the old Spion Kop where the Hereford supporters were, most of which has been renamed the Danger Keep Out End.

It was, of course, best to ignore the fact that the fourth side of the ground is occupied by the cricket square, but that was ever thus. Above all, it was best not to glimpse the football. But there were 5,394 people present, the biggest crowd in the division, the vast majority seduced by a surge of local optimism. In February Northampton had won three games out of four, having failed to win any at all since mid-October, and fallen eight points behind every other club in the Football League. They were effectively in an airtight module, just ready to be blasted off in the direction of Welling and Witton Albion. But in the past month the manager, John Barnwell, has finally been allowed to sign players again, having been barred – because of the club's past financial incompetence – from engaging anyone, even if he cost nothing and was begging for the right to be a Cobbler.

And last week the club were formally removed from the jankers of administration and were released as upright citizens for care in the community. Mere survival has been a total triumph for the board, the supporters and the town.

It was springtime in Abingdon Avenue and the visitors were Hereford, the second-worst team in the League. If Northampton won, the teams would be level on points, with the Cobblers having the easier run-in. It is possible to see skilled football at this level even, on a good day, from the worst teams. This was not a good day. The wind did make control and passing hard but not nearly as hard as the players made it look. Since Northampton had most of the possession, this was primarily their fault. There was some decent running from Mickey Bell and the local boy Darren Harmon, but close to goal the team were collectively inept. It was a bad day too for Efon Elad, the Cameroon Under-21 international (and World Cup contender), whose dreadlocks and exuberance have done much to give Northamptonm their new zest. Somehow he seemed less exotic when one heard he was actually born in Hillingdon – also when one saw that, on this occasion anyway, he could do nothing right.

Hereford showed a minimum of flair but when they got the ball they used it positively. The striker Chris Pike hit the crossbar just after half-time and scored from a cross by Steele after seventy-three minutes. Pickard almost made it 2–0 just before the whistle and no one could have complained. The smallish band of visiting supporters chanted 'Staying Up, Staying Up' as vigorously as if their team were on course for the treble.

Northampton may stay up too if the League sticks to its intention to keep out Kidderminster because their ground is not good enough, which seems a bit tough seen from the County Ground. But, after sixty years of house-hunting, Northampton hope to be in their new council-owned stadium, Sixfields (don't try and say it ten times quickly), by August. There are 5,394 people who will need more persuasion than this to go and join them there. •

Matthew Engel
17 June 1994

Soccer? Who's a succer?

Everything is set. Excitement is mounting. Every hotel room, so it is said, is booked for forty miles around. The great soccer tournament is about to begin and it is all happening right here, sir, in the great state of Illinois.

I refer, of course, to the River City Classic, which takes place in Peoria, Illinois, on the weekend of 29 June, involving 230 school soccer teams from as far afield as St Louis, Missouri, and Madison, Wisconsin.

In the meantime, starting tonight three hours' drive away in Chicago, there is something called the World Cup, involving twenty-four national teams from as far afield as Saudi Arabia and South Korea, though none from the United Kingdom.

Amid all the exhortatory messages – No Smoking! No Parking! Recycle This! Don't Eat That! – that make the modern United States the world's bossiest democracy, the American public has been told endlessly that this is the world's

Eric Cantona: flair du mal.

Picture: Martin Argeles

biggest sporting event. And so it is. The Olympics may be fatter but this makes an infinitely more profound impact. Has there been a solitary moment in Olympic history that can conjure as powerful an instant image for the British TV viewer as the Russian linesman (1966), Bank's save (1970), the Hand of God (1986) or Gazza's tears (1990)?

In virtually every country in the world – even in Africa and Asia, which are not regarded as football's heartlands – the game is either the number one sport or very, very close to it. Except one.

In the world of sports marketing, the Holy Grail, the philosopher's stone, the tic-tac-toe on the fruit machine, is to get to that one and make soccer pay in America. Give us the world's most popular sport and the world's richest market and bring them together, O Genie of the Lamp, and we shall wish for nothing else.

The next thirty-one days, between now and the World Cup final in Los Angeles on 17 July, will decide whether or not that can ever happen. As American politicians, TV executives and entrepreneurs traditionally ask themselves, will it play in Peoria?

Two days ago the president of the United States Soccer Federation, a California lawyer called Alan Rothenberg, announced preliminary plans for Major League Soccer, which is due to start in 1995 – certainly not the first but almost certainly the last attempt to get the game going professionally in a way that will compete with America's traditional sporting obsessions.

After Rothenberg had announced the first seven cities to get franchises for the new league, a woman reporter asked how he could be going ahead with this when the response to the World Cup had been so 'underwhelming'. Rothenberg did not so much give an answer as fling it. 'We've sold 95 per cent of our seats, three and a half million, a million more than in soccer-crazed Italy. Our licensed merchandise programme has exceeded all its budgets. In some places if we quadrupled the size of our stadiums, we couldn't accommodate everyone.'

All this is absolutely true. But the questioner was right too. There is a central paradox about this World Cup that makes it feasible to argue either that this is the best possible place to hold a World Cup, or the worst. The ticket sales have been phenomenal. In which other neutral country, would anyone pay to watch Greece vs. Bulgaria? In Chicago it is a 60,000 sell-out.

Huge crowds lined one of the city's main drags on Wednesday to watch The Parade of the Nations, with local people on floats wearing their ethnic-cliché dress, however inappropriate to the 95 degree heat: triumphalist Swiss with cowbells, Norwegians as Vikings, the pipes and drums of the Chicago Police Department Emerald Society (countries that have not qualified for the World Cup were still invited and the Pakistanis proclaimed themselves world champions of hockey, squash and cricket, but the British had enough discretion to keep a very low profile).

It was a terrific pre-opening ceremony. But one did have the feeling that the parade could have been for anything: the circus come to town or Dan Quayle's presidential campaign or National Pecan Fudge Brownie with Macadamia Nuts Day.

The fact is that 60,000 people is nothing here. America contains multitudes. Precisely that number are supposed to be in town for the National Exposition of Contract Furnishings, all of them deeply into the choices that need to be made about carpet squares and ergonomically designed office chairs. Sixty thousand! Yet the networks are not thought to be keen to make contract furnishings a subject for prime-time television. They are equally wary about association football.

In Peoria (population: 115,000) there are two shops, The Soccer Locker and For Kicks, that sell nothing except equipment for the one sport. 'We've been in business for thirteen years,' says Joan Basso, owner of The Soccer Locker, 'and we're not going out of it.' More children are said to play association rather than American football in Peoria and when the two big high schools, Richwood and Notre Dame – the Knights and the Fighting Irish – play each other they get crowds of around 1,500. There will be loads more at the River City Classic. But this other little competition?

'We've been publishing daily stories on the World Cup for the past two weeks,' said Kirk Wessler, sports editor of the *Peoria Journal-Star*. 'Frankly, we've had no response one way or the other except when we ran a syndicated column from the Detroit paper by a writer who said, "Why should the rest of the world tell the United States what we should be interested in?" and I had one telephone call saying it was an obnoxious piece of garbage.

'I've got five boys myself and four of them play soccer. But even among the kids they play with, there was no talk of the World Cup. And if you went up to them they wouldn't know who the star players were.'

As Peoria goes, so goes the nation. The number of children playing the game has increased hugely over the past twenty-five years. All over America on Saturday mornings, parents stand on touchlines watching their sons and daughters – especially, and this is interesting, daughters – shouting '*off*-ence, Jefferson Junior High', or some such.

But these do not appear to be the people buying World Cup tickets. These are being sold to a rainbow coalition of ethnic Americans, the people who were in the floats at the parade not those who were gawping.

The United States is a permanent international gathering. Anyone officially accredited to the World Cup must sense it at once: April Alvarado takes your picture, Franco Vitale ushers you into line, Vincenzo DeVito processes the ID card and Bernardo De Albegaria sorts out the telephone. But it helps one's understanding of the nation at large's attitude towards the World Cup if you consider the British view of rounders, a childish, sissy game that could not be taken seriously by a grown-up. Here, of course, a butch form of rounders is the most sacred of all national institutions.

Hard by Soldier Field, the American football park where the world champions Germany begin their defence of the title against Bolivia today, is Grant Park. A few dozen Chicago children attending a summer arts camp were there during their lunch break the other day, with a variety of sports equipment. They provided a paradigm of American sporting attitudes. About half chucked an oval football around; about half played impromptu baseball; a lone girl in pink shorts plaintively asked, 'Anyone want to play soccer?' She got one other girl to join her and they retreated to a distant corner. The boys never looked up.

'What do you think of soccer?' I asked Tony (eleven), who was trying to pitch a fastball at the time. 'Sucker?' he replied. 'No, you know, kicking a ball,' 'Oh, yeah,' he said.

'It's kinda cool,' said Adam (twelve). 'I used to play but ... I dunno.' 'I kept getting stepped on,' said J.T. (eleven). 'I just got tired,' said Adam. 'Yeh,' said Dan (twelve), 'the field's too big.' 'I'm glad I don't go to Germany and watch soccer,' said J.T. 'Too violent.'

This is significant because the vague feeling that soccer is girly goes together with the thought that the professional game is surrounded by terrible dangers. It is not just eleven-year-olds who have difficulty grasping the reality of this. The Chicago papers reported the German team's first practice, at a suburban high school, in an awestruck tone that seemed to express vague disappoinment that the hundred or so German-Americans who turned up to watch did not wreck the joint, that the two dozen or so policemen with attack dogs were not required and that there was no immediate role for the Du Page County Emergency Management Incident Command Center, which was stationed behind the goal-mouth.

There is also the view, which seems to be imposed from on high, that the game is boring. Sports columnists, not just in Detroit, compete with each other to come up with sassy, smartass phrases to tell their readers how dreary it all is: 'Hating soccer is as American as Mom's apple pie'; 'If this were a Broadway show it would close in one night.' And so on.

Jerry Trecker, the soccer writer of the *Hartford Courant* in Connecticut, thinks this reflects growing xenophobia. 'We clearly have some of the most knowledgeable soccer people in the world but these people exist outside the American mainstream.

'Language prejudice in the United States has increased dramatically and the non-English-speaking immigrant feels more alienated than he ever did in the past. US youth soccer is a suburban, white phenomenon amoung people who got away from inner cities that used to be black and are now increasingly Hispanic.' It's not the kids who are going to watch the World Cup; it is America's immigrants.

'There were 73,000 at Colombia's game in Boston the other week and they were all routinely called Colombian. They didn't just fly in from Bogota. There were 91,000 in Los Angeles to watch Mexico and they were called Mexicans. They're not Mexicans, they're Americans.'

Trecker thinks this ties in with the US's general withdrawal from the world. 'Before Vietnam, we never had to beat ourselves on the chest and tell each other, "We're great." Now we do. You see this in all its ugliness in the anti-soccer writing. It's *their* game so we have to attack it.'

Trecker has little confidence in Major League Soccer (though his own brother is the PR man). Satellite dishes mean, increasingly, that soccer fans can for a small outlay overdose on Italian, Portuguese, German or even English games. Why should they care about an indigenous league with patchy TV coverage and no ready-made stars? No one expects the US team to do well enough this month to change that.

One sensed that even the League's promoters were not all that enthusiastic. There is an ultra-cynical view that the League will probably never exist, that it is solely a charade for the benefit of the world governing body, FIFA, which insisted on it when the US was awarded the World Cup.

Even as Rothenberg was trumpeting the triumph of the ticket sales he kept using the word 'downsizing', an American word but a very un-American concept. This is what will be done to major stadiums to stop small soccer crowds rattling round in them. There was even a picture of Giants Stadium in New Jersey with all its upper layers blocked off in an attempt to make it more intimate. It will probably have to be renamed Midgets Stadium.

'Downsizing' is not a word that would be used by someone who truly believed the World Cup was going to leave behind a lasting legacy. The tournament begins amid a belief that the Holy Grail will never be found. Anyone want to play contract furnishing? •

Matthew Engel
17 February 1994
....
A limit to Sky's appeal

I t is one of the great moral dilemmas of our time. Do you give in, go out, buy a dish and make the wretched man ever more rich and powerful? Or do you stand righteously aside and find, more and more, that sport is what appears on other people's televisions?

Heaven knows what my answer will be if this Test series gets to 2–2 with everything to play for in Antigua. But after an hour or so spent in front of the one-day international on a neighbour's sofa, I reckon I can hold out a few weeks longer.

Watching cricket is an essentially sociable, fresh-air activity, in which periods of intense concentration need to be mitigated by chatting, snoozing and strolling.

There is no rhythm to televised cricket. Move away from the screen and you lose the thread of the game. And who can sit on a sofa for eight hours just watching cricket? You can, sir? Get a life, never mind a dish, that's my advice.

It is not that Sky's coverage is at all bad. It is now quite a decent blend of Channel Nine's visual sophistication and the BBC's verbal restraint. With David Gower and Michael Holding commentating together we are almost back to the days of dear Jim Laker, who refused to be surprised or excited by anything. ('So the scores are level, one wicket standin', one ball to go and the pavilion's burnin' down. It's turned into a reasonably interestin' finish here.')

All the Sky voices are safe, familiar, BBC-ish, three of them belonging to former England captains: Gower, Boycott and Willis. It is a curious fact that the apotheosis of a cricketing career now consists of climbing into a commentary box and having to think of something snappy to say over a shot of a toddler eating an ice-cream or a woman in a minidress. Dr Johnson, on women preaching and dogs on their hind legs, covered the situation admirably.

Boycott was his usual, kindly positive self. Inside seven minutes he had slagged off Walsh for bowling too slowly and Ambrose for his rotten fielding. Then he was off to fulfil the role of statutory Northerner on Radio 5, the grit amid all the public school voices.

There is a new three-year contract to ensure that *Test Match Special* does still exist next summer, though when Radio 4 listeners discover it is replacing their favourite programmes on Long Wave, some members of the BBC hierarchy may be in almost as much peril as Mark Hebden.

Since it is even more statutory to have an Etonian than a Northerner, it seems reasonable to assume that Henry Blofeld – recently sacked by Sky – will be back to replace the late Brian Johnston. Perhaps Sky felt that Blowers lowered the tone of what, on initial evidence, seems a subdued, competent and decorous form of broadcasting. It is only the adverts that live down to satellite TV's shoddy image.

Do You Want To Get Disgustingly, Horribly, Filthy Rich? Just dial an 0891 number – you could win a quarter of a million, screamed one ad. A better chance of getting filthy rich is acquiring an 0891 number and promoting that sort of scheme. Better still, get the monopoly of satellite broadcasting and make sure the government's in your pocket. Then you might have even *Guardian* readers watching your adverts eventually. •

Gone before

8 June 1994

Dennis Potter

Kenith Trodd

Beneath surprising surfaces much of Dennis Potter's work was about endorsing and revitalising the clichés of popular belief and consolation. For me, his last weeks of life were a glorious revitalisation of the cliché about nothing in life becoming one like the leaving of it. In those three and a half months alone he brought off more than most of us achieve in our whole life.

Against the mortality clock and rising pain which the morphine and heroin cocktails could never get ahead of, he first wrote the best television serial of the last ten years. Then when we all thought that was his and our lot, he sat down and wrote another one that is even better. He then set about pestering in vintage fashion some of the people whose pride it will be to bring those pieces to the screen for notes, offers of rewrites and urgent quizzes to find out whether we were all understanding it properly. He'd already initiated and performed his personal television memorial in an interview which has given hope and insight about death and living to people both near their end and those probably half a century from it. Quite absurdly, against the physical odds, he continued to make weekly visits to London during which he not only disposed of his personal affairs with great panache and compassion but successfully dictated to two television channels exactly how to finance and (unprecedently) co-operate to best realise his posthumous work.

He once told me I'd known him longer than anyone except his mother and he had few other long-term friends. Our relationship was stormy, ludicrous and intermittent, like a misbegotten marriage which never quite works and never quite fails. In that last period we talked as many days as he had the strength and I regard these conversations as real privileges in my own life. Dennis's work will go on speaking for itself for a long time, but I return to cliché to say that great writer he obviously is, but I now think of him also as rather a Great Man. •

Melvyn Bragg

The man I knew was always witty, sometimes acerbic, usually warm, testy now and then, independent-minded, sometimes bloody-minded, a traditionalist, a conservative-anarchist who loved his country but never blindly.

He made a difference to British television. It is right, I think, to seize on this sad, even tragic, loss, in order to point out that there was a time when it was talented individuals who set the tone and the level and the quality in British television. Not bureaucrats; not quangos up and down Whitehall or kitchen Cabinets deep nested inside the broadcasting institutions. But individual programme-makers out there on the screen, leading with their creative chin. Potter's rage against much of the current television establishment was largely based on his apprehension that the day of the free and honest Orwellian voice was being drawn to a close by people who knew how to put up the shutters but had less understanding of how to put on programmes that mattered.

At first because of illness and then from choice he stumbled from journalism into television as a way to make a living and then, also, as a place to make his mark as a writer. He attempted the novel, the theatre and movies, but the great welt of his work was on television. It was a medium he first encountered in the sixties, when it was regarded by many as a snobbishly dismissable little box in the corner. He left it as a medium able to contend in intelligence and reach with anything being done in feature films, on the stage or in the novel.

There was nothing, he decided, that television could not attempt. He sought the fabled memory of childhood through the brilliant device of using adult actors in *Blue Remembered Hills*. He slid from the most mundane dramatic realities into a delightful counterpoint fantasy in *Pennies from Heaven*. In *The Singing Detective* he wove a web as tangled as Le Carré and as labyrinthine as Borges but effortlessly – and all on the television screen. He had failures. But failures in a big and real body of work are usually no more than slippery stepping stones on the way from one territory to another and Potter shifted his territory restlessly.

Thanks to the video revolution, many of his plays will continue to be as available and, I am sure, as often reviewed as anything by his contemporaries. But that, in a way, is almost beside the point.

For the heart of Dennis Potter, to me, was the determination of a vastly talented man to throw all his energies on to what were, when he started, the racing, transient waters of television. The reward was reaching the people of this country.

He gave them everything he had and when he gave his last interview on Channel 4 he was astounded and deeply moved to discover that literally thousands of them wanted to give him back their affection and appreciation. He was a man who treated television as if it were the finest medium in the world and the wide British public as if it were the best audience a writer could have. •

Michael Grade

Dennis never changed in all the years I worked with him. I never found him difficult to work with; he was always rational. He was a man of incredible intelligence and the only way to deal with him was to be utterly straightforward like he was. We started on this note and we always told each other the truth. But we never differed or argued over content – if we argued it was only about money or budgets. He used to call me a cut-throat ex-agent but he liked those discussions, he enjoyed the cut and thrust. When I saw him last I said to him, I'll always remember the good and the bad times, and he laughed and said, 'But especially the bad.'

He was fantastically faithful to television. I could name some pieces by established television writers who did it for the money. Dennis never did. He put his heart and soul into each piece. I just admired the sheer craft and cleverness of his work. Our job [Channel 4's and the BBC's] now is to do justice to *Karaoke* and *Cold Lazarus*.

He inspired a generation of young writers – if you talk to them they'll say they first got excited when they saw Potter's work and the potential of the medium. And he increased the stature and power of the writer in television production. He raised the whole standard of broadcasting and he set a benchmark.

His language was so powerful. What strikes you apart from the wit and intelligence in his final interview is above all his use of words. Yet he was such a great television writer because he wrote in such a visual way. He wrote with a director's eye – he always thought about how the scenes would look and sound. Very few writers can write with such a sense of the pictorial. No one will ever better the body of work he leaves. •

Alan Rusbridger

One of the sadnesses of Dennis Potter's career was the eight-year gap in his work for the BBC before he returned to the fold in 1986 with *The Singing*

Detective. It was worth the wait. The story unfolded in six dense and tortuous episodes, accumulating an audience of nearly 10 million by the end. No television writer ever demonstrated more powerfully that you don't need to be populist to be popular.

The Singing Detective remains a masterpiece of the medium. It piled pastiche upon pastiche – pastiche 'tec, pastiche musical, pastiche hospital drama, pastiche Potter – and then punched you in the stomach while your foot was still tapping.

Underneath the parody was a dark exploration of guilt and the unconscious. Potter was not a man for the Vaselined lens and a fade to black and white. He recognised that memory is a fragmented, scrappy, mixed-up state,* overlaid by subsequent emotions – and by the emotion of recalling the emotion.

The plot was like a giant dot-to-dot puzzle. Bursts of narrative were broken up by fantasy, hallucination, stream of consciousness and dream. For much of the time the main character, Philip Marlow, lay immobile, bedridden, curmudgeonly and teetering on the brink of madness. There was no escape from his past but to lie there and exorcise his childhood guilt by struggling back through his unconscious and yanking it to the surface. To have attracted the sort of audience figures normally reserved for *That's Life* or *Play Your Cards Right* suggested that Potter had tapped into an audience with a great unsatisfied appetite for being made to think.

I remember watching a sneak preview of the final episode just a few hours after it had been edited and dubbed. The audience was made up of the cast, technicians and producers, all seeing it for the first time. At the end they erupted into a prolonged and spontaneous burst of applause. Potter himself had slipped out for a fag. •

Gavin Millar

Before I worked worked with Dennis I was always being told terrifying stories about how difficult he could be and how his words were sacrosanct. But I found him very good to work with. When things didn't work he was always very anxious to help – if he felt you were on his wavelength.

The most important thing for him was the words, and he loved television because he wanted to reach a big audience. If he'd been born 100 years ago he would been a lay preacher. I could see him on the stump or travelling round the country – he was like a mixture of Savonarola and a daily journalist – but television was his way of reaching people with his ideas.

The thing I valued about Dennis most of all was his imagination – he convinced people that it was right to experiment. My regret is the lack of Dennis Potters in the increasing conformity of British television. •

Lynda La Plante

As a writer, he was probably one of my most important influences, because of his inventiveness and his refusal to accept that television was restrictive in any way. He lifted it on to a far higher plane than any other TV writer. There were no boundaries. For me it was very important to have someone right up there battling every inch of the way, and someone who had so much love for television and pride in it as a very important artistic medium.

One of the most extraordinary moments ever on TV was his interview with Melvyn Bragg. A man who was in such terrible pain became electrified when he began to describe his own work. He seemed to just shimmer. If you closed your eyes you could have been listening to a very young twenty-year-old academic because what he was saying was so fresh, so ingenious and so advanced. You could never say you'd seen it all before about a single piece of Potter's work •

Dennis Potter
28 March 1994
....
Smoke screen

It would, of course, be the dear old *Guardian* who, in telling of my terminal cancer, smuggles in a reference to my heavy smoking (25 March). I have cancer of the pancreas with secondaries in the liver, and my beloved cigarettes have nothing to do with it: much less, for sure, than decades of cytotoxic drugs used to contain my other illness. You should amend what you said from 'Mr Potter, who is 58, and is a heavy smoker ...' to 'Mr Potter, who is 58, and regularly eats fresh fruit and vegetables ...' •

Dennis Potter
London W2

Hugo Young
12 May 1994
John Smith

J ohn Smith did not have the chance to be a great leader of the Labour Party. But he was the necessary, probably the inevitable, leader in his time and place. As such he was a brilliant success. He presided over the further transformation of Labour into a believable party of government, and was sure it would reach its destiny next time.

In an age of presidential politics, his death, deeply shocking even if subconsciously half apprehended after his first heart attack, is a terrible blow to the system. It wipes out the alternative leader of a country that shows no sign of believing in the present one. But for Labour his finest legacy is that he will not be impossible to succeed.

Never did a more decent man rise to the top of British politics. He had a rare coherence of morality as well as mind. Although he was a skilful advocate in court, and a wonderful performer in the bear pit, it was the advocacy of social improvement that came from the core of his being, and here his hierarchy of principles never changed.

With unqualified passion, he wanted the betterment of all society, not just part of it. The Scottish belief in community, and in the duty of successful men to advance its cause, came as naturally to him as it once came a certain kind of Tory: the generous, inclusive outlook most public people used to have.

But Smith's consistency was also political. By lucky timing but also by character, he was excused the contradictions that drained so many post-war Labour politicians of their wider credibility. He was a pro-European centre-leftist from the beginning. He did not have to forget what his convictions were, like Harold Wilson; nor change them, leaving the indelible detritus behind, like Neil Kinnock.

It is hard to find any significant subject on which he changed his mind, or had to pretend that he had done so.

His second unique record was as a unifier of the party. There has not been a less divisive Labour leader, and none had fewer enemies. He made the most of the time he came to power. Neil Kinnock had done the dirty work, bequeathing his successor a party it was easy to command. The furies of the left were burned out.

Not that Smith avoided all fearsome battles. This time last year Labour was being torn apart by an argument over trade union domination, and that near-forgotten demon, OMOV – one member one vote. But by comparison with Kinnock, Foot, Callaghan and Wilson, this leader's tragically shortened years were a time of tranquillity, when the party members were finally prepared to let him get on with the job.

There was, therefore, no plotting. For the first time in my memory there was no anti-leader faction. That is one reason why Labour, by the base rules of mass journalism, almost ceased to be reported. Compared with the feuding rabble across the chamber, its MPs looked like the aberrants of politics – undisputing, unimpatient, and utterly unprepared for the fight they must now begin.

Whether this becomes a torment or an opportunity is now the question. It is not too soon to see John Smith as a transitional figure. When the decencies have been done – done with the sincerity the Commons had no difficulty whatever mustering yesterday – you can see it right away.

He ran a half-modernised Labour Party but he was a man of the old politics, the last survivor of the Callaghan cabinet. This was deeply reassuring to the party, and perhaps to the country. He gave Labour a semblance of governing authority, did actually know what it was to govern.

Steeped in Labourism, burnished by the swiftness of a clever Scottish lawyer, he asked the party few awkward questions. With the government in free-fall decline, which it happens to have been almost since he became leader, this comforting style paid dividends.

But it had its limits. It seemed intensely Scottish, growing out of the unshakeable axioms of north-of-the-border socialism, which had remained master of Scotland through all the gyrations further south. Although Labour once had to fight for its life against the Nationalists, the party's *raison d'être* was never in doubt.

However, the very assurance Smith's roots gave him – the same solid confidence that has pushed so many other Scots to the top of the party – perhaps made him less than sensitive to the sources of the English crisis of the left. He would dismiss this by pointing to his numerous neighbours in well-to-do

Edinburgh as proof that he understood the middle classes and could get them to vote for him in Maidstone as easily as Monklands. Not everyone believed this. As yet, Labour has not made convincing inroads south of London.

Whatever the truth, and ceaseless travel to prove the opposite was arguably what killed him, caution and confidence alike persuaded Smith against the need for a radical vision.

Every important choice he made save OMOV, a row he was pushed into against his will, favoured prudence over risk. It was a course that circumstance permitted him. There were grumblings down below, and dark forebodings among some colleagues, but the opinion polls spoke for themselves.

This silence is no longer an option. Fate compels the party to look at itself once more, and make a statement about what it is. The necessity for choice will oblige new contenders to describe their own ideas, in adversarial combat that will pose essentially two alternatives: carrying forward the momentum towards true modernity, or extending the transitional phase Smith thought sufficient to take Labour into power.

By demanding such a debate, John Smith's tragedy need not be the party's catastrophe. Disaster will flow from posturing and acrimony, and nobody is starry eyed enough to think the Kinnock–Smith years vented all such poisons.

Handled sensibly, and producing the right visionary result, the contest could yet make Labour a party for which people will vote with enthusiasm rather than the resignation that now widely obtains.

It will range, essentially, the John Prescott against the Tony Blair school of politics, and those men will surely be among the main names in the field, with Gordon Brown and Robin Cook upholding the claims of the Scottish dynasty.

Since nobody has begun to reckon the odds on a contest – unlike the party that thinks of nothing else – the relative positioning will take time to declare itself. All, in a sense, are equally unequipped to lead. Each candidate, we may be sure, will try to make himself harder to categorise than the conventional wisdom does. They are appealing to a variegated constituency, bereft of many of its old defining symbols and organised blocks.

For my part, I hope the party thinks deeply about what it means to look forward, not back, and seizes its chance to make the positive appeal John Smith had yet to articulate. But two prior thoughts predominate.

The first is that this is a monumentally hard job. Smith did it very well. He was a craftsman in most of the skills required. His bedrock of experience at the front rank of opposition, more than his shortish time in government, gave him a base that protected him against many errors. He knew the ropes, and their limits.

More than that, he had been inspected by the people and not found wanting.

Many pitiless eyes had been run across his life, and he had passed the test. He knew how to be ruthless with his colleagues, but also how to be acceptable to the country. He seemed at ease with himself, a faculty hard to acquire from a cold start in such an exposed position.

Whoever succeeds him will need time to find it, and establish a public reputation still eight parts bank manager, but two parts preacher as well. How all this, meanwhile, affects the other leader, perhaps giving him bizarre respite from his daily agony, is another story. This new Labour leader can only be chosen for the long haul.

But, secondly, the Smith inheritance, like the Smith leadership, brings with it an air of calmness unthinkable three years ago. The party will find it quite hard to resume open warfare. Something deeper than personality, and broader than faction, is moving our politics at this time.

The leader matters. The wrong choice could bring disaster in its train. The system, as much as the party, is owed a leader the whole nation can respect. But the state of things is on his side.

The leader is dead, long live the leader. Without the eighteen month tenure of a brave, accomplished man, that sentiment would have been impossible to set down, except as a sour joke. •

Simon Hoggart
13 May 1994

Sharp wit with an inner fire

The image of a dour Presbyterian lawyer could hardly have been more wrong. What John Smith liked more than anything was what the Irish call the 'crack', that blend of companionship, booze, atmosphere and wit which can lift a conversation into an evanescent work of art.

He was also one of the sharpest and funniest men I ever met. You'd be having an ordinary political chat, and suddenly the zinger would come at you out of the sun. 'Margaret Beckett? Proof that the Rehabilitation of Offenders Act really does work...' The tributes yesterday said that he was without malice. That's not true; every successful politician is malicious, but in his case it was a genial, amiable, constructive malice.

In 1982 I caught a sleeper from Glasgow and saw his name on the manifest. He appeared at the cabin door clanking with miniatures acquired from a friendly steward who knew him well. Ten minutes later there was another knock, and a Scottish Nationalist MP arrived, pulling from what was clearly a remarkable back pocket in his trousers, an entire bottle of whisky.

The conversation was gossipy, funny and extremely malicious, the more so because Scottish Labour politics makes a snakepit look like model of courteous gentility. I got rid of them at Rugby, an hour north of London. Of course, as I tottered on to the platform at Euston I could not, through the hangover, remember a word of what had been said.

After his 1988 heart attack he did cut down considerably on both food and drink. Articles appeared in the papers describing an intake which included bran cereal and skimmed milk. But it was, frankly, rare to see Smith at a party with a glass of skimmed milk in his hand. Like many of us, I suspect he shared the delusion that dry white wine is a non-alcoholic drink.

Like all lawyers he had a store of good legal anecdotes. One of his favourites was about his early days at the bar when he had to defend a particularly unpleasant fifteen-year-old hooligan. The solicitor, a large man who had fought in the Spanish Civil War – on Franco's side – addressed the youth: 'I have managed to obtain, at considerable expense, the services of one of the most eminent advocates at the Scottish Bar, a junior who is undoubtedly destined for high office. So sit in the corner, you wee c**t, and listen to what he says.'

The pose as a boring bank manager was deliberate. Partly it was his background: that was the way people in authority were supposed to behave. Partly it was because, just as John Major won an election by being the un-Thatcher, he wanted to be the un-Kinnock.

But he was also comfy with the style. His political heroes, he said, were Attlee and Truman, both unshowy men who preferred getting the work done to great rhetorical flourishes. In the words of the cliché, he was a great House of Commons man. Just as Dillinger robbed banks because 'that's where the money is', he worked in Parliament because that's where the power is. Innumerable times you'd see him bustling around 'steaming down the Committee Corridor like a small rhinoceros', as one of his colleagues once said.

But there was also rage inside there. Beneath the studious and owlish blink of his public appearances, there was a real hatred of this Conservative government. The constant criticism of him by Labour activists, that he had no fire in his belly, was mistaken. He believed it was absolutely essential to get the present lot out, and that everything, including his own natural inclinations, had to be subordinate to that great cause.

For example, I and other journalists often wrote that he should have used his wit more against John Major. I felt that a leader of the opposition didn't need to be an imitation prime minister; it was his job to lampoon the present incumbent, for his wit to crystallise the country's sense of anger and betrayal. But he said privately that it was essential that he behaved with stern gravitas. 'I must always appear statesmanlike,' he said insistently.

I'm sure that is why he often seemed stilted and slow-footed at Question Time; he was holding back the bubble of his own high spirits. When, in a speech, he could relax and expand, he was a superb parliamentary performer, one of the very few left in the House. In the meantime, he sometimes appeared to want to out-grey John Major. As a senior Tory minister said recently, 'If John Smith were to replace John Major, do you think the financial markets would even notice?'

Yesterday the Prime Minister painted a picture of the two men, convivial and at ease over a behind-the-scenes drink, as their private offices anxiously wondered why the meeting was lasting so long. Smith himself felt differently; he didn't dislike Major in particular, but had little time or affection for him. 'There's nothing to like or dislike there,' he once said.

But he hated the sleaze and corruption which clings to this government, if not personally to its leader. He detested the crookery, the lies, the petty evasions and the featherbedding of rich friends and Tory contributors. He was infuriated by the Nicholas Scott affair, that act of deceit which went against everything he had ever learned. As his friend Menzies Campbell said yesterday, 'He had all the virtues of a Scottish Presbyterian, but none of the vices.'

Well, precious few. I have never known the Commons have the genuine sense of grief we saw yesterday. •

Leader
13 May 1994
••

His mark, one stride from the pinnacle

The world outside, which nowadays has so little respect for politicians, might perhaps have been surprised by the warmth and the poignancy of the tributes paid to John Smith yesterday; not only by close friends and political allies, but by opponents too, within his party and outside it. But no surprise, in truth. It did not need the awful news of his death to establish that here, in the broadest sense of the term, was a good man.

When, at a similar age, Hugh Gaitskell was struck down with similar suddenness, the Liberal leader Jo Grimond said of him that he had joined that considerable band of politicians who had left his mark on history without ever becoming prime minister. That was also true of John Smith long before he became leader. Had it not been for the staunchness which people like Smith – Europeans to their bones and undisguisedly on the right of their party – stuck to Labour through the turmoil of the early eighties while others departed, the party, as a broad-based movement of conscience and reform, might have been shattered.

In the convenient typecasting of politics, he was always portrayed as a kind of careful, stolid, Presbyterian fellow; one of nature's bank managers. To some extent that was true; and after the battles of the Kinnock years, when the party was brought back to the edge of electability but could still not quite cross it, these were virtues of high appropriateness. A man you could trust. A safe pair of hands. Socialism, where is thy sting? But that wasn't anything like the whole story. First, because it missed his sociability, his wit, his frequent cheerfulness, his engaging interest in life. He was not a great platform orator but, in an age which is often said to be devoid of parliamentary stars, he was a star. On his day, and as John Major said in a becoming Commons tribute yesterday, it was often his day, he was devastating – and devastating as much for his humour – as for his analysis. His great weapon was sarcasm; but a sarcasm which even its victims might feel was devoid of real malice, and laced here and there with a touch of ingenious fantasy: another mismatch with the image.

But the image missed something else. It missed the morality. For Smith, politics was always essentially a moral exercise. He would not condone injustice. Injustice clothed in rectitude, defended on grounds of necessity or the greater national good, was to him still injustice. 'In Tory Britain,' he told what we now know was his last Labour conference, 'an angry and disillusioned people are in danger of losing faith in our future. They have seen too often their jobs destroyed, people made homeless, youngsters denied opportunity. They worry, and no wonder they worry, that our society is coming apart, that our very sense of community is being undermined.' He meant to change all that.

'All we can say,' said Grimond of Gaitskell, 'and it is not very much – is that while in Hugh Gaitskell's death there is all too much for tears, there can be nothing but inspiration from the story of his life.' The life of this mountain climber, so cruelly terminated just as the pinnacle seemed to be coming in sight, serves to remind the world that even amidst the stratagems, the duplicities, and the sometimes inevitable shabby compromises, you can get to the top of politics while still remaining yourself. The affection and grief which everywhere greeted the news of his death were proof of how completely John Smith did that. •

W. L. Webb
30 August 1993
....

A thoroughly English dissident

Edward Thompson, who died on Saturday, was the most eloquent historian of his English generation and its best polemical essayist. He was a rare romantic figure among the prosy or jokey generality of post-war British intellectuals. As well as altering the map of English historiography, he was also a formidably effective dissident from contemporary British political culture. After the first phase of the Cold War, he was able by his vivid style and tough argument to win access at least to the print media, as readers of the *Guardian* and *New Society* will best remember.

At the height of his powers and reputation he gave what was to be the last decade of his life to making clear the crippling cost – political, economic and psychic – of the nuclear weapons on which the cold peace precariously rested. It was an intervention which will one day be seen to be as much part of the moral history of his country as his historian's mission to rescue the lives and endeavours of the poor from the dark abyss of time in which the indifference or antagonism of establishment historians had largely been content to leave them.

But although in his clout with the politically frustrated multitudes who turned out for the vast CND rallies of the early 1980s he reminded you of gallant and obdurate central Europeans like Vaclav Havel and Adam Michnik, he was a thoroughly English dissident, a patriot-dissident as well as a socialist-humanist, and the devoted and creative heir to that other line of Englishness that runs from Bunyan and the Levellers, through Blake and Shelley, Tom Paine and William Cobbett, at least as far as William Morris (the subject of his first major work, produced at the age of thirty). Twenty years later he was to describe his political and intellectual formation in an argument with Leszek Kolakowski, another central European former dissident he had long admired:

'I belong to an emaciated political tradition, encapsulated within a hostile national culture which is itself both smug and resistant to intellectuality and failing in self-confidence; and yet I share the same idiom as that of the culture which is my reluctant host ... Take Marx and Vico and a few European novelists away, and my most intimate pantheon would be a provincial tea-party: a gathering of the English and the Anglo-Irish. Talk of free will and determinism, and I think first of Milton. Talk of man's inhumanity, I think of Swift. Talk of morality and revolution, and my mind is off with Wordsworth's 'Solitary'. Talk of the problems of self-activity and creative labour in socialist society, and I am in an instant back with William Morris – a great bustard like myself.'

In fact, with his ardour, wit and rather wild good looks, there was more than a touch of the Byronesque about Edward's dissidence, for all the missionary Methodism in his family and upbringing. There can't have been many young cavalry officers, leading a tank squadron of the swagger 17/21st Lancers at the battle of Cassino, who had been committed communists since the age of sixteen.

Later he would be a leader in another battle, at the front of the exodus from the British Communist Party that followed the revelations of Khrushchev's secret speech to the 20th Congress of the CPSU in 1956. Out of the duplicated (samizdat!) dissident journal *The Reasoner*, which he founded with his wife Dorothy, was to grow *The New Reasoner*, and then not just the *New Left Review* but much of the New Left movement. He and it were committed now to fighting both Stalin's heirs and Nato's military-industrial complex, as Eisenhower called it, as well as what were seen as the cramping consequences for British politics of the Westminster consensus known then as Butskellism.

E. P. Thompson was born in 1924, the son of the writer, poet and former Methodist minister Edward John Thompson and Theodosia Jessup Thompson, who came from an American family of missionaries, diplomats and scholars. Both parents had been missionaries in India but, shortly before Edward was born, his father left the ministry for a fellowship at Oriel College, Oxford, and a university lectureship in Bengali. Gandhi and Nehru were among the steady flow of Indian visitors to their Boars Hill home, while John Masefield, Gilbert Murray and Sir Arthur Evans were neighbours. (Nehru taught Edward how to hold his cricket bat properly.)

Frank, their elder son, also a gifted linguist and poet, who was to die leading an ill-fated Special Operations mission parachuted into Axis Bulgaria to support the partisans, went to Winchester, but Edward was sent to his father's old school, the Methodist Kingswood School in Bath. Both brothers joined the Communist Party as undergraduates, Frank at Oxford, Edward at Corpus Christi, Cambridge, and carried their convictions with them when they went to fight the Nazis, as one can read in the moving wartime letters from Frank, published in *There is a Spirit in Europe*.

This memoir, which Edward and his mother produced in 1947, describing Frank's capture and execution by the Bulgarian government, and adding the letters and some of his poems, gives a hint of the extent to which this admired and beloved elder brother was to be a touchstone for Edward, an emotional and moral reference point in all his writing and political thinking. Together with his experiences in the summer of 1947, first during a visit to Bulgaria with his mother, then working on the great Yugoslav Youth Railway project that brought young socialists from all over Europe and elsewhere to construct the line from Samac to Sarajevo, this influence was to make him responsive and informed (before many others on the British left) about the later political reawakenings in eastern and central Europe.

After serving as a tank commander in North Africa and Italy, he returned to Cambridge in 1946, taking advantage of wartime regulations that allowed him a degree on his first class in part one of the History tripos. He spent his final year reading and researching independently, chiefly in Elizabethan history and literature. His first published work was a short story, and though fiction was not to be his strongest suit – his novel *The Sykaos Papers* (1988) seems to owe something to the 'Canopus in Argo' novels of his quondam *Reasoner* colleague Doris Lessing, but lacks her narrative skill – he was always a writer *and* an historian, with expressive gifts that placed most of his books clearly within the division of literature.

Looking for academic work as the Cold War grew bitter, he was lucky in 1948 as a known communist, to get a job as staff tutor in history and literature in Leeds University's extra-mural department, probably thanks to an old family friend, Guy Chapman, then professor of modern history at Leeds.

Thompson married another social historian, Dorothy Towers, his life-long intellectual and political collaborator. He stayed in the West Riding for seventeen years, teaching, bringing up their three children, and also producing – as well as *The Reasoner* and (with John Saville and Peter Worsley) *The New Reasoner* – his Morris book and what remains his *chef d'œuvre*, *The Making of the English Working Class* (1963), with its vivid re-creation of the lives and thoughts of the generations history chained to the engines of the Industrial Revolution. Like all his major books, both these grew out of smaller projects. The 900 pages on Morris began as a review of an American book that had made him angry. *The Making of the English Working Class* was meant to be chapter one of a textbook on working-class history. *Whigs and Hunters*, that resonant study of the savage working of the 'Black Acts' against poachers, was to have been his contribution to a book of essays on eighteenth-century crime.

In 1965 he was appointed director of the Centre for Social History at Warwick, resigning in 1971 after writing a stinging Penguin Special about the ethos and administrative arrangements of this new 'business university' conveniently sited 'in the mid-Atlantic of the motor industry'. He then started the career as an independent writer and scholar that he increasingly wanted, made possible not least by the salary from Dorothy's full-time academic post.

Now came the period of the heavyweight polemic bouts (chiefly with Perry Anderson and Tom Nairn at the *New Left Reveiw*) over the Paris fashions in neo-Marxism. He considered them to be sterile and unimaginative, remote from understanding of the realm of Utopian desire or any real sympathy for the lives of the oppressed. 'I find,' he wrote in his open letter to Kolakowski, 'in the very vocabulary of this new Marxism, with its obligatory face-making at "humanism", "moralism", etc. – its inability to discuss the arts except by translating them into cerebration – and in its lack of terms with which to handle moral or value-making process, a suggestion that ... [the experience of Stalinism] has passed the new tradition by.'

And then it was the time of Thatcherites and Reaganites, of Cold War two, and a world that seemed more dangerous than it had done for several decades. Of the half-dozen collections of polemical pieces and pamphlets, produced by a Thompson who had enlisted in the cause of demystifying the dark rhetoric of nuclear politics, the first of them, *Writing by Candlelight*, still seems the best. And the best of that collection is the wonderfully quirky and deflationary title essay, looking at the English bourgeoisie in its periodic fits of outraged letterwriting to *The Times* – at the presumptuousness of the servant class asking for more.

Now that the first euphoria of mindless triumphalism about the victory over communism is over, one can already see that posterity will adopt a less condescending attitude than some right-wing politicians now have to what the peace movement achieved. It will come to share Thompson's conviction, stated in the preface to the essays collected in *Customs in Common* (1991), that in fact 'the peace movement made a major contribution to dispersing the Cold War, which had descended like a polluting cloud on every field of political and intellectual life'. What's already clear is the extent to which the intellectual and moral force of his arguments gave confidence to the movement, and gave its case credit among the thinking nation.

He mentions briefly in that preface the ill-health that, with the demands of the peace movement, contributed to the long delay in completing the book, a reticent reference to the battle with illness during the last years of his life that was quite as gallant and taxing as any of his battles with political or academic opponents. •

Mike Ellison
3 March 1994

'Controversialist' Jarman takes his final bow in style

Derek Jarman, the film-maker and hero to Britain's gay community, was receiving visitors to his fisherman's cottage before his funeral yesterday.

Friends, admirers, family and members of the Sisters of Perpetual Indulgence – men dressed in nuns' clothes – came to see him 'lying in state ' in his wooden home on the wasteland of Dungeness, Kent.

In a small back room at the end of a pink corridor lined with books, the artist, who died of Aids eleven days ago, was laid out in a plain open coffin wearing the gold robe of the king in his 1991 film *Edward* II, a necklace and a blue cap inscribed with the word 'controversialist'. His thin hands clutched a small green plastic frog sent to him by an admirer in Japan. Ten candles around a bust on top of a weathered chest containing his CD collection flickered as the draught disturbed purple and blue drapes. An orange-tree stood in a bucket marked £4.

'There are no celebs, it's nice and quiet – what Derek wanted,' said his friend Keith Collins. Visitors wandered through Prospect Cottage, which Jarman bought after being diagnosed HIV-positive in 1986, and the garden of stones, shrubs, sticks and corroding poles, which gave its name to his 1990 movie *The Garden*. A quarter of a mile down a road leading to Dungeness power station, sixty-eight-year-old Doreen Thomas tended her fish counter. She said: 'Derek was not an ordinary guy; he brought a dash of colour here. He didn't come down here to hide like some people would have done. He always gave a wave, he was a nice chap – but I'm a very liberal woman.

'The people here didn't care; and that's saying something – it's a closed community.'

About five miles away from the flat Dungeness landscape, picketed by electricity pylons and dotted with cranes, boats and rusting winching gear, Jarman's funeral was about to start in Old Romney. Some 400 friends filed into eleventh-century St Nicholas's church, while knots of locals gathered over the road. Canon Peter Ford, who conducted the service, said beforehand: 'It has to fit in with the regulations we abide by, although his beliefs were a lot wider than conventional Christianity.'

Mourners included his sister Gaye and her family; Neil Tennant of the Pet Shop Boys; Anthony Page, director of *Middlemarch*; Howard Malin, Jarman's first film producer; Tariq Ali, the writer; Robin Don, a theatre designer; and Jill

Balcon, widow of poet laureate C. Day-Lewis and mother of the Oscar-winning actor Daniel.

Nicholas de Jongh, the theatre critic, one of four friends to address the funeral service, said: 'All down the exciting road Derek travelled as the first and greatest English gay icon; he blazed a trail. He showed what it was in our cruel, unfeeling times to be an outcast, reviled and persecuted for a sexuality in which he rejoiced and saw no shred of evil.' He was buried under a favourite yew tree at the church of St Clement, Old Romney.

Jarman wrote in 1991: 'On 22 December 1986, finding I was body positive, I set myself a target: I would disclose my secret and survive Margaret Thatcher. I did. Now I have set my sights on the millenium and a world where we are all equal before the law.' He died, aged fifty-two, two days before Parliament declined to lower the age of consent for homosexuals to sixteen. •

John Humphrys
24 January 1994

The vibrant voice

Five o'clock in the morning in the rather grubby office of the *Today* programme on the fourth floor of Broadcasting House.

'Morning!' It's sung, rather than spoken, by the figure bouncing through the door. A Pilgrim Father of a figure: bearded, cane in one hand, black wide-brimmed hat perched on his head. A brisk run-down on which famous figure he had had lunch or dinner with the day before and then a quick scan of the papers. 'What a prat! If you'd written that on the *Whitley Bay Seaside Chronicle* forty years ago you'd have been fired!'

It has been like that for nearly twenty years, and now that Brian Redhead has died it feels as though a great hole has been blasted into the side of Broadcasting House. In the forty years since he left the *Whitley Bay Seaside Chronicle* he established himself as the voice of Radio 4, and there were no real challengers to the title.

The natural exuberance that made it possible for Brian to get up at four in the morning year in, year out, and still seem cheerful was one of the things that made

Gone before
....

him different. That, and his sheer love of the job. 'The best job in the world,' he always said. And he really believed it. I sat next to Brian in Studio 4A for eight of those twenty years. Some of the time I wanted to throttle him. Most of the time I tried to work out what made him so good at his job. Oddly, the two qualities went together. Brian truly believed that *Today* needed a star, and he knew he was one. He had never been short of self-confidence. It might have come from a father who had earned his living in a professional boxing ring, until he met his nemesis at the hands of Cast Iron Casey, the Sunderland Assassin. Brian loved telling that story.

He himself, influenced by Scoop Mallory, ace reporter of the *Hotspur*, wanted to be a journalist. Hence the *Chronicle*. But then he was called up for National Service and ended up in Malaya. He was not one of nature's subordinates. He could not see a lot of point in delaying his education pretending to be a soldier in some steamy jungle, so he took himself off to Australia... without bothering to tell his commanding officer.

That earned him a court-martial when they finally caught up with him, but he used to say he defended himself and got off. He was no more compliant at Downing College, Cambridge, when he finally got back to Britain. He was a bright student and did well in the first part of his finals. But he did not approve of the questions in the second part, so he wrote what he wanted to write and ignored the questions. That put paid to his first. Not that it mattered very much. He got a job on the *Manchester Guardian*, and was good at it. But Brian, no good as a subordinate, wasn't much better as a boss either. He fell out with the bureaucrats (he always hated bureaucrats; 'they're all "prats"') and they sacked him. Broadcasting – and the *Today* programme in particular – owes the bureaucrats of the *Manchester Evening News* a debt of gratitude because that was when he joined the BBC. He was already soundly established as the chairman of *A Word in Edgeways*, which he made, in the words of its producer, Michael Green, 'an unrehearsed intellectual adventure'. He tried his hand at television – as a reporter on the old *Tonight* programme – but it wasn't until he joined *Today* that he found his real home. His partnership with John Timpson lasted thirteen years and they, and the programme, became a national institution.

So what did Redhead have? The ability to infuriate, for sure. If you did not happen to come from Macclesfield or care about traffic jams on the M6, you might curse him over the cornflakes. If you were a politician with a grievance you might write to the director-general and demand he be sacked for his latest outrage, and many did. They were wrong. They hated him for the very reason that so many others loved him. He was brilliant at puncturing pomposity and exposing the weakness in an argument.

True, he loved the occasional aside that gave his bosses ulcers: 'It's the boat race at the weekend. In the old days it divided the nation. Now we leave that to the government.' But his questions were, as far as it is possible to be in this seat-of-the-pants business, fair. And those politicians who were rash enough to challenge his professional impartiality usually lived to regret it.

Nigel Lawson must still be licking his wounds – from when he suggested Redhead was a lifelong supporter of the Labour Party, and got both barrels. Peter Lilley suggested Redhead voted Labour. It so happened that he tended to vote Tory – but only because his MP was Nicholas Winterton, friend and defender.

The fact is, Brian was not ideological; he was a pragmatist. If Thatcherite capitalism delivered the goods (i.e. the jobs) that was fine. If he appeared to be tougher with the government than with the opposition, that was because 'governments DO things; oppositions can only TALK about doing things'. If he offered a Tory government the occasional hostage to fortune, that had more to do with ego than politics.

And that is what so often made you want to throttle him. I lost count of the number of times I would wait to hear the private thoughts of one of the great and the good as he passed through the studio – and instead got Brian's thoughts, telling the great man what he ought to be doing.

He knew perfectly well the dangers of celebrity, and he often protested that he tried very hard not to be one. He affected to despise television because, if you weren't careful, 'you begin to behave like a fellow looking in the mirror all the time and doing impressions of yourself. And you finish up not knowing who you are.' Brian hugely enjoyed his fame, but he was not corrupted. He was the ultimate professional. And he would regard that as the greatest compliment of all. •

Polly Toynbee
14 September 1993
....

Raging at the dying of the light

'Something horrible has happened,' Liz Forgan said. She had trouble getting the words out. Jill Tweedie had just told her that twenty-four hours previously she had been diagnosed as having motor neurone disease. Incurable, fatal, horrible and relatively rapid. Of diseases to strike, this is one of the very worst. But Jill, a life force of exuberant energy, a survivor of disasters that would have destroyed lesser women? Unthinkable. We may fear cancer or heart attacks for ourselves or our friends, but not a savage, rampant, wasting disease that destroys the whole body and paralyses.

Jill, Liz and I all worked together on the *Guardian* women's page. Liz as editor, Jill and I as columnists. Jill wrote her brilliant *Faint-Hearted Feminist* columns in those days, under Liz's aegis (later turned into a television sitcom with Lynn Redgrave, and Posy Simmonds and I appeared on the same Monday page, all of us friends ever since. But Jill was the beacon.

Though gripped by fear and horror, Jill wanted everyone to know at once, didn't want to keep having to break the news to people. She wanted to write this article herself, and tried, but found she couldn't. I can see why. It's the most difficult piece I've ever been asked to write. Striking the right note, she said, was so hard. It came out flippant and plucky because she didn't want to sound self-pitying. But she doesn't want to put on a brave act either. Why should she? Goddammit, she has been plunged into a grotesque mental torture chamber, she says, without hope or light.

The diagnosis came two months ago, abrupt, shocking, without preparation. There had been intimations that something was wrong. Her breathing had changed, she was constantly tired and breathless, but the GP's stethoscope and a chest X-ray found nothing. A lifetime of smoking have, ironically, left not a blemish on her lungs. In mid-June, at the party to celebrate the publication of the first part of her autobiography, *Eating Children*, she could hardly climb the stairs and was exhausted. It was Jon Snow at that party who realised then she might be seriously ill.

He asked a friend, a consultant neurologist, to see her. He turned up out of the blue on her doorstep, examined her, and then told her to come into the hospital at once for tests. There followed reflex tests, the usual knocking on knees and elbows, the pencil up the soles of the feet and, more unnerving, a gazing hard at the arms and legs, looking for the feared signs, a faint fluttering of the muscles beneath the skin, a slight twitch. And there were more high-tech tests too, an electro-cardiogram, another that punctured little holes in her muscles. They injected a chemical into her veins, pressed down on her arm, and were plainly distressed with the results. Typically Jill dismissed herself from hospital after the first night (true, there had been no sheets or pillow cases in the ward and tiny portions of disgusting food delivered at entirely random and varying hours of the day). But she returned each morning as a day patient, angry and frustrated at the long waits and the inefficiency of it all. Not a good patient patient.

They were looking for something, anything, she later realised, any symptom that could possibly lead to any other diagnosis. But there was none. At the end of the five days she was summoned to the consultant's small, stuffy room. 'He was jovial, bluff, cheery, full of pleasantries about holidays,' she says. 'So I knew it would be something ghastly. Then he just said the words, "You've got motor neurone." I was numb. I felt like someone in a bad B-movie when I asked, "How long have I got?" but it was all I could say. "Can't tell," he said, and I was utterly taken aback by that. "What do you mean you can't tell? Is it a month, or ten years?" Twice he said, "I can't tell. There's no way of knowing." When she pressed later for the actuarial statistics, she squeezed out the fact that most people die within one to three years of diagnosis, but some few last for twenty years, like Stephen Hawking, a name that resurfaces uncomfortably time and again.

But he told her there was no treatment of any kind, nothing that made a jot of difference. There was no cure, only research, dimly on the horizon, linked to Alzheimer's research projects. What more? It's rare, only 5,000 people in the UK have it. And it never, never retreats or goes into remission, though its inevitable progress may speed up or slow down.

The consultant drew diagrams of ganglions, neurones and so on, which she didn't in the least understand. Dumbly, she thanked him and she and Alan [Brien, her husband, the writer and journalist] were shown out to sit on two chairs outisde. No comfort, no advice, just the appalling brutish fact. They sat there staring ahead, with nothing but despair and shock. And at that moment a brisk white-overalled woman appeared down the corridor with a tape measure, and started to measure Jill's legs and back. 'What are you doing?' Jill asked. 'Just measuring you for a wheelchair. It can take two months for them to be delivered so it's best to get it done now.' Brutal, cruel treatment, within minutes of being told the news.

Yet worse was to come. She and Alan were next ushered down into a large basement room. 'A horrible, horrible room, you have no idea of the shock,' she says. 'It was like an Ideal Home exhibition for torture chambers.' Bedrooms, bathrooms and kitchens had been laid out there, displaying a variety of handrails, hoists, seats that go up and down in the bath, lifts, and kettleholders. 'I sat down at a table and started to cry.'

Two days later, not even two months later, the brand-new wheelchair was delivered and dumped in the front hall when Jill was alone in the house. 'I just stood there and stared at it. When Alan came in he bundled it away and hid it somewhere, I don't know where.' Another cigarette, another sip of wine. 'But how can it be that if you have cancer these days they thrust counselling at you at every stage, about everything from your sex life to your children. Why has none of that gentleness filtered down to other departments dealing with people with terminal conditions. And with cancer at least there's a chance you might get better.' Since then she has come to know and like that consultant, who is so solicitous that he makes regular visits to her home. She thinks he broke the news so badly because he hated having to do it.

But why did they tell her at all? What is the point? Perhaps, with her journalistic curiosity, she would have demanded the truth from them. But only if she had really wanted to know. It would have been her choice.

There is no disguising that the last two months have been spent hanging above a black pit of despair, saved, she says 'only by the continual company and loving kindness of friends, with their everyday life-giving laughter and gossip'. But she is honest, with herself, with everyone, with this interview. She doesn't want to pretend, though others often do. People say the most extraordinary things to jolly her along. 'Well, we're all dying aren't we?' or 'Just live for the moment.' Jill explodes: 'Live for the moment! Live for the moment! What on earth does that mean? Each moment is full of the future, thinking of plans and pleasures ahead. Just listen to anyone talk, and you know.'

Or people talk to her in hushed voices, wanting her to be saintly, spiritual, as if she already had one foot on the other side, and something special to impart. 'Sod that,' she says. Suffering does not ennoble, we agree. 'I don't want to be uplifted, or uplifting, I just want to go on being me.' As for the idea that this is some kind of 'opportunity for personal growth', to hell with that too. 'Religious belief,' she says, vaguely, 'would, I suppose, be a comfort.' But we agree that this is not acceptable, no deathbed conversions here, die as you lived. 'And,' she adds, 'if there's any silver lining to knowing you're dying, it's not the love of some vague God, but the love of human beings that's vital, and having time to tell them you love them too.'

And if any reader feels moved to send Jill any uplifting tracts, religious or meditational, they may receive a call from me on their doorstep, minded to knock them on the nose for their effrontery. Evangelists and proselytisers do get a gleam in their eye when they think they've got you at rock bottom.

Jill laughed when I told her about an appalling interview I did once with a woman who had been more than twenty years in an iron lung, a torment to herself, her family and her miserable husband. She said to me with a beatific smile from inside her iron cocoon, 'You know why I keep going? Because I know the good I do to able-bodied people like you. You look at me and I make you appreciate the value of your life, compared to mine, and it makes you happy.' Jill does not relish becoming a sacrificial emblem. And then there is Stephen Hawking. Time and again people searching vainly for something hopeful to say wax lyrical on the miracle of a life so helpless yet still so full of purpose and genius: 'See what he's done, see the worth of living. You can still write. Look at him.' She looks, and the sight leaves her aghast.

Jill finds walking very difficult, and getting up and down stairs impossible without help. Friends call to offer help with cooking, cleaning, driving or anything to feel useful. Alan says, 'I tell them all to go out and buy Jill's book, get their friends to buy it and write a note to Jill about it.'

She sits on her sofa, painfully thin, without appetite, yet, as ever, beautiful. And, as ever, the very best company there is. For however hard she tries to describe despair, in creeps the wit, the perceptions, the penetrating determination to get to the heart of things, that urge to turn things on their head and twist every proposition through a hundred prismatic, gleaming beams of light. (Oh, Jill! How can this be happening to you?) And still, generous and not in the least self-obsessed, she draws out of us, her friends, our own worries, our own comparatively piffling unhappinesses, and dispenses as ever the very best, most human, advice. She doesn't deserve this, I think, full of anger. Good God, hasn't she had enough? As her recent book so movingly describes, at fifty-seven she's had a hard life, a cruel father, a cot death baby, and her next two children stolen away until adulthood by their father to an unknown destination; of four children only one brought up by her. Greek choruses wouldn't do justice to this monstrosity.

But justice of course has nothing whatsoever to do with it, unless you are religious. There is no plan, no reason, no cause. This is just random, just chance. But the one thing she never thinks is 'Why me?' because that isn't the point either. 'Why me?' implies 'Why not someone else?' and that is not her cast of mind.

'In the old days,' one doctor said to her, 'we would have fudged this diagnosis.' But it is the modern trend among doctors and ethics committees to tell all. They no longer seek to be patronising, all-powerful arbiters of their patients' lives, treating them as children to be protected from frightening truths. I often hear the thoughtful ones saying that facing death is a very important part of life, and they themselves would want to know, to participate in it, to contemplate it, and to end their lives with knowledge and insight. Noble thoughts expounded with all the rationality of a healthy beating heart and death an unthinkable millennium away. Not right here, and now, with the chill hand of the grim reaper grasping at the throat.

We talk of my husband, Peter, who died suddenly last year. I (and he, in a way) made the opposite choice. Throughout four days in an intensive care unit, desperately weaker by the day, he did not choose to know. He did not ask the questions that would have told him the truth. Had he demanded to know, he would have been told, but he didn't. Yet from all he had said before about death and illness, from everything I knew of him, I would have sworn he would have seized upon the awful facts immediately. I would have expected him to understand at once, and press the question until he knew how very few days he had left. But he didn't. He chose to think an operation would save him, chose to talk of his convalescence, of plans, of the future. And I forbade any doctor to tell him anything more unless he asked. So he had no last dying days to contemplate his life, we had no goodbyes, and he died gently without panic or fear. And I do not regret that. The best death is a death you never get to experience.

But many would disagree, the leading lights in the hospice movement among them. Religious people, and others of a contemplative turn of mind, manage to regard death as an integral part of living, a part of the meaning of life. But Jill is not that way inclined, and we agree that parting for ever from everyone you love is an abomination to be evaded in both thought and deed. People complain that these days we are not equipped for death. It is a taboo. We are not used to people dying, other than the very old. But were people ever 'good at it'? When children died regularly, and disease or childbirth swept people away randomly and often in the flood of life, there was plenty of convenient ritual to cope with it. But there was also all that wild superstition and religion to try to paper over the abyss. Was that 'better'? I doubt it. Sugary promises of an afterlife where we shall all meet again in a great celestial *Guardian* women's page in the sky certainly wouldn't do much to help make sense of the meaning of life.

So how should we face it, we rationalists, for us, for our loved ones? Raging feels right at present. Jill is for the Roman way. 'If I can die at a time of my own choosing, then I shall feel I have gained some control over my life again. If I know I can die when I want, then at least I have something.' And sometimes now she wishes she had killed herself on the day she was diagnosed, for it is so much harder to pick a time, to choose a moment, as week follows week. But she is certain that the time will come when that is what she will do, because she cannot, quite reasonably, face the thought of total incapacity, and if anyone says Stephen Hawking again ...

One friend did come round hesitantly with a bottle of morphine, but she was dubious about it, said she'd had it over six years now and it had probably gone off, at which they both laughed a good deal. Alan says he will support whatever Jill decides to do, but adds, 'I want every month with her I can get.' 'But I'm not much use to you,' Jill says. 'I'm pretty poor value.' 'Nonsense!' Alan says. 'I like looking after you, loving you. True, I don't know where half the things in the house are, but I'm learning, and anyway, what does it matter, compared to being with you?' Jill smiles, wanly. 'Self-pity is the worst, isn't it? So destructive, with nowhere to go. But I feel I see things as they are at the moment. Nature doesn't give a sod, just goes on telling you to live. People say to me, "You know, it's amazing what you get used to. I never thought my old mother would bear someone taking her to the loo, but she did. She got used to it." Well, I don't want to get used to it.' And she's frightened of getting it wrong, 'Frightened of going on beyond the time I should have had the courage to stop it.'

The isolation is another thing. She is over there on the dying side, and we are still here, on the living side. She cannot bear to think we look at her as a thing apart, untouchable, in a realm of horror we cannot enter. But then, it *is* difficult for us to enter. I cannot pretend to her presumptiously that I can know how she feels, or what it means. We may all have had moments of panic about dying, fearful midnight intimations of mortality, but I imagine that's nothing like the real and certain knowledge. She does not want to be counselled by some death expert, because she bristles at the thought that a healthy person can do much for her, let alone tell her how to die, or how to be less depressed about dying. Jill says enviously of Peter, 'He died in the fullness of life, people remembering him as he was, well and active. I want to be remembered like that, not as a pathetic invalid. I get stoned a bit on cannabis now and then, and that eases things, along with the warmth of other people. But otherwise if I'm left alone the panic attacks starts, the ferrets start nibbling at my brain. It's mental not physical anguish I suffer at the moment.'

Jill has always been the pioneer. In her *Guardian* columns one of the first to blast the world with piercingly observed mockery and outrage at the way women were treated, in childbirth, at home, at work and everywhere. Motherhood took on a whole new dimension under her pen. Every difficult stage in her life she explored and mined for the illumination of others. The other day one nurse in the hospital suddenly and spontaneously hugged her, an old reader who had lived her life through much of Jill's writing, like so very many women of our era. Now, how bitter, Jill is out ahead of us again, telling us about dying before we want to know. Telling it with all the usual clarity and honesty. No, there is no mystery, no mystique, only this.

Why write about it, why describe this agonising and utterly meaningless catastrophe? Because, she says, she wants it described honestly for once, for others who may feel the same way and feel ashamed. Articles like this are supposed to be uplifting. After all, what is the point of protesting about death? Better to try to find meaning in it, surely? This is the point in the story where I should draw a deep breath and leave you, dear reader, with a wise and improving thought or two. Through all this suffering we learn ... What? With the wound comes the bow ... Does it, hell? In the midst of death there is life ... Where? No, only rage, rage against the dying of the light. •

Frank Keating
11 December 1993
....
Talking a very good game

Over two decades ago Granada TV decided to devote a full peak-hour transmission to debating that hardy perennial 'the lost soul of British soccer'. For some misguided reason, they chose to bribe with fifty guineas this camera-shy, tongue-tied correspondent to sit on the studio stage and field questions from a live audience. (In those days, £52 10s would buy many a crate of brown ale.)

There would also be another on the panel, a fellow journalist then but one who had been a shining, celebrated and resonantly famed captain and player a few years before.

Danny Blanchflower was waiting for me at Euston and with scarcely even a 'hi' he was already in full, unstoppable and glorious spate about football and life, football and the world, football and the universe. On the train, the buffet car was entranced as Blanchflower continued his merrily gushing tutorial about the game's innate goodness as well as the creeping cynicism that threatened it. By Crewe, he was chairing a full-scale debate which seemed by now to be involving half the train's passengers, men, women and children.

Your totally silent and even bedazzled correspondent just grinned and nodded alongside the great man. Before the daunting evening debate in front of the cameras, Danny did not even take breath while we were being made up – sitting in the next chair, charmingly and persuasively demanding of the make-up girl that she fully comprehend that 3–3– 4 was by far the most efficient formation for any decent team to play the game and that Sir Alf's 4–3–3 was far more debilitating to the welfare of the British people than Mr Heath's fiscal policies and his three-day week.

Lights, camera, action. My mouth was dry with nerves. Were my flies undone? Please don't ask me the first question...

In the event, no remote worries at all. Even those more general questions which the chairman (I think it was the lisping Mike Scott) addressed directly to me – 'Is the press to blame in any way?' or 'Is the coaching wrong in our schools?' – were mercifully and garrulously fielded, with the eruptive alacrity and certainty of a Randall in the covers in his prime, by the astonishingly erudite and knowing Ulsterman alongside me.

The truth is, I did not have to utter a finished sentence in the whole hour, unless you count the nervously grinning 'good evening', a likewise, but relieved, 'goodnight' and a few 'well, Mike, that's a very interesting question from the floor, I'm glad that chap in the red pullover asked me that, er...' before Danny's full spate rushed in.

The fifty guineas were handed over and the incredible Blanchflower irrepressibly continued into the early hours in the lounge bar of the Midland Hotel. Bless him, and the ever-rewarding memory of him.

The British game has had few one-offs as potent as Blanchflower. But how our grandest figures are so readily and quickly consigned to forgotten and sepia-washed history.

The newly minted (and always unmissable) edition of *The Book of Football Quotations* (by Phil Shaw and Peter Ball) was brought out last month by Stanley Paul. In the ten years since its first, there have been umpteen reprints.

In the very first, in 1984, the index has Blanchflower's wit and wisdom with far and away the most entries – more than Brian Clough and Sir Alf Ramsey, the runners-up. The latest edition has excised every one of Blanchflower's contributions. Such is the way of the world.

In the first edition, Blanchflower represents the book's ballast – from page 14 to page 209: 'George Best makes a greater appeal to the senses than Finney or Matthews did. His movements are quicker, lighter, more balletic. He offers grander surprises to the mind and the eye. He has ice in his veins, warmth in his heart, and timing and balance in his feet.'

Perhaps the last entry of that first edition sums up what happened before the wretched illness closed in on poor, good, lovely companionable Danny. It illustrates too why he was so wantonly wasted as a broadcasting pundit.

The fact is, he was *too* good. He said what he thought. If a match was tripe, he told the viewers so. This was how the appalled American producer Bill Bergesch phrased it: 'Blanchflower killed every soccer sportcast for us. He pointed out all the bad things. He was so honest it hurt us. His job was to promote the sport. That's what we were paying him to do.'

It was the same when he was a Fleet Street columnist. If his beguiling but always resplendently witty, barbed and trenchant pieces were so much as tweaked – let alone rechiselled as sometimes – by a subeditor worried about readers' sensibilities, then Danny would come into the pub in an expansively cold fury, and take from his pocket his latest resignation letter.

It ran to many pages – every word dripping with glorious poster-paint passion. About the rights of man, honesty and integrity of the beautiful game. His beautiful game. •